THE RULES
OF ART

Genesis and Structure
of the Literary Field

MERIDIAN

Crossing Aesthetics

Werner Hamacher

& David E. Wellbery

Editors

Translated by
Susan Emanuel

*Stanford
University
Press*

*Stanford
California
1995*

THE RULES
OF ART

Genesis and Structure
of the Literary Field

Pierre Bourdieu

Stanford University Press
Stanford, California
© 1992 Editions du Seuil
This translation and Introduction © 1996
    Polity Press
First published in France as *Les Règles de l'art*
    by Editions du Seuil
Originating publishers of English edition:
    Polity Press in association with Blackwell
    Publishers
First published in the U.S.A. by Stanford
    University Press, 1996
Printed in Great Britain
Cloth ISBN 0–8047–2568–3
Paper ISBN 0–8047–2627–2

This book is printed on acid-free paper.

C'est en lisant qu'on devient liseron.

RAYMOND QUENEAU

Contents

Translator's Preface

~∞~

Tackling a major opus by Pierre Bourdieu is particularly daunting since he has been so well served by many previous English translators. I owe a debt to my predecessors, even if I have not always followed their precedents.

The Rules of Art is a complex book which spans too many academic fields for any one translator to claim particular expertise. In the Prologue, a reading of Gustave Flaubert's *Sentimental Education*, and in the first part, about the conquest of autonomy in the field of cultural production, Bourdieu invites us on a 'walk through the woods' of the literary and artistic fields in the second half of the nineteenth century, including byways forgotten even by those well versed in French literary history. Portions of part II, which lays the foundation of what he calls a 'science of works of art' and of part III, an analysis of the pure aesthetic and alternatives to it, have appeared previously in a variety of contexts, but they have since been revised in the writing of this work.

I have respected Bourdieu's 'hierarchy of text', in which he complements the main argument with illustrative text in smaller type, and both are supported by a network of footnotes, many of them pithy, now moved to the end of the text. Several chapters have appendices which furnish concrete examples or push an argument in a polemical direction. His footnotes are so rich that I have hesitated to add to their number, except for occasional glosses of his key theoretical terms for those new to his thought, and of literary or artistic movements where these seemed essential. For his citations, I have endeavoured to discover English editions, and if I could not find one, I have reproduced his reference and translated the quoted passages myself. In general, his style in French has a willed 'literariness' about it, which I have attempted to preserve, sometimes keeping his plays on words by putting his French in italics and parentheses after English renderings which cannot do them justice. Readers will be aware – and Bourdieu's self-reflexiveness does not allow us to forget – that this book is written within a charged intellectual field both in France, where sociology often struggles within a hierarchy that puts philosophy at the pinnacle of thought, and in Europe, where a basis for collective action by scholars and artists, such as he tries to provide in his Postscript, is rendered more difficult by competitiveness within their fields and threats to their autonomy emanating from outside.

I wish to thank Armand Mattelart for daring me when I first read the book to contact Bourdieu, who patiently answered the queries I brought to him. This project would have been impossible without the selfless patience of Shoggy Waryn of MIT, a second reader who accompanied me through every page, Ann Bone, whose contribution extended beyond simple copy-editing, and Kerry Emanuel, whose soft heart and customized software took much of the pain out of a labour of love.

Preface

～⌇～

Angel. Eminently suitable for love and literature.

GUSTAVE FLAUBERT, *Dictionary of Received Ideas*

Not *everything* appears in the collection of foolish quotations, so there's hope.

RAYMOND QUENEAU

'Shall we allow the social sciences to reduce literary experience – the most exalted that man may have, along with love – to surveys about our leisure activities, when it concerns the very meaning of our life?'[1] Such a question, lifted from one of the innumerable timeless and nameless defences of reading and of culture, would certainly have unleashed the furious mirth that the well-meaning commonplaces of his day inspired in Flaubert. And what to say of such shopworn tropes of the scholastic cult of the Book, or of such supposedly Heideggerian-Hölderlinian revelations, each worthy of enriching the 'Bouvardo-Pécuchetian anthology' (the phrase is Queneau's) as these: 'To read is first of all to be torn out of oneself, and of one's world';[2] 'It is no longer possible to be in the world without the help of books';[3] 'In literature, essence is revealed at a stroke; it is given in all its truth, with all its truth, like the very truth of the being which reveals itself'?[4]

If it seems to be necessary to begin by evoking some of these vapid reflections on art and life, the unique and the common, literature and science, the (social) sciences which may well elaborate laws but only by losing the 'singularity of experience', and literature which elaborates no laws but which 'deals always with the individual person, in his absolute singularity',[5] it is because, indefinitely reproduced by and for scholarly liturgy, they are also inscribed in all minds fashioned by the School. Functioning as filters or screens, they continually threaten to block or confound the understanding of scientific analysis of books and of reading.

Does the claim for the autonomy of literature, which found its exemplary expression in Proust's *Contre Sainte-Beuve*, imply that the reading of literary texts should be exclusively literary? Is it true that scientific analysis is doomed to destroy that which makes for the specificity of the literary work and of reading, beginning with aesthetic pleasure? And that the sociologist is wedded to relativism, to the levelling of values, to the lowering of greatness, to the abolition of those differences which make for the singularity of the 'creator', always located in the realm of the Unique? And all because the sociologist is thought to stand on the side of the greatest number, the average, the mean, and thus of the mediocre, the minor, the *minores*, the mass of petty, obscure actors, justly unrecognized, and to be an ally of what is repugnant to the 'creators' of an era, the content and the context, the 'referent' and the *hors-texte*, beyond the pale of literature?

For a good number of accredited writers and readers of literature, not to mention philosophers, of greater or lesser standing, who, from Bergson to Heidegger and beyond, intend to assign science a priori limits, the case is already made. And countless are those who forbid sociology any profaning contact with the work of art. We might cite Gadamer, who places at the outset of his 'art of understanding' a postulate of incomprehensibility or, at the very least, of inexplicability: 'The fact that the work of art represents a challenge to our understanding because it *indefinitely escapes all explanation*, and offers an *ever insurmountable resistance* to whoever would translate it into the identity of a concept, has been precisely for me the point of departure for my hermeneutic theory.'[6] I will not debate this postulate (but does it even bear debating?). I would simply ask why so many critics, so many writers, so many philosophers take such satisfaction in professing that the experience of a work of art is ineffable, that it escapes by definition all rational understanding; why they are so eager to concede without a struggle the defeat of knowledge; and where does their irrepressible need to belittle rational understanding come from, this rage to affirm the irreducibility of the work of art, or, to use a more suitable word, its transcendence.

Why such insistence on conferring upon the work of art – and upon the understanding it calls for – this *status of exception*, if not in order to stamp with prejudicial discredit the (necessarily laborious and imperfect) attempts of those who would submit these products of human action to the ordinary treatment of ordinary science, and thereby assert the (spiritual) transcendence of those who know how to *recognize* that transcendence? Why such implacable hostility to those who try to advance the understanding of the work of art and of aesthetic experience, if not because the very ambition to produce a scientific analysis of that *individuum ineffabile* and of the *individuum ineffabile* who produced it, constitutes a mortal threat to the pretension, so common (at least among art lovers) and yet so 'distinguished', of thinking of oneself as an ineffable individual, capable of ineffable experiences of that ineffable? Why, in short, such *resistance to analysis*, if not because it inflicts upon 'creators', and upon those who seek to identify with them by a 'creative' reading, the last and perhaps the worst of those wounds inflicted, according to Freud, upon narcissism, after those going under the names of Copernicus, Darwin and Freud himself?

Is it legitimate to invoke the experience of the lover, to make of love, as an astonished abandon to the work grasped in its inexpressible singularity, the only form of understanding which accords with the work of art? And to see in the scientific analysis of art, and of the love of art, the form *par excellence* of scientistic arrogance, which, under cover of explaining, does not hesitate to threaten the 'creator' and the reader in their liberty and their singularity? Against all those defenders of the unknowable, bent on manning the impregnable ramparts of human liberty against the encroachments of science, I would oppose this very Kantian thought of Goethe's, which all natural scientists and social scientists could claim as their own: 'Our opinion is that it well becomes man to assume that there is something unknowable, but that he does not have to set any limit to his inquiry.'[7] I think that Kant expresses well the image that scientists have of their enterprise when he suggests that the reconciliation of knowing and being is a sort of *focus imaginarius*, the imaginary from which science must measure itself without ever being able to reach it (despite the illusions of absolute knowledge and the end of history, more common among philosophers than among scientists . . .). As for the threat that science might pose to the liberty and singularity of the literary experience, it suffices, to do justice to the matter, to observe that the ability, procured by science, to explain and understand that experience – and thus to give oneself the possibility of a genuine freedom from one's determinations – is offered to all those who want to and can appropriate it.

A more legitimate fear might be that science, in putting the love of art under its scalpel, might succeed in killing pleasure, and that, capable of delivering understanding, it might be unable to convey feeling. So one can only approve of an effort like that of Michel Chaillou, when – basing himself on the primacy of feeling, or emotional experience, of *aisthesis* – he offers a literary evocation of the literary life, strangely missing from the 'literary' histories of literature.[8] By contriving to reintroduce into an apparently self-contained literary space what one may call, with Schopenhauer, the *parerga et paralipomena*, the neglected 'margins' of the text, all that ordinary commentators leave aside, and by evoking, by the magic virtue of nomination, that which made (and was) the life of authors – the humble domestic details, picturesque if not grotesque or 'crotesque' [squalid], of their existence amid its most ordinary setting – he subverts the ordinary hierarchy of literary interests. Armed with all the resources of erudition, not in order to contribute to the sacralizing celebration of the classics, to the cult of ancestors and of the 'gift of the dead', but to summon and prepare the reader to 'clink glasses with the dead', as Saint-Amant said, Chaillou thus tears fetishized texts and authors from the sanctuary of History and academicism, and sets them free.

How could the sociologist, who must also break with idealism and literary hagiography, not feel an affinity with this 'carefree knowledge' [*gai savoir*], which relies on the free associations made possible by a liberated and liberating usage of historical references in order to repudiate the prophetic pomp of the grand critiques of authors and the sacerdotal droning of scholarly tradition? However, contrary to what the common image of sociology might lead one to believe, the sociologist cannot be completely content with the literary evocation of literary life. If attention to the perceptible is perfectly suitable when applied to the text, it does lead to neglect of the essential when it bears on the social world within which the text is produced. The task of bringing authors and their environments back to life could be that of a sociologist, and there is no shortage of analyses of art and literature whose purpose is the reconstruction of a social 'reality' that can be understood in the visible, the tangible, and the concrete solidity of daily experience. But, as I shall try to demonstrate throughout this book, the sociologist – close in this respect to the philosopher according to Plato – stands opposed to 'the friend of beautiful spectacles and voices' that the writer also is: the 'reality' that he tracks cannot be reduced to the immediate data of the sensory experience in which it is revealed; he aims not to offer (in)sight, or feeling, but to construct systems of intelligible relations capable of making sense of sentient data.

Is this to say that one is once more returned to the old antinomy of the intelligible and the sensible? In fact, it will be up to the reader to judge if, as I believe (having experienced it myself), scientific analysis of the social conditions of the production and reception of a work of art, far from reducing it or destroying it, in fact intensifies the literary experience. As we shall see with respect to Flaubert, such analysis seems to abolish the singularity of the 'creator' in favour of the relations which made the work intelligible, only better to rediscover it at the end of the task of reconstructing the space in which the author finds himself encompassed and included as a point. To recognize this point in the literary space, which is also the point from which is formed a singular point of view *on* that space, is to be in a position to understand and to feel, by mental identification with a constructed position, the singularity of that position and of the person who occupies it, and the extraordinary effort which, at least in the particular case of Flaubert, was necessary to make it exist.

The love of art, like love itself, even and especially of the *amour fou* kind, feels founded in its object. It is in order to convince oneself of being right in (or having reasons for) loving that such love so often has recourse to commentary, to that sort of apologetic discourse that the believer addresses to himself or herself and which, as well as its minimal effect of redoubling his or her belief, may also awaken and summon others to that belief. This is why scientific analysis, when it is able to uncover what makes the work of art *necessary*, that is to say, its informing formula, its generative principle, its *raison d'être*, also furnishes artistic experience, and the pleasure which accompanies it, with its best justification, its richest nourishment. Through it, sensible love of the work can fulfil itself in a sort of *amor intellectualis rei*, the assimilation of the object to the subject and the immersion of the subject in the object, the active surrender to the singular necessity of the literary object (which, more often than not, is itself the product of a similar submission).

But is this not paying too high a price for the intensification of experience, to have to confront the reduction to historical necessity of something that wants to be lived as an absolute experience, freed from the contingencies of a genesis? In reality, to understand the social genesis of the literary field – of the belief which sustains it, of the language game played in it, of the interests and the material or symbolic stakes engendered in it – is not to surrender to the pleasure of reduction or destruction (even if, as Wittgenstein suggests in his 'Lecture on ethics',[9] the effort to understand no doubt owes something to the 'pleasure of destroying prejudices' and to the 'irresistible seduction' exercised by 'explanations of the type "this is *only* that"', especially by way of antidote to the pharisaical complacencies of the cult of art).

To seek in the logic of the literary field or the artistic field – paradoxical worlds capable of inspiring or of imposing the most disinterested 'interests' – the principle of the work of art's existence in what makes it historic, but also transhistoric, is to treat this work as an intentional sign haunted and regulated by something else, of which it is also a symptom. It is to suppose that in it is enunciated an expressive impulse which the imposition of form required by the social necessity of the field tends to render unrecognizable. Renouncing the angelic belief in a pure interest in pure form is the price we must pay for understanding the logic of those social universes which, through the social alchemy of their historical laws of functioning, succeed in extracting from the often merciless clash of passions and selfish interests the sublimated essence of the universal. It is to offer a vision more true and, ultimately, more reassuring, because less superhuman, of the highest achievements of the human enterprise.

Acknowledgements

I would like to thank Marie-Christine Rivière for her help in the preparation and organization of the original manuscript of this book.

Pierre Bourdieu

Flaubert, Analyst of Flaubert

A Reading of Sentimental Education

～∞～

One does not write what one wants.

GUSTAVE FLAUBERT

Sentimental Education, that book on which a thousand commentaries have been written, but which has undoubtedly never been truly read, supplies all the tools necessary for its own sociological analysis:[1] the structure of the book, which a *strictly internal* reading brings to light, that is, the structure of the social space in which the adventures of Frédéric unfold, proves to be at the same time the structure of the social space in which its author himself was situated.

One might think perhaps that it is the sociologist, in projecting questions of a particular sort, who turns Flaubert into a sociologist, and one capable, moreover, of offering a sociology of Flaubert. And there is a risk that the method of proof itself, which is to be based on constructing a model of the immanent structure of the book – in order to re-engender and so to understand the principle at work behind the whole story of Frédéric and his friends – may appear as the height of scientistic excess. Yet the strangest thing is that this structure – which strikes one as self-evident the moment it is spelled out – has eluded the most attentive interpreters.[2] This obliges us to raise more particularly than usual the problem of 'realism' and of the 'referent' of literary discourse. What indeed is this discourse which speaks of the social or psychological world *as if it did not speak of it*; which *cannot speak* of this world except on condition that it only speak of it as if it did not speak of it, that is, in a *form* which performs, for the author and the reader, a *denegation* (in the Freudian sense of *Verneinung*) of what it expresses? And should we not ask ourselves if work on form is not what makes possible the partial anamnesis of deep and repressed structures, if, in a word, the writer most preoccupied with formal research – such as Flaubert and so many others after him – is not actually driven to act as a *medium of those structures* (social or psychological), which then achieve objectification, passing through him and his work on inductive words, 'conductive bodies' but also more or less opaque screens?

Above and beyond the fact that it compels us to pose these questions and examine them, *in situ*, as it were, the analysis of the book ought to allow us to take advantage of the properties of literary discourse, such as its capacity to reveal while veiling, or to produce a de-realizing 'reality effect', in order to introduce us gently, with Flaubert the socioanalyst of Flaubert, to a socioanalysis of Flaubert, and of literature.

Places, investments, displacements

This 'long-haired youth of eighteen', 'who had recently matriculated', whom his mother, 'having provided him with just sufficient to cover his expenses, had packed ... off to Le Havre to visit an uncle who, she hoped, would be putting her son in his will', this bourgeois adolescent who thinks 'of an idea for a play, of subjects for a painting, of future passionate affairs of the heart',[3] has come to the point in a career from which he can encompass with one gaze that totality of powers and possibilities open to him and the avenues to take him there. Frédéric Moreau is, in a double sense, an indeterminate being, or better yet, determined to indetermination, both objective and subjective. Set up in the freedom which his situation as heir to property [*rentier*] assures him, he is governed, right down to the feelings of which he is apparently the subject, by the fluctuations of his financial investments [*placements*], which define the successive orientations of his choices.[4]

The indifference which he sometimes betrays for the common objects of bourgeois ambition[5] is a secondary effect of his dreamed love for Madame Arnoux, a kind of imaginary support for his indetermination. 'What is there for me to do in the world? Others strain after wealth, fame, power. I have no profession; you are my exclusive occupation, my entire fortune, the aim and centre of my life and thoughts.'[6] As for the artistic interests which he expresses from time to time, they do not have enough constancy and consistency to offer a base of support for a higher ambition capable of positively thwarting vulgar ambition: he who, from his first appearance, 'thought of the plot of a play and of subjects for paintings', and at other times 'dreamt of symphonies', 'wanted to paint' and composed verses, begins one day 'to write a novel called *Sylvio, a Fisherman's Son*', in which he depicts himself, with Madame Arnoux; then he 'rents a piano and composes German waltzes'; then converts to painting, which brings him closer to Madame Arnoux, only to return to the writing ambition, this time with a History of the Renaissance.[7]

Frédéric's entire existence, like the whole universe of the novel, is organized around two poles, represented by the Arnoux and the Dambreuses: on the one side, 'art and politics', and on the other 'politics and business'. At the intersection of the two universes, at least in the beginning, that is, before the revolution of 1848, there stands, besides Frédéric himself, only father Oudry, a guest at the Arnoux', but as a neighbour. The key characters, notably Arnoux and Dambreuse, function as symbols charged with marking and representing the pertinent positions in the social space. They are not '*caractères*' in the manner of La Bruyère, as Thibaudet believes, but rather symbols of a social position (the work of writing thus creates a universe saturated with significant details, and therefore more signifying than true to life, as testified by the abundance of pertinent indices it offers to analysis).[8] Thus, for example, the different receptions and gatherings are entirely signified, and differentiated, by the drinks served there, from Deslauriers's beer to Dambreuse's 'grand vins de Bordeaux', passing through Arnoux's 'vins extraordinaires', lipfraoli and tokay, to Rosanette's champagne.

One may thus construct the social space of *Sentimental Education* by relying for landmarks on the clues that Flaubert supplies in abundance and on the various 'networks' that social practices of cooptation such as receptions, soirées and friendly gatherings reveal (see the diagram).

At the three dinners hosted by the Arnoux,[9] we meet, besides the stalwarts of *L'Art Industriel* – Hussonnet, Pellerin, Regimbart and, at the first, Mlle Vatnaz – regulars such as Dittmer and Burrieu, both painters; Rosenwald, a composer; Sombaz, a caricaturist; Lovarias, a 'mystic' (present twice); and, finally, occasional guests like Anténor Braive, a portrait painter; Théophile Lorris, a poet; Vourdat, a sculptor; Pierre-Paul Meinsius, a painter; to whom should be added, at such dinners, a lawyer, Maître Lefaucheux, and two art critic friends of Hussonnet's, a paper maker and father Oudry.

At the opposite extreme, the receptions at the Dambreuses,[10] the first two separated from the others by the revolution of 1848, gather together, besides generically defined characters, such as a former cabinet member, the *curé* of a large parish, two civil servants, 'proprietors' and famous personalities of the worlds of art, science and politics ('the great Mr A., the famous B., the intelligent C., the eloquent Z., the wonderful Y., the old stagers of the centre left, the

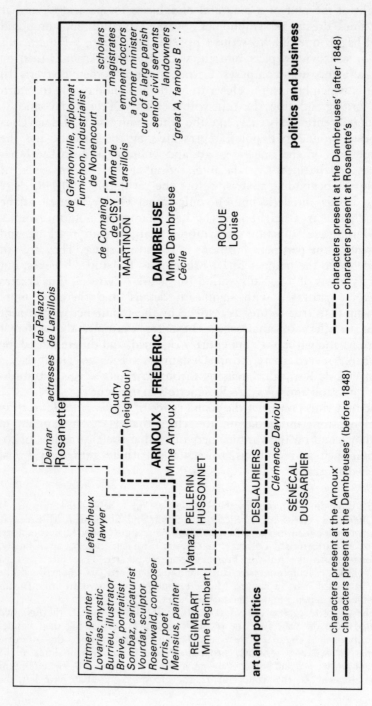

art and politics

Dittmer, painter
Lovarias, mystic
Burrieu, illustrator
Braive, portraitist
Sombaz, caricaturist
Vourdat, sculptor
Rosenwald, composer
Lorris, poet
Meinsius, painter

REGIMBART
Mme Regimbart

Lefaucheux
lawyer

Vatnaz

PELLERIN
HUSSONNET

DESLAURIERS

Clémence Daviou

SÉNÉCAL
DUSSARDIER

Delmar
Rosanette
actresses

de Palazot
de Larsillois

Oudry
(neighbour)

ARNOUX
Mme Arnoux

FRÉDÉRIC

de Grémonville, diplomat
Fumichon, industrialist
de Nonencourt

de Comaing
de CISY

MARTINON

Mme de
Larsillois

DAMBREUSE
Mme Dambreuse
Cécile

ROQUE
Louise

scholars
magistrates
eminent doctors
a former minister
curé of a large parish
senior civil servants
landowners
'great A, famous B . . .'

politics and business

--------- characters present at the Arnoux'
————— characters present at the Dambreuses' (before 1848)

-- -- -- characters present at the Dambreuses' (after 1848)
- - - - - characters present at Rosanette's

Figure 1 The field of power according to *Sentimental Education*

paladins of the right, the veterans of the middle way'), Paul de Grémonville, a diplomat; Fumichon, an industrialist; Mme de Larsillois, the wife of the prefect; the Duchesse de Montreuil; M. de Nonencourt; and finally (besides Frédéric) Martinon, Cisy, M. Roque and his daughter. After 1848, we shall also see at the Dambreuses' M. and Mme Arnoux, Hussonnet and Pellerin, converted, and lastly Deslauriers, introduced by Frédéric into the service of M. Dambreuse.

At the two receptions given by Rosanette, one at the time of her liaison with Arnoux,[11] the other at the end of the novel, when she plans to marry Frédéric,[12] one encounters actresses, the actor Delmar, Mlle Vatnaz, Frédéric and certain of his friends, Pellerin, Hussonnet, Arnoux, Cisy and, lastly, the Comte de Palazot and characters also encountered at the Dambreuses', Paul de Grémonville, Fumichon, M. de Nonencourt, and M. de Larsillois, whose wife frequents the salon of Mme Dambreuse.

The guests of Cisy all belong to the nobility (M. de Comaing, present also at Rosanette's, etc.) with the exception of his tutor and of Frédéric.[13]

At the soirées of Frédéric, one finds once more Deslauriers, accompanied by Sénécal, Dussardier, Pellerin, Hussonnet, Cisy, Regimbart and Martinon (these last two being absent from the last soirée).[14]

Finally, Dussardier assembles Frédéric and the petit-bourgeois fraction of his friends, Deslauriers, Sénécal, as well as an architect, a pharmacist, a wine merchant and an insurance employee.[15]

The pole of political and economic power is marked by the Dambreuses, who are from the start constituted as the supreme goals of political and amorous ambition ('A millionaire – just think of it. Make sure you can get into his good books! And his wife's too! Become her lover!'[16]). Their salon receives 'men and women knowledgeable about life', that is, about business, totally excluding, before 1848, artists and journalists. Conversation there is serious, boring, conservative: the Republic is declared impossible in France; journalists ought to be gagged; decentralization is urged, with the redistribution of the surplus urban population to the countryside; the 'lower classes' are castigated for their vices and needs; people chat about politics, elections, amendments and further amendments; prejudices against artists are voiced. The rooms are overflowing with art objects. The rarest delicacies are served there: bream, venison, crayfish, accompanied by the best wines, in the most beautiful silver dishes. After dinner, the men talk among themselves, standing up; the women are seated in the background.

The opposite pole is marked, not by a great revolutionary or established artist, but by Arnoux, an art dealer, who, in this function, is the representative of money and business dealings at the heart of the universe of art. Flaubert is perfectly clear on this in his notebooks; M. Moreau (the original name of Arnoux) is an 'industrialist of art', then a 'pure industrialist'.[17] The oxymoron of words is there to emphasize, as much in the designation of his profession as in the title of his journal *L'Art Industriel*, the double negation inscribed in the formula of this double being, indeterminate, like Frédéric, and therefore fated to ruin. As 'neutral territory where rival factions could rub shoulders',[18] the 'hybrid establishment' which is *L'Art Industriel* offers a meeting place for artists occupying opposite positions, advocates of 'social art', exponents of art for art's sake, or writers consecrated by the bourgeois public. Talk there is 'free', which means wilfully obscene ('Frédéric was astonished by the cynicism of these men'), always paradoxical; manners there are 'simple' but one does not detest affecting a 'pose'. There one eats exotic dishes and one drinks 'extraordinary wines'. There one becomes impassioned about aesthetic or political theories. There one is on the left, or rather for the Republic, like Arnoux himself, or even socialist. But *L'Art Industriel* is also an artistic industry capable of economically exploiting the work of artists because it is an authority for the consecration which governs the production of writers and artists.[19]

Arnoux was in a certain manner predisposed to fulfil the function of art dealer, only able to ensure the success of his enterprise by dissimulating to himself its truth, that is, its exploitation, by a permanent double game between art and money.[20] This dual being, 'with his innate combination of sincerity and commercial guile',[21] of calculated avarice and 'madness' (as Mme Arnoux would define it[22] but also Rosanette[23]), that is, of extravagance and generosity as much as of impudence and impropriety, accumulates for his own sake, at least for a while, the advantages of two antithetical logics. There is the logic of disinterested art, which knows only symbolic profits, and there is the logic of commerce: his duality, more profound than all manner of duplicity, allows him to catch artists at their own game, that of disinterestedness, confidence, generosity, friendship ('Arnoux loved him – Pellerin – even while exploiting him'[24]) and thereby to leave them the best part, the wholly symbolic profits of what they themselves call 'glory',[25] reserving for himself the material profits made on their work. Businessman and merchant among people who owe to *themselves* the refusal to acknowledge [*reconnaître*], or to be aware of [*connaître*] their material interest, he is destined to appear to artists as a bourgeois and to the bourgeois as an artist.[26]

Situated between bohemia and 'society', the 'demi-monde' – represented by Rosanette's salon – recruits simultaneously from the two opposed universes: 'The courtesans' drawing rooms – their importance dates from this period – served as neutral territory on which reactionaries of different parties could meet.'[27] This intermediate and slightly shady world is dominated by 'free women', thus capable of carrying out the function of go-betweens between the 'bourgeois', simply dominant, and the artists, dominant–dominated (the wife of the 'bourgeois', dominated – as a woman – among the dominants, also fulfils this function, on another level, with her salon). Often of lower-class extraction, these 'girls' of luxury, and even of art, such as the dancers and actresses, or La Vatnaz, half kept woman, half woman of letters, who are paid to be 'free', engender freedom by their fantasies and their extravagance (the homology with bohemia is striking, or even with the more established writers, who, such as Baudelaire or Flaubert, are questioning at the same time the relation between their function and that of the 'prostitute'). Everything there is permitted which would be unthinkable elsewhere, even at the Arnoux',[28] not to mention the salon of the Dambreuses: incongruities of language, puns, boasts, 'lies taken for truth, improbable asser-tions', misdemeanours ('people threw oranges or corks; people left their seats to chat with someone else'). This 'milieu made for pleasure'[29] holds concurrently the advantages of the two opposed worlds, conserving the freedom of one and the luxury of the other, without the concomitant privations, since some abandon there their forced asceticism and others their mask of virtue. And it is to 'this little family party', as Hussonnet says ironically,[30] that the 'girls' invite the artists among whom they sometimes recruit their para-mours (here, Delmar) and the bourgeois who support them (here, Oudry); but this inverted family reunion, where the liaison of money and reason serves to maintain the heart's relations, remains once more dominated, like a black mass, by what it denies: all the bourgeois rules and virtues are banished, except respect for money, which may, as virtue does in other cases, prevent love.[31]

The question of inheritance

In thus laying out the two poles of the field of power, a true *milieu* in the Newtonian sense,[32] where social forces, attractions or repulsions, are exercised, and find their phenomenal manifestation in the form of psychological motivations such as love or ambition, Flaubert institutes the conditions of a kind of sociological experimentation: five adolescents – including the hero, Frédéric – provisionally assem-bled by their situation as students, will be launched into this space, like particles into a force-field, and their trajectories will be deter-mined by the relation between the forces of the field and their own inertia. This inertia is inscribed on the one hand in the dispositions they owe to their origins and to their trajectories, and which imply a tendency to persevere in a manner of being, and thus a probable trajectory, and on the other in the capital[33] they have inherited, and which contributes to defining the possibilities and the impossibilities which the field assigns them.[34]

A field of possible forces exercised on all bodies entering it, the field of power is also a field of struggle, and may thus be compared to a game: the dispositions, that is to say the ensemble of incorporated properties, including elegance, facility of expression or even beauty, and capital in its diverse forms – economic, cultural, social – constitute the trumps which will dictate both the manner of playing and success in the game – in short, the whole process of *social ageing* which Flaubert calls 'sentimental education'.

As if he had wanted to expose to the forces of the field a collection of individuals possessing, in different combinations, the aptitudes representing in his eyes the conditions for social success, Flaubert thus 'constructs' a group of adolescents such that each of its members is united with each of the others and separated from all the others by an ensemble of similarities and differences distributed in a fairly systematic manner: Cisy is very rich, noble, endowed with relations and distinguished (handsome?), but not very intelligent or ambitious; Deslauriers is intelligent and animated by a fierce will to succeed, but he is poor, lacking in relations and without looks; Martinon is rich enough, handsome enough (at least he brags about it), intelligent enough, and bent on success; Frédéric has, as the saying goes, everything going for him – relative wealth, charm, and intelligence – except the will to succeed.

In this game which is the field of power, the stakes are evidently *power* which must be conquered or maintained, and those who enter it can differ in two relations: firstly, from the standpoint of inheritance, which means advantages; secondly, from the viewpoint of the disposition of the heir in relation to it, which means the 'will to succeed'.

What makes an heir disposed to inherit or not? What drives him to simply maintain the inheritance or to augment it? Flaubert gives some elements of an answer to these questions, notably in the case of Frédéric. The relation to inheritance is always rooted in the relation to the father and the mother, overdetermined figures in whom the psychic components (of the sort psycho-analysis describes) are intertwined with the social components (of the sort sociology analyses). The ambivalence of Frédéric with respect to his inheritance, source of his tergiversations, may find its principle in his *ambivalence* towards his mother, a double personage, obviously feminine, but also masculine in that she substitutes for the disappeared father, bearer of the customary social ambition. Widow of a 'plebeian' husband who 'was killed by a sword blow during her pregnancy, leaving her a compromised fortune', this female head of the household, born to a family of the minor provincial nobility, had transferred to her son all her ambitions of social re-establishment and never ceased reminding him of the imperatives of the worlds of business affairs and money, which apply also to affairs of the heart. Even so, Flaubert suggests (notably in the evocation of the final meeting: he felt 'an indefinable feeling, a repugnance akin to a dread of committing incest') that Frédéric had transferred his love for his mother to Mme Arnoux, responsible for the victory of reasons of love over those of business.

Thus a first division is effected between the 'petits-bourgeois' who have no other resources than their (good) will, Deslauriers and Hussonnet,[35] and the heirs. Among the latter, there are heirs who come to terms with it, either by contenting themselves with maintaining their position, like Cisy, the aristocrat, or by trying to augment it, like Martinon, the conquering bourgeois. Cisy has no other *raison d'être*, in the economy of the novel, than to represent one of the possible dispositions with respect to inheritance and, more generally, with respect to the system of inheritable positions: he is the unproblematic heir, who contents himself with inheriting because, given the nature of his inheritance, his wealth, his titles, but also his intelligence, there is nothing else for him to do than that, nothing else for him to do either *for* that. But there are also heirs with stories, those who, like Frédéric, refuse, if not to inherit, at least to be inherited by their inheritance.

The transmission of power between generations always represents a critical moment in the history of domestic units, among other reasons because the relation of *reciprocal appropriation* between the material, cultural, social and symbolic patrimony and the biological individuals fashioned by and for the appropriation finds itself provisionally in peril. The tendency of patrimony (and thus of the whole social structure) to continue in its state cannot be realized unless the inheritance inherits the heir, unless, by the mediation notably of those who are provisionally responsible for it and who must assure their succession, 'the dead (that is, property) seizes the quick (that is, a proprietor disposed and able to inherit).'

Frédéric does not fulfil those conditions: a possessor who does not intend to let himself be possessed by his possessions, without however renouncing them, he refuses to get in line, to provide himself with the two properties which alone can confer on him, in these times and in this milieu, the instruments and insignia of social existence, to wit an 'estate' and a wife endowed with income.[36] Frédéric wants to inherit without being inherited. He lacks what the bourgeois call a serious side, that aptitude to be what one is: the social form of the principle of identity which alone may establish an unequivocal social identity.

In proving himself incapable of taking himself seriously, of identifying himself by anticipation with the social existence which is destined for him (for example, that of the 'intended' of Mlle Louise[37]) and thereby giving guarantees of future seriousness, he de-realizes the 'serious' and all the 'domestic and democratic virtues'[38] – virtues of those who, identified with what they are, do what should be done and are devoted to what they do, whether 'bourgeois' or 'socialists'.

So while everything else makes him similar, Martinon is, in this respect, the perfect antithesis of Frédéric. If, in the final analysis, he is the one who ends up by winning, it is because he takes the roles seriously whereas Frédéric merely plays at them: Flaubert, who, from his first appearance, notes that he wanted 'already to appear serious',[39] indicates for example that, during the first reception of the Dambreuses, amid the laughter and 'daring pleasantries', 'Martinon alone remained serious',[40] whereas Frédéric chatted with Mme Dambreuse. In a general way, in similar circumstances, Martinon always tries to convince 'serious people' of his 'seriousness'; as opposed to Frédéric, who flees to women from the boredom of masculine conversation ('As all this bored Frédéric, he went over to the women'[41]).

Frédéric's disdain for *serious* people, who, like Martinon, are always disposed to adopt enthusiastically the states of being to which they are promised and the women who are promised to them, is compensated by the irresolution and insecurity that he feels in the face of a universe without marked goals or reliable landmarks. He incarnates one of the manners, and not the least common, of experiencing bourgeois adolescence, which may be lived and expressed, according to the moment or to the epoch, in the rhetoric of aristocratism or in the phraseology of populism, strongly tinged, in both cases, with aestheticism.

A potential bourgeois and a provisional intellectual, obliged to adopt or to mime for a while the poses of an intellectual, he is predisposed to indeterminacy by this double contradictory determination: placed at the centre of a field of forces owing its structure to the opposition between the pole of economic or political power and the pole of intellectual or artistic prestige (in which the force of attraction receives a reinforcement from the very logic of the student milieu), he is situated in a zone of social weightlessness in which the forces which will carry him in one direction or another are provisionally balanced and cancelled.

In addition, through Frédéric, Flaubert carries on the interrogation into what makes adolescence a *critical moment*, in a dual sense. 'Entering into life', as one says, means to accept entering into one or another of the social games which are socially recognized, and engaging in the inaugural *investment*, both economic and psychological, which is implied in the participation in the *serious games* of which the social world is composed. This belief in the game, in the value of a game, and of its stakes, is manifested above all, as with Martinon, in seriousness, indeed in the very spirit of seriousness, this propensity to take seriously all things and people – especially oneself – socially designated as serious, and them alone.

Frédéric does not manage to invest himself in one or another of the games of art or money that the social world proposes. Rejecting the *illusio* as an illusion unanimously approved and shared, hence as an *illusion of reality*, he takes refuge in true *illusion*, declared as such, whose form *par excellence* is the novelistic illusion in its most extreme forms (with Don Quixote or Emma Bovary, for example). The entry into life as entry into the illusion of the real guaranteed by the whole group is not self-evident. And novelistic adolescences, such as those of Frédéric or Emma, who, like Flaubert himself, take fiction seriously because they do not manage to take the real seriously, remind us that the 'reality' against which we measure all fictions is only the universally guaranteed referent of a collective illusion.[42]

Thus, with the polarized space of the field of power, the game and the stakes are set in place: between the two extremes there is total incompatibility, and one cannot gamble at both tables except by risking losing everything by wanting to win everything. With the description of the properties of the adolescents, the cards are dealt. The game can commence. Each of the protagonists is defined by a sort of generative formula, which does not need to be made completely explicit, and even less so formalized, in order to orient the choices of the novelist (the formula functions rather like the practical intuition of the habitus[43] which, in daily experience, permits us to sense or to comprehend the conduct of people familiar to us). Actions, interactions, relations of rivalry or conflict, or even the happy or unhappy happenstances which make up the course of different life histories, are just so many occasions to manifest the essence of characters by deploying the formula across time in the form of a story [*histoire*].

Thus, each of the behaviours of every single character will come to refine the system of differences which oppose each to all the other members of the experimental group, without ever really adding to the initial formula. In fact, each of them is whole in each of his manifestations, a *pars totalis* predisposed to function as a sign immediately intelligible by all the others, past or future. Thus, Martinon's neat 'beard along the line of the jaw' announces all his subsequent behaviour, from the pallor, sighs and lamentation by which he betrays, on the occasion of the riot, his fear of being compromised, or the prudent contradiction which he offers to his comrades when they attack Louis-Philippe – an attitude that Flaubert himself relates to the docility which served him in escaping detentions during his college years and in pleasing his law professors now – right down to the serious face he puts on, both in his behaviour and in his ostentatiously conservative speeches, at the Dambreuse soirées.

If *Sentimental Education* – necessarily a story of a group whose elements, united by an almost systematic set of combinations, are subjected to an ensemble of forces of attraction or repulsion exercised over them by the field of power – may be read as a history, it is because the structure which organizes the fiction, and which grounds the illusion of reality it produces, is hidden, as in reality, beneath the interactions of people, which are structured by it. And since the most intense of these interactions are sentimental relations, foregrounded in advance for attention by the author himself, one understands how they have completely obscured the basis of their own intelligibility from the eyes of commentators whose 'literary sense' hardly inclines them to look for the key to sentiments in social structures.

What precludes the characters from having the abstract appearance of combinations of parameters is also, paradoxically, the narrowness of the social space in which they are placed: in this finite and closed universe, very similar, despite appearances, to that of crime novels where all the characters are enclosed on an island or in an isolated manor, the twenty protagonists have strong chances of meeting each other, for better or worse, and hence of developing in a necessary adventure all the implications of their respective 'formulas', which enclose in advance the episodes of their interactions, for example the rivalry for a woman (between Frédéric and Cisy for Rosanette, or between Martinon and Cisy for Cécile) or for a position (between Frédéric and Martinon with respect to the protection of M. Dambreuse).

From a preliminary comparative overview of trajectories, one learns that 'Cisy will not finish his law studies'. And why should he? Having fooled around over the time of a Parisian adolescence, as the tradition of the time expected, with people, customs and heretical ideas, he will not waste time finding the direct path which takes him to the future implicated in his past, that is, to the 'château of his ancestors' where he will end up, as he should, 'sunk into religion and father of eight children'. A pure example of simple reproduction, he is equally well opposed to Frédéric, the heir who refuses the inheritance, as to Martinon who, wanting to do everything possible to augment it, puts a will to succeed into the service of his inherited capital (of wealth and relations, beauty and intelligence), a will whose equivalent is only found among the petits-bourgeois and which will assure him the highest of the objectively offered trajectories. The *determination* of Martinon, strict inverse of the indetermination of Frédéric, doubtless owes an important part of its efficacy to the symbolic effects accompanying any action marked by this sign: the particular modality of practices which make manifest the disposition with respect to the stakes, 'seriousness', 'conviction', 'enthusiasm' (or inversely 'frivolity', 'insolence', 'casualness'), constitutes the surest testimony of the recognition of coveted positions, hence the submission to the order into which one wants to integrate, the very thing each socially constituted body requires above all from those who will have to reproduce it.

The relation between Frédéric and Deslauriers sketches the opposition between those who inherit and those who inherit only the aspiration to possess, that is, between the bourgeois and the petit-bourgeois. Hence the adventure at the house of the Turkish woman: Frédéric has the money, but lacks the audacity; Deslauriers, who does dare, doesn't have the money, and can only follow him in his flight.

The social distance which separates them is recalled many times, in particular by means of the opposition between their tastes: Deslauriers has aesthetic aspirations of the first degree and ignores the refinements of snobbery ('A poor man, he hankered after luxury in its most obvious form'[44]): ' "If I were you," said Deslauriers, "I'd prefer to buy myself some silver plate," revealing, by this taste for sumptuous display, the man of humble origin.'[45] In fact, he 'longed for wealth, as a means of gaining power over men', whereas Frédéric imagines the future as an aesthete.[46] Moreover, Frédéric demonstrates several times that he is ashamed of his relation with Deslauriers[47] and even gives him evidence openly of his disdain.[48] And Flaubert, as if to recall the principle of Deslauriers's whole conduct (and its difference from that of Frédéric), makes the question of *inheritance* the cause of the failure which puts an end to his university ambitions: presenting himself at the competitive examinations for teaching posts 'with a thesis on the right of making a will, in which he maintained that this right should be restricted as far as possible', 'as luck would have it, he had drawn by lot, as the subject for this lecture, the Statute of Limitations,' which gave him the opportunity to prolong his diatribe against inheritance and heirs; confirmed by this failure in the same 'unfortunate theories' which merited the setback, he advocates the abolition of collateral succession, making an exception only for Frédéric . . .[49] Certain commentators – and Sartre himself – have seriously wondered about the existence of a homosexual relationship between Frédéric and Deslauriers, on the strength, precisely, of one of the passages in *Sentimental Education* in which the objective structure of the relation between classes shows through the most clearly in the interaction between the individuals: 'Then his thoughts turned to Frédéric's physical appearance, which had always exerted an almost feminine charm on him.'[50] Which is in reality no more than a relatively stereotyped manner of enunciating the social difference between a corporal hexis[51] and the manners which, being situated in the order of refinement and elegance, put Frédéric on the side of the feminine, if not effeminacy, as one sees in this other passage: 'He had made another acquaintance at the Law School. This was Monsieur de Cisy, the scion of a noble family, who was like a girl, his manners were so gentle.'[52] To the difference in their manners should be added the more fundamental difference in their relation to money, Frédéric obviously possessing, as Pierre Coigny observes, 'a feminine notion of money, which he makes an instrument of pleasure and luxury more than of power'.[53]

The principle of the singular relation between the two friends is inscribed in the relation between the bourgeoisie and petite bourgeoisie: the aspiration which leads one to identify with, to put oneself in the place of, to take oneself for another is constitutive of petit-bourgeois pretension, and more widely, of the position of *pretender* (or of the second, the 'double'). One thinks inevitably of the ambiguous action that Deslauriers undertakes in Frédéric's name towards Mme Arnoux, of his deliberations at the moment when he tries to appropriate to himself Frédéric's two 'chances', M. Dambreuse and Mme Arnoux, to take his place by putting himself into his place, or of the strategy he employs towards Louise, the 'promised' of Frédéric whom he will end up marrying: 'He had begun, not only by singing his friend's praises but by copying his ways and expressions as far as he could.'[54]

The proclivity of Deslauriers to identify himself with Frédéric, to espouse his cause, to imagine that 'he was the other, by a strange mental process which combined resentment and sympathy, imitation and audacity',[55] cannot be divorced from a sharp awareness of the difference which separates him from Frédéric, a *sense* of the social distance which obliges him to keep his distance, even in imagination. Knowing that what is good for one is not necessarily good for the other, he keeps his place even when he is replacing the other: 'In ten years, Frédéric had to be a deputy; in fifteen a minister; why not? With his father's money, which would come to him soon, he could begin by starting a newspaper; that would be the first step; after that they would see. As for Deslauriers's own ambition, it remained a chair at the Law School.'[56] If he allies his ambitions with those of Frédéric, it is always to subordinate to them his own realistic and limited projects: 'You really must get into that circle. You can introduce me later on.'[57] He has ambitions *for* Frédéric: but that means that he *lends* Frédéric not merely *his* ambitions, properly speaking, but those that he would feel fully justified in having *if only* he had the means that Frédéric has: 'An idea occurred to him: to go and see Monsieur Dambreuse and ask for the secretary's post for himself. But the post was sure to be conditional on the purchase of a certain number of shares. He realized *the folly* of his plan and said to himself: "Oh, no! That would be wrong of me." Then he racked his brains to find a way of recovering the fifteen thousand francs. A sum like that was *nothing for Frédéric*. But *if he had had it*, what a lever it would have been!'[58] The ease of the prestigious heir, who can fritter his inheritance or give himself the luxury of refusing it, does not reduce the objective distance which separates him from the pretenders: an implicit condemnation of anxious and nervous *arrivisme*, it can only add shameful hate to an envy that cannot be confessed.

The desperate hope of being another turns easily into the despair of failing at it, and ambition by proxy ends in *moral indignation*: Frédéric, having what he has, ought to have the ambitions Deslauriers holds for him; or else Deslauriers, being what he is, ought to have the means Frédéric does. We must again follow Flaubert: 'And the former clerk waxed indignant that the other's fortune was so large. "The use he makes of it is pitiful. He's selfish to the core. Oh, what do I care about his fifteen thousand francs?"'[59] Here one arrives at the principle of the *dialectic of resentment* which condemns in the other the possession one desires oneself. 'Why had he lent them? For love of Madame Arnoux. She was his mistress: Deslauriers had no doubt of that. "That's another thing for which money comes in useful." Hatred flooded into his mind.' The unhappy passion for inaccessible possessions and the extorted admiration that goes along with it are fated to end in hatred of the other, the only way of escaping hatred of oneself when envy attaches itself to properties – notably corporal or *incorporated*, such as manners – that one cannot appropriate, without nevertheless being able to abolish all desire for appropriation (thus it is that the indignant condemnation of the 'brilliant', frequent among pedants, as Flaubert would have said, is more often than not merely the inverted form of an envy which has nothing to oppose to the dominant value other than an antivalue, the 'serious', defined by the *privation* of the condemned value).

But resentment is not the only outcome; it develops in alternation with voluntarism: 'But was not resolution the essential factor in every undertaking? And since, given sufficient resolution, one could overcome any obstacle . . .'[60] What it would be sufficient for Frédéric to merely want, Deslauriers must obtain by force of will, even if he would have to take the place of Frédéric. This typically petit-bourgeois vision which makes social success depend on personal will and individual goodwill, this anxious ethic of effort and merit which carries resentment to its reverse, is extended logically in a vision of the social world which combines *artificialism* with cryptocratic obsession – half optimistic, since determination and intrigue can accomplish anything, and half desperate, since the secret springs of this mechanism are left to *plotting* among the initiated. '*Never having seen society* except through the fever of his ambition, Deslauriers *pictured it* as an *artificial creation*, functioning in accordance with mathematical laws. A dinner in town, a meeting with an important official, the smile of a pretty woman, could, through a series of actions following logically upon one another, produce amazing results. Certain Paris drawing-rooms were like those *machines* which take in material in its raw state and give it out with its value increased a hundred fold. He believed in courtesans advising diplomats, in rich marriages obtained by intrigue, in the genius of criminals, in the submissiveness of fortune to a strong will.'[61] It is thus that the world of power appears when it is perceived from outside, and especially from afar and from below, by someone who aspires to enter it: in politics as elsewhere, the petit-bourgeois is condemned to *allodoxia*, an error of perception and of appreciation which consists in *recognizing* one thing for another.[62]

Resentment is a submissive revolt. Disappointment, by the ambition it betrays, constitutes an admission of gratitude. Conservatism was never mistaken about this: it knows enough to see there the highest tribute rendered to the social order, that of vexation and frustrated ambition; just as it knows how to detect the truth of more than one juvenile revolt in the trajectory which leads from the rebellious bohemianism of adolescence to disillusioned conservatism or to reactionary fanaticism in maturity.

Hussonnet, the other petit-bourgeois whom Flaubert, as we have seen, has trouble distinguishing from Deslauriers, had early on undertaken a literary career: the typical incarnation of this bohemia, fated to material privations and to intellectual disappointments, that Marx called the *Lumpenproletariat* and Weber the 'proletaroid intelligentsia', he maintains himself for long years in the condition of a 'garçon de lettres', busy with writing 'rejected vaudevilles' and turning out lyrics. From setback to setback, from the failed journal to the weekly planned for the indefinite future,[63] this slightly optimistic adolescent, who has neither the material means (income) nor the intellectual capacity indispensable for long remaining in a state of awaiting the recognition of the public, becomes an embittered man, ready to denigrate everything, in his contemporaries' art as in revolutionary action.[64] In time, he finds himself installed in the post of organizer of a reactionary circle,[65] an intellectual who has tried and given up everything, especially intellectual things, and who is now ready for anything, even for writing the biographies of captains of industry,[66] in order to win the 'high place' from whence he would dominate 'all the theatres and the whole of the press'.[67]

That leaves Frédéric; an heir who does not want to become what he is, that is, a bourgeois, he oscillates between mutually exclusive strategies and, carried along by his refusal of the possibilities offered to him – notably by means of marriage to Louise – he ends by compromising all his chances of reproduction. The contradictory ambitions that carry him successively towards the two poles of the social space, to an artistic career or to business, and, in parallel, to the two women associated with these positions, are the distinctive feature of a being *without gravity* (another word for seriousness), incapable of posing the slightest resistance to the forces of the field.

All that he can oppose to these forces is his inheritance, which he uses to defer the moment when he will be heir, in order to prolong the state of indetermination which defines him.

When he is for the first time 'ruined, robbed, done for', he renounces Paris and everything associated with it, 'art, learning, and love',[68] to resign himself to the law office of Maître Prouharam; but, once he inherits from his uncle, he takes up again the Parisian dream which appears to his mother, responsible for calling him to order, that is, to objective chances, as 'an absurd folly'. A fresh collapse of his shares makes him decide to return to the provinces, the maternal home, and Mlle Roque, that is, to his 'natural place' in the social order. 'At the end of July an inexplicable slump occurred in Northern Railway shares. Frédéric had not sold his, and he lost sixty thousand francs at one blow. His income was considerably reduced as a result. He must either cut down his expenditure, or adopt a profession, or make a rich marriage.'[69]

Deprived of any strength of his own, whether in terms of the tendency to continue in the dominant position which characterizes heirs disposed to conform, or of the aspiration to accede to it which defines the petit-bourgeois, he defies the fundamental law of the field of power and attempts to evade the irreversible choices which determine social ageing and to reconcile contraries, art and money, all-consuming passions and rational love. And he sees this clearly when, at the end of the novel, learning from his innumerable failures, he attributes his defeat to 'the lack of a straight line'.

Incapable of determining himself, of kissing good-bye to one or the other of the incompatible possibilities, Frédéric is a dual being, with or without duplicity, and hence fated to misunderstanding and mix-ups, whether spontaneous, provoked or exploited, or to the double game of a 'double existence'[70] that the coexistence of separate universes makes possible and which permits the deferral, for a time, of determinations.

It is by a first misunderstanding that the dramatic mechanism which organizes the whole work is announced. Deslauriers, who turns up at Frédéric's at a moment when the latter is preparing to go out, believes that he is going to dine at the Dambreuses' and not at the Arnoux', and jokes: 'Anybody would think you were getting married!'[71] The mix-ups continue with a misunderstanding that is cynically maintained by Frédéric, when Rosanette believes that he is crying as she is for their dead child, whereas he is thinking of Mme Arnoux;[72] and also when Rosanette, whom Frédéric receives in the apartment prepared for Mme Arnoux, interprets for herself kindnesses and tears destined for another, without Frédéric doing anything to disabuse her. There is a misunderstanding again when Frédéric accuses Rosanette of having launched against Arnoux (that means against Mme Arnoux) legal proceedings for which in fact Mme Dambreuse is responsible.[73] Frédéric's amorous comedy of errors gives meaning to the implicit chiasma in Rosanette's cry from the heart: 'Why should you go and amuse yourself with respectable women?'[74] There is a mix-up organized by Martinon who, with the unwitting complicity of Frédéric, only too happy to be seated near Mme Arnoux, takes his place so as to be seated next to Cécile.[75] Martinon also organizes another knowing mix-up: once more with the complicity of his victim, he pushes Mme Dambreuse into Frédéric's arms, yet he pays court to Cécile, whom he will marry, thus inheriting through her the fortune of M. Dambreuse, which he had pursued first via Mme Dambreuse, who is finally disinherited by her husband at the very moment Frédéric inherits her.

Frédéric seeks in the strategies of the double game (or self-division) the means of maintaining himself for a while in the bourgeois universe which he recognizes as 'his natural environment'[76] and which procures for him 'a feeling of contentment, of profound satisfaction'.[77] He tries to reconcile the contraries by reserving for them separate spaces and times. At the price of a rational division of his time and a few lies, he manages to combine the noble love of Mme Dambreuse, the incarnation of bourgeois respectability 'whose name appeared in fashion magazines'[78] and the playful love of Rosanette, who falls for him with an exclusive passion at the very moment he discovers the charms of double inconstancy: 'he repeated to one the vow he had just made to the other; he sent them two similar bouquets, wrote to both of them at the same time, then made comparisons between them; but there was a third woman who was always in his thoughts. The impossibility of possessing her served as a justification for his deceitful behaviour, which sharpened his pleasure by providing constant variety.'[79] The same strategy occurs in politics where he involves himself in a candidature 'supported by a Conservative and extolled by a Radical'[80] which will also end in failure: 'Two new candidates appeared, one a Conservative, the other a Radical; a third would have no chance, whatever his politics. It was Frédéric's fault; he had let his opportunity slip; he ought to have come earlier and bestirred himself.'[81]

Necessary accidents

But the possibility of the *accident*, the unforeseen collision of socially exclusive possibles, is also inscribed in the coexistence of independent series. The sentimental education of Frédéric is the progressive learning about the incompatibility between two universes, between art and money, pure love and mercenary love; it is the story of structurally necessary accidents which determine social ageing by determining the telescoping of structurally irreconcilable possibles which were allowed to exist in an equivocal state by the double games of 'double existence': the successive meetings of independent causal series annihilate little by little all the 'lateral possibles'.[82]

By way of verifying the proposed model, it may suffice to observe that the structural necessity of the field, which wrecks the disordered ambitions of Frédéric, will defeat the essentially contradictory enterprise of Arnoux: veritable structural twin of Frédéric, the art dealer is, like him, a double being, representing money and business in the universe of art.[83] While he can defer for a while the fatal outcome to which he is destined by the law of the incompatibility among universes by playing, like Frédéric, a permanent double game, Arnoux is doomed to ruin by his indetermination and his ambition to reconcile contraries: 'Since his mind was incapable of reaching the peaks of high art and not philistine enough to aim purely at profit, he was falling between two stools and heading for disaster.'[84] It is remarkable that one of the last positions that Deslauriers and Hussonnet dangle before Frédéric, by contrast with those he has discounted in administration or business, is completely similar to the one previously occupied by Arnoux: 'You must give a dinner once a week. That's absolutely indispensable, even if it costs you half your income. People will want to be invited; it will be a meeting-place for others, a lever for you; and using the two handles of literature and politics to manipulate public opinion, we'll have Paris at our feet within six months, you'll see!'[85]

To understand this sort of game of 'loser takes all' which is Frédéric's life, one must have in mind on the one hand the link Flaubert establishes between the forms of love and the forms of love of art which are in the midst of being invented, at more or less the same time, and in the same world – that of bohemia and artists – and on the other hand the relation of inversion which opposes the universe of pure art and the world of business. The game of art is, from the point of view of business, a game of 'loser takes all'. In this economic world turned upside down, one cannot conquer money, honours (it is Flaubert who said that 'honours dishonour'), women (legitimate or illegitimate), in short, all the symbols of worldly success, success in high society and success in this world, without compromising one's salvation in the hereafter. The fundamental law of this *paradoxical* game is that there one has an interest in distinterestedness: the love of art is a crazed love [*l'amour fou*], at least when one considers it from the viewpoint of the norms of the ordinary, 'normal' world put on to the stage by the bourgeois theatre.

It is through this similarity between the forms of love of art and the forms of love that the law of the incompatibility between the universes is realized. In effect, in the order of ambition, the swinging oscillations between art and power tend to tighten up the further on one gets in the story; this is so even though Frédéric continues to swing for a long time between a position of power in the world of art and a position in administration or business (that of secretary general in the firm run by M. Dambreuse, or that of auditor to the Council of State). In the sentimental order, on the contrary, swings of greater amplitude, between crazed love and mercenary love, are played out to the end; Frédéric is placed between Mme Arnoux, Rosanette and Mme Dambreuse, whereas Louise (Roque), the 'promised one', the most probable possible, is never more than a refuge for him and a revenge in times when his stocks are literally and figuratively low.[86] And most of the accidents, which close down the space of possibles, will occur through the intermediary of these three women; more specifically, accidents will arise from the relationship that, through these women, unites Frédéric to Arnoux or to M. Dambreuse, to art and to power.

These three feminine figures represent a system of possibles, each of them defining herself by opposition with the two others: 'When he was with her [Mme Dambreuse] he did not feel that overwhelming ecstasy which impelled him towards Madame Arnoux, nor the happy excitement which Rosanette had caused him at first. But he desired her as an exotic, refractory object, because she was noble, because she was rich, and because she was devout . . .'[87] Rosanette is contrasted with Mme Arnoux as the easy girl compared with the inaccessible woman whom one refuses in order to continue day-dreaming of her and loving her in the unreality of the past; as the 'worthless girl' compared with the priceless woman, sacred, 'saintly':[88] 'the one playful, wild, amusing; the other grave and almost religious.'[89] On the one hand, someone whose social truth (a 'trollop'[90]) is always recalled (from such a mother one may accept only a son, and he – she suggests it herself, acknowledging thereby her indignity – will be called Frédéric like his father). On the other hand, someone whom everything predestines to be a mother,[91] and of a 'little girl' who would resemble her.[92] As for Mme Dambreuse, she is equally well contrasted with the one as with the other: she is the antithesis of all forms of 'fruitless passions',[93] as Frédéric says, 'follies' or 'crazed love', which bring bourgeois families to despair because they destroy ambition. In her, as in Louise, but at a level of superior achievement, the antinomy of power and love, of the sentimental attachment and the business connection, is abolished: Mme Moreau herself can only applaud, reawakened to her loftiest dreams. But, while it brings power and money, this bourgeois love, in which Frédéric will see retrospectively 'a slightly shameful specu-lation',[94] inversely does not procure either delight or 'rapture', and must even draw its substance from authentic loves: 'He made us of his old love. He told her about all the emotions which Madame Arnoux had once aroused in him – his yearnings, his fears, his dreams.'[95] 'He admitted at that moment what he had refused to acknowledge until then – the disillusionment of his senses. This did not prevent him from simulating ardent passion; but in order to feel it, he had to summon up the image of Rosanette or Madame Arnoux.'[96]

The first accident which will put an end to Frédéric's artistic ambitions occurs when it is necessary to choose between three possible destinations for the fifteen thousand francs he has just received from his notary:[97] whether to give them to Arnoux to help him to escape bankruptcy (thereby saving Mme Arnoux), entrust them to Deslauriers and Hussonnet and launch himself into a literary enterprise, or bring them to M. Dambreuse for investment.[98] 'He stayed at home, cursing Deslauriers, for he wanted to keep his promise and yet help Arnoux at the same time. "What if I approached Monsieur Dambreuse? But under what pretext could I ask him for money? On the contrary, I ought to be taking him some money for his coal shares!" '[99] And the misunderstanding is prolonged: Dambreuse offers him the post of secretary general when in reality he has come to intercede for Arnoux at the request of Mme Arnoux.[100] Thus, it is from the relation which unites him with Arnoux, that is to the world of art, through the passion he feels for his wife, that there arises for Frédéric the ruin of his artistic possibles, or more exactly the collision of the three mutually exclusive possibles which possess him: *l'amour fou*, principle and expression of the rejection of being an heir, hence of ambition; the contradictory ambition for power in the world of art, that is, in the universe of non-power; and the wavering and defeated ambition for real power.

Another accident, born of the double game and of comedy of errors, puts a definite end to all double games: Mme Dambreuse, who has learned that the twelve thousand francs that Frédéric had borrowed from her under false pretences were destined to save Arnoux, and so Mme Arnoux,[101] has put up to auction, on the advice of Deslauriers, the goods of the Arnoux couple; Frédéric, who suspects Rosanette of this action, breaks off with her. And it is the final meeting, archetypal manifestation of this structure, which assembles Mme Dambreuse and Rosanette around the 'relics' of Mme Arnoux. To the purchase by Mme Dambreuse of the casket of Mme Arnoux, which reduces the symbol and the love it symbolizes to its value in money (a thousand francs), Frédéric retaliates by the rupture, and re-establishes Mme Arnoux in her status as priceless object 'by sacrificing a fortune to her'.[102] Placed between the woman who buys love and the one who sells it, between two incarnations of bourgeois love, the good match and the mistress, complementary and hierarchized, moreover, as the *monde* and the *demi-monde*, Frédéric affirms a pure love, irreducible to money and any objects of bourgeois interest, a love for a thing which, after the fashion of the pure work of art, is not for sale and is not made to be sold. Just as pure love is art for the sake of the art of love, art for art's sake is the pure love of art.

There is no better testimony of all that separates literary writing from scientific writing than this capacity, which it alone possesses, to concentrate and condense in the concrete singularity of a sensitive figure and an individual adventure, functioning both as metaphor and as metonymy, all the complexity of a structure and a history which scientific analysis must laboriously unfold and deploy. Thus it is that the sale at auction telescopes in an instant the whole story of the casket with the silver clasps, which itself condenses the whole structure and story of the confrontation between these three women and what they symbolize: at the first dinner in the rue de Choiseul, at the Arnoux', it is there, on the mantelpiece; Mme Arnoux takes from it the bill for the cashmere that Arnoux had given to Rosanette. Frédéric will spot it, at Rosanette's, in the second antechamber, 'between a vase full of visiting cards and a writing case'. And it is logically the witness and the prize of the ultimate confrontation between the three women, or, more exactly, of the final confrontation of Frédéric *with* the three women, which happens over this object and cannot fail to evoke the 'theme of the three caskets' analysed by Freud.

We know that Freud, taking as his point of departure a scene from Shakespeare's *The Merchant of Venice* where the suitors must choose between three caskets, one of gold, one of silver and the third of lead, shows that this theme in fact deals with the 'choice that a man makes between three women', the caskets being 'symbols of the essential of femininity, hence of woman herself'.[103] One may suppose that, by means of the mythic schema unconsciously put to work to evoke this sort of rape of the dreamed purity of Mme Arnoux, represented by the mercenary appropriation of her casket, Flaubert involves a homologous social scheme as well, to wit, the opposition between art and money. He can thus produce a representation of a wholly essential region of the social space which at first seems absent: the literary field itself, which is organized around the opposition between pure art, associated with pure love, and bourgeois art, under its two forms, mercenary art that can be called major, represented by the bourgeois theatre and associated with the figure of Mme Dambreuse, and minor mercenary art, represented by vaudeville, cabaret or the serial novel, evoked by Rosanette. There again, one has to suppose

that it is by means of and for the sake of the elaboration of a story
that the author is led to uncover the most deeply buried structure –
the most obscure because it is the most directly linked to his primary
investments – which is at the foundation of his mental structures and
his literary strategies.

The power of writing

One is thus led to the true site of the relation, so often evoked,
between Flaubert and Frédéric. In place of the customary complacent
and naive projections of an autobiographical type, one should in fact
perceive an enterprise of *objectification of the self*, of autoanalysis, of
socioanalysis. Flaubert separates himself from Frédéric, from the
indetermination and powerlessness which define him, in the very act
of writing the story of Frédéric, whose impotence manifests itself,
among other things, by his inability to write, to become a writer.[104]
Far from suggesting the identification of the author with the character, it is certainly to register more clearly how far he is separating
himself from Gustave and his love for Mme Schlésinger by the very
act of writing the story of Frédéric that Flaubert indicates that
Frédéric undertakes to write a novel, quickly abandoned, which takes
place in Venice and whose hero 'was himself, the heroine, Madame
Arnoux'.[105]

Flaubert sublimates the indetermination of Gustave, his 'profound
apathy',[106] in the retrospective appropriation of himself that he
ensures by writing the story of Frédéric. Frédéric loves in Mme
Arnoux 'the woman in romantic novels';[107] he will never find again
in real happiness all ideal happiness;[108] he becomes inflamed with 'an
indescribable feeling of retrospective lust'[109] during the literary evocation of royal mistresses; he conspires – by his clumsiness, his
indecisiveness, or his daintiness – with the objective circumstances
that come to delay or prevent the satisfaction of a desire or the
fulfilment of an ambition.[110] And one thinks of the phrase at the very
end of the novel, concluding the nostalgic recollection by Frédéric
and Deslauriers of their disastrous visit to the house of the Turkish
woman: 'That was our best time!'[111] This rout of naiveté and purity
is retrospectively revealed as a fulfilment: in fact, it condenses
Frédéric's whole story, that is, the experience of the virtual possession
of a plurality of possibles between which one will not and cannot
choose, an experience that, by the indetermination that it determines,
is at the root of powerlessness. It is this desperately retrospective
revelation that is the destiny of all those who can only live their lives

in the future anterior tense, in the manner of Mme Arnoux evoking her relation with Frédéric: 'Never mind, we shall really and truly have loved each other!'[112]

One could cite twenty phrases from his *Letters* where Flaubert seems to speak precisely Frédéric's language: 'Many things that leave me cold when I see them or when others talk about them enrapture me, irritate me, or hurt me if I speak of them, and especially if I write.'[113] 'You can depict wine, love, women and glory on the condition that you're not a drunkard, a lover, a husband, or a private in the ranks. If you participate actively in life, you don't see it clearly: you suffer from it too much or enjoy it too much. The artist, to my way of thinking, is a monstrosity, something outside nature.'[114] But the author of *Sentimental Education* is precisely someone who knew how to make an artistic project out of the 'inactive passion' of Frédéric.[115] Flaubert could not say: 'Frédéric, *c'est moi*.' By the very act of writing a story which could have been his, he shows that this story of a failure could not be the story of the person who wrote it.

Flaubert has turned to good account what Frédéric took to be destiny: the rejection of social determinations, the ones attached, like bourgeois maledictions, to a social position, as well as properly intellectual features such as membership of a literary group or a review.[116] He tried throughout his life to keep himself in that indeterminate position, that *neutral place* where one can soar above groups and their conflicts, the struggles waged by different species of intellectuals and artists among each other, and those which pit them all against different varieties of 'owners'. *Sentimental Education* marks a privileged moment in that endeavour: the aesthetic intention and the neutralization which it implements in the novel apply to the very possibility which he had to deny to be constituted himself – to wit, the passive indetermination of Frédéric, which is the spontaneous equivalent, and therefore a failed one, of the active indeterminacy of the 'creator' he is labouring to create. The immediate compatibility of all the social positions which, in ordinary existence, cannot be simultaneously (or even successively) occupied, between which one had better choose, and by which, whether one wishes it or not, one is chosen – it is only in and by literary creation that one may live that compatibility.

'That is why I love Art. There, at least, everything is freedom, in this world of fictions. There, one is satisfied, does everything, is both a king and his subjects, active and passive, victim and priest. No limits; humanity is for you a puppet with bells you make ring at the end of his sentence like a buffoon with a kick.'[117] One thinks, too, of the imaginary biographies which Saint Antony retrospectively gives himself: 'I might as well have stayed with the monks of Nitria [. . .] But

I would have served my brothers better by simply becoming a priest [. . .] It was up to me to become . . . say . . . a grammarian, or a philosopher [. . .]. Better have been a soldier. [. . .] Neither was there anything to stop me from putting down money for a post as toll-gatherer on some bridge.'[118] Among the numerous variations on the theme of compossible existences, one remembers this passage from a letter to George Sand: 'I do not experience, as you do, that sense of a life that is beginning, the stupefaction of an existence freshly unfurling. It seems to me, on the contrary, that I have always existed! And I am *possessed* by memories that go back to the Pharoahs. I see myself at different moments of history, very clearly, in various guises and occupations. My present self is the result of all my vanished selves. I was boatman on the Nile, *leno* [procurer] in Rome at the time of the Punic Wars, then Greek rhetorician in Suburra, where I was devoured by bedbugs. I died, during the Crusades, from eating too many grapes on the beach in Syria. I was pirate and monk, mountebank and coachman – perhaps Emperor of the East, who knows?'[119]

Writing abolishes the determinations, constraints and limits which are constitutive of social existence: to exist socially means to occupy a determined position in the social structure and to bear the marks of it, especially in the form of verbal automatisms or mental mechanisms;[120] it also means to depend on, to hold to and to be held by, in short, *to belong to* groups and be enclosed in networks of relations which have objectivity, opacity and permanency, and which show themselves in the form of obligations, debts, duties – in short controls and constraints. As with Berkeleyan idealism, the idealism of the social world supposes both the overview and absolute viewpoint of the sovereign spectator, freed from dependence and from work through which the resistance of the physical and the social world makes itself felt, and thus capable, as Flaubert says, 'of placing oneself in one bound above humanity and having nothing in common with it other than a relation of the eye'. Eternity and ubiquity, these are the divine attributes with which the pure observer endows himself. 'I saw other people live, but with another life than mine: some believed, others denied, still others doubted, and others finally didn't care about those things at all and went about their business, that is, selling in their shops, writing their books or crying in their pulpits.'[121]

One recognizes, here again, Flaubert's fundamental relation to Frédéric as the possibility, simultaneously surpassed and conserved, of Gustave. Through the character of Frédéric, which he could have been, Flaubert objectifies the idealism of the social world which is expressed in the relationship of Frédéric to the universe of positions offered to his aspirations, and in the dilettantism of the bourgeois adolescent provisionally free of social constraints, 'with no one to care for, with no hearth or home, with no faith or law', as Sartre says in *La Mort dans l'âme*. By the same token, the *social ubiquity* that

Frédéric pursues is inscribed in the social definition of the writer's trade, and it will henceforward be part of the representation of the artist as the uncreated 'creator', with neither attachments nor roots, orienting not only literary production but a whole way of living the situation of an intellectual.

But it is difficult to put aside the question of the social determinations of ambition, to tear oneself out of all determinations and to soar in thought over the social world and its conflicts. What Frédéric's story reminds us of is that intellectual ambition may be only the imaginary inversion of the failure of temporal ambitions. Is it not significant that Frédéric, who, while at the summit of his trajectory, does not hide his disdain for his friends, failed revolutionaries (or revolutionary failures), never feels himself as much an intellectual as when his business affairs are going badly? Disconcerted by the reproach of M. Dambreuse regarding his shares and by the allusions of Madame Dambreuse to his carriage and to Rosanette, he defends among bankers the positions of the intellectual, concluding 'I don't care a damn about business!'[122]

And how could the writer avoid asking himself whether the contempt of the writer for the 'bourgeois' and for the temporal possessions imprisoning him – property, titles, decorations, women – does not owe something to the resentment of the 'bourgeois' *manqué*, led to convert his failure into the aristocratism of an elective renunciation? 'Artists: Praise their disinterestedness,' says the *Dictionary of Received Ideas*. The cult of disinterestedness is the principle of a prodigious reversal, which turns poverty into rejected riches, hence spiritual riches. The poorest of intellectual projects is worth a fortune – the fortune which is sacrificed to it. Better still, there is no temporal fortune which can rival it, since it would always be preferred anyway ... As for the autonomy which is supposed to justify this imaginary renunciation of an imaginary wealth, is it not the conditional freedom, limited to its separate universe, which the 'bourgeois' assigns it? Does not the revolt against the 'bourgeois' remain governed by what it contests, as long as it ignores the principle, truly *a contrario*, of its existence? How can one be sure that it is not still the 'bourgeois' who, in keeping him at a distance, allows the writer to distance himself from *him*?[123]

Flaubert's formula

Thus, through the character of Frédéric and the description of his positioning in the social space, Flaubert delivers the generative formula which is the basis of his own novelistic creation: the double refusal of opposed positions in different social spaces and of the corresponding taking of positions which is at the foundation of an objectifying distance with respect to the social world.

'Frédéric, caught *between two dense masses*, did not budge; in any case, he was fascinated and enjoying himself tremendously. The wounded falling to the ground, and the dead lying stretched out, did not look as if they were really wounded or dead. He felt as if he were watching a *play*.'[124] One could take an inventory of the innumerable attestations of this *aesthetic neutralism*: 'I feel no more pity for the lot of the modern working classes than for that of the ancient slaves who turned the millstones. I am no more modern than I am ancient, no more French than Chinese.'[125] 'The only things that exist for me in the world are splendid poetry, harmonious, well-turned, singing sentences, beautiful sunsets, moonlight, pictures, ancient sculpture, and strongly marked faces. Beyond that, nothing. I would rather have been Talma than Mirabeau, because he lived in a sphere of purer beauty. I am as sorry for caged birds as for enslaved human beings. In all of politics, there is only one thing that I understand: the riot. I am as fatalistic as a Turk, and believe that whether we do everything we can for the progress of humanity, or nothing at all, makes no whit of difference.'[126] And to George Sand, who excited his nihilistic verve, Flaubert writes: 'Ah, how tired I am of the ignoble worker, the inept bourgeois, the stupid peasant and the odious ecclesiastic! This is why I am losing myself, as much as I can, in antiquity!'[127]

The double refusal is no doubt also at the root of all the character couplets which function like generative schemas of the novelistic discourse: Henry and Jules of the first *Sentimental Education*, Frédéric and Deslauriers, Pellerin and Delmar in the actual *Sentimental Education*, and so forth. It is affirmed once again in Flaubert's taste for symmetries and antitheses (particularly visible in the scenarios of *Bouvard and Pécuchet* published by Demorest), antitheses between parallel things and parallels between antithetical things, and above all for the crossed trajectories which lead so many of Flaubert's characters from one extreme to another in the field of power, with all the sentimental recantations and all the correlative political changes of mind, which are in fact simple developments in time, in the form of biographical processes, of the same chiasmatic structure. In *Sentimental Education* there is Hussonnet, a revolutionary who becomes a conservative ideologist, and Sénécal, a republican who as police agent in the service of the coup d'état cuts down his old friend Dussardier on the barricade.[128]

But the clearest proof of this generative scheme, the veritable principle of Flaubertian invention, is revealed in the notebooks in which Flaubert outlines the scenarios of his novels, where the structures that writing blurs and dissimulates through the imposition of form are apparent in all their clarity. There, on three occasions, two couples of antithetical characters with intersecting trajectories are fated to all the changes of direction and repudiations, pirouettes and *volte-faces*, especially from left to right, that are so beguiling to bourgeois disenchantment. I must quote in its entirety the project 'The oath of friends', in which Flaubert dramatizes two of these changes of heart so dear to him, in a social space rather similar to that of the *Education*.

THE OATH OF FRIENDS

An [industrial] <tradesman>, opaque, making a great fortune

couple ⎰ a man of letters at first poet ... then tumbled-
down journalist becomes famous
a true poet – increasingly refined and obscure
– concrete
doctor
jurist man of the law. notary

couple ⎰ Lawyer – republican. becoming Minister.
work of the family to demoralize him (ern.
knighthood)
a true republican all utopias successively

(Emm. Vasse)
ends up on the guillotine
employed in an office

The degradation of Man by Woman. – The Hero-democrat, <lettered> free-thinker <& poor> in love with a great Catholic lady. Modern philosophy and religion in opposition, – and filtering into each other.
He is virtuous at first to earn her. <she is his ideal> then seeing that it is of no use, he becomes dishonest. & reveals himself at the end by an act of devotion. – he saves her during the Commune in which he participates, turning later against the commune and getting killed by the Versaillais.
He is at first an <unpublished> lyric poet – then <unpro-duced> playwright – then <unnoticed> novelist – then journalist. [then] <will become> a civil servant at the fall of the empire. – He turned to power during the Olivier Ministry.
So She [will] <want to> give him his daughter

A liberal (a little <becoming more and more> sceptical) the Catholic woman corrupts him slowly
– She loses her faith.
He is ruined.

Durry, *Flaubert et ses Projets inédits*, p. 111; pp. 258–9

Everything leads us to think that the work of writing ('the torments of style' that Flaubert so often mentions) aims first of all to master the uncontrollable effects of the ambivalent relation towards all those who gravitate within the field of power. This ambivalence that Flaubert shares with Frédéric (in whom he objecti-fies it), and which means that he can never identify completely with any of his characters, is undoubtedly the practical basis of the extreme care he takes in controlling the distance inherent in the situation of the narrator. The concern to avoid the *confusion of*

personas to which novelists so often succumb (when they put their
.thoughts into the minds of characters), and to maintain a distance
even in the decisive identification that leads to true understanding,
seems to be the common root of a whole set of stylistic traits
discovered by different analysts: for example, the deliberately
ambiguous use of a *citation* which may have the value of either
ratification or derision, and expresses both hostility (the theme of
the 'collection of foolish quotations')[129] and identification; the complex linking of direct speech, indirect speech and free indirect speech
which allows him to vary in an infinitely subtle manner the distance
between the subject and the object of the tale and the narrator's
point of view on the characters ('Of all Frenchmen, the one who
trembled the most was Monsieur Dambreuse. The new state of
affairs not only threatened his fortune but, far worse, contradicted
his experience. Such a splendid system! Such a wise king! What
could have happened? The world was coming to an end! The very
day after the Revolution he dismissed three servants, sold his horses,
bought a soft hat to wear in the street, and even thought of letting
his beard grow . . .'[130]); the use of *as if* ('So he shuddered, seized by
an icy sadness, as if he had seen entire worlds of misery and despair
. . .'), which, as Gérard Genette observes, 'introduces a hypothetical
vision'[131] and explicitly reminds us that the author is attributing to
characters some probable thoughts instead of 'lending them his own
thoughts', without his being aware of it and, in any case, without
letting it be known; the use, noted by Proust, of verbal tenses, and
in particular the imperfect and the simple past, each to mark variable
distances from the present for the narration and for the narrator's
voice; the recourse to dots which, like immense points of suspension,
open a space for silent reflection by the author and the reader; and
finally, the 'generalized asyndeton' identified by Roland Barthes,[132] a
negative manifestation – hence unperceived – of the withdrawal of
the author, which is marked by a suppression of these miniscule
logical interventions, the linking particles, through which are introduced, in an imperceptible way, relations of causality or finality,
opposition or similitude, and which insinutates a whole philosophy
of action and of history.

Thus the double distance of social neutrality and constant balan-
cing between identification and hostility, and between the support and
the derision that it favours, predisposed Flaubert to produce the
vision of the field of power that he offers in *Sentimental Education*.
It is a vision that one could call sociological if it were not set apart
from a scientific analysis by its form, simultaneously offering and
masking it. In fact, *Sentimental Education* reconstitutes in an extra-

ordinarily exact manner the structure of the social world in which it was produced and even the mental structures which, fashioned by these social structures, form the generative principle of the work in which these structures are revealed. But it does so with its own specific means, that is, by giving it to be *seen* and *felt* in *exemplifications* (or, better, *evocations* in the strong sense of incantations capable of producing effects, notably *on the body*), in the 'evocatory magic' of words apt to 'speak to the sensibilities' and to obtain a belief and an imaginary participation *analogous* to those that we ordinarily grant to the real world.[133]

The sensitive translation conceals the structure, in the very form in which it presents it, and thanks to which it succeeds in producing a *belief effect* (more than a reality effect). And it is probably this which means that the literary work can sometimes say more, even about the social realm, than many writings with scientific pretensions (especially when, as here, the difficulties that must be overcome in acceding to knowledge are not so much intellectual obstacles as the resistances of the will). But it says it only in a mode such that it does not truly say it. The unveiling finds its limits in the fact that the writer somehow keeps control of the return of the repressed. The putting-into-form operated by the writer functions like a generalized euphemism, and the reality de-realized and neutralized by literature that he offers allows him to satisfy a desire for knowledge ready to be satisfied by the sublimation offered him by literary alchemy.

In order to unveil completely the structure that a literary text could only unveil by veiling, the analysis should reduce the story of an adventure to the protocol of an experimental montage. It is appreciated that this has something profoundly disenchanting about it. But the hostile reaction it arouses requires the question of the specificity of literary expression to be posed clearly: imposing form also implies respecting formalities [*mettre des formes*], and the denegation that literary expression performs is what permits the limited manifestation of a truth which, put otherwise, would be unbearable. The 'reality effect' is that very particular form of belief that literary fiction produces, through a disclaimed reference to the reality designated, which allows us to know everything by refusing to know what really is. A sociological reading breaks the spell. By interrupting the complicity that unites author and reader in the same relation of denegation of the reality expressed by the text, it reveals the truth that the text enunciates but in such a way that it does not say it; moreover, sociological reading *a contrario* brings to light the truth of the text itself, whose specificity is defined precisely by the fact that it does not say what it says in the same way as the sociological reading does.[134] The form in which literary objectification is enunciated is no doubt what permits the emergence of the deepest reality, the best hidden (here, the structure of the field of power and the model of social ageing), because that is the veil which allows the author and reader to dissimulate it and to close their eyes to it.

The charm of the literary work lies largely in the way it speaks of the most serious things without insisting, unlike science according to Searle, on being taken completely seriously. Writing offers the author and the reader the possibility of a mature understanding which is not half-hearted. Sartre said in his *Critique of Dialectical Reason*, on the subject of his first readings of the works of Marx: 'I understood everything and I understood nothing.' Such is the understanding of life that we have from reading novels. One may 'live all lives', in Flaubert's phrase, by writing or reading, only because they are so many ways of not truly living it. And when we come to really live what we have lived a hundred times in reading novels, we must commence from the beginning our 'sentimental education'. Flaubert, the novelist of the novelistic illusion, introduces us to the principle of that illusion. In reality as in novels the characters who are called romanesque, and among whom we should also include the authors of novels – 'Madame Bovary, *c'est moi*' – are perhaps those who take fiction seriously, not, as it is said, to escape the real and seek evasion in imaginary worlds, but because, like Frédéric, they cannot manage to take reality seriously, because they cannot appropriate the present in the way it presents itself, the present in its insistent – and terrifying – presence. At the basis of the functioning of all social fields, whether the literary field or that of power, there is the *illusio*, the investment in the game. Frédéric is one who does not manage to invest himself in any of the games of art or money that the social world produces and proposes. His Bovaryism is grounded in the powerlessness to take the real – that is, the stakes of games called serious – seriously.

The novelistic illusion that in its most radical forms may extend, as with Don Quixote or Emma Bovary, to the complete abolition of the frontier between reality and fiction thus finds its principle in the experience of reality as an illusion: if adolescence appears as the romanesque age *par excellence*, and if Frédéric appears as the exemplary incarnation of that age, it is perhaps because the entry into life, or rather, into one or other of the social games the social world offers for our investment, does not always go without saying. Frédéric – like all difficult adolescents – is a formidable analyst of our deepest relationship to the social world. To objectivize the novelistic illusion, and especially the relation to the so-called real world it assumes, is to remind ourselves that the reality against which we measure all fictions is merely the recognized referent of an (almost) universally shared illusion.

Appendix 1

Summary of Sentimental Education

Frédéric Moreau, a student in Paris around 1840, meets Madame Arnoux, the wife of the editor of an art magazine, who has a gallery of paintings and engravings in Montmartre. He falls in love with her. He nourishes vague desires simultaneously literary, artistic and worldly. He tries to introduce himself into the household of Dambreuse, a worldly banker, but disappointed by the welcome he receives falls back into uncertainty, idleness, solitude and daydreams. He frequents a whole group of young people who will gravitate around him: Martinon, Cisy, Sénécal, Dussardier, and Hussonnet. He is invited to the Arnoux' home and his passion for Mme Arnoux is renewed. On holiday at his mother's in Nogent, he learns of the precarious situation of his fortune and meets the young Louise Roque, who falls in love with him. As soon as an unexpected legacy makes him rich, he leaves again for Paris.

He finds Mme Arnoux, whose welcome disappoints him. He meets Rosanette, a demi-mondaine, mistress of Monsieur Arnoux. He is torn between diverse temptations, tossed from one to another: on the one hand, Rosanette and the charms of the luxurious life; on the other, Mme Arnoux, whom he tries in vain to seduce; and finally, the rich Mme Dambreuse, who could help him to realize his worldly ambitions. After a long series of hesitations and procrastinations, he returns to Nogent, having decided to marry M. Roque's daughter. But he leaves again for Paris: Marie Arnoux agrees to a rendez-vous. He waits in vain while fighting goes on in the streets (it is 22 February 1848). Disappointed and angry, he will console himself in Rosanette's arms.

A witness to the revolution, Frédéric visits Rosanette assiduously: he has a son by her who soons dies. He also frequents the salon of the Dambreuses.

He becomes the lover of Mme Dambreuse, and after the death of her husband, she proposes marriage to him. But, in a sudden outburst, he breaks off first with Rosanette and then with Mme Dambreuse, but not to run to Mme Arnoux again – after the bankruptcy of her husband, she has left Paris. He returns to Nogent, having decided to marry the Roque girl. But in the meanwhile she has married his friend Deslauriers.

Fifteen years later, in March 1867, Mme Arnoux visits him. They confess their love for each other, recalling the past. They separate for ever.

Two years later, Frédéric and Deslauriers review their failure. All they have left is the memories of their youth; the most precious one, that of a visit to the house of the Turkish woman, is the story of a rout: Frédéric, who had the money, fled the brothel, frightened by the sight of so many women on offer; and Deslauriers had been forced to follow him. They conclude: 'Yes, that was our best time!'

Appendix 2

Four Readings of Sentimental Education

This is a time when one is gladly revolutionary in art and in literature, or at least believes oneself so, since one takes for daring gestures and immense progress everything which contradicts the accepted ideas of the two generations which preceded the one which is reaching maturity. Then, as now and in every age, one is duped by words, one gets enthusiastic about empty phrases, one lives on illusions. In politics, a Regimbart or a Sénécal are types we still find and we will continue to see as long as men continue to frequent brasseries and clubs; in the world of business and finance, there have always been people like Dambreuse and Arnoux; among painters, Pellerins; Hussonnets are still the plagues of editors' offices; and yet, all the above are of their own time and not of today. But they have such humanity that we perceive in them enduring characters who each constitute, instead of a novelistic personage destined to die with his contemporaries, a type which survives his century. And what can we say of the protagonists, Frédéric, Deslauriers, Mme Arnoux, Rosanette, Mme Dambreuse, Louise Roque? No larger novel has ever offered to the reader such a quantity of figures so marked by characteristic traits.

> R. Dumesnil, *En marge de Flaubert*
> (Paris: Librairie de France, 1928), pp. 22–3

The three loves of Frédéric, Mme Arnoux, Rosanette, Mme Dambreuse, could be, by sleight of hand, characterized under the three names of beauty, nature and civilization [...]. At the centre of the picture there are light values. At the edges, dark values, more secondary figures; on the one hand there is the group of revolutionaries, on the other the group of bourgeois, in other words, people of progress and people of order. Right and left, these political realities are here considered as the values pertaining to the artist, and Flaubert sees in them an opportunity to dramatize once more, as in Homais and Bournisien,[135] the two alternate masks of human folly. [. . .] These figures cluster together in the manner in which they recall and complement each other, but they do not belong to the core and the subject of the novel, and one could detach them without appreciably altering the principal design.

A. Thibaudet, *Gustave Flaubert*
(Paris: Gallimard, 1935), pp. 161, 166, 170

What does the title signify? The sentimental education of Frédéric Moreau is his education *by* sentiment. He learns to live, or more exactly, he learns what existence is, by experiencing love, love affairs, friendship, ambition . . . And this experience ends in total failure. Why? First, because Frédéric is, above all, an imaginative person in the bad sense of the word, who daydreams existence instead of lucidly grasping its necessities and limits; then because he is, to a large extent, the masculine replica of Emma Bovary; and finally, and as a consequence, Frédéric is a *waverer*, most of the time *incapable* of taking a decision, except for excessive and extreme decisions made on impulse.

Does this lead one to say that *Sentimental Education* ends in nothingness? I don't think so. Because there is Marie Arnoux. This pure figure *redeems*, so to speak, the whole novel. Marie Arnoux is, we may be certain, Elisa Schlesinger, but one cannot help thinking that she is an Elisa singularly idealized. While Mme Schlesinger was in many respects a very respectable woman, nevertheless what one knows of her, despite everything – her attitude, at the very least equivocal, during her liaison with Schlesinger, and the fact (at least probable) that she had been, at some moment, the mistress of Flaubert – leaves us to think that ultimately Marie Arnoux is undoubtedly the feminine ideal of Flaubert rather than a faithful and authentic image of his 'grand passion'. That does not prevent Marie Arnoux such as she is from remaining – in the middle of a world teeming with *arrivistes*, with the vain, the sensual, the high living, the daydreamers, or the oblivious – a profoundly human figure, composed of tenderness, of resignation, of firmness, of silent suffering and of goodness.

J.-L. Douchin, Foreword to *L'Éducation sentimentale*
(Paris: Larousse, coll. 'Nouveaux Classiques Larousse', 1969), pp. 15–17.

To what extent is the love he bears him homosexual? In his excellent article 'Le Double Pupitre', Roger Kempf has very ably and judiciously established the 'androgyny' of Flaubert. He is man and woman; I have specified above that he wants to be a woman in the hands of women, but it could well be that he may have experienced this avatar of vassality as an abandonment of his body to the desires of the lord. Kempf gives some disturbing citations, the following in particular, which he finds in the second *Education*: 'The day of Deslauriers's arrival, Frédéric allowed himself to be invited by Arnoux . . .'; perceiving his friend, 'he began to tremble like an adulterous woman under the gaze of her husband.' And: 'Then Deslauriers thought of Frédéric's person itself. It had always exercised on him "a nearly feminine charm."' Here we have a pair of friends between whom, 'by a tacit consent, one would play the wife and the other the husband.' Rightly, the critic adds that 'this distribution of rôles is very subtly demanded' by Frédéric's femininity. And Frédéric in the *Education* is the chief incarnation of Flaubert. Conscious of this femininity, we may say he internalizes it by making himself Deslauriers's wife. Gustave very skillfully shows us how Deslauriers is excited by his wife Frédéric, but we never see Frédéric enraptured with the virility of his husband.

J.-P. Sartre, *The Family Idiot: Gustave Flaubert 1821–1857*, trans. Carol Cosman (Chicago: University of Chicago Press, 1981), vol. 2, p. 380.

Appendix 3

The Paris of Sentimental Education

In the geographical triangle whose corners are represented by the world of business (IV on the map, the 'Chaussée d'Antin', the Dambreuse residence), the world of art and of successful artists (V, the 'Faubourg Montmartre', with *L'Art Industriel* and the successive residences of Rosanette) and the student milieu (II, the 'Quartier Latin', the initial residence of Frédéric and of Martinon) can be seen a structure which is quite simply that of the social space of *Sentimental Education*. This universe as a whole is objectively defined in its turn by a double relation of opposition, though one never evoked in the work itself, on the one hand to the old aristocracy of the 'Faubourg St-Germain' (III), often mentioned by Balzac and totally absent from *Sentimental Education*, and on the other to the 'classes populaires', the working classes (I): in fact, the zones of Paris which were the site of the decisive revolutionary events of 1848 are excluded from Flaubert's novel (the descriptions of the first incidents in the Latin Quarter[136] and of the troubles at the Palais-Royal bring us back to the districts of Paris constantly evoked in the rest of the novel). Dussardier, the sole representative in the novel of the popular classes, works at first in the rue de Cléry.[137] The site of Frédéric's arrival in Paris, on the way back from Nogent, is also situated in this area (rue du Coq-Héron).

The 'Latin Quarter', the area of academic study and of 'beginnings in life', is the residence of students and 'working girls' [*'grisettes'*] whose social

This note, prepared and discussed on the occasion of a seminar on the social history of art and literature at the École Normale Supérieure (1973), was compiled in collaboration with J.-C. Chamboredon and M. Kajman.

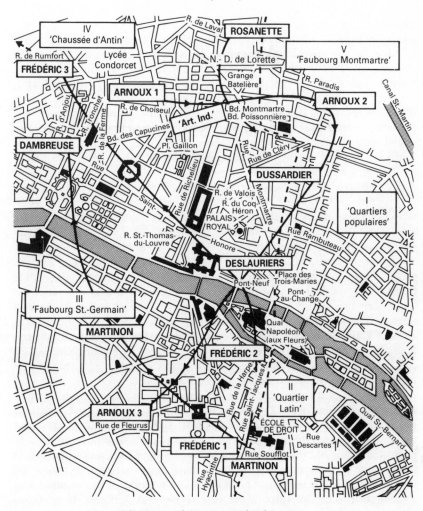

The Paris of *Sentimental Education*

image is being constituted at the time (with, in particular, the *Contes et Nouvelles* of Alfred de Musset, notably 'Frédéric et Bernerette' which appeared in the *Revue des Deux Mondes*). The social trajectory of Frédéric is sketched out there: he inhabits successively the rue Saint-Hyacinthe,[138] then quai Napoléon,[139] and dines regularly in the rue de la Harpe.[140] The same with Martinon.[141] In the social image of Paris that littérateurs were in the course of constructing, and to which Flaubert tacitly refers, the 'Latin Quarter', site of the *fête galante*, of artists and *grisettes* of the 'bohemian life', is strongly opposed to the high place of aristocratic asceticism which is the faubourg Saint-Germain.

The 'Chaussée d'Antin', which means in the universe of *Sentimental*

Education the zone constituted by the streets Rumfort (with Frédéric's hotel), d'Anjou (Dambreuse) and de Choiseul (Arnoux), is where the members of the new ruling fraction of the dominant class reside. This 'new bourgeoisie' is opposed both to the demi-monde of the 'Faubourg Mont-martre' and especially to the old aristocracy of the 'Faubourg Saint-Germain', among other things by the composite character of the population which resides there (as witnessed in the novel by the social distance between Frédéric, Dambreuse and Arnoux) and by the mobility of its members (Dambreuse comes there, Frédéric only gets there after his inheritance, Martinon arrives there by marriage and Arnoux will soon be excluded from it). This new bourgeoisie, which intends to safeguard or create the marks of the old lifestyle of the faubourg Saint-Germain (for example by acquiring very grand town houses), is no doubt, in part, the product of a *social reconversion* which is translated into a *spatial translation*;[142] 'M. Dambreuse was really the Comte d'Ambreuse; but, after 1825, he had gradually abandoned both his title and his party, and had turned his attention towards commerce';[143] and a little later, to mark simultaneously the links and the geographical and social *rupture*: 'By flattering the duchesses, she [Mme Dambreuse] soothed the rancour of the noble faubourg and created the impression that Monsieur Dambreuse might yet repent and render useful service.' The same system of ties and oppositions can be read in the coat-of-arms of Dambreuse, both heraldic mark and label of a knight of industry. The allusion to the committee of the rue de Poitiers,[144] meeting place of all conservative politicians, would confirm if required that it is in this part of Paris that from now on 'everything will be played out.'

The 'Faubourg Montmartre', where Flaubert situated *L'Art Industriel* and the successive domiciles of Rosanette, is the appointed residence of successful artists (it is there for example that Feydeau and Gavarni reside; the latter will in 1841 launch the term 'lorette' to designate the demi-mondaines who haunt the sector of Notre-Dame de Lorette and the place Saint-Georges). In the manner of Rosanette, who in some ways is its literary transfiguration, this quartier is the site of the residence or meeting place of financiers, successful artists, journalists, and also actresses and 'lorettes'. These demi-mondains and demi-mondaines, who, like *L'Art Industriel*, are located halfway between the bourgeois quartiers and the popular ones, are opposed just as much to the bourgeois of the 'Chaussée d'Antin' as to the students, to the *'grisettes'* and the failed artists – whom Gavarni harshly derided in his caricatures – of the 'Latin Quarter'. Arnoux, who at the time of his splendour participates by his residence (rue de Choiseul) and his place of work (boulevard Montmartre) in the universe of money and the universe of art, finds himself first sent back towards the faubourg Montmartre (rue Paradis),[145] before being thrown into the absolute outsiderdom of the rue de Fleurus.[146] Rosanette, too, circulates in the space reserved for 'lorettes', and her decline is marked by a progressive slide to the east, that is to the boundaries of the working-class areas: rue de Laval;[147] then rue Grange-Batelière;[148] and finally, boulevard Poissonnière.[149]

Thus, in this *structured and hierarchized space*, ascending and descending social *trajectories* are clearly distinguished: from south to north-west for the former (Martinon and, for a while, Frédéric), from west to east and/or from north to south for the latter (Rosanette, Arnoux). The failure of Deslauriers is marked by the fact that he never leaves the point of departure, the quartier of students and failed artists (place des Trois-Maries).[150]

PART I

Three States
of the Field

~∞~

Artists. All charlatans.
Praise their disinterestedness.

GUSTAVE FLAUBERT

We are workers of luxury. Thus nobody is rich enough to pay us. When you want to earn money with your pen, you have to do journalism, serials or the theatre. *Bovary* brought me 300 francs, which I had to PUT UP, and I will never make a cent from it. Right now I manage to pay for my paper, but not the errands, trips and books that I need for my work; and, in the end, I find that all right (or I pretend to find it all right), because I don't see what relation there is between a five-franc coin and an idea. You have to love Art for Art's sake; otherwise, the humblest job is worth more.

GUSTAVE FLAUBERT

I

The Conquest of Autonomy

The Critical Phase in the Emergence of the Field

~∞~

It is painful to note that we find similar errors in two opposed schools: the bourgeois school and the socialist school. 'Moralize! Moralize!' cry both with missionary fervour.

CHARLES BAUDELAIRE

> Leave everything.
> Leave Dada.
> Leave your wife, and your mistress.
> Leave your hopes and your fears.
> Sow your children in the corner of a wood.
> Leave the prey for the shadow.
> Leave if need be an easy life, what you are
>   offered for a future situation.
> Hit the road.

ANDRÉ BRETON

The reading of *Sentimental Education* is more than a simple preamble aiming to prepare the reader to enter into a sociological analysis of the social world in which it was produced and which it brings to light. It requires the interrogation of the particular social conditions which are at the origin of Flaubert's special lucidity, and also the limits of that lucidity. Only an analysis of the genesis of the literary field in which the Flaubertian project was constituted can lead to a real understanding of both the generative formula at the core of the book and Flaubert's craftsmanship in *putting it to work [la mettre en oeuvre*], objectifying in one fell swoop this generative structure and the social structure of which it is the product.

We know how much Flaubert contributed, along with others, notably Baudelaire, to the constitution of the literary field as a world apart, subject to its own laws.. To reconstruct Flaubert's point of view, that is, the point in the social space from which his vision of the world was formulated, and that social space itself, is to have a real chance of placing ourselves at the origins of a world whose functioning has become so familiar to us that the regularities and the rules it obeys escape our grasp. And returning to the 'heroic times' of the struggle for independence, when the virtues of revolt and resistance had to assert themselves clearly in the face of a repression exercised in all its brutality (especially during the trials), also means rediscovering the forgotten – or repudiated – principles of intellectual freedom.

A structural subordination

To understand the experience that writers and artists may have had of the new forms of domination they found themselves subjected to in the second half of the nineteenth century, and the horror the figure of the 'bourgeois' sometimes inspired in them, we need to have some idea of the impact of the emergence of industrialists and businessmen of colossal fortunes (like the Talabots, the de Wendels, or the Schneiders). Fostered by the Second Empire's industrial expansion, they were self-made men, uncultured *parvenus* ready to make both the power of money and a vision of the world profoundly hostile to intellectual things triumph within the whole society.[1]

One can cite the testimony of André Siegfried speaking of his own father, an entrepreneur in textiles: 'In his education, culture counted for nothing. To tell the truth, he never had intellectual culture and didn't worry about having any. He was educated, remarkably informed, knew everything he needed for acting on the spot, but the disinterested taste for things of the mind remained foreign to him.'[2] In the same way, André Motte, one of the great patrons of the North, writes: 'I repeat each day to my children that the title of *bachelier* [high school graduate] will never put a piece of bread into their mouths; that I sent them to school to allow them to taste the pleasures of intelligence, and to put them on their guard against all false doctrines, whether in literature, philosophy or history. But I add that it would be very dangerous for them to give themselves over to the pleasures of the mind.'[3]

The reign of money is asserted everywhere, and the fortunes of the newly dominant class, either industrialists making unprecedented profits from technical transformations and state subsidies, or occasionally small speculators, are flaunted in the luxurious mansions of Haussmann's Paris and in the splendour of carriages and dress. The practice of having an official candidate in elections allows new men to be given political legitimacy along with membership in the legislative body, and a large proportion of these are businessmen; it forges tight links between the political world and the economic world, extending progressively to a press becoming increasingly read and increasingly profitable.

The exaltation of money and profit serves the strategies of Napoleon III: in order to secure the loyalty of a bureaucracy not yet fully converted to the 'impostor', he rewards his supporters with sumptuous emoluments and lavish gifts; he increases the number of celebrations in Paris, and in Compiègne, where he invites (in addition to editors and the patrons of the press) those society writers and painters who are the most compliant and conformist, such as Octave Feuillet, Jules Sandeau, Ponsard, Paul Féval, and Meissonier, Cabanel, Gérôme, and those most disposed to behave like courtesans, as when Octave Feuillet and Viollet-le-Duc stage, with the help of Gérôme or Cabanel, 'tableaux vivants' on subjects borrowed from history and mythology.

We are far from the learned societies and the clubs of aristocratic society of the eighteenth century, or even of the Restoration. The relationship between cultural producers and the dominant class no longer retains what might have characterized it in previous centuries, whether that means direct dependence on a financial backer (more common among painters, but also occurring in the case of writers), or even allegiance to a patron or an official protector of the arts. Henceforward it will be a matter of a veritable *structural subordination* which acts very unequally on different authors according to their position in the field. It is instituted through two principal mediations: on the one hand, the market, whose sanctions and constraints are exercised on literary enterprises either directly, by means of sales figures, numbers of tickets sold and so forth, or indirectly, through new positions offered in journalism, publishing, illustration and all forms of industrialized literature; and on the other hand, durable links, based on affinities of lifestyle and value systems, and operating especially through the intermediary of the salons, which unite at least a portion of the writers to certain sections of high society, and help to determine the direction of the generosities of state patronage.

In the absence of true specific apparatuses of consecration (the universities, for example, with the exception of the Collège de France, have no influence in this field), political authorities and members of the imperial family exercise a direct hold on the literary and artistic field, not only by the sanctions which hit newspapers and other publications (lawsuits, censorship, etc.), but also through the material and symbolic profits they are in a position to distribute: pensions (like the one Leconte de Lisle secretly received from the imperial regime), access to the opportunity to be performed in the theatres and concert halls or to exhibit in the Salon de Peinture et de Sculpture (whose control Napoleon III tried to wrest away from the Académie Française), not to mention salaried posts or commissioned offices (like the post of senator granted to Sainte-Beuve), and honorific distinctions, such as appointment to the academies and institutes.

The tastes of the self-made men installed in power lean in the direction of the novel, in its most facile forms – like the serialized novels [*feuilletons*], which are argued over at court and in ministries, and which give rise to lucrative publishing houses. In contrast, poetry, still associated with major romantic battles, with bohemia and with partisanship on behalf of the disfavoured, becomes the object of a deliberately hostile policy, notably on the part of the Minister of State – as evidenced for example by the lawsuit aimed at poets, or by the persecutions of editors such as Poulet-Malassis, who had published a whole poetic avant-garde, notably Baudelaire, Banville, Gautier, Leconte de Lisle, and who was driven to bankruptcy and debtors' prison.

The constraints inherent in belonging to the field of power also apply to the literary field owing to exchanges that are established between the powerful – for the most part upstarts in search of legitimacy – and the most conformist or the most consecrated of writers, notably through the subtly hierarchized universe of the salons.

The Empress surrounds herself, at the Tuileries, with society writers, critics and journalists, all of them as notoriously conformist as Octave Feuillet, who was made responsible for organizing spectacles at Compiègne. Prince Jérôme vaunts his liberalism (for example, he gives a banquet in honour of Delacroix – which does not stop him from receiving Augier) by keeping at his side, at the Palais-Royal, a Renan, a Taine or a Sainte-Beuve. Princess Mathilde, finally, affirms her originality in relation to the imperial court by receiving, in a very selective manner, writers such as Gautier, Sainte-Beuve, Flaubert, the Goncourt brothers, Taine and Renan. Then, further from the court, one finds salons like that of the Duc de Morny, protector of writers and artists; that of Mme de Solms, who, in bringing together personalities as heterogeneous as Champfleury, Ponsard, Auguste Vacquerie and Banville, attracts that prestige attached to a place of opposition; that of Mme d'Agoult, where the liberal press gathers; that of Mme Sabatier, where the friendship between Flaubert and Baudelaire is forged; those of Nina de Callias and Jeanne de Tourbey, both rather heterogeneous assemblages of writers, critics and artists; and finally, that of Louise Colet, frequented by the followers of Victor Hugo and the survivors of Romanticism, but also by Flaubert and his friends.

These salons are not only places where writers and artists can gather together as kindred spirits and meet the powerful – thereby making real, through direct interactions, the continuity from one end of the field of power to the other. They are not merely élitist refuges where those who feel threatened by the eruption of industrialized literature and journalist-writers can give themselves the illusion of reliving (without really believing in it) the aristocratic life of the eighteenth century, a life which is often evoked nostalgically by the Goncourts: 'This bear-cage of nineteenth-century men of letters is curious when you compare it to the society life of littérateurs of the eighteenth century, from Diderot to Marmontel; today's bourgeoisie scarcely seeks out a man of letters except when he is inclined to play the role of mysterious creature, buffoon or guide to the outside world.'[4]

The salons are also, through the exchanges that take place there, genuine articulations between the fields: those who hold political power aim to impose their vision on artists and to appropriate for themselves the power of consecration and of legitimation which they hold, notably by means of what Sainte-Beuve calls the 'literary press';[5] for their part, the writers and artists, acting as solicitors and intercessors, or even sometimes as true pressure groups, endeavour to assure for themselves a mediating control of the different material or symbolic rewards distributed by the state.

The salon of the Princess Mathilde is the paradigm of these *bastard institutions*, whose equivalents can be found in the most tyrannical regimes (fascist or Stalinist, for example) and where exchanges are instituted which it would be false to describe in terms of 'rallying' (or, as one would say after 1968, of 'recuperation') and in which the two camps find some definite advantages. It is often among these personages caught in a double bind – powerful enough to be taken seriously by writers and artists, without being sufficiently so to be taken seriously by the powerful – that arise gentle forms of ascendancy that prevent or discourage the complete *secession* of the holders of cultural power and that bog them down into these confused relations, founded on gratitude as well as guilt over compromises and shady deals, with a power of intercession perceived as a last recourse, or at the very least an exceptional measure, suitable to justify concessions of bad faith and to provide an excuse for heroic ruptures.

This profound imbrication of the literary field and the political field is revealed at the time of Flaubert's trial, an occasion for the mobilization of a powerful network of relations uniting writers, journalists, senior civil servants, major bourgeois who support the Empire (his brother Achille especially) and members of the court – and happening in spite of all differences in taste and lifestyle. That said, in this great chain there are straightforward exclusions. In the first rank is Baudelaire, proscribed from the court and the salons of the members of the imperial family; unlike Flaubert, he loses his trial, because he does not want to fall back on the influence of a family of the haute bourgeoisie, and he smacks of heresy because he mixed with bohemia. However, the ranks also include realists like Duranty, and later Zola and his group (although many of the old guard of the 'second bohemia' like Arsène Houssaye, have entered the ranks of the powerful littérateurs). There are also some who are simply left out, like the Parnassians,[6] often, it is true, of petit-bourgeois origins and bereft of social capital.

Like the routes of domination, the routes of autonomy are complex, if not impenetrable. And the struggles at the heart of the political field – like the one which pits the Empress Eugénie, a foreigner, upstart and bigot, against Princess Mathilde, formerly received by the Faubourg Saint-Germain and long since well acquainted with the Parisian salons, protectress of the arts, liberal guardian of French values – may indirectly serve the interests of the writers most concerned about their literary independence: under the protection of the powerful, the latter can obtain the material or institutional resources that they cannot expect from either the market, that is, the newspaper publishers, or, as they quickly understood after 1848, from the commissions monopolized by their most destitute competitors from bohemia.

Although she is no doubt not so far removed in her real tastes (for the serial novel, the melodrama, Alexander Dumas, Augier, Ponsard and Feydeau) from the Empress whom she impugned as frivolous, the Princess Mathilde wants to give her salon a very high literary profile. Advised in the choice of her guests by Théophile Gautier, who had come to her in 1861 to seek her assistance in finding an employment capable of freeing him from journalism, and by Sainte-Beuve, who was a very famous man in the 1860s, reigning over the *Constitutionnel* and the *Moniteur*, she means to act as a patroness and protectress of the arts. She constantly intervenes to secure favours or protection for her friends: obtaining a seat in the Senate for Sainte-Beuve, the prize of the Académie Française for George Sand, the Légion d'Honneur for Flaubert and Taine, fighting to secure for Gautier first a post, then the Académie, interceding for *Henriette Maréchal* to be performed at the Comédie-Française, and protecting, through the intermediary of her lover Neiuwerkerke, whose taste she followed in painting, official painters like Baudry, Boulanger, Bonnat or Jalabert.[7]

Thus it is that the salons, which distinguish themselves more by whom they exclude than by whom they include, help to structure the literary field (as journals and publishers will do in other states of the field) around great fundamental oppositions: on the one hand the eclectic and fashionable hacks assembled in the court's salons, and on the other the great élitist writers, grouped around Princess Mathilde and at the Magny dinner table (headed by Gavarni, the great friend of the Goncourts, Sainte-Beuve and Chennevières, and including Flaubert, Paul Saint-Victor, Taine, Théophile Gautier, Auguste Neffetzer, editor-in-chief of *Le Temps*, Renan, Berthelot, Charles Edmond, editor of *La Presse*), and finally the bohemian set.

The effects of structural domination are also exercised through the press: in contrast to that of the July Monarchy, which was very diversified and highly politicized, the press of the Second Empire, under the permanent threat of censorship, and quite often under the direct control of bankers, is obliged to offer accounts of official events in a weighty and pompous style; it has to sacrifice itself to vast and inconsequential literary and philosophical theories, and to a pompousness worthy of Bouvard and Pécuchet. The 'serious' journals themselves give space to the serials, light boulevard chronicles and jottings which dominate the two most celebrated creations of the period, *Le Figaro* – whose founder, Henri de Villemessant, spreads the tidbits he manages to collect in the salons, cafés and behind the scenes in the theatres, dividing them between the rubrics of 'échos', 'chronicles', 'letters' – and *Le Petit Journal*, a deliberately apolitical penny paper, which gives pride of place to more or less fictionalized stories of a sensational nature.

The directors of the papers, habitual guests of all the salons and intimates of the political ruling class, are flattered personalities, whom no one dares defy, especially the writers and artists who know that an article in *La Presse* or *Le Figaro* creates a reputation and opens a future. It is through these papers, and the serials of which they have an endless supply and which are read by everybody, from the common people to the bourgeoisie, from ministerial offices to the court, that, as Cassagne puts it, 'industrialism has penetrated literature itself after having transformed the press.'[8] The industrialists of writing follow public taste and manufacture written works in a cursive style, of popular appearance, but not excluding either the 'literary' cliché or the search for stylistic effect, 'whose value is routinely measured by the amount these works have earned'.[9] As an example, every day Ponson du Terrail managed to write a different page each for *Le Petit Journal*, *La Petite Presse*, a literary daily, *L'Opinion Nationale*, a political daily which was pro-imperial, *Le Moniteur*, the Empire's official journal, and *La Patrie*, a very serious political daily. Through their roles as critics, the writer-journalists set

themselves up, in all innocence, as the measure of everything in art
and literature, thereby authorizing themselves to disparage everything
that surpasses them and to condemn all initiatives which might
question the ethical dispositions influencing their judgements and
which above all express the limits and even the intellectual mutila-
tions inscribed in their trajectory and their position.

Bohemia and the invention of an art of living

The development of the press is one index among others of an
unprecedented expansion of the market for cultural goods, linked by
a relationship of circular causality to the inflow of a substantial
population of young people without fortunes, issuing from the middle
or popular classes of the capital and especially the provinces, who
come to Paris trying for careers as writers and artists – careers which
until then had been more strictly reserved for the nobility or the
Parisian bourgeoisie. Despite the multiplication of positions offered
by the development of trade, in fact business and the civil service
(especially the education system) cannot absorb all those with diplomas from secondary schools, whose numbers are increasing rapidly
throughout Europe in the first half of the nineteenth century, and will
see a new rise in France under the Second Empire.[10]

The gap between the supply of dominant positions and the demand for them
is particularly marked in France because of the effect of three specific factors:
first, the relative youth of the administrative personnel coming out of the
Revolution, the Empire and the Restoration, which for a long time blocks access
to those careers open to the children of the small and middle bourgeoisie – in the
army, medicine, the administration – to which should be added the competition
from aristocrats who are regaining administrative positions and barring the
route to professionals ['*capacités*'] coming from the bourgeoisie; secondly, a
centralization that concentrates those with diplomas in Paris; and finally, the
exclusivity of the grande bourgeoisie. The latter, made especially sensitive by
revolutionary experiences, perceives any form of upward mobility as a threat to
the social order (as evidenced by Guizot's speech before the Chamber of Deputies
on 1 February 1836 on the unsuitable character of humanities teaching) and tries
to reserve eminent positions, especially in the upper echelon of the administration, to its own children – among other things, by trying to conserve the
monopoly of access to classical secondary education. In fact, under the Second
Empire, in keeping with economic growth, the personnel in secondary education
continues to grow (going from 90,000 in 1850 to 150,000 in 1875), as do those
in higher education, especially in the literary and scientific fields.[11]

These newcomers, nourished in the humanities and in rhetoric but
deprived of the financial means and the social protection indispens-

able for taking advantage of their degrees, find themselves pushed towards literary professions, which are surrounded with every prestige of romantic triumph and which, in contrast to the more bureaucratized professions, do not require any qualification guaranteed by scholarity, or else pushed towards the artistic professions exalted by the success of the Salon. It is clear in fact that, as always, supposedly morphological factors (and in particular those relating to the *sizes* of the populations concerned) are themselves subordinate to social conditions such as, in this particular case, the prodigious prestige of the career of painter or writer: 'Even those among us who were not of that craft', writes Jules Buisson, 'only thought about things in order to write about them.'[12]

These morphological changes are no doubt one of the major determinants (or at least a precondition) of the process of autonomization of the literary and artistic fields and the correlative transformation of the relation between the world of art and literature and the political world. To understand this transformation, one might think of it by analogy with the oft-analysed shift from the servant, attached by personal ties to a family, to the free worker (of which Weber's agricultural labourer is a particular case) who, freed from the ties of dependence which limited or prevented the free sale of his labour, is available to put himself on the market and to undergo its anonymous constraints and sanctions, often more pitiless than the gentle violence of paternalism.[13] The major virtue of this comparison is to put us on guard against the widespread inclination to reduce this fundamentally ambiguous process solely to its alienating effects (in the tradition of the British Romantics analysed by Raymond Williams): we forget that it exercised liberating effects, too, for example by offering the new 'proletaroid intelligentsia' the possibility of earning a living (no doubt a rather miserable one) from all the small jobs linked to industrial literature and journalism, although the new possibilities thereby acquired could also be the basis of new forms of dependence.[14]

With the assemblage of a very numerous population of young people aspiring to live by art, and separated from all other social categories by the art of living they are in the course of inventing, a genuine society within society makes its appearance. Even if, as Robert Darnton has shown, it was taking shape, on a much smaller scale, as early as the end of the eighteenth century, a society of writers and artists in which scribblers and daubers predominate, at least numerically, has something extraordinary about it, something without precedent, and it gives rise to much investigation, first of all among its own members. The bohemian lifestyle, which has no doubt made an important contribution (with fantasy, puns, jokes, songs, drink and love in all forms) to the invention of the artistic lifestyle, was elaborated as much against the dutiful existence of official painters and sculptors as against the routines of bourgeois life. Making the art of living one of the fine arts means predisposing it to enter into literature; but the invention of the literary personage of bohemia is not simply a fact of literature: from Murger and Champfleury to Balzac and to the Flaubert of the *Sentimental Education*, novelists contribute greatly to the public recognition of this new social entity – especially by inventing and spreading the very notion of bohemia – and to the construction of its identity, values, norms and myths.

The assurance of being collectively keepers of excellence with respect to lifestyle is expressed everywhere, from Murger's *Scenes of Bohemian Life* to Balzac's *Treatise of the Fashionable Life*. Thus, according to Balzac, in a universe divided into 'three classes of being' – 'the man who works' (which throws in together the labourer, mason, soldier, small retailer, office clerk and even the doctor, lawyer, large merchant, country squire and bureaucrat), 'the man who thinks', and 'the man who does nothing' and devotes himself to the 'elegant life' – 'the artist is the exception: his idleness is a form of work, and his work a rest; he is elegant and casual in turn; he puts on, according to whim, the labourer's smock, or decides on the tail coat worn by the man of fashion. He does not follow the rules. He imposes them. Whether occupied in doing nothing or meditating a masterpiece without appearing to be occupied; whether he drives a horse with a wooden bit or holds the reins of an elegantly equipped britschka, whether he doesn't have twenty centimes on him or throws away handfuls of gold, he is always the expression of a great thought and he dominates society.'[15] Force of habit and complicity prevent us from seeing everything that is at stake in a text like this, that is, the work of constructing a social reality in which we participate more or less as intellectuals by affiliation or by aspiration, and which is nothing other than the social identity of the intellectual producer. The reality designated by words in ordinary usage – writer, artist, intellectual – has been made by cultural producers (Balzac's text is only one among thousands), by normative statements, or better yet, by performative ones like this one. Under the guise of saying what is, these descriptions aim to make us see and make us believe, to make the social world be seen in conformity with the beliefs of a social group that has the singularity of having a quasi-monopoly on the production of discourse about the social world.

An ambiguous reality, bohemia inspires ambivalent feelings, even among its most passionate defenders. In the first place this is because it defies classification: near to the 'people', with whom it often shares misery, it is separated from them by the art of living that defines it socially and which, even if ostentatiously opposed to the conventions and proprieties of the bourgeoisie, is situated nearer to the aristocracy or the grande bourgeoisie than to the orderly petite-bourgeoisie, notably in the matter of relations between the sexes, where it experiments on a large scale with all the forms of transgression (free love, venal love, pure love, eroticism) which it institutes as models in its writings. All this is no less true of its most destitute members who, strong in their cultural capital and the authority born of being *taste-makers*, succeed in providing themselves at the least cost with audacities of dress, culinary fantasies, mercenary loves and refined leisure, for all of which the 'bourgeois' pay dearly.

But adding to its ambiguity, bohemia does not stop changing in the course of time, as it grows numerically and as its prestige (or mirages) attracts destitute young people, often of provincial and working-class origin, who around 1848 dominate the 'second bohemia'. In contrast to the romantic dandy of the 'golden bohemia' of the rue de Doyenné, the bohemia of Murger, Champfleury or Duranty constitutes a veritable intellectual reserve army, directly subject to the laws of the market and often obliged to live off a second skill (sometimes with no direct relation to literature) in order to live an art that cannot make a living.

In fact, the two bohemias coexist in practice, but with different social weights at different times: the 'proletaroid intellectuals', who are often so miserable that, in taking themselves for object, according to the tradition of romantic memoirs like Musset's, they invent what will be called 'realism', live alongside, and may also clash with, delinquent or downgraded bourgeois possessing all the properties of the dominants save one: poor relations of the great bourgeois dynasties, aristocrats ruined or in decline, foreigners and members of stigmatized minorities such as the Jews. These 'penniless bourgeois', as Pissarro put it, or those whose income serves only to finance a lost cause, seem to be adjusted in advance, in their double or divided habitus, to the position of a double bind, that of being the dominated among the dominants, which destines them to a sort of objective indetermination, hence a subjective one, never as visible as in the simultaneous or successive fluctuations of their relationship with the powerful.

The rupture with the 'bourgeois'

The relations the writers and artists maintain with the market, whose anonymous sanction may create unprecedented disparities among them, certainly helps to shape the ambivalent picture they have of the 'public' at large, both fascinating and despised. They confuse the 'bourgeois', who are enslaved by the vulgar concerns of commerce, with the 'people', who are given over to the stupefying effect of productive activities. This double ambivalence inclines writers and artists to form an ambiguous image of their own position in the social space and of their social function: this explains why they are given to wide oscillations when it comes to politics, and why – as the numerous changes of regime intervening between the 1830s and 1880s can attest – they tend to slide, like iron filings, towards the pole of the field that is momentarily strong. Thus, when in the last years of the July Monarchy the centre of the field's gravity is displaced to the left, we observe a general slide towards 'social art' and socialist ideas (Baudelaire himself speaks of the 'puerile Utopia of the school of *art for art's sake*'[16] and takes a violent stand against pure art). Tipping the other way, under the Second Empire, without rallying openly behind it, and sometimes proclaiming, as with Flaubert, the greatest contempt for 'Badinguet', a number of defenders of pure art assiduously frequent one or another of the salons run by great personages of the imperial court.

But the society of artists is not merely a laboratory where this singular art of living that is the style of an artist's life is being invented as a fundamental dimension of the enterprise of artistic creation. One of its major functions, and yet one always overlooked, is to be its own market. This society offers the most favourable and comprehensive welcome to the audacities and transgressions that writers and artists introduce, not only into their works but also into their existence (itself conceived as a work of art); the rewards of this privileged market, if they do not manifest themselves in cold cash, have at least the virtue of assuring a form of social recognition for those who otherwise appear (that is, to other groups) as a challenge to common sense. The cultural revolution which gave rise to this inverse world (the literary and artistic field) could only succeed because the great heresiarchs, in their will to subvert all the principles of vision and division, could count if not on the support, at least on the *attention* of all those who, in entering into the universe of art in the process of formation, had tacitly accepted the possibility that everything there was possible.

Thus it is clear that the literary and artistic field is constituted as such in and by opposition to a 'bourgeois' world which had never before asserted so bluntly its values and its pretension to control the instruments of legitimation, both in the domain of art and in the domain of literature, and which, through the press and its hacks, now aims to impose a degraded and degrading definition of cultural production. The distaste mixed with contempt inspired in writers (Flaubert and Baudelaire notably) by this regime of upstarts with no culture, entirely governed by the false and the dubious, and the credit granted by the court to the most common literary works, the very ones the press serve as a vehicle for and celebrate, combined with the vulgar materialism of the new masters of the economy and the sycophantic servility of quite a number of writers and artists, have in no small way contributed to favouring a break with the ordinary world that is inseparable from the constitution of the world of art as a world apart, an empire within an empire.

'Everything was false,' says Flaubert in a letter to Maxime Du Camp dated 28 September 1871:[17] 'a false army, false politics, false literature, false credit, and even false courtesans.' And he develops the theme in a letter to George Sand:[18] 'All was false! False realism, false army, false credit, and even false harlots [. . .]. And this falseness [. . .] was applied especially in the manner of judging. They extolled an actress not as an actress, but as a good mother of a family. They asked art to be moral, philosophy to be clear, vice to be decent, and science to be within the range of the people.' And says Baudelaire: 'The 2 December has physically apoliticized me. There are no more great ideas.' One could also cite, although it comes much later, a text by Bazire on the subject of Manet's *Jesus Mocked by the Soldiers*, which well expresses the particular horror aroused by the cultural atmosphere of the Second Empire: 'This Jesus, who truly suffers at the hands of the brutal soldiers, is a man instead of a god but was accepted as neither . . . People were fanatical about prettiness, and would have liked to see appealing faces on all the figures, victim and executioners alike. There is and always will be a group of people who need to have nature embellished and who will have nothing to do with art unless it is a lie. Such a point of view flourished at that time: the Empire had idealized tastes and hated to see things as they are.'[19]

How could we suppose that the political experience of this generation, with the failure of the revolution of 1848 and the coup d'état of Louis-Napoleon Bonaparte, and then the long period of desolation that was the Second Empire, did not play a role in the elaboration of the disenchanted vision of the political and social world which went hand in hand with the cult of art for art's sake? This exclusive religion is the last recourse of those who reject submission and resignation: 'The moment was disastrous for verse,' as Flaubert wrote in a preface to the 'last songs' of his friend Louis Bouilhet. 'Imagination, like courage, was singularly flattened, and the public was not disposed, any more than the powers that be, to permit independence of mind.'[20] When the people had manifested a political immaturity only equalled by the cynical cowardice of the bourgeoisie, and humanist dreams and humanitarian causes had been held up to ridicule or dishonoured by those very people who were supposed to be defending them – journalists selling themselves to the highest bidder, former 'martyrs of art' turned guardians of artistic orthodoxy, littérateurs pandering to a false idealism of escapism in their 'respectable' plays and novels – then one may say, with Flaubert, that 'nothing is left' and 'for us the only way is to shut ourselves up and keep our noses to our work, like moles.'[21]

And in fact, as Albert Cassagne observes, 'they will devote themselves to independent art, to pure art, and since art has to have a subject, they will either find this subject in the past, or else they will take it from the present, but making of it simple objective representations which are thoroughly disinterested'.[22] 'Renan's thoughts sketch out the evolution that will lead to dilettantism ("Since 1852, I have become all curiosity"); Leconte de Lisle buries his humanitarian dreams under Parnassian marble; the Goncourts repeat that "the artist, the man of letters and the scholar should never get mixed up in politics: it is a storm they should let pass over them."'[23]

While accepting these descriptions, we must challenge the idea that they tend to imply, of a direct determination by economic and political conditions: it is from the very particular position that they occupy in the literary microcosm that writers such as Flaubert, Baudelaire, Renan, Leconte de Lisle or Goncourt become aware of a political conjuncture which, grasped through the categories of perception inherent in their dispositions, allows and encourages their inclination to independence (whereas other historical conditions might have repressed or neutralized that inclination – for example by reinforcing the dominated positions in the literary field and in the social field, as on the eve of 1848, or in the days after it).

Baudelaire the founder

This analysis of the relations between the literary field and the field of power, which puts the stress on the forms (patent or latent) and on the effects (direct or inverted) of dependence, should not make us forget one of the major effects of the functioning of the literary world as a field. There is no doubt whatsoever that *moral indignation* against all forms of submission to the forces of power or to the market – whether it is a matter of careerist assiduity which makes certain littérateurs (one thinks of a Maxime du Camp) pursue privileges and honours, or the subservience to the demands of the press and of journalism which pushes writers of serialized fiction and vaudeville into an undemanding literature devoid of style – has played a determining role with writers such as Baudelaire or Flaubert in the daily resistance which led to a progressive affirmation of the autonomy of writers; and it is certain that, in the heroic phase of the conquest of autonomy, the ethical rupture is always, as one sees clearly with Baudelaire, a fundamental dimension of all aesthetic ruptures.

But it is no less certain that indignation, revolt and contempt remain negative principles, contingent and conjunctural, too directly dependent on the particular dispositions and virtues of individuals and no doubt too easily reversed or overturned, and that the reactional independence which they arouse remains too vulnerable to enterprises of seduction or annexation by the powerful. Practices which are regularly and durably emancipated from constraints and from direct or indirect pressures from temporal powers are not possible unless they can find their principle not in the fluctuating inclinations of moods or the voluntarist revolutions of morality, but in the very necessity of a social universe which has as a fundamental law, as a *nomos*, independence with respect to economic and political power; unless, to put it another way, the specific *nomos* which constitutes the literary or artistic order as such finds itself instituted both in the objective structures of a socially governed universe and in the mental structures of those who inhabit it and who tend by this fact to accept as evident the injunctions inscribed in the immanent logic of its functioning.

It is only in a literary and artistic field which has achieved a high degree of autonomy, as will be the case in France in the second half of the nineteenth century (especially after Zola and the Dreyfus Affair), that all those who mean to assert themselves as fully fledged members of the world of art, and above all those who claim to occupy the dominant positions in it, will feel the need to manifest their independence with respect to external powers, political or economic. Then, and only then, will indifference with respect to power and honours – even the most apparently specific, such as the Académie, or even the Nobel Prize – and distance with respect to the powerful and their values be immediately understood, and even respected, and therefore rewarded, and consequently those qualities will tend to impose themselves more and more forcefully as the practical maxims of legitimate conduct.

In the critical phase of the constitution of an autonomous field claiming the right to define for itself the principles of its legitimacy, those who contribute to the questioning of literary and artistic institutions (in which the overthrow of the Académie de Peinture and the Salon mark the high point) and to the invention and imposition of a new *nomos* have come from the most diverse positions: in the first place, from among the over-abundant youth of the Latin Quarter who denounce and sanction, notably in the theatre, compromises with power; from the realist circle of Champfleury and Duranty, who pit their politico-literary theories against the conformist 'idealism' of bourgeois art; finally and especially, from the upholders of art for art's sake. In fact, what Baudelaire, Flaubert, Banville, Huysmans, Villiers, Barbey and Leconte de Lisle have in common, over and above their differences, is being engaged in a labour that is located at the antipodes of a production subservient to the powerful or to the market; and despite their discreet concessions to the seductions of the salons (or even, as with Théophile Gautier, of the Académie), they are the first to formulate clearly the canons of the new legitimacy. It is they who, making a break with the dominants over the principle of the existence of the artist as artist, institute it as a rule of operation of the field in the process of formation. Thus Renan can prophesy: 'If the revolution is led in an absolutist and Jesuitical direction, we will react with intelligence and liberalism. If it is made for the benefit of socialism, we will react in the direction of the civilization and intellectual culture which will be bound to suffer at first from this excess . . .'

If, in this collective enterprise with no explicitly planned scheme or expressly designated leader, one had to choose a sort of founding hero, a *nomothète*, and an initial founding act, one could think only of Baudelaire and, among other creative transgressions, of his candidacy to the Académie Française, both perfectly serious and parodic at the same time. By a decision reached after mature deliberation, even in its intention to outrage (it is Lacordaire's seat that he chooses to bid for), and fated to appear just as bizarre, if not scandalous, to his friends in the subversive camp as to his enemies in the conservative camp who are loyal to the Académie and before whom he chooses to present himself (he will visit them one by one), Baudelaire defies the whole established literary order. His candidacy is a veritable symbolic attack, and is much more explosive than all the transgressions with no social consequences that, nearly a century later, will be called 'actions' in painting circles: he calls into question and puts to the challenge the mental structures, the categories of perception and of appreciation, which, being adjusted to social structures by a congruence so profound that they escape the scrutiny of the most apparently radical critique, are the basis of an unconscious and immediate submission to the cultural order – a visceral adherence which is betrayed for example in the 'astonishment' of a Flaubert, who was nevertheless eminently capable of comprehending the Baudelairean provocation.

Flaubert writes to Baudelaire, who had asked him to recommend his candidature to Jules Sandeau: 'I have so many questions to ask you and my astonishment has been so profound that a whole volume would not suffice!'[24] And to Jules Sandeau, with a very Baudelairean irony: 'The candidate asks me to tell you "what I think of him". You must know his work. As for me, certainly, if I were a member of the honourable assembly, I would like to see him seated between Villemain and Nisard! What a scene!'[25]

In presenting his candidature to an institution of consecration still widely recognized as such, Baudelaire, who was more aware than anyone of what sort of welcome would be offered him, affirms the right to consecration conferred on him by the recognition he enjoys in the narrow circle of the avant-garde; in forcing this body, discredited in his own eyes, to show in the plain light of day its incapacity to recognize him, he also affirms the right, and even the duty, incumbent on the bearer of the new legitimacy to overturn the scale of values, obliging even those who do recognize him, and whom his act disconcerts, to admit that they still recognize that old order more than they thought. By an act contrary to good sense, senseless, he undertakes to institute the anomie that, paradoxically, is the *nomos* of this paradoxical universe that will come to be the literary field when it achieves full autonomy, to wit, the free competition among creator-prophets freely asserting the extraordinary and singular *nomos*, without precedent or equivalent, which properly defines them. This is what he said to Flaubert in his letter of 31 January 1862: 'How could you have failed to guess that [the name] Baudelaire meant: Auguste Barbier, Théophile Gautier, Banville, Flaubert, Leconte de Lisle, in short, *pure literature*?'[26]

Moreover, the ambivalence of Baudelaire himself – while affirming to the end the same obstinate rejection of the 'bourgeois' life, he remains despite everything concerned about social recognition (did he not dream once of the Légion d'Honneur, or, as he writes to his mother, of directing a theatre?) – shows clearly how very difficult it was for the founding revolutionaries (the same swings can be observed in Manet) to make the breaks needed to install a new order. In the same way as the elective transgression of an innovator (one thinks of Manet's *Dead Bullfighter*) may appear as the awkwardness of incompetence, so the deliberate failure of a provocation remains simply a failure, at least in the eyes of the Villemains or even the Sainte-Beuves. The latter concludes his article in the *Constitutionnel* about the Académie elections with these remarks full of perfidious condescension: 'What is certain is that M. Baudelaire gains from being seen; whereas one was expecting to see a strange and eccentric man, one finds oneself in the presence of a polite, respectful, exemplary candidate, a gentle boy, of refined language and completely classical in formal appearance.'[27]

It is probably not easy, even for the creator himself in the intimacy of his experience, to discern what it is that separates the failed artist, a bohemian who prolongs adolescent revolt beyond a socially assigned limit, from the 'accursed artist', provisional victim of the reaction aroused by the symbolic revolution that he effects. As long as everyone does not recognize that new principle of legitimacy which permits a sign of future election to be perceived in present maledic-tion, and as long as a new aesthetic regime is not yet installed in the field – and beyond it, in the field of power itself (the problem will pose itself in the same terms to Manet and to those refused by the Salon) – then the artist-heretic is doomed to an extraordinary incertitude, the principle of a terrible *tension*.

Baudelaire, no doubt because he lived, with the lucidity of begin-nings, all the contradictions – experienced as so many *double binds* – inherent in a literary field in the process of formation, saw better than anyone the link between transformations of the economy and society and the transformations of the artistic and literary life which confront the pretenders to the status of writers or artists with two alternatives: either degradation, the famous 'bohemian life', made up of material and moral misery, sterility and resentment; or a sub-mission to the tastes of the dominants, just as degrading, through journalism, the serial or the boulevard theatre. A ferocious critic of bourgeois taste, Baudelaire is equally vigorous in his opposition to the 'bourgeois school' of the 'knights of good sense', led by Émile Augier, and the 'socialist school', both of them accepting the same (moral) password: 'Moralize! Moralize!'

In his article on *Madame Bovary* in *L'Artiste*, he writes: 'For several years, the share of interest the public accords spiritual things has significantly diminished; its budget of enthusiasm is still shrinking. The last years of Louis-Philippe had witnessed the final explosions of a spirit that could still be stimulated by the play of the imagination; but the new novelist found himself confronting a society that was completely jaded – worse than jaded – degraded and greedy, abhorring only the imaginary and caring only for material possessions.'[28] Similarly, once again allying himself with Flaubert, who in letter after letter (to Louise Colet especially) rails against the 'pretty' and the 'sentimental', Baudelaire – in a draft of a response to an article by Jules Janin on Heine – denounces the taste for the pretty, the gay, the charming, which leads to preferring the joy of French poets over the melancholy of foreign poets (he is thinking of those who, like Béranger, can exalt the 'charming intoxication of twenty years of age').[29] And he exhibits fury worthy of Flaubert towards those who accept servicing bourgeois taste, in the theatre especially: 'For some time, a great craze for respectability has dominated the theatre as well as the novel [. . .] One of the proudest supporters of bourgeois respectability, one of the champions of *good sense*, M. Émile Augier, has written a play, *La Ciguë*, in which a young man, rowdy, drunken, and dissolute [. . .] finally takes a fancy to the pure eyes of a young girl. Great profligates have been known to seek painful, unknown pleasures in asceticism [. . .]. That would be beautiful, although rather commonplace. But that would be too much for M. Augier's virtuous public. I believe he wanted to prove that in the long run we always have to *settle down . . .*'[30]

He lives and describes with stunning lucidity the contradiction he had discovered in his painful and rebellious apprenticeship to the literary life at the heart of bohemia in the 1840s: the tragic humiliation of the poet and the exclusion and malediction he suffers are imposed by exterior necessity at the same time as they present themselves to him, by an interior self-necessity, as the condition of accomplishing his work. The experience and the awareness of this contradiction mean that, unlike Flaubert, Baudelaire places his whole existence and his entire work under the banner of defiance and rupture, and also that he knows that there is no other way for him and does not want to be recuperated.

While Baudelaire's position in the field is comparable to that of Flaubert, he brings to it a heroic dimension, founded no doubt on his relationship with his family, and at the time of his trial this will lead him to take a very different attitude from that of Flaubert, who was ready to play on the bourgeois worthiness of his lineage, and it is also responsible for Baudelaire's long descent into the misery of bohemian life. We must cite the letter he writes to his mother when he was 'worn out with weariness, worry and hunger': 'Send me [. . .] enough to let me survive for three weeks [. . .] I believe so firmly in my timetable and in the strength of my willpower that I know *for a fact* that if I could succeed in leading a regular life, for two or three weeks, *my intelligence would be saved.*'[31] While Flaubert comes out of the *Madame Bovary* trial enhanced by the scandal, lifted to the ranks of the greatest writers of the age, Baudelaire experiences, after the trial of *Les Fleurs du mal*, the fate of a 'public' man but a stigmatized one, excluded from good society and the salons frequented by Flaubert, and banned from the literary universe by the mainstream press and magazines. In 1861 the second edition of *Les Fleurs du mal* is ignored by the press, hence by the public, but establishes its author in literary circles, where he still has numerous enemies. As a result of the continuous challenge he throws down to the 'right-thinking' in his life as much as in his work, Baudelaire incarnates the most extreme position of the avant-garde, that of revolt against all authorities and all institutions, beginning with literary institutions.

He is certainly led to put a gradual distance between himself and the realist or humanitarian complacencies of bohemia, a flabby and uncultivated world, whose insults confuse the great romantic creators with the ever-so-honest plagiarists of embourgeoised literature, and he opposes to it the work which must be done in suffering and despair, as with Flaubert at Croisset.

In the 1840s, Baudelaire marks his distance with respect to the realist bohemia by the symbolic impact of his external appearance, opposing to the slovenliness of his companions the elegance of the dandy, the visible expression of the tension which never ceases to haunt him. He belabours the realist ambitions of Champfleury who, 'since he minutely studies it [. . .] believes he has grasped an external reality'; he rails against realism, 'a repulsive insult [. . .] which for the ordinary man signifies not a new means of creation, but a minute description of trivial details.'[32] In his description of 'realist youths, giving themselves over, on leaving infancy, to realist art (new things require new words)', he cannot find words harsh enough, despite the friendship for Champfleury that he will never relinquish: 'What distinctly characterises them is a decided, inborn hatred of museums and libraries. Yet they have their classics, Henri Murger and Alfred de Musset in particular [. . .] From [Murger's] complete confidence in genius and inspiration, they derive the right not to submit to any mental gymnastics [. . .]. They are bad mannered, have stupid love affairs, are as conceited as they are lazy.'[33]

But he never renounces what he has acquired by his passage through the most disinherited regions of the literary world, which are thus the regions most favourable to a critical and global perception – disenchanted and complex, criss-crossed by contradictions and paradoxes – of this world itself and the whole social order. Moral deprivation and misery, even while they constantly threaten his mental integrity, appear to him as the only possible site for freedom and the only legitimate principle of an inspiration inseparable from an insurrection.

Unlike Flaubert, who follows an aristocratic tradition, it is not in the salons or in correspondence that he wages his fight, but in the heart of that world of 'déclassés', in the words of Hippolyte Babou, who form a heterogeneous army of the cultural revolution. Through him, it is the whole of bohemia – despised and stigmatized (even down to the tradition of authoritarian socialism, prompt to recognize there the interloper of the *Lumpenproletariat*) – and the 'accursed artist' who find themselves rehabilitated. (We see this in a letter to his mother of 20 December 1855 where he contrasts 'the admirable poetic faculty, the neatness of ideas and the power of hope that constitute [his] capital', that is to say, the specific capital guaranteed by an autonomous literary field, with the 'ephemeral capital that he lacks to keep himself, so as to work in peace far from the damned carrion of the proprietor'.)[34] Breaking with the naive nostalgia of a return to aristocratic patronage in the manner of the eighteenth century (often evoked by writers nevertheless near to him in the field, such as the Goncourts or Flaubert), he formulates an extremely realistic and farsighted definition of what the literary field will become. Thus, in mocking the decree of 12 October 1851, designed to encourage 'authors of plays with a moral and educational purpose', he writes: 'There is something in an official prize which offends man and humanity, and obscures the modesty of virtue [. . .]. As for writers, their prize is in the esteem of their peers and in the cash registers of booksellers.'[35]

In trying to gather together and to understand the different actions taken by Baudelaire, in his life as in his work, to affirm the independence of the artist, and in not selecting just those rejections which, after him, became integral to the writer's existence – rejection of family (birth or membership), rejection of career, rejection of society and so on – there is a risk of seeming to return to the hagiographic tradition which takes as its principle the illusion of seeing in the objectively congruent outcomes of a habitus the willed coherence of a project. How could we not perceive, however, something like a policy of independence in the acts that Baudelaire undertook regarding publishing and criticism? We know that at a time when the growth of 'commercial' literature is making fortunes for a few large publishing houses – Hachette, Lévy and Larousse – Baudelaire chooses to associate, for *Les Fleurs du mal*, with a small publisher, Poulet-Malassis, who frequents the cafés of the avant-garde. Refusing the more favourable financial conditions and the incomparably wider distribution offered him by Michel Lévy, precisely because he is afraid of a mass exposure of his book, he takes up with a smaller publisher, but one who is himself engaged in the struggle on behalf of young poetry (he will publish notably Asselineau, Astruc, Banville, Barbey d'Aurevilly, Champfleury, Duranty, Gautier, Leconte de Lisle) and fully identified with the interests of his authors (this way of demonstrating his option of rupture contrasts with Flaubert's strategy of publishing with Lévy and in *La Revue de Paris*, even though he despises the editorial board, composed as it is of *arrivistes* like Maxime Du Camp, and partisans of 'useful' art).[36] Obeying one of those emotional attachments both profoundly willed and uncontrollable, reasonable without being thought out, which are the 'choices' of the habitus ('with you, I will be honestly and elegantly produced'), Baudelaire effects for the first time the break between commercial and avant-garde publishing, thereby contributing to the upsurge of a field of publishers homologous with that of writers; at a stroke, he achieves a structural liaison between the publisher and the writer at the front line [*de combat*] (an expression which is not excessive if one remembers that Poulet-Malassis was roundly condemned for the publication of *Les Fleurs du mal* and obliged to go into exile).

The unitary course of radicalism is expressed in the conception of criticism that Baudelaire elaborated. It seems as if he was renewing the tradition which at the time of Romanticism associated artists and writers in an ideal community, grouped in the same circles or around a magazine like *L'Artiste*, and which incited many writers to take up art criticism – going too far, in a sense, since a number of them forgot everything about the old ideal. However, substituting the theory of 'correspondances' for the vague notion of a common ideal, Baudelaire denounces the incompetence and especially the lack of understanding of critics who try to measure individual works against formal and universal rules. He dispossesses the art critic of the role of judge conferred by, among other things, the academic distinction between the phase of the work's conception, superior in dignity, and the subordinate phase of its execution, the place of technique and know-how, and instead asks that the critic submit in some way to the work, but with a wholly new intention of creative readiness, striving to bring to light the deepest intentions of the painter. This radically new definition of the role of the critic (until then largely confined to paraphrasing the informational content, especially historical, of the painting) is logically inscribed in the process of the institutionalization of the anomie that is the correlative of the formation of a field in which each creator is authorized to establish his own *nomos* in a work, bringing along with it the principle (without antecedent) of his own perception.

The first calls to order

Paradoxically, the out-of-the-ordinary acts of prophetic rupture that the founding heroes must carry out in fact work to create the conditions necessary for making the heroes and heroism of these beginnings redundant: in a field reaching a high degree of autonomy and self-awareness, it is the mechanisms of competition themselves which authorize and favour the ordinary production of out-of-the-ordinary acts, founded on the rejection of temporal satisfactions, worldly gratifications and the goals of ordinary action. The calls to order and the sanctions (the most terrible of which is discredit, the exact equivalent of an excommunication or a bankruptcy) are the automatic product of the competition that particularly pits the consecrated authors, those most exposed to the seduction of worldly compromises and temporal honours which are always suspected of being compensations for renunciations or repudiations, against the newly arrived, who by their position are less subject to solicitations of the outside world, and who tend to contest established authorities in the name of values (disinterestedness, purity, etc.) which the latter proclaim, or are called on to impose.

Symbolic repression is exercised with special rigour on those who endeavour to arm themselves with external (hence 'tyrannical', in Pascal's sense) authorities or powers in order to triumph in the field.

This is the case with all the intermediary personages situated between the artistic field and the economic field – the publishers, gallery owners or theatre directors, not to mention the civil servants in charge of administering state patronage – with whom the writers and artists often maintain (there are exceptions such as the publisher Charpentier) relations of either latent or occasionally open violence. As witness, Flaubert, who himself had many quarrels with his publisher, Lévy, writes like this to Ernest Feydeau, who is preparing a biography of Théophile Gautier: 'You should convey that he was exploited and tyrannized by all the newspapers for which he wrote; Girardin, Turgan and Dalloz were torturers to our poor old man, which we bemoan [. . .]. A man of genius, a poet with no income and who is of no given political party, he was forced to write for the papers in order to live; so, this is what befell him. In my opinion, this is the *spirit* in which you should do your study.'[37]

To take just one example, borrowed from Flaubert's age, one may here evoke the person of Edmond About, a liberal writer for the *Opinion Nationale*, who was a veritable *bête noire* for the whole literary avant-garde, for a Baudelaire, a Villiers or a Banville – they said of him that he 'was naturally made for borrowing received opinions'; despite the 'spiritual impertinences' of his articles for the *Figaro*, he was reproached for having sold his pen to the *Constitutionnel*, whose subservience to the powerful was well known, and especially for incarnating the treachery of opportunism and servility, or simply of frivolity, which disfigures all values, and above all those it vaunts. When in 1862 he puts on *Gaëtana*, all the youth of the Left Bank mobilize to heckle it, and after four turbulent evenings the play is withdrawn.[38] There were countless plays (for example *La Contagion* by Émile Augier) which were booed and scuttled by mercenary cabals or claques of rowdy art students.

But there is no better proof of the effectiveness of the calls to order inscribed in the very logic of the field as it moves towards autonomy than the recognition that the authors who appear to be the most directly subordinate to external demands or exigencies, not only in their social behaviour but in their work itself, are more and more often forced to grant to the specific norms of the field; as if, in order to honour their status as writers, they must manifest a certain distance from the dominant values. Thus, if one only knows them through the sarcasms of Baudelaire or Flaubert, it comes as something of a surprise when one discovers that the most typical representatives of the bourgeois theatre offer, far from unequivocal praise of bourgeois life and values, a violent satire on the very foundations of that existence and of the 'lowering of manners' imputed to certain personages of the court and the imperial bourgeoisie.

Thus the same Ponsard who, with his *Lucrèce*, presented at the Théâtre-Français in 1843 (the year *Les Burgraves* failed), had appeared as the herald of the neoclassical reaction against Romanticism, and who had been accordingly named as head of the 'School of good sense', under the Second Empire attacks the ravages of money: in *L'Honneur et l'Argent* he becomes indignant against people who prefer dignities and riches dishonestly acquired to an honourable poverty; in *La Bourse* he castigates cynical speculators, and in his last play, a drama entitled *Galilée* performed in 1867, the year of his death, he makes a plea for the freedom of science.

In the same way, Émile Augier, who has a Parisian grand bourgeois background (born in Valence, he had been raised in Paris), who came into the repertory of the Comédie-Française in 1845 with *Un Homme de bien* and *La Ciguë* and who had written *Gabrielle*, a work performed in 1849 as the paradigm of the anti-romantic bourgeois comedy, turns into a painter of the evils caused by money. In *La Ceinture dorée* and *Maître Guérin* he dramatizes grand bourgeois gentlemen of dishonestly acquired fortunes who suffer at the hands of their children of overly delicate virtue. In *Les Effrontés*, *Le Fils de Giboyer* and *Lions et Renards*, plays created in 1861, 1862 and 1869, he attacks shady businessmen who exploit journalism, illegal deals, and illicit trading, and he deplores the success of unscrupulous rogues.[39]

Even though also intended as warnings to the bourgeoisie, these concessions that the authors most typical of bourgeois theatre feel bound to make to anti-bourgeois values attest to the fact that no one can any longer completely ignore the fundamental law of the field; the writers furthest in appearance from the values of pure art in fact recognize this – even if only in their manner, always a little shameful, of transgressing it.

We note in passing something that is not acknowledged by the argument that the sociology (or social history) of literature, often identified with a certain kind of literary statistics, would somehow have the effect of 'levelling' artistic values by 'rehabilitating' second-rate authors. Everything inclines us to think that, on the contrary, one loses the essence of what makes for the individuality and even the greatness of the survivors when one ignores the universe of contemporaries with whom and against whom they construct themselves. Besides the fact that they are marked by their membership in a literary field and thus enable us to grasp its impact and, at the same time, its limits, such authors, condemned by their failures or successes of doubtful merit, and simply and purely fated to be erased from the history of literature, also affect the functioning of the field by their very existence and by the reactions they arouse. The analyst who only knows about those authors from the past who have been recognized by literary history as worthy of being conserved is embracing an intrinsically vicious form of understanding and explanation. Such an analyst can only register, unwittingly, the way the ignored authors have affected, by the logic of action and reaction, the authors to be interpreted – the ones who, by their active rejection, have contributed to the others' disappearance from history. This is to preclude a true understanding of everything in the work of the survivors themselves that is, like their rejections, the indirect product of the existence and action of the vanished authors. This is never more clearly seen than in the case of a writer such as Flaubert, who defines and constructs himself in and through the whole series of double negations with which he counters contrasting pairs of styles or authors – like Romanticism and realism, Lamartine and Champfleury, and so forth.

A position to be made

From the 1840s onwards, and especially after the coup d'état, the influence of money, exercised notably through dependence on it of the press, itself subject to the state and the market, and the fascination, encouraged by the splendour of the imperial regime, with pleasures and banal entertainments, in the theatre especially, favoured the expansion of a commercial art which was directly subject to audience expectations. Faced with this 'bourgeois art', a 'realist' current perpetuates itself with difficulty as a current which prolongs and transforms the tradition of 'social art' – to use the labels of the day. Against one and the other was defined, in a double refusal, a third position, that of 'art for art's sake'.

This prevalent taxonomy, born of the struggle over classification occurring in the literary field, has the virtue of reminding us that, in a field still being constituted, the internal positions must first of all be understood as so many specifications of the generic position of writers (or the literary field) in the field of power, or, if you like, as so many particular forms of the relationship objectively established between writers as a whole and temporal power.

The representatives of 'bourgeois art', who are for the most part writers for the theatre, are tightly and directly linked to the dominant class, as much by their origins as by their lifestyle and value system. This affinity, which is the very basis of their success in a genre that supposes direct communication, and therefore ethical and political complicity, between author and audience, assures them not only of great material profits – the theatre is by far the most profitable of literary activities – but also of all sorts of symbolic profits, beginning with the emblems of bourgeois consecration, particularly membership in the Académie. Like those in painting such as Horace Vernet and Paul Delaroche, then Cabanel, Bouguereau, Baudry and Bonnat, and those in the novel such as Paul de Kock, Jules Sandeau, Louis Desnoyers and so on, it is authors such as Émile Augier or Octave Feuillet who offer to bourgeois audiences plays perceived as 'idealist' (by contrast with the current called 'realist', but just as 'moral' and moralizing, which will be represented in the theatre by Dumas fils and his *La Dame aux camélias* and also, but in another mode, by *Henriette Maréchal* by the Goncourt brothers): this watered-down Romanticism, whose generative formula is well described by Jules de Goncourt when he calls Octave Feuillet 'a Musset for all the family', subordinates the most frenzied novelistic style to bourgeois tastes and norms, celebrating marriage, good management of patrimony and honourable settlements on children.

Thus, in *L'Aventurière*, Émile Augier combines the sentimental reminiscences of Hugo and Musset with praise for high morals and family life, and with a satire on courtesans and a condemnation of love late in life.[40] But it is with *Gabrielle* that the restoration of 'healthy and respectable' art attains the summit of bourgeois anti-Romanticism: this verse play, performed in 1849, concerns a bourgeois wife, married to a notary who is too prosaic for her taste, who, on the point of yielding to a poet, a friend of 'fields prostrating themselves to the sun', suddenly discovers that true poetry lies in hearth and home; falling into the arms of her husband, she cries:

Oh, father of the family, oh poet, I love you.

This line seems written to enter into the parodies of the 'Garçon'; Baudelaire, in an article in *La Semaine Théâtrale* of 27 November 1851 entitled 'The respectable drama and novel', commented on it as follows: 'A notary! Can you see that respectable housewife cooing amorously on her husband's shoulder and looking languishingly at him as in the novels she has read! Can you see all the notaries in the theater applauding the author who treats them as his equals by avenging them on all those indigent rascals who believe that a poet's craft consists in expressing the lyric emotions of the heart in a rhythm determined by tradition!'[41] The same moralizing intention is affirmed by Dumas fils who pretends to aid in transforming the world by a realist picture of the problems of the bourgeoisie (money, marriage, prostitution and so on) and who, opposing Baudelaire and the separation of art and morality he proclaims, will state in the preface to his 1858 play *Le Fils naturel*: 'All literature which does not aim at perfectibility, the raising of moral standards, the ideal – and in a word, the useful – is a scrawny, unhealthy, stillborn literature.'

At the opposite pole of the field, there are the supporters of social art, who had their hour on the eve of and just after the February

Days of 1848: republicans, democrats and socialists such as Louis Blanc and Proudhon, and also Pierre Leroux and George Sand who, notably in their *Revue Indépendante*, flattered Michelet and Quinet, Lamennais and Lamartine and, to a lesser degree, the too tepid Hugo. They condemn the 'egotistical' art of the supporters of 'art for art's sake' and demand that literature fulfil a social or political function.

In the social effervescence of the 1840s, also marked by manifestos in favour of social art emanating from the Fourierists and Saint-Simonians, there appeared 'popular' poets such as Pierre Dupont, Gustave Mathieu[42] or Max Büchon, translator of Hebel, and the 'worker-poets' patronized by George Sand and Louise Colet.[43] In the small circles of bohemia, in cafés like the Voltaire and the Momus, or at the editorial offices of small literary journals like the *Corsaire-Satan*, gather writers as different as A. Gautier, Arsène Houssaye, Nerval, all survivors of the first bohemia, and also Champfleury, Murger, Pierre Dupont, Baudelaire and Banville and dozens of others who have fallen into obscurity (like Monselet or Asselineau). These authors temporarily brought together are destined for divergent fates, like Pierre Dupont and Banville, the plebeian producer of cheap couplets and the republican aristocrat enamoured of classical form, or like Baudelaire and Champfleury, whose very close friendship, forged around Courbet (they will meet again over the magazine *L'Atelier*) and the mystical exchanges of their 'Wednesdays', will survive the disagreement over 'realism'.

In the 1850s the position is occupied by the second bohemia, or at least by a 'realist' tendency which is forming there and whose theoretician is Champfleury. This 'singing and wineladen' bohemia[44] extends the circle of the *Corsaire-Satan*. It holds its meetings on the Left Bank, at the Andler brasserie (and a few years later at the Brasserie des Martyrs), grouping together around Courbet and Champfleury popular poets, painters such as Bonvin and A. Gautier, the critic Castagnary, the fantastical poet Fernand Desnoyers, the novelist Hippolyte Babou, the publisher Poulet-Malassis and sometimes, despite his theoretical disagreements, Baudelaire. With its easygoing lifestyle and spirit of camaraderie, with the enthusiasm and passion of theoretical discussions on politics, art and literature, this open assembly of young people, writers, journalists, painters and students, founded on daily reunions in a café, favoured an ambience of intellectual exaltation contrasting in every way with the reserved and exclusive atmosphere of the salons.

No doubt the solidarity that these 'proletaroid intellectuals' manifest with respect to the dominated owes something to their provincial and working-class ties and attachments: Murger was the son of a concierge, Champfleury's father was secretary in the mayor's office in Laon, Barbara's a small merchant of musical instruments in Orléans, that of Bonvin a gamekeeper, that of Delvau a tanner in the faubourg Saint-Marcel, and so forth. But, contrary to what they wanted (and led others) to believe, this solidarity is not just the direct effect of loyalty, of inherited dispositions: it is also rooted in the experiences associated with the fact of occupying, at the heart of the literary field, a dominated position which is clearly not unconnected with their position in terms of origin, and, more precisely, to the dispositions and the economic and cultural capital they have inherited from it.

We may borrow from Pierre Martino this evocation of Murger's social properties as an exemplary representative of the category: 'He was the son of a concierge and certainly destined for an entirely different career than that of editor of *La Revue des Deux Mondes*; it is his mother's ambition that helped him make, after many miseries, this sudden break; he was sent to college; he sometimes recalled this maternal decision without enthusiasm and implored humble parents to allow their children to remain the same. His studies were irregular and incomplete; the child scarcely profited from them; he read the poets for the most part, and began to write verses. He never thought of making up this lost education; his ignorance was remarkable: he admired with respect and ingenuousness one of his friends who had read Diderot, but he didn't wish to imitate him. His judgement, even in his maturity, lacked vigour: when he touched on social, political, religious and even literary questions, his thoughts were singularly impoverished. How would he find the time and the means to give his mind serious nourishment? After a break with his father, he took refuge with one of the 'water drinkers', and he was in the grip of true misery, which took away his health, sent him several times into hospital, and led him to die at the age of forty, worn out by privation. The success of his books, after ten very hard years, brought him only small ease, and the wherewithal to live alone in the country. His experience of the world was as incomplete as his education; the only reality he knew was his own bohemian life, and what he could see of peasant ways in the neighbourhood of his house at Marlotte, and so he often repeated himself.'[45]

Champfleury, a close friend of Murger, presents very similar characteristics: his father is secretary at the mayor's office in Laon, and his mother has a small store. His studies are cursory, then he leaves for Paris where he obtains a small job as a delivery boy for booksellers. He and some friends from a restaurant compose the circle called the 'water drinkers'. He writes art criticism for *L'Artiste* and *Le Corsaire*. In 1846 he enters the Society of Men of Letters. He writes serials for serious magazines. In 1848, he takes refuge in Laon, but receives two hundred francs from the provisional government. Back in Paris, in the 1850s, he sees a lot of his old friends Baudelaire and Bonvin, as well as Courbet. He writes much in order to live (novels, reviews, scholarly essays). He becomes known as the 'chief of the Realists', which causes him trouble with the censors. Thanks to Sainte-Beuve, in 1863 he obtains the licence of the Funambules Theatre, but only for a short time. In 1872, he becomes curator at the Sèvres museum.[46]

Even though they define themselves by their refusal of the two polar positions, those who are going gradually to invent what will be called 'art for art's sake' (and at the same time, the norms of the literary field) have in common with social art and with realism the fact that they, too, are violently opposed to the bourgeoisie and bourgeois art: their cult of form and impersonal neutrality makes them appear as the defenders of an 'immoral' definition of art, especially when those such as Flaubert seem to place their formal research in the service of a debasing of the bourgeois world. The word 'realism', no doubt more or less as vaguely characterized in the taxonomies of the time as any of its equivalents today (like 'gauchiste' or radical), allowed it to encompass in the same condemnation not only Courbet, the initial target, and his defenders, with Champfleury at their head, but also Baudelaire and Flaubert – in short, all those who, in form or substance, seemed to threaten the moral order and thereby the very foundations of the established order.

At Flaubert's trial, the closing speech of the assistant public prosecutor Pinard denounces 'realist painting' and invokes the morality that 'stigmatizes realist literature'; Flaubert's lawyer is obliged to recognize in his defence that his client belongs to the 'realist school'. The reasons adduced for the judgment twice take up the terms of the accusation, and insist on 'the vulgar and often shocking realism of the character portrayals'.[47] In the same fashion, in the judgment condemning *Les Fleurs du mal*, we read that Baudelaire is guilty of a 'crude realism which offends modesty' and leads to 'the arousal of the senses'.[48] In general, a number of historical debates, about art especially, but also other matters, would find themselves clarified, or more simply annulled, if one could bring to light, in each case, the complete world of distinct and often contrasting significations which all the relevant concepts – 'realism', 'social art', 'idealism', 'art for art's sake' – are given in social struggles within the entire field (where they often function, originally, as terms of denunciation or insults, as here with the notion of realism) or within the subfield of those who claim them as emblems (such as the different defenders of 'realism' in literature, painting, theatre, etc.). Nor should we forget that the meanings of these words, eternalized in theoretical discussion by dehistoricizing them (this dehistoricization, often the simple effect of ignorance, being one of the important conditions of a debate called 'theoretical'), constantly change in the course of time, as do the fields of corresponding struggles and the relations of force between users of considered concepts, who never overlook so completely the previous history of the taxonomies they are using as when they construct genealogies, more political than scientific, with the purpose of giving symbolic force to their present usages.

But in a way, as witnessed by the trials mounted against them, whose serious side should not be underestimated, the proponents of 'pure art' go much further than their apparently more radical fellow-travellers: aesthetic detachment – constituting, as we shall see, the veritable principle of the symbolic revolution they are carrying out –

leads them to break with the moral conformism of bourgeois art without falling into that other form of ethical complacency illustrated by the proponents of 'social art' and the 'realists' themselves when, for example, they exalt the 'superior virtue of the oppressed', as does Champfleury, according the people 'a sentiment for great things that makes them superior to the best judges.'[49]

That said, the frontier between the spirit of ironic provocation and rebellious transgression is blurred, corresponding to less difference between a moderate openness to the literary avant-garde characterizing the former, and the spirit of contestation, more political than aesthetically radical, asserted by the latter. Without doubt, after the coup d'état the differences of lifestyle associated with social origins relayed by position in the field favoured the constitution of distinct groups. On the one side, writers who are already more or less consecrated and dedicated to art for art's sake gather at the two brasseries Divan Le Peletier and the Paris and at *La Revue de Paris* – writers such as Banville, now adopted by the major reviews, Baudelaire, Asselineau, Nerval, Gautier, Planche, the de la Madelène brothers, Murger (once he is famous), Karr, de Beauvoir, Gavarni, the Goncourts and so forth. On the other side, at the Andler and Martyrs brasseries the 'realists' meet: Courbet, Champfleury, Chenavard, Bonvin, Barbara, Desnoyers, P. Dupont, G. Mathieu, Duranty, Pelloquet, Vallès, Montégut, Poulet-Malassis and so on. All the same, the two groups are not rigorously separated and there are frequent movements from one to another: Baudelaire, Poulet-Malassis, Ponselet, who are the most to the left politically, make frequent incursions into the Andler brasserie, as do Chenavard, Courbet and Vallès to the Divan Le Peletier.

Rather than a ready-made position which only has to be taken up, like those founded in the very logic of social functioning, through the social functions they fulfil or lay claim to, 'art for art's sake' is a *position to be made*, devoid of any equivalent in the field of power and which might not or wasn't necessarily supposed to exist. Even though it is inscribed in a potential state in the very space of positions already in existence, and even though certain of the romantic poets had already foreshadowed the need for it, those who would take up that position cannot make it exist except by making the field in which a place could be found for it, that is, by revolutionizing an art world that excludes it, in fact and in law. They must therefore invent, against established positions and their occupants, everything necessary to define it, starting with that unprecedented social personage who is the modern writer or artist, a full-time professional, dedicated to one's work in a total and exclusive manner, indifferent to the exigencies of politics and to the injunctions of morality, and not recognizing any jurisdiction other than the norms specific to one's art.

The double rupture

The occupants of this contradictory position are destined to oppose, according to two different relationships, different established positions and hence to try to reconcile the irreconcilable, that is, the two opposed principles governing their double rejection. In opposition to 'useful art', the official and conservative variant of 'social art', of which Maxime Du Camp, a close friend of Flaubert's, was one of the most notorious defenders, and in opposition to bourgeois art, the consenting or unconscious vehicle of an ethical and political *doxa*, they call for ethical freedom, even prophetic provocation; they want above all to assert a distance from all institutions – the state, the Académie, journalism – but without recognizing themselves for all that in the spontaneous carelessness of the bohemians, who also claim the values of independence but in order to legitimate either transgressions without properly aesthetic consequences or pure and simple regressions to the facile and the 'vulgar'.

If they reject the bourgeois life to which they were destined, meaning both career and family, it is not to trade one slavery for another by accepting, in the manner of Gautier and so many others, the servitudes of the literary industry and journalism, nor to place themselves in the service of a cause, no matter how noble or generous. In this sense, the political attitude of Baudelaire, especially in 1848, is exemplary: he does not fight for the republic, but for the revolution, one he loves as a sort of art for the sake of revolt and transgression. In their concern to situate themselves on a plane above ordinary alternatives, to surmount them by flying over them, they impose an extraordinary discipline on themselves, one which is deliberately assumed against the facile options that their adversaries on all sides permit themselves. Their autonomy consists in an obedience freely chosen, but unconditional, to the new laws they invent and that they wish to make triumph in the Republic of Letters.

It follows that they are fated to feel with renewed intensity the contradictions inherent in the status of 'poor relations' of the bourgeois family which is inscribed in the dominated position that the field of cultural production occupies in the midst of the field of power. (This means that one may impute to this position the essence of what Sartre, in the case of Flaubert, attributes to the relationship to the family and class of origin.) And perhaps it is not excessive to see in the poem significantly titled 'Héautontimoroumenos' ('he who punishes himself') a symbolic expression of the extraordinary tension resulting from the contradictory relationship of participation–exclusion that links Baudelaire both to the dominants and the dominated:

> I am the wound, and yet the knife!
> The smack and yet the cheek that takes it!
> The limb, and yet the wheel that breaks it,
> The torturer and he who is flayed![50]

For those who suspect me of reading something into the text (a fault customarily levelled at inspired interpreters), I shall cite the following statement which one would be wrong to see as a simple provocation by aesthetic cynicism (which it is as well), and in which Baudelaire, after the revolution of 1848, identifies himself with the two camps: 'I would have wanted to be in turn torturer and victim, to know the sensations that one has in both cases.'

Baudelaire's very aesthetic undoubtedly finds its basis in the double rupture that he achieves and that is especially manifest in a sort of permanent exhibition of paradoxical singularity: dandyism is not only the will to stand out and to astonish, an ostentation of difference or even the pleasure of displeasing, the concerted intention to disconcert, to scandalize, by voice, gesture, sarcastic pleasantry; it is also and above all a whole ethical and aesthetic posture extended to a culture (and not a cult) of the self, that is to say, to the exaltation and the concentration of emotional and intellectual capacities. A hatred of flabby forms of Romanticism, which holds sway within the school of good sense – when for example an Émile Augier becomes the defender of a poesy dedicated to 'true feelings', that is, to healthy passions of love for family and society – greatly influences his condemnation of improvisation and lyricism to the benefit of work and research; but at the same time, a rejection of facile transgressions, usually confined to the ethical plane, is the basis of the will to inject contention and method into even this controlled form of freedom which is the 'cult of the manifold sensation'.

It is in this geometric space between contraries, that has nothing of the 'juste milieu' of Victor Cousin, that Flaubert too is situated, along with others such as Gautier, Leconte de Lisle, Banville, Barbey d'Aurevilly and so on, very different one from another and never constituting a real group.[51] And I will cite only one particularly exemplary formulation of these double rejections that are found in all domains of existence, from politics all the way to aesthetics proper, and whose formula could be put like this: I detest X (a writer, manner, movement, theory, etc.; here, realism, Champfleury), but I detest just as much the opposite of X (here, the false idealism of an Augier or a Ponsard who, like me, is opposed to X, that is, to realism and to Champfleury; but also, in addition, to Romanticism, like Champfleury): 'Everyone thinks I am in love with reality, whereas actually I detest it. It was in hatred of realism that I undertook this book. But I equally despise the false brand of idealism which is such a hollow mockery in the present age.'[52]

This generative formula, which is the transformed form of the contradictory properties of the position, allows us to reach a truly genetic understanding of a number of the particularities inherent in the position-takings of the occupants of this position, a re-creative understanding which is quite different from some kind of projective empathy. I am thinking, for example, of their political neutrality, which shows itself in the complete eclecticism of their relationships and friendships and which is associated with the refusal of any engagement in action ('Foolishness', in Flaubert's celebrated phrase, 'consists in wanting to draw conclusions'), of any official consecration ('Honours dishonour,' he also said), and above all of any kind of ethical or political preaching, whether glorifying bourgeois values or instructing the masses in republican or socialist principles.

The concern to keep one's distance from all social roles (and the gathering places where the people occupying them commune) requires a refusal to bow to the expectations of the public, to follow them or to lead them, in the way the authors of successful plays or serials do. Flaubert, who undoubtedly goes further than anyone else with this bias in favour of indifference, reproaches Edmond de Goncourt for addressing the public in the preface to the *Frères Zemganno* to explain to them the aesthetic intentions of the play: 'Why do you need to speak to the public? It is not worthy of our confidences.'[53] And he writes to Renan, on the subject of the *Prière sur l'Acropole*: 'I do not know if there exists in French a more beautiful page of prose! [. . .] It is splendid and I am sure that the bourgeois don't understand a word of it. So much the better!'[54] The more the artist affirms himself as such by affirming his autonomy, the more he constitutes the 'bourgeois' (which term encompasses, as it does for Flaubert, 'the bourgeois in overalls and the bourgeois in frock coat') as the 'Boeotian' or 'Philistine', inapt at loving the work of art, at appropriating it in a real way, that is, symbolically.

'I include in the word "bourgeois" the bourgeois in overalls as well as the bourgeois in frock coat. It's we, we alone – that is, the educated – who are the People, or, to put it better, the tradition of Humanity.'[55] Or again: 'Yes, they will give me hell – count on them. *Salammbô* will annoy the bourgeois, that means the whole world . . .'[56] 'The bourgeois, which means practically the whole world: bankers, exchange agents, notaries, dealers, shopkeepers and the others, whoever was not part of the mysterious circle and earned his living prosaically.'[57] If pure artists are carried along by their hatred of the 'bourgeois' to proclaim their solidarity with those proscribed by the brutality of interests and prejudices – the bohemian, the acrobat, the ruined noble, the big-hearted servant girl and the prostitute, a kind of figure symbolic of the relation of the artist to the market – they can also be brought to approach the 'bourgeois' when they feel threatened by bohemia.[58]

The horror of the *bourgeois* is nourished in the very heart of the artistic microcosm – chief horizon of aesthetic and political conflicts – by the execration of the 'bourgeois artist'; by his success and notoriety, almost always paid for by his servility to the public or the powers that be, he is a reminder of the possibility always open to the artist of turning art into commerce or of making himself the organizer of the pleasures of the powerful, in the fashion of Octave Feuillet and his friends. 'There is something a thousand times more dangerous than the bourgeois,' says Baudelaire in *Les Curiosités esthétiques*, 'and that is the bourgeois artist, who was created to interpose himself between the artist and genius, hiding one from the other.' But the 'pure' writers are also led by their very demanding conception of artistic work to hold the literary proletariat in a professional's contempt, which undoubtedly underlies the picture they form of the 'populace'. The Goncourts denounce in their *Journal* 'the tyranny of the brasseries and bohemia over all real workers', and they contrast Flaubert with the 'great men of bohemia', like Murger, to justify their conviction that 'you have to be an honest man and an honourable bourgeois to be a man of talent.' As for Baudelaire and Flaubert, who, in spite of themselves, are placed by the dominant perspective, within and outside the field, among the 'realists' – these two are opposed to the vague humanism of the proponents of social art and the Proudhonian realists by the rigour of their professional ethic, leading them to refuse to identify freedom with carelessness, and by the aristocratism of their personal ethic, inspiring in them the same horror of all forms of 'Pharisaism', whether conservative or progressive. Thus, for example, when Hugo writes to him that he 'never said Art for Art's sake', but 'Art for Progress's sake', Baudelaire (who in a letter to his mother speaks of *Les Misérables* as a 'squalid and inept book') redoubles his contempt for the political priesthood of the romantic magus. After the militant period of 1848, he joins Flaubert in a disenchantment leading to a rejection of any connection with the social world and to an undifferentiated condemnation of all those who sacrifice to the cult of good causes, like George Sand, his bête noire. He agrees with Flaubert to hold in contempt the proponents of 'social Catholicism', that monstrous coupling (to cite freely a letter from Flaubert to George Sand) of the 'Immaculate Conception and lunch boxes for workingmen.'[59]

'I have just swallowed Lamennais, Saint-Simon, and Fourier, and am now going over all of Proudhon. [...] One salient feature is common to them all: hatred of liberty, hatred of the French Revolution and of philosophy. All those people belong to the Middle Ages; their minds are buried in the past. And what schoolmasters! What pedants! Seminarians on a spree, bookkeepers in delirium! The reason for their failure in '48 was that they stood outside the mainstream of tradition. Socialism is one face of the past, just as Jesuitism is another. Saint-Simon's great teacher was M. de Maistre, and how much Proudhon and Louis Blanc owe to Lamennais has never been sufficiently told.'[60] We remember that in *Sentimental Education* Flaubert encompasses in the same disdain conservatives attached to the bourgeois order and reformers infatuated with chimeras. Baudelaire, here again, proves himself much more radical than Flaubert, notably regarding George Sand: silly, ponderous, gossipy, 'she displays when discussing morality the same depth [...] as concierges' daughters and harlots'; a 'theologian of judgement', she 'suppresses hell by friendship for humankind'. He habitually denounces the 'heresy of teaching a lesson', the view that the aim of poetry is 'a lesson of some sort'. He also takes just as violently against Veuillot who had attacked art for art's sake and of whom he says that he is 'utilitarian like a democrat'.[61]

An economic world turned upside down

The symbolic revolution through which artists free themselves from bourgeois demand by refusing to recognize any master except their art produces the effect of making the market disappear. In fact they could not triumph over the 'bourgeois' in the struggle for control of the meaning and function of artistic activity without at the same time eliminating the bourgeois as a potential customer. At the moment when they argue, with Flaubert, that 'a work of art [...] is beyond appraisal, has no commercial value, cannot be paid for,' that it is *without price*, that is to say, foreign to the ordinary logic of the ordinary economy, they discover that it is effectively *without commerical value*, that it has no market. The ambiguity of Flaubert's phrase, saying two things at once, leads to the uncovering of a sort of infernal mechanism, which is set up by artists and in which they find themselves caught: making a necessity of their virtue, they can always be suspected of making a virtue of necessity.

Flaubert felt this principle of the new economy very keenly: 'If one does not address the crowd, it is right that the crowd should not pay one. It is political economy. But, I maintain that a work of art (worthy of that name and conscientiously done) is beyond appraisal, has no commercial value, cannot be paid for. Conclusion: if the artist has no income, he must starve! They think that the writer, because he no longer receives a pension from the great, is very much freer, and nobler. All his social nobility now consists in being the equal of a grocer. What progress!'[62] 'The more one puts conscience into one's work, the less use it is. I would maintain this axiom with my neck under the guillotine. We are workers of luxury; thus nobody is rich enough to pay us. When you want to earn money with your pen, you have to do journalism, serials, or the theatre.'[63]

This antinomy of modern art as pure art is displayed in the fact that, as the autonomy of cultural production grows, the interval of time necessary for works to impress on the public (most of the time against the critics) the concomitant norms of their perceptions is seen to grow likewise. This temporal gap between supply and demand tends to become a structural characteristic of the field of limited production: in this economic universe (actually anti-economic) which is established at the economically dominated but symbolically dominant pole of the literary field – in poetry with Baudelaire and the Parnassians, and in the novel with Flaubert (despite the *succès de scandale*, and based on a misunderstanding, of *Madame Bovary*) – producers may have only their competitors as clients, at least in the short run. Thus, when under the Second Empire, with the establishment of censorship, the major journals were closed to young writers, we witness a proliferation of small reviews, for the most part doomed to an ephemeral existence, whose readers are recruited from among the contributors and their friends. Therefore producers have to accept all the consequences of the fact that the only remuneration they can count on will be necessarily deferred – as opposed to 'bourgeois artists' who are assured of an immediate clientele, or to mercenary producers of commercial literature, such as the authors of vaudevilles or popular novels, who can make substantial incomes from their production while assuring themselves of a reputation as a social or even socialist writer, like Eugène Sue.

Eugène Sue is probably one of the first, if not the first, to have tried, more unconsciously than consciously, to compensate for the discredit attached to 'popular' success by invoking a vaguely socialist philosophy. The extraordinary interest he aroused by applying the procedures of the historical novel to a depiction of the dominated classes, and thus offering the bourgeois subscribers to the *Constitutionnel* a fresh form of exoticism, also had another side in the accusations often levelled at him of immorality and of violating good taste. 'Socialism', as with realism in the case of Champfleury, allowed the inauguration of a popular 'novel of manners' in what was both an aesthetic and a political

gambit; which meant that Eugène Sue, if one can believe Champfleury, was
worth reading by the bourgeois as a 'moral novelist'.

Some writers, such as Leconte de Lisle, go so far as to see in
immediate success 'the mark of intellectual inferiority'. And the
Christlike mystique of the 'artiste maudit', sacrificed in this world
and consecrated in the one beyond, is no doubt just the transfiguration into the ideal, or into a professional ideology, of the specific
contradiction of the mode of production which the pure artist aims
to establish. One is in fact in an economic world inverted: the artist
cannot triumph on the symbolic terrain except by losing on the
economic terrain (at least in the short run), and vice versa (at least in
the long run).

It is this paradoxical economy that gives inherited economic
properties all their weight – also in a very paradoxical manner – and
in particular a private income, the condition of survival in the absence
of a market. In more general terms (and against the mechanistic
representation of the influence of social determinations which is too
often accepted within social history or in the sociology of art and
literature), the probable effects of the properties attached to agents –
whether in an objective state, such as economic capital and securities,
or in an incorporated state, such as dispositions constitutive of the
habitus – depend on the state of the field of production. In other
words, the same dispositions may engender the taking of very
different if not contrary positions, for example on the political or the
religious terrain, according to the states of the field (and this is
sometimes so even within a single lifespan, as witnessed by the
numerous ethical or political 'conversions' that can be observed in
the years from 1840 to 1880).

This refutes, for a start, the tendency to make of social origin an independent
and transhistoric explanatory principle – in the manner, for example, of those
who establish a universal opposition between patrician writers and plebeian
ones. If one ceaselessly has to combat the tendency to reduce an explanation
relying on the *relation between a habitus and a field* to a direct and mechanical
explanation by 'social origin', it is undoubtedly because this form of simplistic
thinking is encouraged by the habits of ordinary polemic that make frequent use
of the genealogical insult ('son of a bourgeois!') and also by certain research
practices, just as evident in monographs ('the man and his work') as in statistics.

As in *Sentimental Education*, 'inheritors' hold a decisive advantage
when it comes to pure art: inherited economic capital, which removes
the constraints and demands of immediate needs (those of journalism,
for example, which overcame a Théophile Gautier) and makes it

possible to 'hold on' in the absence of a market, is one of the most important factors in the differential success of avant-garde enterprises, with their doomed or else very long-term investments. 'Flaubert', Théophile Gautier told Feydeau, 'was smarter than us, [. . .] he had the intelligence to come into the world with some patrimony, a thing which is absolutely indispensable to anyone who wants to make art.' And Flaubert would not have denied this, since he wrote to Feydeau at the time of the death of 'good Théo' about using the exploitation that the latter suffered his whole life as the basis of a biography conceived as 'vengeance'. And there is no better illustration of the condition of 'literary labourer' experienced by Gautier, who was obliged after 1837 to produce his theatrical notices for *La Presse* every week, than the conflicts between him and the director of the paper, Émile de Girardin, notably on the occasion of his trip to Spain, or than Maxime Du Camp's description of his stay in the Orient: 'Each stage of his journey was counted by the pages of copy he sent to his paper: he valued the kilometers by the number of lines that they cost him.'[64]

It is once again money (inherited) that guarantees freedom with respect to money. All the more so since, in giving assurances, guarantees and safety nets, a fortune confers that audacity which fortune smiles on – without doubt more in matters of art than anywhere else. It spares 'pure' writers the compromises to which an absence of income exposes them, as witness the famous pension of Leconte de Lisle or the efforts of Flaubert on behalf of his friend Bouilhet, less wealthy than he: 'Now, about the question of *living*. I promise you that Mme Str[oehlin] could perfectly well ask the Emperor in person for the *place* that you wish. Keep your eye open for one over the next three weeks. Mention your father's service record on the sly. We'll see. You could ask for a pension, but you would have to pay for that in the currency of your trade, that is, in cantatas, epithalamia, etc. – no, never.'[65]

But Flaubert is no doubt also fully justified in getting indignant at the 'convenient barb' ('you are lucky to be able to work without rushing, thanks to your income') his colleagues 'throw back at him'. But if there is no doubt that the objective freedom an income secures in relation to temporal powers and to the powerful may favour subjective freedom, it remains true that it is not a necessary condition (and even less a sufficient one) for independence, or for *indifference* towards worldly seductions of even the most specific kind, such as critical praise and literary success, which only can be assured by an undivided investment in a true intellectual project. 'Success, time, money, publication are relegated to the lowest level of my mind, off on some very vague horizons that are of no concern to me whatever. All that seems to me dull as dishwater, and unworthy (I repeat the word, *unworthy*) of exciting one's brain about. The impatience of literary folk to see themselves in print, acted, known, praised, I find astonishing – like a madness. That seems to me to have no more to do with a writer's work than dominoes or politics. Voilà. Anybody can do as I do – work just as slowly as I, and better. All you have to do is rid yourselves of certain tastes, and sacrifice a few pleasures. I am not at all virtuous, but I am consistent. And though I have great needs (which I never mention), I would rather be a wretched monitor in a school than write four lines for money.'[66]

Maybe there is here, for those who want it, a rather indisputable criterion of value for all artistic production and, more generally, for intellectual production: to wit, the investment in a work which is measurable by the cost in effort, in sacrifices of all kinds and, definitively, in time, and which goes hand in hand with the consequent independence from the forces and constraints exercised outside the field, or, worse, within it, such as the seductions of fashion or the pressures of ethical or logical conformism – for example, the required themes, obigatory subjects, conventional forms of expression and so forth.

Positions and dispositions

It is only when one has characterized the different positions that one can come back to particular agents and to different personal properties that more or less predispose them to occupy these positions and to realize the potentialities inscribed there. It is remarkable that the whole assembly of champions of 'art for art's sake', who are objectively very close in the political and aesthetic positions they take up,[67] and who, without forming a group properly speaking, are linked together by relations of mutual esteem and sometimes friendship, also remain very close to each other in their social trajectory (just as, we recall, the champions of 'social art' or 'bourgeois art' were).

So, Flaubert and Fromentin are sons of important provincial doctors, Bouilhet is also the son of a doctor, but of lesser standing (and dying young), Baudelaire the son of a bureau chief in the high legislative Assembly (who claimed to be a painter) and son-in-law of a general, Leconte de Lisle the son of a planter from La Réunion, whereas Villiers de L'Isle-Adam comes from a very old noble family and Théodore de Banville, Barbey d'Aurevilly and the Goncourts from families of the minor provincial nobility. Regarding several among them, biographers note that the fathers 'wanted a high social position for them' – which explains no doubt why almost all of them took up or pursued law studies (like Frédéric ...): this is true of Flaubert, Banville, Barbey d'Aurevilly, Baudelaire and Fromentin.

Both the talented bourgeoisie and the traditional nobility have in common the favouring of aristocratic dispositions which lead these writers to feel equally alienated from the demagogic declarations of the proponents of 'social art', whom they identify with the journalistic plebs of bohemia,[68] and the facile entertainments of 'bourgeois artists', who, coming for the most part from the financial bourgeoisie, are in their eyes merely merchants in the temple, past masters of the art of recuperating, by caricaturing them, the values of the great romantic tradition.

Being almost equally endowed with economic and cultural capital, writers from the central positions at the heart of the field of power (like the sons of doctors or members of the 'intellectual' or liberal professions, called in the language of the time 'capacités') seem predisposed to occupy a homologous position in the literary field. Thus the double orientation of the investments of Flaubert's father Achille-Cléophas (bearing on both the education of children and land ownership) corresponds to the indecision of the young Gustave as he confronts an *embarras du choix* between equally probable futures: 'Grand avenues still remain open to me, already trodden paths, habits for sale, job positions, a thousand slots that can be filled with imbeciles. Therefore I will be a cog in society, I will take my place. I will be an honest man, dutiful and everything else you want, I will be like any other, *comme il faut*, like everyone, either lawyer, doctor, subprefect, notary, solicitor, some judge, a stupidity like all stupidities, a man of the world or of the office, which is even more stupid.'[69]

The reader of Sartre's *The Family Idiot* is more than a little surprised when, in a letter from Achille-Cléophas to his son, ritual observations (though not without intellectual pretension) on the virtues of travelling suddenly take on a typically Flaubertian tone, with a vituperative remark about a grocer: 'Profit from your trip and remember your friend Montaigne, who reminds us that we travel mainly to observe the humours of nations and their mores, and to "rub and sharpen our wits against other brains". See, observe and take notes; do not travel like a grocer or a salesman.'[70] This programme for a literary voyage and the very form of the references to Montaigne ('your friend'), which allows us to suppose that Gustave shared his literary tastes with his father, lead us to doubt, despite what Sartre suggests, that Flaubert's literary 'vocation' could have found its origin in the 'paternal curse' and in the unhappy relationship with an older brother who outshone him academically and conformed better to the paternal image of success;[71] in any case they testify to the fact that the inclinations of the young Gustave certainly received the understanding and support of Dr Flaubert, and that the latter, if we are to believe this letter and also, among other clues, the frequency of the references to poets in his medical thesis, was not insensitive to the prestiges of the literary enterprise.

But this is not all, and at the risk of pushing a little too far the search for an explanation we may, in reinterpreting Sartre's analysis, notice the homology occurring between the relationship of the artist as the 'poor relation' of the 'bourgeois' or of the 'bourgeois artist', and the relation of Flaubert to his older brother, designated by his precedence of birth to perpetuate the bourgeois lineage by pursuing an honourable career that Gustave, too, ought to have embraced;[72] and we may hypothesize that this superimposition of redundant determinations might have inclined Flaubert to search for and produce the position of writer, of pure writer, and to feel in a singularly acute manner the contradictions inscribed in that position, where they attain their highest degree of intensity.

Flaubert's point of view

At this point, the analysis characterizes in generic fashion the position occupied by Flaubert, among others, and it only partially grasps his particularity, notably because it does not enter into the specific logic of the work itself, understood in terms of its properly artistic genesis. One can almost hear Flaubert when he asked, after having reproached the critics of his time for simply replacing the grammarian type of criticism in the manner of La Harpe with a historical criticism in the manner of Sainte-Beuve or Taine, 'Where do you know [of] a criticism? Who is there who is anxious about the work in *itself*, in an intense way? They analyse very keenly the setting in which it is produced and the causes leading to it; but as for the unknowing [*inscient*] poetics? Where does it come from? And the composition and style? The author's point of view? Never!'[73]

To answer the challenge one must, taking Flaubert at his word, reconstitute the artistic *viewpoint* from which the 'unknowing poetics' is defined, and which, as the *view from a point* in the artistic space, characterizes it exclusively. More precisely, we must reconstruct the space of the artistic *position-takings*, both actual and potential, which was the context for the formulation of the artistic project, and which we may assume, as a hypothesis, is homologous with the space of positions in the field of production itself, as it has been roughly described. To construct the author's viewpoint in this sense is, if you will, *to be put in his place*, but through an approach which is totally different from the sort of projective identification 'creative' criticism strives for.

Paradoxically, we can only be sure of some chance of participating in the author's subjective intention (or, if you like, in what I have called elsewhere his 'creative project') provided we complete the long work of objectification necessary to reconstruct the universe of positions within which he was situated and where what he wanted to do was defined. In other words, one cannot take the author's point of view (or that of any other agent) and come to an understanding – but an understanding very different from that enjoyed, in practice, by the person who actually occupies the point under consideration – unless the author's situation in the space of constitutive positions within the literary field is grasped anew: it is this position that, on the basis of the structural homology between the two spaces, is at the root of the 'choices' this author makes in a space of artistic position-takings (with respect to content and form), defined, themselves also, by the differences that unite and separate them.

When Flaubert embarks on writing *Madame Bovary* and *Sentimental Education*, he actively situates himself, by choices (implying the same number of refusals) in the space of the possibles offered him. To understand these choices is to understand the differential signification that characterizes them within the universe of compossible choices and the intelligible relationship that joins this differential meaning to the difference between the author of these choices and the authors of choices different from his. To give a more concrete idea of this project, we may cite a letter addressed to Flaubert on 7 February 1880 in which Paul Alexis tries to justify the preface he has written for a collection of his stories: 'If every author had done as much for each of his books, and with such sincerity and naiveté, even with his tongue in his cheek, what a precious mine of information for criticism, for literary history! Example: in the preface to *Madame Bovary* this piece of information: "The irritation produced in me by the bad writing of Champfleury and the so-called realists has not been without influence in the production of this book. Signed: Gustave Flaubert." What light that would shed on the literary history of the second half of the nineteenth century! What idiocies spared future teachers of rhetoric!'[74] But, lacking 'sincere and naive' replies to a methodical questionnaire about the ensemble of landmarks, beacons or foils with respect to which the creative project is defined we have to rely on spontaneous declarations, hence often partial and imprecise ones, or on indirect clues in order to try to reconstitute both the conscious and unconscious parts of the way the writer's choices were shaped.

The hierarchy of genres, and within them the relative legitimacy of styles and authors, is a fundamental dimension of the space of possibles. Even though it is a stake in struggles at all times, it presents itself as a given which must be reckoned with, whether in order to oppose it or to transform it. In choosing to write novels, Flaubert laid himself open to the inferior status associated with belonging to a minor genre. In fact, the novel was perceived as an inferior genre, or rather, to use Baudelaire's words, a 'routine genre', a 'bastard genre',[75] despite the acknowledged prestige of Balzac, who, by the way, himself scarcely liked to define his books as novels (he almost never uses this term, unless to designate the subgenre à la Walter Scott or a philosophical-fantastical book like *La Peau de chagrin*). The Académie Française, which held the novel in suspicion, waits until 1863 to crown a novelist – and then it is Octave Feuillet . . .[76] And the preface to *Germinie Lacerteux*, the manifesto of the realist novel, must still claim for 'the Novel (with a capital)' the status of a 'great serious form'.

But, through what he invests in his choice – that is, a transformed definition of the novel involving a denial of the rank it has been assigned in the hierarchy of genres – Flaubert contributes to transforming the novel and to transforming the social representation of the genre, starting with his colleagues – all novelists with any ambition, notably the naturalists, treat him as the head of the movement. The recognition he obtains from the best-known writers and critics, and through them, the world of the salons (where, as we have seen, the 'realist' novelists and even the most eminent representatives of the officially dominant genre, the Parnassian poets, are excluded) allows him to impose respect for the genre well beyond the intellectual field properly speaking – and it is a genre already endowed with a long history and distinguished founding fathers, including some he claims himself, like Cervantes, and others who have made an impression on all cultivated minds, like Balzac and Musset. And thus Gustave Planche can write: 'The novel [. . .] today treads the highest peaks of philosophy and poetry.'[77]

At the time when Flaubert embarks on writing his first novel, there is no novelist with the scope of Balzac, but there are, in no particular order, Octave Feuillet, Sandeau, Augier, Féval, About, Murger, Achard, de Custine, Barbey d'Aurevilly, Champfleury, Barbara, and one should add to these, as Jean Bruneau observes,[78] all the second-rank Romantics, today totally forgotten, but who were best-sellers then, such as Paul de Kock, Janin, Delavigne, Barthélemy, and so on. In this confused universe, at least looking confused to us, Flaubert knows how to recognize his own. He reacts violently against everything that we could call 'genre literature' – by an analogy (one he suggests himself[79]) with genre painting – such as vaudeville, historical novels à la Dumas, comic opera, not forgetting, obviously, novels à la Paul de Kock (*Mon Voisin Raymond*, *La Pucelle de Belleville*, *Le Barbier de Paris*, etc.) that flatter the public by reflecting back its own image in the form of a hero with a psychology directly transcribed from the daily life of the petite bourgeoisie. He also rails against the idealist platitudes and the sentimental outpourings of an Augier or a Feuillet: the latter will have an immense success in 1858, that is after the appearance of *Madame Bovary*, with *Le Roman d'un jeune homme pauvre*, a Romanesque tale of the woes of Maxime Odiot, Marquis de Champcey d'Hauterive, who, ruined by his father and obliged to earn his living as steward to the Laroque family, ends by marrying the Laroque heiress, after extravagant vicissitudes.

But he does not fall either into the camp of novelists labelled 'realist', such as Duranty, Champfleury (or, at the other extreme, that of bourgeois art, Feydeau, About or Alexandre Dumas fils), who are opposed to the same adversaries as he is, but who define themselves above all against Romanticism and against all the major professionals of literature, among whom he would place himself: 'For almost all of them, the absence of classical studies means that, not knowing what metaphysics or psychology or logic are, they do not know how to analyse and how to think. You hear them pronounce the names of Stendhal, Mérimée, Sainte-Beuve, Renan, Berthelot, Taine; but with the exception of Joseph Delorme and the author of *Colomba*, the names were all they knew.'[80]

The first realists, that is, the section of the second bohemia who were accustomed to gather round Courbet and Champfleury in the 1850s, in the Brasserie Andler in rue Hautefeuille or, on the Right Bank, at the Brasserie des Martyrs (people like Duranty, Barbara, Desnoyers, Dupont, Mathieu, Pelloquet, Vallès, Montégut, Silvestre, and also, from the artists and art critics, Bonvin, Chenavard, Castagnary, Préault), are separated, as we have seen, by a whole cluster of social properties, and in particular by their social origin and their meagre cultural capital, from the two camps to which they are opposed on the terrain of symbolic struggles. What unites them, apart from the closeness of their habitus, are an anticonformist rejection of the official conservatism, making them plunge into every current that is slightly new, a taste for exact observation, a defiance with respect to lyricism, a belief in the powers of science, a certain pessimism, and perhaps above all a refusal of any hierarchy in objects or styles – a rejection which finds its expression in the right to say everything and in the right of everything to be said.

Flaubert and 'realism'

Duranty and Champfleury wanted a literature of pure observation, social, popular, excluding all erudition, and they took style for a secondary property. Better at declaiming in the Brasserie des Martyrs against Ingres and the official fine arts, along with Courbet, Murger and Monselet – that is, at demolishing rather than constructing – they are mediocre theoreticians, only slightly cultivated, who bring to the intellectual field petit-bourgeois dispositions that are perceived as such: a serious mind and militant inclinations, often rather sectarian, which are antithetical and antipathetic to aesthetic casualness. Moreover, as they draw no distinction between the political field and the artistic field (this is the very definition of social art), they also import modes of action and forms of thought current in the political field, conceiving literary activity as engagement and collective action, founded on regular meetings, slogans, programmes.

Their role is decisive at the beginning: it is they who in the 1850s express and organize the youthful revolt and create the discussion places where new ideas are developed, starting with the very idea of a party of novelty which would come to be called the avant-garde. But, as often happens in the history of intellectual movements (one thinks for example of the recent history of the feminist movement), the enthusiasm and passion of the leaders and militants opens the way and then cedes place to the professionalism of creators who have the economic and cultural means to realize in their works those literary and artistic utopias that their less advantaged precursors have already canvassed in cafés and newspapers (like Duranty, who had circulated his critical views in the press); the very means to return once more, at a higher level of exigency and accomplishment, to the aristocratic freedoms and values of the eighteenth century.

The opposition between art and money, which emerged as one of the fundamental structures of the dominant vision of the world at the same time as the literary and artistic field asserted its autonomy,[81] prevents agents and also analysts (especially when their specialty and/or literary inclinations lead them to an idealized vision of the condition of the artist in the eighteenth century) from perceiving that, as Zola says, 'money has emancipated the writer, money has created modern letters.'[82] In terms very close to those Baudelaire employed, Zola recalls in fact that it is money which has freed the writer from dependence on aristocratic patronage and public powers and, against the proponents of a romantic conception of the artistic vocation, he calls for a realist perception of the possibilities that the reign of money affords the writer: 'One must accept without regret or childishness, one must recognize the dignity, the power and justice of money, one must abandon oneself to the new spirit . . .'[83] (These quotes and references are borrowed from an article by W. Asholt[84] which analyses the positions of Vigny (in his preface to *Chatterton*, 1834), Murger (in his preface to *Scènes de la vie de bohème*, 1853), Vallès (in his preface to *L'Argent*, 1860) and Zola on the relations between the writer and money.)

Designated as the head of the realist school after the success of *Madame Bovary*, which coincides with the decline of the first realist movement, Flaubert waxes indignant: 'Everyone thinks I am in love with reality whereas actually I detest it. It was in hatred of realism that I undertook this book. But I equally despise the false brand of idealism which is such a hollow mockery in the present age.'[85] This formula (whose value as matrix I have already mentioned) conveys the principle of the totally paradoxical (almost 'impossible') position that Flaubert is going to constitute; the character it has of being unclassifiable is manifest in the indecisive debates that he arouses between those who want to pull him towards realism and those who, more recently, have wanted to annex him to formalism (and to the 'Nouveau Roman'). It is also manifest in the fact that people often resort to oxymorons in order to characterize him: Francisque Sarcey called him 'the neo-Parnassian of prose', and a historian speaks of him in terms of 'realism of art for art's sake'.[86] But, for that, he would have to combine the attributes of the realists, who are today totally forgotten (except for Courbet, who *mutatis mutandis* is a little to Manet what Champfleury was to Flaubert), and of those who were quite opposite to them in so many ways, starting with their social position and vision: Gautier (the author of the preface to *Mademoiselle de Maupin*, and the 'impeccable master' of pure form), Baudelaire, and even the Parnassians. This is not to mention Romantics like Chateaubriand, and all the great ancestors, ignored or renounced by the lovers of novelty at all cost, the Boileaus, La Fontaines or Buffons to whom Flaubert resorts assiduously, thereby inscribing his work in the history of literature instead of simply 'placing himself' within contemporary letters – as do those who are concerned about making a place there, with reference to a certain public – and contributing thereby to the autonomization of the field.

Flaubert, we know, said he had written *Madame Bovary* 'in hatred of realism'. And, in fact, preaching, demonstration and declamation, and all the petit-bourgeois dispositions expressed in them, is what

Flaubert tries to escape in that absolute impassiveness which so shocks commentators, progressives as much as conservatives, beginning with Champfleury and Duranty: 'There is neither emotion, feeling nor life in this novel, but rather a great arithmetical force which has measured and assembled every possible gesture, gait or unevenness of ground in the given characters, events and locations. This book is a literary application of the calculus of probabilities.'[87]

The space of position-takings that analysis reconstitutes does not present itself as such to the writer's consciousness; that would oblige us to interpret his choices as conscious strategies of distinction. It emerges here and there, in fragments, notably in moments of doubt about the reality of the difference that the creator intends to assert in his work itself, and quite apart from any deliberate quest for originality. 'I am afraid of becoming another Paul de Kock or producing a kind of chateaubriandized Balzac.'[88] 'What I am currently writing risks being like Paul de Kock's work if I do not give it a deeply literary form. But how to render trivial dialogue that is well written?'[89] And the permanent struggle on two fronts that is implicated in a project founded on a double refusal contains the danger of constantly falling between Scylla and Charybdis: 'I pass alternately from the most extravagant emphasis to the most academic platitude. It reads like Pétrus Borel and Jacques Delille by turns.'[90] But the threat to artistic identity is never as great as when it is presented in the form of an encounter with an author occupying a position in the field which is apparently very close to his own. This is the case when Bouilhet draws Flaubert's attention to *Les Bourgeois de Molinchart*, a novel by Champfleury that was appearing in serialized form in *La Presse* and whose subject, a provincial adultery, is very close to that of *Madame Bovary*.[91] In fact, Flaubert undoubtedly finds this an occasion to affirm his difference: 'I wrote *Madame Bovary* to annoy Champfleury. I wanted to show that bourgeois dreariness and mediocre sentiments could sustain beautiful language.'[92]

Better still, he invents in practice, in the work by which he creates himself as a 'creator', the veritable principle of this difference: a singular relationship, which makes up the Flaubertian tonality, between the refinement of the writing and the extreme platitude of a subject which he happens to have in common with the realists, the Romantics, or even the boulevard authors;[93] a sort of *dissonance*, by which we are reminded at every moment of the ironic or even parodic distance of the writer from what he writes, or from other manners of writing, such as, in this case, the insipid sentimentality of Champfleury's novels or Duranty's novellas. Zola felt this tension keenly, as well as the aristocratic loftiness which is at the root of it and which does not preclude a strength of negation on a par with that of the realists: 'Yes, the big word is spoken out loud: Flaubert was a bourgeois, and the most worthy, the most scrupulous, the most orderly you could want. He often said so himself, proud of the esteem he enjoyed, his entire life ordered around work, which did not prevent him from slitting the throat of the bourgeois, of striking out at them on every occasion with his lyrical fits of anger [. . .]. Happily, alongside the impeccable stylist, the rhetorician crazy about perfection, there is a philosopher inside Flaubert. He is the grandest naysayer we have had in our literature. He professes veritable nihilism – an ism that would have infuriated him – and he did not write a page that did not plunge deep within our emptiness.'[94]

One can, by the way, find a proof *a contrario* of the creative virtue of this tension in the extreme feebleness of Flaubert's theatrical works, where, quite precisely, it comes undone. If Flaubert, author of several plays that met with resounding failure, did lamentably badly in the theatre, it is undoubtedly because the contempt he had for the Ponsards, Augiers, Sardous, for Dumas fils and other successful vaudeville writers (all of them, according to him, only good enough to portray puppets and pull their strings, and who left him with an overly simple idea of the theatre) led him to lapse into exaggerating everything that in his eyes defined the inner logic of the theatre.[95] This can be seen in *Le Candidat*, a satire on politics written in two months, in which he has a go at all parties – at the Orléanistes, at the partisans of the Comte de Chambord, at reactionaries of all stripes as well as at the republicans – and in which he chose to 'do it crudely', to overload traits, to dramatize one-dimensional characters near to caricature, to inflate by using stage whispers insights into actions already too obvious, and to indulge in schematic demonstration. In short, once he accepts rivalling successful authors instead of appropriating their project by redefining it against them, that is, against the facilities they commit, Flaubert ceases writing like Flaubert.

'Write the mediocre well'

'Write the mediocre well':[96] this formula in the form of an oxymoron concentrates and condenses his whole aesthetic programme. It gives a fair idea of the almost impossible situation in which he has placed himself in trying to reconcile contraries – that is, requirements and experiences ordinarily associated with opposing regions of the social space and of the literary field, and hence socio-logically irreconcilable ones. And thus he is going to establish, in the lowest and most trivial forms of a literary genre held as inferior – that is to say, in the subjects commonly treated by the realists, as witness the encounter with *Les Bourgeois de Molinchart* by Champfleury – the highest requirements that had ever been asserted even in the noble genre *par excellence*, such as the descriptive distance and the cult of form imposed in poetry by Théophile Gautier, and after him the Parnassians, in order to combat the sentimental effusion and the stylistic facilities of Romanticism.

This tour de force revealed by analysis is not willed as such. Flaubert does not pit Gautier against Champfleury, or vice versa, nor does he aim to reconcile contraries or to combat the excess of the one with the excess of the other. He opposes both of them, and he constructs himself as much against Gautier and Pure Art as against realism. Near, here again, to Baulelaire or Manet, he feels as much antipathy for the false materialism of a realism that wants to ape the real and that overlooks its true *matter*, that is to say the language that *writing* worthy of the name treats as resonant material (the 'blasting mouth') charged with meaning, as he feels for the adulterated and gratuitous idealism of bourgeois art: 'Art should not be toyed with, even if I am a partisan just as passionate about the doctrine of art for art's sake, understood in my own manner (of course).'[97]

Flaubert calls into question the very fundamentals of the current way of thinking, that is to say, the common principles of vision and division that, at any one moment, ground the consensus about the common meaning of the world: poetry against prose, the poetic against the prosaic, lyricism against vulgarity, conception against execution, idea against writing, subject against technique, and so on; he revokes the limits and the incompatibilities that ground the perceptual and communicative order on the prohibited that is the sacrilege of the mixture of genres or the confusion of orders, prose applied to the poetic and especially poetry applied to the prosaic. In this sense, one could agree with the first critics of *Madame Bovary* who saw in this book (in the manner of Manet's critics denouncing in the painter of Olympia the representative of 'democracy within art')[98] the first expression of a democracy in letters (so long as one does not make the link these critics were evidently establishing between democracy or democrats in politics, on the one hand, and 'democracy' or 'democrats' in the literary field, on the other). But one cannot make a break with the 'logical conformism' and 'moral conformism' that are at the basis of the social and mental order without suffering consequences. And it is understandable that the enterprise may have appeared constantly to itself as a form of *folly*: 'It is perhaps absurd to want to give prose the rhythm of verse (keeping it distinctly prose, however) and to write of ordinary life as one writes history or epic (but without falsifying the subject). I often wonder about this. But on the other hand it is perhaps a great experiment, and very original too!'[99]

To want, as he says again, 'to blend lyricism and the vulgar' is to undergo the untenable and disturbing testing which goes with the task of effecting the collision of opposites. In fact, all the time he is writing *Madame Bovary* he does not stop mentioning his suffering, which sometimes turns into despair: he compares himself to a clown performing a tour de force, obliged to execute 'furious gymnastics'; he blames the 'fetid' and 'dissolute' material for preventing him from blasting away on lyrical themes, and he awaits with impatience the moment when he can once more get drunk on fine style. But he says over and over that he does not know, properly speaking, what he is doing, or what the outcome will be of the effort against nature, against his nature anyway, which he is forcing on himself. 'What this book will be, I don't know; but I can say that it will be written.' The only assurance in the face of the unthinkable is the feeling of a tour de force conveyed by the experience of the immensity of the effort, corresponding to the extraordinary difficulty of the enterprise: 'I will have done true writing, which is rare.' 'True writing': for any mind structured according to the principles of vision and division shared by all those who get involved between 1840 and 1860 in the grand battle over 'realism', the expression is by all evidence an *oxymoron*. To say of a book, or rather a piece of writing, as does Flaubert, that 'it is written' has nothing to do with tautology. It is to affirm more or less what Sainte-Beuve means when, with respect to *Madame Bovary*, he declares: 'A precious quality distinguishes M. Gustave Flaubert from other more or less exact observers, who, these days, pride themselves on faithfully rendering reality, and sometimes succeed at it: he has style.'[100]

This then is the singularity of Flaubert, if we may believe Sainte-Beuve: he produces writings taken to be 'realistic' (no doubt by virtue of their object) which contradict the *tacit* definition of 'realism' in that they are written, that they have 'style'. This is something, as we see more clearly now, which by no means goes without saying. The programme announced in the formula 'write the mediocre well' is here deployed in its truthfulness: it is a matter of nothing less than *writing* the real (and not describing it, imitating it, or letting it somehow produce itself as a natural representation of nature); that is to say, it is a matter of making that which properly defines literature, but with respect to the real that is most dully real, the most ordinary, the most whatever is, in contrast to the ideal, not made to be written.[101]

The challenge to the prevailing forms of thought presented by the symbolic revolution and the absolute originality of what it engenders have as their counterpart the absolute solitude implied by transgressing the limits of the thinkable. This thought which has thus become its own measure cannot really expect that minds structured according to the very categories that it challenges will be able to think this unthinkable. So it is noticeable that critical judgements, when applying to works the principles of division that these works undermine, undo the inconceivable combination of contraries, reducing it to one or the other of the opposed terms. Thus this critique of *Madame Bovary*, trusting in ordinary associations, infers from the vulgarity of objects a vulgarity of style: 'The style of Champfleury (that says it all) – common to pleasure, and trivial, lacking force or breadth, without grace or delicacy. Why should I fear revealing the most outstanding fault of a school which does have its good qualities? The Champfleury school, which we clearly see Flaubert belonging to, considers that style is not good enough for it; it snaps its fingers at it, looks down on it, is full of sarcasm for authors *who write*. Write? What for? Let me be understood, that's enough! But it is not enough for everybody. If Balzac sometimes wrote badly, he always had style. This is what the Champfleurists don't dare acknowledge.'[102]

So there are those who, privileging content, associate *Madame Bovary* with *Les Bourgeois de Molinchart* by Champfleury, with *Les Amours vulgaires* by Vermorel or with *La Bêtise humaine*, a satire on bourgeois life by Jules Noriac – references which must have struck at Flaubert's heart – and on the other hand, people like Pontmartin, putting together the novels of Flaubert and of Edmond About in the same article entitled 'Le roman bourgeois et le roman démocrate', or who, like Cuvillier-Fleury in *Les Débats* of 26 May 1857, link Flaubert and Dumas fils. ('Look,' writes Flaubert, 'someone affects to confuse me with young Alex. Now my Bovary is a Lady of the Camellias. Bang!')

But there are also rarer critics, who are more attentive to tone and style and situate Flaubert in the line of the formalist poets. Whereas Champfleury deplores the abuse of description and Duranty the absence of 'sentiment, emotion, life', Jean Rousseau, in *Le Figaro* of 27 June 1858, sees in Gautier the direct inspiration for Flaubert's descriptive style. And Charles Monselet, a renegade from the realist group now become one of the incarnations of the boulevard spirit, dramatizes in a satire entitled *Le Vaudeville du crocodile* a Flaubert and a Gautier who declare they want to suppress humanity in favour of description: 'In an Egyptian vaudeville,' says the Gautier figure, 'there should be neither men nor women; human beings spoil the landscape, they cut off the lines disagreeably, they alter the smooth curve of the horizon. Man is out of place in nature.' And the Flaubert character replies, 'Yes, by Jove!'[103]

It is not surprising that Baudelaire is the only one to avoid this divided view, and to restore in his receiving it the experience of the tension that is at the root of the tour de force that consists of extracting a universal from 'that subject [which] is the most hackneyed, the most prostituted, the most like the hurdy-gurdy's stalest tune – adultery': 'a style that is vigorous, picturesque, subtle, and exact', finding 'the most ardent and the most heated emotions in the most trite love affair'.[104].

What makes for the radical originality of Flaubert, and what confers on his work its incomparable *value*, is that it makes contact, at least negatively, with the totality of the literary universe in which it is inscribed and whose contradictions, difficulties and problems he takes complete responsibility for. It follows that the only chance of truly recapturing the singularity of his creative project and fully accounting for it depends on proceeding exactly inversely to those who are content with chanting the litanies of the Unique. It is by completely historicizing it that one can completely understand how he tears himself away from the strict historicity of less heroic destinies. The originality of his enterprise cannot be truly extracted unless, instead of making an inspired but incomplete guess about such and such a position in the actual field (like the Nouveau Roman – labelled by the famous but poorly interpreted phrase of the 'book about nothing'), we reinsert it into the historically reconstituted space inside of which it was constructed; if, in other words, taking the viewpoint of a Flaubert who was not yet Flaubert, we try to discover what the young Flaubert was obliged to do and wanted to do in an artistic world not yet transformed by what he did – as is the world to which we tacitly refer him in treating him as a 'precursor'. It is in fact our familiar world that prevents us from understanding, among other things, the extraordinary effort that he had to make, the unprecedented resistances that he had to overcome, starting within himself, in order to produce and impose what today, in large part thanks to him, seems to us to be something that can be taken for granted.

In truth, there does not exist in the field one pertinent possible he does not refer himself to in practice, and sometimes explicitly so. First of all there are those possibles which have already been mentioned, such as the insipid Romanticism of the bourgeois theatre or the 'respectable novel' (to quote Baudelaire), or Champfleury's realism or even Vermorel's (he would have taken, according to Luc Badesco,[105] the opposite course to the author of *Amours vulgaires*, in his portraits of Tricochet and Gaston especially). To these should be added all those he explicitly acknowledged: obviously Gautier, the Quinet of the *Ahasverus* that he knows by heart, and all the poets who, as with Boileau whom he rereads ceaselessly, provide him with antidotes to the bland language of *Graziella*, the clichés of *Jocelyn* and the sentimental outpourings of Musset, whom he reproaches for having only ever sung about his own passions; Baudelaire; Villiers de L'Isle-Adam, with whom he communed in the cult of style, a passion for antiquity and a love of the outrageous remark and caricature; and Heredia, whose preface to the translation of the *Journal de Bernal-Diaz* he admires. Nor should we forget Leconte de Lisle who, despite his disdain for the novel, related his admiration for *Salammbô* and *Les Trois Contes*, and who, in the 1850s, had formulated in various prefaces an aesthetic based, like Flaubert's own, on condemnation of romantic sentimentalism and the poetry of social propaganda; he and Flaubert share a concern for impassivity, the cult of rhythm and plastic exactitude, and also a love of erudition.

In this age when philologists, notably Burnouf, with his *Introduction à l'histoire du bouddhisme*, and even more the historians (Michelet in particular, whose *Histoire romaine* he admired in his youth), are fascinating to writers, in particular to his friends Théophile Gautier and Louis Bouilhet (whose first book *Melaenis*, appearing in 1851, is an archaeological tale), Flaubert takes on an immense labour of research, notably in the preparation of *Salammbô*. His contemporaries see in him a poet doubled with a scholar (Berlioz, who addresses him as a 'scholar poet', consults him over the costumes for *Les Troyens à Carthage*, and his friend Alfred Nion regrets that his modesty prevented him from accompanying the text of *Salammbô* with erudite notes).[106]

But the era is also that of Geoffroy Saint-Hilaire, Lamarck, Darwin, Cuvier, of theories of the origins of species and evolution: Flaubert, who also wants to overcome the traditional opposition between art and science, like the Parnassians, borrows from the natural and historical sciences not only their erudite knowledge but also their characteristic mode of thought and the philosophy drawn from them – determinism, relativism, historicism. He finds there among other things a legitimation of his repugnance for the preaching of social art and his taste for the cold neutrality of the scientific viewpoint: 'What is beautiful in the natural sciences is that they do not want to prove anything. And what breadth of facts and what immensity of thought!

We should treat mankind like mastodons and crocodiles!' Or again: 'treating the human soul with the impartiality that one puts into the physical sciences.'[107] What Flaubert learned from the school of biology, from Geoffroy Saint-Hilaire especially, 'this great man who has shown the legitimacy of monsters',[108] leads him very close to the key Durkheimian dictum 'social facts should be treated like things' that he puts into operation with much rigour in *Sentimental Education*.

One feels that Flaubert is wholly there, in this universe of relationships that would have to be explored one by one, in their double dimension, both artistic and social, and that he nevertheless remains irreducibly beyond it: is this not because the active integration that he effects implies an overcoming? In situating himself, as it were, at the geometric intersection of all perspectives, which is also the point of greatest tension, he forces himself in some fashion to raise to their highest intensity the set of questions posed in the field, to play out all the resources inscribed in the space of possibles that, in the manner of a language or a musical instrument, is offered to each writer, like an infinite universe of possible combinations locked in a potential state within the finite system of constraints.

Return to *Sentimental Education*

It is no doubt *Sentimental Education* that offers the most accomplished example of this confrontation with the set of pertinent position-takings. By its subject, the work is inscribed at the intersection of the romantic and realist traditions: on the one hand, Musset's *La Confession d'un enfant du siècle* and Vigny's *Chatterton*, but also the so-called intimist novel that, as Jean Bruneau notes, 'recounts events of daily life and asks the essential questions about them' and which, 'down-to-earth and often moralizing', prefigures the realist novel and the thesis novel;[109] and on the other hand, the second bohemia, whose intimate journal in the romantic manner (as with Courbet's intimist painting of the world familiar to the painter) is converted into the realist novel when, with *Les Scènes de la vie de bohème* by Murger and especially *Les Aventures de Mariette* and *Chien-Caillou* by Champfleury, it registers in a faithful manner the often sordid reality of rawboned daubers' lives, their garrets, watering-holes and love affairs ('It is in reality the saddest life,' writes Champfleury in a letter of 1847, 'consisting of not dining, not having boots, and making about all that a quantity of paradoxes.')

In tackling such a subject, Flaubert comes up against not only

Murger and Champfleury, who are not of his stature: he also confronts Balzac, not just the Balzac of *Un Grand Homme de province à Paris*, the story of nine poor young men, or *Un Prince de la bohème*, but more especially the author of *Le Lys dans la vallée*. The great precursor is explicitly invoked, in the book itself, by means of Deslauriers's advice to Frédéric, 'Remember Rastignac in the *Comédie humaine*.' This reference by one character in a novel to another character in a novel marks the access of the novel to a reflexivity that, we know, is one of the foremost manifestations of the autonomy of a field: the allusion to the internal history of the genre, a sort of wink at a reader able to appropriate this history of works (and not only the story/history recounted in this work), is even more significant in that it is inscribed in a novel that encloses within itself a reference – a negative one – to Balzac. In the fashion of Manet, who introduces into a tradition of rather scholastic imitation a form of distanced imitation, ironic if not parodic, Flaubert performs with regard to the founding father of the genre a deliberately ambiguous bow, which perfectly fits the ambivalent admiration he holds for him. As if to make clearer his rejection of the Balzacian aesthetic, he takes a subject typical of Balzac but erases its Balzacian resonances, thus showing that one can make a novel without 'doing a Balzac' or even, as the defenders of the Nouveau Roman liked to say, that 'one can henceforth no longer do a Balzac' (or do a Walter Scott, as in the 'Légende de Saint Julien' in the *Trois Contes*, where the parodic intention is signalled by direct allusions). As with Manet's references to the grand masters of the past, Giorgione, Titian or Velázquez, Flaubert's references speak both reverence and distance, marking that rupture in the continuity, or that continuity in the rupture, which makes up the history of a field reaching autonomy. This is the complexity of the artistic revolution: under pain of excluding oneself from the game, one cannot revolutionize a field without mobilizing or invoking the experiences of the history of the field, and the great heretics – Baudelaire, Flaubert or Manet – inscribe themselves explicitly in the history of the field, mastering its specific capital much more completely than their contemporaries, so that revolutions take the form of a return to sources, to the purity of origins.

Flaubert does not compete with Balzac (emulation is a sort of defeated identification that leads to dissolution within alterity) and his profound choices undoubtedly owe nothing to the search for distinction. The work necessary for 'doing a Flaubert' – and for making Flaubert – implies a taking of distance from Balzac that does not need to be conceived as such – even if one cannot totally exclude, with either Flaubert or Manet, an intention to mystify the reader or the viewer by this play on irony, or parody: how for example can one not see in *Un Coeur simple* an affectionate parody of George Sand? And we know that Flaubert had anticipated presenting his *Diction-naire des idées reçues* in a preface 'so phrased that the reader does not know whether his leg was being pulled'.

In placing the reference to Rastignac in the mouth of Deslauriers, an accomplished incarnation of the petit-bourgeois, Flaubert author-izes us to see in Frédéric – as everything else suggests – the 'counter-part' (as the logicians say) of Rastignac, and this does not mean a failed Rastignac, or even an anti-Rastignac, but rather an equivalent of Rastignac in another possible world, the one Flaubert creates, and which as such competes with the one by Balzac.[110] Frédéric contrasts with Rastignac in a universe of possible literary worlds that really exists, at least in the minds of commentators, but also in the universe of a writer worthy of the name. What separates the 'conscious' writer from the 'naive' writer is precisely that the former masters the space of possibles well enough to sense the meaning that the possible which the writer is in the midst of realizing may acquire from its being put into a relationship with other possibles, and in order to avoid undesirable links which might sidetrack the intention. As proof there is this note by Flaubert in the notebook published by Mme Durry: 'Beware of *Le Lys dans la vallée.*' And could Flaubert not have been thinking as well of *Dominique* by Fromentin, and especially of *Volupté* by Sainte-Beuve, one of those anticipated readers all writers have in mind and even write for, especially when they are writing against them: 'I made *Sentimental Education* in part for Sainte-Beuve. He died without seeing a line of it.'[111] And how could he not have had in mind *Les Forces perdues* by Maxime Du Camp, that book borrowing from shared memories that appeared in 1866 and of which he said to George Sand that it resembled in many respects the *Education* he was working on?[112]

But this is not all. In choosing to write, with the impassivity of a paleontologist and the refinement of a Parnassian, the novel of the *modern* world, without overlooking a single one of the burning events that divide the literary and political worlds – the 1848 revolution, the artistic debates of the day about 'worker poets', industrial art, the comparison of 'village songs' to the 'lyrics of the nineteenth century' – he smashes a whole series of obligatory associ-ations: the ones that tie the so-called 'realist' novel to the 'literary rabble' or to 'democracy', the 'vulgarity' of objects to the 'baseness' of style, or the 'realism' of the subject to humanist morality. He breaks in one stroke all interdependencies founded on support for one or another of the constitutive terms of convenient pairs of contraries: thus, more than with *Madame Bovary*, he is fated to disappoint all those who expect literature to demonstrate something, to disappoint defenders of the moral novel as well as proponents of the social novel, conservatives and republicans, those who are sensitive to the triviality of the subject as well as those who reject the aesthetic coldness of the style and the deliberate flatness of the composition.

This series of ruptures of all relationships that, like moorings, could attach the work to groups, to their interests and their habits of thought explains better than the conjuncture (which is often invoked) the reception given by critics to the book, no doubt one of the worst received and also the most inadequately read in Flaubert's whole oeuvre. These ruptures are totally analogous with those accomplished by science, but are not willed as such and operate at the deepest level of the 'unknowing poetics', that is to say, in the work of writing and the work of the social unconscious fostered by the work on form, the instrument of an anamnesis that is both favoured and limited by the denegation involved in the imposition of form. The writing is by no means an outpouring, and there is a gulf between Flaubert's objecti-fication operating in the *Education* and Gustave's subjective projec-tion onto the character of Frédéric seen by commentators in it: 'One does not write what one wants,' says Flaubert. 'And it is true. Maxime [Du Camp] writes what he wants to, or close to it. But that is not writing.'[113] Nor is it a pure documentary account, as those sometimes seen as his disciples seem to think: 'Goncourt is very happy when he has seized upon a word in the street that he can stick in a book, and I am well satisfied when I have written a page without assonances or repetitions.'[114]

The imposition of form

It is not by chance that the quasi-explicit project of adding up requirements and constraints which seem irreconcilable, being asso-ciated with opposite positions in the literary space (hence with the generative dispositions of 'antipathies' and 'incompatibilities of tem-perament', of exclusions and exclusivities), leads with *Sentimental Education* to an extraordinarily successful (and quasi-scientific) objectification of Flaubert's social experiences and the determinations weighing on them, including those attaching to the writer's contradic-tory position in the field of power. The work of writing leads Flaubert to objectify not only the positions to which he is opposed in the field together with the people occupying them (like Maxime Du Camp, whose liaison with Mme Delessert furnishes him with the generative scheme for the relationship between Frédéric and Mme Dambreuse), but also, through the system of relationships that links him with other positions, the whole space in which he is himself enclosed, and hence his own position and his own mental structures. In the chiasmatic structure that is obsessively repeated throughout his work, and under the most diverse forms – doubled characters, intersecting trajectories, etc.[115] – and in the very structure of the relationship he draws between Frédéric and the benchmark characters in *Sentimental Education*, Flaubert objectifies the structure of the relationship that unites him, as a writer, to the universe of positions constitutive of the field of power or, what amounts to the same thing, to the universe of positions homologous with preceding ones in the literary field.

If he is able to overcome by his work as a writer the incompatibilities instituted in the social world in the form of groups, circles, schools and so forth, and also instituted in the mind (not excluding his own) in the form of principles of vision and division (such as those pairs of notions as -isms that he so detested), it is perhaps for this reason. In contrast to the passive indetermination of Frédéric, the active rejection of all determinations associated with a determined position in the intellectual field,[116] to which he was inclined by his social trajectory and the contradictory properties that were at its core, predisposed him to a higher and broader view of the space of possibles, and at the same time to a more complete use of the freedoms concealed by the constraints.

Thus, far from annihilating the creator by the reconstruction of the universe of social determinations that exert pressure on him, and reducing the work to the pure product of a milieu instead of seeing in it the sign that its author has known how to emancipate himself from it (as Proust seemed to fear in *Contre Sainte-Beuve*), sociological analysis allows us to describe and to understand the specific labour that the writer had to accomplish, both against these determinations and thanks to them, in order to produce himself as creator, that is, as the *subject* of his own creation. It even allows us to take account of the difference (ordinarily described in terms of *value*) between works that are the pure product of a milieu and a market, and those that must produce their market and may even contribute to transforming their milieu, thanks to the work of emancipation of which they are the product and which is accomplished, in part, through the objectification of that milieu.

It is not by chance that Proust is not the absolutely unproductive writer who is the narrator of *À la recherche du temps perdu*. Proust the writer is what the narrator becomes in and through the work that produces the *Recherche*, and that produces him as a writer. It is this liberating rupture, creative of the creator, that Flaubert symbolized in dramatizing, in the shape of Frédéric, the powerlessness of a being manipulated by the forces of the field – and this, in the very work whereby he surmounted that powerlessness by evoking the adventure of Frédéric, and, beyond it, the objective truth of the field in which he was writing this story and which, because of the conflict among its rival powers, could have reduced him, like Frédéric, to powerlessness.

The invention of the 'pure' aesthetic

The logic of the double refusal is at the root of the invention of the pure aesthetic that Flaubert achieves, but in an art like the novel that seems dedicated – more or less to the same degree as painting, where Manet will achieve a similar revolution – to the naive search for the illusion of reality. Realism is in effect a partial and abortive revolution: it does not really challenge the confusion of aesthetic value and moral (or social) value that Victor Cousin erected as a 'theory', and that still influences critical judgement when it expects a novel to carry a 'moral lesson' or when it condemns a work for its immorality, its indecency or its indifference. If realism questions the existence of an objective hierarchy of subjects, it is only to invert it, out of a concern to rehabilitate or to take revenge (critics speak of a 'rage to disparage') – not to abolish it. This is why one tends to recognize the existence of a hierarchy in the nature of the social milieux represented rather than in the more or less 'low' or 'vulgar' ways of representing them (which often go together): 'Realism, at the time the word started to be used, had only one meaning: the appearance in a novel of characters who were formerly despised [. . .]. Realism, *La Revue des Deux Mondes* asserts, is the "depiction of particular worlds and demi-mondes".'[117] Thus Murger himself is perceived as realist because he presents 'mediocre subjects' and heroes who dress badly, speak disrespectfully of everything and are unaware of social proprieties.

This privileged link with a particular category of objects must be broken by Flaubert in order to generalize and radicalize the partial revolution that realism effected. In particular, this is why – as Manet will do when confronted with a similar problem – he depicts at the same time, and sometimes in the same novel, the highest and lowest, the noblest and the most vulgar, bohemia and high society. Like Manet (in a painting such as *La Blonde aux seins nus*, for example), he subordinates literal and literary interest in the subject to its interest for representation, he sacrifices sensuality or sentimentality to the sensibility of the literary or pictorial medium – which leads him to reject subjects which touch us too emotionally or to treat them in such a manner as to lower their dramatic interest by a sort of *muting* effect.

While the pure gaze can attach a special interest to objects socially designated as hateful or contemptible (such as Boileau's serpent or Baudelaire's carrion), by reason of the challenge they represent and the prowess they call for, it deliberately ignores all the non-aesthetic differences between objects, and so it may find in the bourgeois universe, notably because of the privileged link that unites it to bourgeois art, a particular occasion to affirm its irreducibility. 'In literature there are not', says Flaubert, 'beautiful subjects for art and [. . .] So Yvetot is as good as Constantinople.'[118] The aesthetic revolution cannot be carried out except aesthetically:[119] it is not sufficient to constitute as beautiful that which is excluded by the official aesthetic, to rehabilitate modern, base or mediocre subjects; a power must be affirmed that belongs to art to constitute everything aesthetically by virtue of form ('to write the mediocre well'), to transmute everything in a work of art by the efficacy peculiar to writing. 'It is for this reason that there are no noble subjects or ignoble subjects; from the standpoint of pure Art one might almost establish the axiom that there is no such thing as subject – style in itself being an absolute manner of seeing things.'[120]

But it is not sufficient either to affirm, as do the Parnassians, or even Gautier, the primacy of pure form that, becoming an end in itself, says nothing other than itself. No doubt someone could contradict me here with the famous 'book about nothing', so enchanting to the theoreticians of the Nouveau Roman and the semiologists, or with Baudelaire's oft-quoted passage from the article devoted to Gautier in Crépet's *Anthologie des poètes français*: 'Poetry [. . .] has no goal other than itself; [. . .] and no poem will be so great, so noble, so truly worthy of the name Poetry as that which will have been written solely for the purpose of writing a poem.'[121] In both cases, one condemns oneself to a partial and mutilated reading if one does not hold together the two facets of a truth determined and defined by opposing two opposite errors. Thus, against all those who 'imagine that the aim of poetry is a lesson of some sort, that it must now fortify the conscience, now perfect morals, now *prove* something or other which is useful', in short, against 'the heresy of teaching a lesson', common to Romantics and realists, and its corollaries, 'the heresies of passion, truth, morality',[122] Baudelaire places himself alongside Gautier. But even while praising him he dissociates himself imperceptibly from Gautier, by lending him (in a strategy classic to prefaces) a conception of poetry which is not in the least formalist – his own: 'If one considers that with this marvelous faculty [style and knowledge of the language], Gautier combines an immense innate understanding of universal *correspondences* and symbolism, that repertory of all metaphor, one will realize why, without fatigue as without fault, he can always define the mysterious attitude which the objects of creation assume in men's eyes. There is in the work, in the *Logos*, something *sacred* which forbids us to turn it into a game of chance. To know how to use a language is to practice a kind of evocatory magic.'[123]

It is not, it seems to me, to force the meaning of the last sentence to see there the programme of an aesthetic founded on the reconciliation of possibles unduly separated by the dominant representation of art: a *realist formalism*. What does Baudelaire say in fact? Paradoxically, it is pure work on pure form, a formal exercise *par excellence*, that causes to surge up, as if by magic, a real more real than that which is offered directly to the senses and before which the naive lovers of reality stop, ready to bring in outside moral or political significations which, like the caption of a painting, guide the gaze and divert it from the essential. In contrast to a Parnassian and to Gautier, Baudelaire wants to abolish the distinction between form and substance, style and message: he demands of poetry that it integrate the spirit and a universe conceived as a reservoir of symbols whose language can capture the hidden meaning by drawing on the inexhaustible depths of the universal analogy. The divinatory search for equivalences among data collected by the senses allows them to recover the 'expansion of infinite things' by conferring on them, by the power of the imagination and by the grace of language, the value of symbols capable of melting into the spiritual unity of a common essence. Thus, to the sentimental lyricism of Romanticism (French, at least), that conceives of poetry as the refined expression of feelings, and to the pictorial and descriptive objectivism of Gautier and of the Parnassians that renounces the search for a reciprocal penetration of mind and nature, Baudelaire opposes a sort of mysticism of sensation enlarged by the game of language: an autonomous reality, with no referent other than itself, the poem is a creation independent of creation, and nevertheless united with it by profound ties that no positivist science perceives, and which are as mysterious as the correspondences uniting between themselves beings and things.

This is the same formalist realism defended by Flaubert with completely different expectations, and in a particularly difficult instance, since the novel is seemingly given to the search for the reality effect at least as rigorously as poetry is given to the expression of sentiment. His mastery of all the requirements of form allows him to assert almost limitlessly the power he possesses to constitute aesthetically any reality in the world, including those which, historically, realism had taken as its chosen objects. Moreover, as we have seen, it is in and through the work on form that evocation (in Baudelaire's strong sense) is effected, the evocation of this real which is more real than are sensory appearances given over to a simple realistic description. 'The idea is born from the form': the work of writing is not a simple execution of a project, a pure imposition of form onto a pre-existing idea, as classical doctrine believes (and as the painting academy still teaches), but a veritable search, similar in its way to that practised by initiatory religions, and destined in some fashion to create conditions favourable to the evocation and the growth of the idea that is none other, in this case, than the real. To reject the stylistic proprieties and conventions of the established novel and to reject its moralism and sentimentalism is all of a piece. It is through work on the written language, involving at the same time and in turn resistance, struggle and submission, a handing over of oneself, that works the evocatory magic which, like an incantation, makes the real rise up. It is when writers manage to let themselves be possessed by words that they discover that words think for them and reveal the real to them.

The research that could be called formal on the composition of the work, the articulation of the stories of different characters, the correspondence between the settings or situations and the behaviours or 'character types', as well as on the rhythm or the colour of phrases, the repetitions and assonances that must be hunted out, the received ideas and conventional forms that must be eliminated, is all part of the conditions of the production of a reality effect more profound than the one analysts ordinarily designate by this term. Unless one sees as a sort of completely unintelligible miracle the fact that analysis can discover in the work – as I have done for *Sentimental Education* – profound structures inaccessible to ordinary intuition (and to the reading of commentators), it must be acknowledged that it is through this work on form that the work comes to contain those structures that the writer, like any social agent, carries within him in a practical way, without having really mastered them, and through which is achieved the anamnesis of all that ordinarily remains buried, in an implicit or unconscious state, underneath the automatisms of an emptily revolving language.

Finally, to make of writing an indissolubly formal and material search, trying to use the words which best evoke, by their very form, the intensified experience of the real that they have helped to produce in the very mind of the writer, is to oblige the reader to linger over the perceptible form of the text, with its visible and sonorous material, full of correspondences with a real that is situated simultaneously in the order of meaning and in the order of the perceptible, instead of traversing it as if it were a transparent sign, read and yet unseen, in order to proceed directly to the meaning. It constrains the reader to discover there the intensified vision of the real that has been inscribed by the magical evocation involved in the work of writing. We can cite a critic of the time, Henry Denys, who describes well the effect Flaubert's first novel might have produced in comparison with painting: 'it contains dazzling pages of audacity and truthfulness. In addition, the everlasting friends within this fiction with rosy fingers, whose head rests in the half-light and the rest of the body in gauzy folds, would perhaps be upset by too harsh a light: the long use of falsifying glasses has given them a weak look, indecisive and superficial.'[124] And it is doubtless because he succeeds truly in obtaining from the reader, by the force peculiar to the writing, this intensified look at an intensified representation of the real – and of a real methodically overlooked by ordinary convention and proprieties – that Flaubert (like Manet, who did more or less the same thing in his sphere) arouses the indignation of readers who are nevertheless full of indulgence towards works which are devoid of the evocatory magic of his writing. This explains, too, why critics, however accustomed to the precious eroticism of 'respectable' novelists and official painters, have been so numerous in denouncing what they call Flaubert's 'sensualism'.

The ethical conditions of the aesthetic revolution

The revolution of the gaze effected in and through the revolution in writing both presupposes and brings forth a rupture of the link between the ethical and the aesthetic, which goes hand in hand with a total conversion of lifestyle. This conversion, to be accomplished in the aestheticism of the artistic lifestyle, could only be half completed by the realists of the second bohemia, because they were blinkered by the question of the relations between art and reality, between art and morality, but also and especially by the limits of their petit-bourgeois ethos, which prevented them from accepting its ethical implications. All the partisans of social art, whether it is Léon Vasque talking of *Mademoiselle de Maupin*, or Vermorel judging Baudelaire, or Proudhon stigmatizing the habits of artists, see very clearly the ethical foundations of the new aesthetic: they denounce the perversion of a literature that 'becomes venereal and turns to the aphrodisiac'; they condemn the 'minstrels of the ugly and squalid', combining 'moral ignominies' and 'physical corruptions'; they are especially indignant that there are method and artifice in this 'cold, reasoned, studied depravity'.[125] Scandalously perverse indulgence, but also scandalously cynical indifference to infamy and scandal. One such critic, in an article on *Madame Bovary* and the 'physiological novel', reproaches Flaubert's pictorial imagination for 'shutting itself in the physical world as if it were an immense attic peopled with models that all have the same value in his eyes'.[126]

In fact, the pure gaze which in those days it was a matter of *inventing* (instead of being content with putting it to work, as today), at the cost of breaking the links between art and morality, requires a posture of impassivity, indifference and detachment, if not a cynical casualness which is poles apart from the double ambivalence, composed of horror and fascination, of the petit-bourgeois with respect to the 'bourgeois' and the 'people'. For example, it is Flaubert's violent anarchistic humour, his sense of transgression and the joke, along with this capacity to hold himself at a distance, which allow him to draw the most beautiful aesthetic effects from the simple description of human suffering. Thus, when he regrets that with *Les Amoureux de Sainte-Périne* Champfleury had spoiled a good subject, he states: 'For I don't see that it is comic: I should have made [it] atrocious and lamentable.'[127] And we can once more evoke that letter in which he encourages Feydeau, then at the side of his dying wife, to draw an artistic profit from this experience: 'You are having and you are going to have "important" experiences, and you are going to be able to turn them into "important" writings. It's a high price to pay. The bourgeois little suspect that we give them our hearts to eat. The race of gladiators is not dead; every artist is one. He amuses the public with his agonies.'[128]

Aestheticism taken to its limit tends towards a sort of moral neutralism, which is not far from an ethical nihilism. 'The only way to live in peace is to place yourself in one leap above all of humanity, and to have nothing to do with it but an ocular relation. This would scandalize the Pelletans, the Lamartines and the whole sterile and *dried-up* race (inactive in the public good as in the ideal) of humanitarians, republicans, etc. – Too bad! They should start paying their debts before preaching charity. Be just respectable, before wanting to be virtuous. Fraternity is one of the most beautiful inventions of social hypocrisy.'[129] This freedom with respect to the moral proprieties and humanitarian conformities binding 'respectable' people into Pharisaism is no doubt what profoundly unites the group of guests at the Magny dinners, where, between literary anecdotes and obscene stories, the separation of art and morality is advocated. It is this which grounds the particular affinity between Baudelaire and Flaubert, which the latter invokes when he writes to Ernest Feydeau, during the editing of *Salammbô*: 'I am reaching rather dark tones. We are starting to wade through gore and to burn the dying. Baudelaire would be happy!' And the aesthetic aristocratism which is stated here in the mode of a provocative sally is betrayed in a more discreet and no doubt more authentic manner in a judgement on Hugo such as this one, very close to that formulated by Baudelaire: 'Why did he sometimes proclaim such a ridiculous morality which so diminished him? Why the politics? Why the Académie and the received ideas, the imitation, etc.?'[130] Or on Erckmann-Chatrian: 'How very boorish! Here are two nuts, who have very plebeian souls.'[131]

Thus the invention of the pure aesthetic is inseparable from the invention of a new social personality, that of the great professional artist who combines, in a union as fragile as it is improbable, a sense of transgression and freedom from conformity with the rigour of an extremely strict discipline of living and of work, which presupposes bourgeois ease and celibacy[132] and which is more characteristic of the scientist or the scholar. The great artistic revolutions are not the act either of the (temporally) dominant, who here as elsewhere have no quarrel with an order that consecrates them, or of the simply dominated, who are usually condemned by their conditions of existence and dispositions to a routine practice of literature and who may supply troops equally to the heretics or to the guardians of the symbolic order. Revolutions are incumbent on those hybrid and unclassifiable beings whose aristocratic dispositions, often associated with a privileged social origin and with the possession of large symbolic capital (in the case of Baudelaire and Flaubert, a sulphurous prestige straight away ensured by scandal), underpin a profound 'impatience with limits', social but also aesthetic limits, and a lofty intolerance of all compromises with the times. 'To seek an honour no matter what, seems to me, besides, an act of incomprehensible modesty.'[133]

This distance from all positions that favours formal elaboration – it is the work on form which inscribes it into the work itself. It is the pitiless elimination of all 'received ideas', all the typical commonplaces of any group and all the stylistic traits marking or betraying

adherence to or support for one or another of the attested positions
or position-takings; it is the methodical use of a free indirect style
that leaves as indeterminate as possible the relationship of the
narrator to the facts or persons of which the tale speaks. But nothing
is more revealing of Flaubert's point of view than the *very ambiguity
of viewpoint* marked in the *composition* so characteristic of his
books, and so it is with *Sentimental Education*, which critics have
often reproached for being made out of a series of 'bits put together',
by virtue of the absence of a clear hierarchy of details and incidents.[134]
As Manet will do later, Flaubert abandons the unifying perspective
taken from a fixed and central point of view in favour of what one
could call, with Panofsky, an 'aggregated space', meaning a space
made of juxtaposed pieces and without a privileged point of view. In
a letter to Huysmans about *Les Soeurs Vatard*, he writes that it
'lacks, like *Sentimental Education*, the falseness of perspective! There
is no progression of effect.'[135] And we may remember that declaration
he made one day to Henry Céard, again about the *Education*: '"It is
a condemned book, my dear friend, because it does not do *that*" –
and, joining his long hands elegant in their robustness, he simulated
the shape of a pyramid.'[136] The rejection of a pyramid construction,
that is, one with an ascending convergence towards an idea, a
conviction, a conclusion, itself contains a message, and no doubt the
most important, that is to say a vision – if not to say a philosophy –
of the story/history [*histoire*], in the dual meaning of the word. A
bourgeois who is fervently anti-bourgeois, Flaubert has at the same
time absolutely no illusions about the 'people' (although Dussardier,
the sincere and disinterested plebeian – who, believing he is defending
the Republic, kills a heroic insurgent – turns out to be an abused
innocent and the only luminous figure in the *Education*). But, in his
absolute disenchantment, he preserves an absolute conviction concerning the task of the writer. Against all preachers with sterling
souls descending from Lamennais (antithesis of Barbès of whom he
says to George Sand: 'he loved freedom, that one, and without
mincing words, like a man of Plutarch'), he asserts, in the only way
that matters, that is, *without mincing words*, and by the very
structure of his discourse, his refusal to grant the reader the false
satisfactions offered by the false Pharisaic humanism of the vendors
of illusions. That text which in refusing to 'make a pyramid' and to
'open up perspectives' declares itself as a discourse of the here and
now, and from which the author is effaced (though like Spinoza's
God, he remains immanent and coextensive with his creation), there,
then, is Flaubert's point of view.

2

The Emergence of a
Dualist Structure

~∞~

> If I had Paul Bourget's fame, I would show myself every night
> in a G-string in a burlesque show and I guarantee I would be
> big box-office.
>
> ARTHUR CRAVAN

Having evoked the state of the intellectual field in the phase of its formation – a heroic period when the principles of autonomy that will later be converted into objective mechanisms, immanent in the logic of the field, still reside to a large extent in agents' dispositions and actions – in this chapter the wish is to propose a model of the *state* of the literary field as it is established in the 1880s. In fact, one would need to construct a true chronicle of events to get a concrete appreciation of how this universe, anarchic and wilfully libertarian in appearance (which it also is, thanks in large part to the social mechanisms that authorize and favour autonomy), is the site of a sort of well-regulated ballet in which individuals and groups dance their own steps, always contrasting themselves with each other, sometimes clashing, sometimes dancing to the same tune, then turning their backs on each other in often explosive separations, and so on, up until the present time . . .

The particularities of genres

The progress of the literary field towards autonomy is marked by the fact that, at the end of the nineteenth century, the hierarchy among genres (and authors) according to specific criteria of peer judgement is almost exactly the inverse of the hierarchy according to commercial success. This is different from what was to be observed in the seventeenth century, when the two hierarchies were almost merged, with those most consecrated among people of letters, especially poets and scientists, being the best provided with pensions and profits.[1]

From the economic point of view, the hierarchy is simple, and relatively constant, despite conjunctural fluctuations. At the summit stands the theatre, providing large and immediate profits for a very small number of authors in return for a relatively small cultural investment. At the bottom of the hierarchy, there is poetry which, with very few exceptions (such as some successes in verse theatre), procures extremely small profits for a small number of producers. Situated in an intermediate position, the novel can assure large profits to a relatively large number of authors, but only so long as it extends its public well beyond the literary world itself (to which poetry is confined) and beyond the bourgeois world (as is the case for theatre), that is, to the petite-bourgeoisie or even, especially by the intermediary of municipal libraries, as far as to the 'labour aristocracy'.

From the point of view of the criteria of appreciation that dominate inside the field, things are less simple. Nevertheless, we see by a number of indices that, under the Second Empire, the summit of the hierarchy is occupied by poetry. Consecrated as the art *par excellence* by the romantic tradition, it retains all its prestige; despite fluctuations – with the decline of Romanticism, never totally equalled by Théophile Gautier or Parnassus, and with the rise of the enigmatic and sulphurous figure of Baudelaire – it continues to attract a large number of writers, even if it is almost totally devoid of a market: most poetic works reach at most a few hundred readers. At the opposite end, the theatre – with its direct exposure to the immediate sanction of the bourgeois public, its values and orthodoxies – procures, besides money, the institutionalized consecration of the academies and official honours. As for the novel, situated in a central position between the two poles of the literary space, it presents the largest dispersion from the viewpoint of symbolic status: even though it has acquired its marks of nobility, at least within the field, and even beyond it, with Stendhal and Balzac and especially Flaubert, it remains associated with the image of mercantile literature, tied to journalism by the *feuilleton* (serial). It acquires considerable weight in the literary field when with Zola it achieves the success of exceptional sales (hence very substantial earnings that allow it to break free from the press and the serial), reaching a much wider public than any other mode of expression, but without letting go of specific requirements regarding form (it will even manage to obtain through the society novel a bourgeois consecration until then reserved to the theatre).

One can assess the chiasmatic structure of this space, in which the hierarchy according to commercial profit (theatre, novel, poetry) coexists with an inverted hierarchy according to prestige (poetry, novel, theatre), by a *simple model* taking account of two principles of differentiation. On the one hand, the different genres, considered as economic enterprises, are distinguished in three respects: firstly, as a function of the price of the product or the act of symbolic consumption, relatively high in the case of theatre or the concert, low in the case of the book, the musical score or the museum or gallery visit (with the unit cost of a painting putting pictorial production in a completely separate situation); secondly, as a function of the numbers and the social qualities of the consumers, hence of the size of the economic but also symbolic profits (linked to the social standing of the public) assured by these enterprises; thirdly, as a function of the length of the production cycle, and in particular how quickly profits, material as much as symbolic, are obtained and for how long they are guaranteed.

On the other hand, to the extent that the field progressively gains in autonomy and imposes its own logic, these genres also grow more distinct from each other, and more clearly so, according to the degree of intrinsically symbolic credit they possess and confer, this tending to vary in inverse relation to economic profit. In effect, the credit attached to any cultural practice tends to decrease with the numbers and especially the social spread of the audience, because the value of the credit of recognition ensured by consumption decreases when the specific competence recognized in the consumer decreases (and even tends to change sign when it descends below a certain threshold).

This model takes account of the major oppositions among genres, but also the more subtle differences observed inside the same genre, as it does of the diverse forms that the consecration accorded to genres or authors may assume. It is in effect the social quality of the audience (measured principally by its volume) and the symbolic profit it assures which determine the specific hierarchy established among works and authors within each genre, with the hierarchized categories detected there corresponding rather closely to the social hierarchy of the respective audiences. This can be clearly seen in the case of theatre, with the opposition between classical theatre, boulevard theatre, vaudeville and cabaret, or more sharply still in the case of the novel, where the hierarchy of specialties – the society novel that will become the psychological novel, the naturalist novel, the novel of manners, the regionalist novel, the popular novel – corresponds quite directly with the social hierarchy of the readerships concerned, and also, rather closely, with the hierarchy of the social universes represented in them, and even with the hierarchy of authors according to social origin and sex.

It also allows us to understand similarities and differences between the novel and the theatre. Boulevard theatre, able to provide established authors with considerable economic profits thanks to repeated performances of the same work before a limited and bourgeois public, brings to authors, almost all of them from the bourgeoisie, one form of social respectability, that consecrated by the Académie. The very particular social characteristics of playwrights result from the fact that they are the product of a two-stage selection: the theatres being very few and their directors having an interest in keeping plays on the bill for as long as possible, the authors must first face a terrible competition for their work to be staged, and there the major trump is the social capital of relationships within the theatrical milieu; they must then face the competition for an audience, and there there is the factor (besides mastery of the tricks of the trade, itself also linked to familiarity with the world of the theatre) of closeness to the values of the audience, largely bourgeois and Parisian, and hence more 'distinguished' socially than culturally.

In contrast, the novelists cannot realize profits equal to those of playwrights unless they reach a 'broad audience' [*le grand public*], which means, as the pejorative connotations of the expression indicate, exposing oneself to the discredit attached to commercial success. Thus it is that Zola, whose novels met the most compromising success, no doubt owes his escape from the social destiny marked out for him by his large print runs and his vulgar subjects in part to the conversion of the 'commercial', negative and 'vulgar' into the 'popular', charged with all the positive prestiges of political progressivism – a conversion made possible by the role of social prophet that was vested in him at the heart of the field and which was acknowledged well beyond it with the help of militant devotion (and also, but much later, of professional progressivism).[2]

The extraordinary seduction exercised on Zola by the *Introduction à l'étude de la médecine expérimentale* cannot only be explained by the immense prestige enjoyed by science in the 1880s, notably through the influence of people such as

Taine, Renan, and also Berthelot (a scientist who makes himself the prophet of a veritable religion of science).[3] Was he naive enough to believe – a reproach often made – that Claude Bernard's method could be applied directly to literature? In any case, everything leads us to believe that the theory of the 'experimental novel' offered him a privileged means of neutralizing the suspicion of vulgarity attached to the social inferiority of the milieux that he depicted and of the readers his books reached. In claiming to draw inspiration from the model of eminent doctors, he identified the gaze of the 'experimental novelist' with the *clinical gaze*, establishing between the writer and his object the objectifying distance which separates the leading lights of medicine from their patients. This concern to keep a distance is never as evident as in the contrast that he maintains (and which will be abolished by Céline, among others) between the language put into the mouths of working-class characters and the narrator's remarks, the latter always marked by signs of great literature – in their rhythm, which is that of the written word, or in the traits typical of sustained style, such as the use of the *passé simple* tense and indirect speech. Thus someone who in his manifesto *Le Roman expérimental* loudly proclaimed the independence and dignity of the man of letters, affirms in his work itself the superior dignity of literary culture and language, by which he should be recognized and for which he claims recognition. In this way he designates himself as the author *par excellence* of popular education, itself totally founded on the acknowledgement of that cutting-off which is at the basis of the respect for culture.

Differentiation of genres and unification of the field

The Symbolist reaction against naturalism – and also, in the case of poetry, against the positivism that weighs on Parnassian poetry through the superstitious insistence on the precise fact or document, and on Orientalism and Hellenism – cannot be understood as a direct effect of a transformation of mentalities itself reflecting economic and political changes – that is to say, it cannot be understood by leaving out the *specific* logic and history of the field. It is likely that the 'spiritualist renaissance' observed in the whole field of power, linked to the renewal of an idealism associated with the cult of Wagner and the Italian primitives, and which in the literary field takes the form of a renewal of mysticism (with the Union for Moral Action of Paul Desjardins, for example), sometimes mixed with an urbane anarchism of the salon,[4] furnished the conditions favourable to the appearance and the relative success of the Symbolist movement (and of innumerable small related movements, such as Florian-Parmentier's 'Impulsionism' which, against 'scientific materialism, experimental fanaticism, and intellectualism', elaborates a philosophy close to that of Bergson). The social and even political dimension of this reaction is in fact rather evident: it pits an artistic and spiritualist art which cultivates the sense of mystery against a social and materialist art based on science. (Political progressivism is more associated with aesthetic conservatism, and is found for example among the old social Parnassians or in different bizarre schools such as Jules Romains's 'Unanimism', which claims inspiration from Tarde, Le Bon and naturalism, or such as 'Paroxysm', 'Dynamism', 'Proletarianism' and so forth.)

But the Symbolist reaction is not completely comprehensible unless it is considered in relation to the specific crisis undergone by literary production in the 1880s, a crisis whose effects on the different literary genres are felt to a greater degree the more economically viable they are.[5] Poetry, despite the force of attraction accrued by the novel, continues to draw a large share of new entrants and has nothing much to lose, it is true, since it has hardly any customers outside the producers themselves; the immanent logic of the permanent differentiation of styles favours the rise, along a route opened by Baudelaire, of a Symbolist school breaking with the belated Parnassians or naturalists who render sorry political, philosophical or social speeches into verse. By contrast, the naturalist novelists, especially those of the second generation, are very directly hit by the crisis and their conversions are no doubt also reconversions aiming to respond to the new expectations of the cultivated public, linked especially to the 'spiritualist renaissance': some (like Huysmans) are converted to a 'spiritualist naturalism', while others – like Paul Bonnetain, J.-H. Rosny, Lucien Descaves, Paul Margueritte and Gustave Guiches, the authors of the 'Manifeste des cinq contre la terre' (Manifesto of the Five against the Earth) published in *Le Figaro* on 18 August 1887 – participate in the spiritualist reaction against Zola and naturalism.

For their part, a number of the writers who had been drawn at first to poetry now reinvest in the 'idealist' and 'psychological' novel a cultural capital and above all a social capital greater than that of their naturalist competitors:[6] thus André Theuriet imports into the novel the tradition of intimist poetry, and Paul Bourget, a disciple of Taine who, like Anatole France, André Theuriet and Barbey d'Aurevilly, had begun his literary career with the publication of collections of poetry (*La Vie inquiète*, 1875; *Edel*, 1878; *Les Aveux*, 1882), makes himself the analyst of the refined sentiments of characters confined to a mondain setting, thus opening the way to novelists such as Barrès, Paul Margueritte, Camille Mauclair, Édouard Estaunié or even André Gide, certain of whose novels, by their style and lyricism, can be read as poems in prose. This has the effect of causing a division of the novel into competing schools (which is already present in poetry) with, at the opposite pole to the new currents, the social or regional novel coming out of naturalism, and the thesis novel.

As for the theatre, a domain reserved for writers of bourgeois origins, it also becomes a refuge for unlucky novelists and poets, of petit-bourgeois or working-class origin for the most part; but they come up against barriers to entry which are characteristic of the genre, to wit, the gentle means of exclusion by which the closed club of theatre directors, accredited authors and critics block the aspirations of new arrivals. No doubt because it is more directly subject to the constraints of the demand from a principally bourgeois (at least in origin) clientèle, theatre is the last to experience an autonomous avant-garde, and it is one which, for the same reasons, will always remain fragile and threatened. Despite the initial failures of the Goncourt brothers (in 1865 with *Henriette Maréchal*) and of Zola (with *Thérèse Raquin* in 1873, *Les Héritiers Rabourdin* in 1874, *Bouton de rose* in 1878, *L'Assommoir* in 1879, etc.), the moves by the naturalists, Zola especially,[7] to overthrow the hierarchy of genres by transferring onto the terrain of the theatre the symbolic capital acquired with a new audience (who read his novels but who do not go to the theatre) does not remain totally without effect: in 1887, Antoine founds his Théâtre-Libre, the first enterprise to really defy the economic constraints in a sector of the field where until then they had reigned undisputedly, and where they will also manage to triumph, since the venture was abandoned in 1896 by its director, scuppered by debts of a hundred thousand francs.

But the rupture out of which a new position is found to be created, one opposed both to the declamatory tradition of the Comédie-Française and to the casual elegance of boulevard actors, is sufficient to give rise to the most characteristic effects of the functioning of a universe as a field. On the one hand, the Théâtre d'Art of Paul Fort, which will become the Théâtre de l'Oeuvre of Lugné-Poe (a renegade from the Théâtre-Libre), is set up on the model of the Théâtre-Libre but against it, reproducing in the subfield of theatre thus instituted the oppositions between naturalists and Symbolists that henceforth divide the whole field. On the other hand, in constituting as such the problem of *mise en scène* and in posing various stagings as so many *artistic games*, that is as *systematic* sets of explicitly *chosen* responses to a set of problems which tradition was not aware of or to which it responded without posing them, André Antoine questions a doxa that was unquestioned as such, and he sets the whole game in motion, to wit, the history of *mise en scène*.

At a stroke he gives rise to a *finite space of possible choices* which theatrical research has not yet finished exploring, the universe of pertinent problems on which any director *worthy of the name* must take a position, whether willingly or not, and which different directors will disagree about: questions bearing on the scenic space, on the relationship (which Antoine thought more necessary) between the design of the set and the characters (he advocates exactitude), the question of the text and the starkness or theatricality of the interpretation, the question of the interaction between actors and spectators (with the hall put into darkness and – as against playing to the audience, which breaks the theatrical illusion – the theory of the 'fourth wall'), the question of lighting and sound, and so forth.[8]

The best evidence of the hold Antoine won over the field that he thus brought into existence lies in the fact that, as observers who are the least inclined to a sociological vision of the history of the theatre have indicated, his adversaries at the Théâtre de l'Oeuvre confront each of his position-takings with an antagonistic one: they offer the ostentation of 'theatricality' (with Jarry especially) against the illusionism of the 'natural', 'suggestion' against verisimilitude, 'theatre of imagination' against 'theatre of observation', the primacy of speech against the primacy of décor, 'metaphysical man' against 'physiological man', 'a theatre of the soul' (in the expression of Édouard Schuré) against a theatre of the body and its instincts, symbolism against naturalism – all these antitheses being carried along by playwrights and directors who, like Paul Fort and Lugné-Poe, stand in a similar relationship of opposition to Antoine and his playwrights from the view of social origins (while Antoine had only a primary education, Lugné-Poe, whose father made his career in banking, notably as deputy director of the Société Générale in London, is a former pupil of the Lycée Condorcet).

Thus, between the beginning of the century, with poetry, and the 1880s, with theatre (described by Zola, in reply to Huret, as 'always behind the rest of literature'), there develops at the heart of each genre a more autonomous sector – or, if you will, an avant-garde. Each of the genres tends to cleave into a research sector and a commercial sector, two markets between which one must be wary of establishing a clear boundary, since they are merely two poles, defined in and by their antagonistic relationship, of the same space. This process of differentiation of each genre is accompanied by a process of unification of the whole set of genres, that is, of the literary field, which tends more and more to organize itself around common oppositions (for example, in the 1880s, the one between naturalism and Symbolism): in effect, each of the two opposed sectors of each subfield (for example, the director's theatre) tends to become closer to the similar sector of the other genres (the naturalist novel in Antoine's case or Symbolist poetry in Lugné-Poe's) than the opposite pole of the same subfield (boulevard theatre). In other words, the opposition between genres loses its structuring efficacy in favour of the opposition between the two poles present in each subfield: the pole of pure production, where the producers tend to have as clients only other producers (who are also rivals), and where poets, novelists and theatrical people endowed with similar position characteristics find each other, though they may be engaged in relations that may be antagonistic; and the pole of large-scale production, subordinated to the expectations of a wide audience.

Art and money

From now on, the unified literary field tends to organize itself according to two independent and hierarchized principles of differentiation: the principal opposition, between pure production, destined for a market restricted to producers, and large-scale production, oriented towards the satisfaction of the demands of a wide audience, reproduces the founding rupture with the economic order, which is at the root of the field of restricted production. This principle of differentiation is intersected by a secondary opposition that is established, within the subfield of pure production, between the avant-garde and the consecrated avant-garde. There is, for example, in the period under consideration, the opposition between the Parnassians and those called the 'Decadents', themselves virtually divided, along a third dimension, according to differences of style and literary project which correspond to differences in social origin and lifestyle.

Long considered as the lost children of Parnassus (present among the thirty-seven poets published in the first two editions of the collection titled *Le Parnasse contemporain*, they are excluded from the third edition, which gives them the status of martyrs), Verlaine and Mallarmé begin to attract attention in the middle of the 1880s, and receive their *nom de guerre* from a polemical parody, *Les Déliquescences d'Adoré Floupette, poète décadent*, a collection of satiric verses by Gabriel Vicaire and Henri Beauclair appearing in 1885 which ridicules the poetry of Verlaine, Mallarmé and their imitators. At first objectively united by their common opposition to their elders, the Parnassians (and assembled in battle order by Verlaine who includes in *Les Poètes maudits* Mallarmé, Rimbaud and Tristan Corbière), the two poets, Mallarmé and his Symbolists, Verlaine and his Decadents, gradually grow apart until they confront one another over a series of stylistic and thematic contrasts (that of the Right Bank and the Left Bank, the salon and the café, pessimistic radicalism and prudent reformism, an explicit aesthetic founded on hermeticism and esoterism versus an aesthetic of clarity and simplicity, of naiveté and emotion) which corresponds to social differences (the majority of the Symbolists come from the middle or grande bourgeoisie or the nobility and have studied in Paris, often the law, whereas the Decadents

high degree of consecration (old)

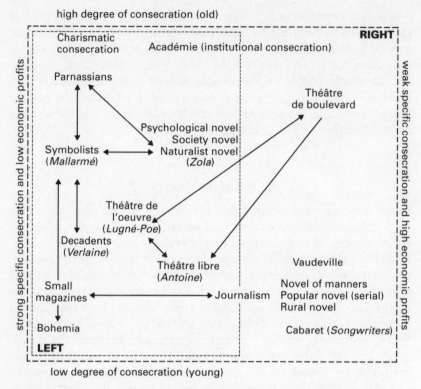

Figure 2 The literary field at the end of the nineteenth century (detail)

come from the working class or petite bourgeoisie and are poorly endowed with cultural capital).[9]

Differences in the *degree of consecration* in fact separate *artistic generations*, defined by the interval (often very short, sometimes barely a few years) between styles and lifestyles that are opposed to each other – as 'new' and 'old', original and 'outmoded'. These arbitrary dichotomies are often almost empty of meaning, but are sufficient to classify and give existence to, with the least amount of effort, the groups designated – rather than defined – by labels intended to produce the differences that they pretend to enunciate.

The fact that social age is largely independent of biological age is never seen as clearly as in the literary field, where generations may be separated by less than a decade (as is the case with Zola, born in 1840, and his recognized disciples from the Soirées de Médan such as Alexis, born in 1847; Huysmans, in 1848; Mirbeau, in 1848; Maupassant, in 1850; Céard, in 1851; Hennique, in 1851). The same thing is true of Mallarmé and his first followers. Another example is

Paul Bourget, one of the principal defenders of the 'psychological novel', who is only twelve years away from Zola. Zola does not fail to notice this disconnection between social age (of position) and chronological or 'real' age: 'In dwelling on such foolishness, such nonsense, at so grave a moment in the evolution of ideas, they give me the impression, all these young people who are aged between thirty and forty, of nutshells dancing on Niagara Falls! They have nothing under them except gigantic and hollow pretension!'[10]

The occupants of avant-garde positions who are not yet consecrated, and especially the older ones (biologically) among them, have an interest in reducing the second opposition to the first, and in making the success or recognition that certain avant-garde writers may obtain in the long term appear as the effect of a repudiation or a compromise with the bourgeois order. They can rely on the fact that while bourgeois consecration and the economic profits or temporal honours which mark it (the Académie, prizes and so forth) go by priority to writers producing for the bourgeois market and the consumer's market, they also affect the most conformist section of the consecrated avant-garde. Thus the Académie Française has always given a seat to a small number of 'pure' writers, for example Leconte de Lisle, head of the Parnassians, who in 1852, in the preface to *Poèmes antiques*, posed as a prophet, restorer of a lost purity and adversary of fashion, and who finishes up in the Académie, decorated with the Légion d'Honneur. *A contrario*, those who want at any price to avoid assimilation to bourgeois art and the effect of social ageing it determines must refuse the social signs of consecration – decorations, prizes, academies and all kinds of honours.

The temporal structures and forms of change that were installed much earlier in the domain of poetry, destined to be responsive to the rhythm of revolutions (romantic, Parnassian, Symbolist), now make themselves felt in the novel as well, with the advent of naturalism, and even in the theatre with the advent of the role of director [*metteur en scène*] and the revolution it introduces. In the case of poetry, the rhythm of revolutions (planned, if not successful) accelerates and at the beginning of the century 'literary anarchy', as some call it, reaches its height: the 'Congress of Poets', held in Paris at the École des Hautes Études Sociales on 27 May 1901 to foster an attempt at fraternization, closes in tumult and battle. The schools multiply, leading to one schism after another: Synthesism with Jean de la Hire, Integralism with Adolphe Lacuzon in 1901, Impulsionism with Florian-Parmentier in 1904, Aristocratism with Lacaze-Duthiers in 1906, Unanimism with Jules Romains, Sinceritism with Louis Nazz, Subjectivism with Han Ryner, Druidism with Max Jacob, Futurism with Marinetti in 1909, Intensism with Charles de

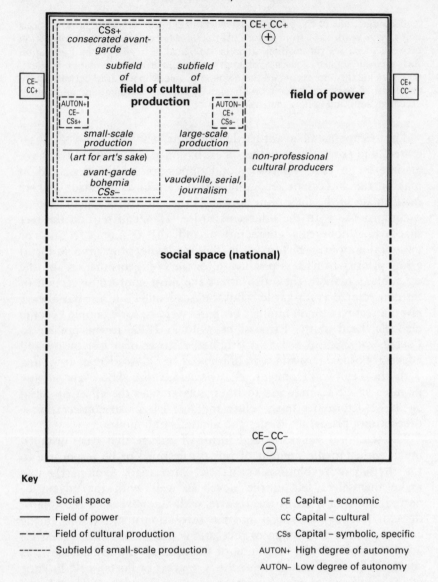

Figure 3 The field of cultural production in the field of power and in social space

Saint-Cyr in 1910, Floralism with Lucien Rolmer in 1911, Simultaneism with Henri-Martin Barzun and Fernand Divoire in 1912, Dynamism with Henri Guilbeaux in 1913, Freneticism, Totalism, etc.[11] Some justify their impatience to accede to the succession by drawing on the logic of permanent revolution that has become the functioning law of the field and do not hesitate to say that twenty-five years is too long a term of survival for a literary generation.[12] Sectarian frenzy, reminiscent of avant-garde political sects, leads to schisms instigated by self-proclaimed leaders: the Decadents engender Symbolism, which engenders Magnificism, Magism, socialism, anarchism and the Roman School. Very few of the movements manage to establish themselves, and most leaders of schools remain without disciples, almost all of them disappearing into oblivion. Everywhere, the inaugural rupture engenders its repetition in a new rupture.

In the case of the novel, the naturalist revolution engenders, in time, the reaction of the 'psychologists', and in the case of the theatre, as we have seen, the appearance of Antoine's Théâtre-Libre almost immediately provokes the creation of Lugné-Poe's Théâtre de l'Oeuvre, a projection into the new space opened up by Antoine of the opposition (transcending generic frontiers) between naturalism and Symbolism (as a result of this double rupture, poetry asserts its domination over the novel, with Huysmans, and over the theatre, with Maeterlinck). Each successful revolution legitimates itself, but legitimates, too, revolution as such, even if merely a revolution against the aesthetic forms that it imposed. The demonstrations and the manifestos of all those who, from the start of the century, endeavour to impose any new artistic regime, designated by a concept ending in an ism, bear witness that revolution tends to impose itself as the *model* of access to existence in the field.

An exemplary case, which has been called the 'crisis of naturalism', is none other than the set of symbolic strategies, partially effective, by which a set of writers and critics, some of whom come out of naturalism, assert their right to succession in a sort of symbolic coup d'état: that is to say, in addition to the five authors of the manifesto of 18 August 1887, there is Brunetière, who writes an article on 1 September 1887 on the bankruptcy of naturalism; Paul Bourget who, in the preface to *Le Disciple* of 1889, stands up against triumphant naturalism; and Jules Huret himself with his famous survey (first example of those performative interrogations, often practised since, that tend to produce the effects they pretend to register), in which he gives all the pretenders, Huysmans for example, the opportunity to say that 'naturalism is finished.'[13] Thus a schema of thought is constituted and as it spreads among writers, journalists and that part of the public most worried about its cultural distinction, it leads to a conception of the literary life, and more generally of all of intellectual life, as being within the logic of fashion, allowing the condemnation of a tendency, a current, a school, by arguing merely that it is 'outmoded'.

The dialectic of distinction

From the reading of some of the books of that era or immediately afterwards[14] and their detailed accounts of all the literary schools, it is difficult not to draw an impression that we are dealing with a universe which is subject, in an almost mechanical fashion, to the law of action and reaction – or, if one wants to include intentions and dispositions, of pretension and distinction. There is no action by an agent that is not a reaction to all the others, or to one or another among them: neo-Romanticism rejects Symbolist obscurity and tries to reconcile poetry and science; Moréas's 'Roman' school opposes Symbolism by returning to classicism; Fernand Gregh's 'humanism' rejects Symbolism as obscure and inhumane; Morice's 'neo-classical renaissance' is opposed wholesale to everything that is new, and so forth.

It is understandable how one could place at the turn of the century, as Robert Wohl does, the emergence of a very marked tendency to think of the whole social order in terms of a scheme of division into generations (following the logic which often makes intellectuals extend to the whole social world the characteristics of their own microcosm):[15] it is in effect the moment when this division tends to generalize itself to the whole field of cultural production. This occurs especially with the revolt declared in the books by Agathon (the pseudonym of Henri Massis, born in 1886, and Alfred de Tarde, born in 1880), *L'Esprit de la nouvelle Sorbonne* (1911) and *Les Jeunes Gens d'aujourd'hui* (1913), against the scientist thought of the Renans and Taines which had dominated the whole intellectual field in the 1880s and which conquers the university field through the founders of the new sciences and the new university, such as Durkheim, Seignobos, Aulard, Lavisse, Lanson and Brunot. In this critical phase of a permanent struggle that transposes the opposition between right and left, Catholics and atheists, to the core of the intellectual field, the fundamental divisions that will become the structuring principles of later visions of the world are asserted in all their clarity: the rejection of reason or intelligence in the name of the heart or of faith leads to an anti-rationalism or an irrationalism that valorizes comprehension against explanation, rejects science and especially social science – and most especially 'teutonic' sociology – for its reductionism, positivism and materialism, exalts 'culture' against the soulless erudition of the 'intellectual technicians' and their file cards, and aims to restore the national ideal – that is to say, the classical humanities, Latin and Greek, the pantheon of French authors and also, on another plane, sports and virile virtues.

The opposition between the incumbents and the pretenders instals at the very core of the field a tension between those who try to overtake their rivals and those who wish to avoid being overtaken, as if it were a race. This happens with Zola and Maupassant when they respond to the success of the psychological novel by changing their theme and style, with *Le Rêve* and *Une Vie*, as if to realize by anticipation the project of their competitors: 'Besides, if I had time, I would myself do what they want to do,' Zola replied to Huret's survey, meaning that he himself would effect that outmoding of naturalism, that is to say, of himself, that his adversaries were trying to effect against him.[16]

Specific revolutions and external changes

If the permanent struggles between possessors of specific capital and those who are still deprived of it constitute the motor of an incessant transformation of the supply of symbolic products, it remains true that they can only lead to deep transformations of the symbolic relations of force that result in the overthrowing of the hierarchy of genres, schools and authors when these struggles can draw support from external changes moving in the same direction. Among these changes, the most determining is no doubt the growth (linked to economic expansion) of the educated population (at all levels of the school system) that underlies two parallel processes: the rise in the number of producers who can live by their pen or draw subsistence from the small jobs offered by cultural enterprises (publishing houses, papers, etc.); and the expansion of the market of potential readers who are thus offered to successive pretenders (Romantics, Parnassians, naturalists, Symbolists, etc.) and their products. These two processes are obviously linked to each other to the extent that it is the growth of the market of potential readers that, in allowing the development of the press and the novel, permits the multiplication of the small jobs available in them.

More generally, although largely independent of them *in principle*, the internal struggles always depend, *in outcome*, on the correspondence that they maintain with the external struggles – whether struggles at the core of the field of power or at the core of the social field as a whole. So the naturalist revolution was made possible by the meeting between, on one hand, the new dispositions that Zola and his friends could introduce into the field of production, and on the other, the objective chances that guarantee the conditions of achievement of these dispositions: to wit, on the one hand, a lowering of the barrier to entry into the literary professions linked to the relatively favourable situation of the market for intellectual work (in the larger sense), offering the jobs necessary to guarantee a minimum of resources to writers deprived of private income (like Zola himself, employed by the Librairie Hachette from 1860 to 1865 and contributor to several newspapers), and on the other hand a literary market in expansion, hence more numerous and more socially varied readers, therefore a market that is potentially inclined to welcome new products.

Just as with the success of naturalism, the backlash that militates against it in the 1880s is not to be understood as a direct effect of external changes, whether economic or political. The 'crisis of naturalism' correlates with a crisis of the literary market, that is, more precisely, the disappearance of the conditions that in the preceding era had favoured the access of new social categories to consumption and, in parallel, to production. And the political situation (the multiplication of labour exchanges, the development of the CGT trade union and the socialist movement, the Anzin strike, Fourmies, etc.), which is not unconnected to the spiritualist renewal within the bourgeoisie (and the very numerous conversions of writers), can only encourage those at the core of the field who, carried along by the internal logic of the competitive fight, stand up against the naturalists (and, through them, against the cultural pretensions of the rising fractions of the petite-bourgeoisie and the bourgeoisie). There is no doubt that the climate of spiritual restoration helps to favour the return to forms of art that, like Symbolist poetry or the psychological novel, carry to the highest degree the reassuring denial of the social world.

There is still the question of how the 'creative project' can arise from the convergence of the particular dispositions that a producer (or a group of producers) brings into the field (due to his previous trajectory and his position in the field) and the space of possibles inscribed in the field (what one puts under the vague term of artistic or literary tradition). In the particular case of Zola, one would have to analyse what in the writer's experience (we know in particular that he had been condemned to long years of misery by the early death of his father) might have favoured the development of the rebellious way of seeing economic and social necessity (or even inevitability) that his whole work expresses, and the extraordinary power of rupture and resistance (no doubt arising from the same dispositions) that was necessary for him to achieve this body of work and to defend it against the whole logic of the field. 'A book', he wrote in *Le Naturalisme au théâtre*, 'is nothing more than a battle fought against conventions.' Only the conjunction of an exceptionally favourable set of circumstances and an inflexible indifference to the tacit injunctions of the literary field and, after the success of *L'Assommoir*, to all manifestations of hatred or contempt could have made possible such defiance of some of the most fundamental norms of literary decorum, and above all his durable success.

The invention of the intellectual

But it is probable that Zola would not have escaped the discredit to which he was exposed by his successful sales, or the suspicion of vulgarity they implied, if he had not succeeded (without having sought it) in changing, at least partially, the principles of perception and appreciation then current; notably he constituted as a deliberate and legitimate choice the stance of independence and dignity appropriate for a man of letters, by putting his own kind of authority at the service of political causes. To achieve that, Zola needed to produce a new figure, that of the intellectual, by inventing for the artist a mission of prophetic subversion, inseparably intellectual and political, which had to be able to make everything his adversaries described as the effect of a vulgar or depraved taste appear as an aesthetic, ethical and political stance, and one likely to find militant defenders. Carrying to term the evolution of the literary field towards autonomy, he tries to extend into politics the very values of independence being asserted in the literary field. This is what he accomplishes when, during the Dreyfus Affair, he manages to import into the political field a problem constructed according to the principles of division characteristic of the intellectual field and to impose on the social universe as a whole the unwritten laws of that world which is a particular one but has the particularity of laying claim to the universal.[17]

Thus, paradoxically, it is the autonomy of the intellectual field that makes possible the inaugural act of a writer who, in the name of norms belonging to the literary field, intervenes in the political field, thus constituting himself as an intellectual. 'J'accuse' is the outcome and the fulfilment of a collective process of emancipation that is progressively carried out in the field of cultural production: as a prophetic rupture with the established order, it reasserts against all reasons of state the irreducibility of the values of truth and justice and, at the same stroke, the independence of the guardians of these values from the norms of politics (those of patriotism, for example) and from the constraints of economic life.

The intellectual is constituted as such by intervening in the political field *in the name of autonomy* and of the specific values of a field of cultural production which has attained a high degree of independence with respect to various powers (and this intervention is unlike that of the politician with strong cultural capital, who acts on the basis of a specifically political authority, acquired at the price of a renunciation of an intellectual career and values). In this way, the intellectual stands in contrast to the eighteenth-century writer, prebendary of the state, socially credited with a recognized but subordinated function, strictly enclosed within the realm of diversion and thus removed from the burning questions of politics and theology; the intellectual also contrasts with the aspiring legislator who aims to exercise a spiritual power in the realm of the political and rival the prince or the minister on their own territory, in the manner of Rousseau writing a constitution for Poland; and finally, the intellectual contrasts with those who, having bartered status (often of second rank) in the intellectual field for a position in the political field, then break more or less ostentatiously with the values of their original universe and, intent on asserting themselves as men of action, are often the most inclined to denounce the idealism or lack of realism of 'theoreticians' in order to give themselves a better right to betray the values inscribed in those theories. Enclosed within his own order, with his back against his own values of freedom, disinterestedness and justice, precluded by them from abdicating his specific authority and responsibility in exchange for necessarily devalued profits or temporal powers, the intellectual asserts himself against the specific laws of politics (those of *Realpolitik* and reasons of state[18]) as defender of universal principles that are in fact the result of the universalization of the specific principles of his own universe.[19]

The invention of the intellectual accomplished with Zola does not only presuppose the prior autonomization of the intellectual field. It is also the outcome of another, parallel process of differentiation, that which leads to the constitution of a corps of professional politicans, and which exercises indirect effects on the constitution of the intellectual field.[20] The liberal fight against the Restoration and the overture made to men of letters in the Orléanist period had favoured, if not a politicization of intellectual life, at least a sort of lack of differentiation between literature and politics, as the flowering of literary politicians and political littérateurs such as Guizot, Thiers, Michelet, Thierry, Villemain, Cousin, Jouffroy and Nisard bears witness. The 1848 revolution, disappointing or disturbing the liberals, and especially the Second Empire, sent most writers into a sort of political quietism, inseparable from a lofty withdrawal towards art for art's sake, defined as against 'social art'. We recall Baudelaire fulminating against the socialists: 'Zealously bludgeon the shoulders of the anarchist!'[21] Or Leconte de Lisle teaching a lesson to Louis Ménard, who had remained faithful to his political ideals: 'Are you going to spend your life worshipping Blanqui, who is neither more nor less than a sort of revolutionary hatchet, useful in its place, I grant you, but still a hatchet! Get out! The day you have written a good book, you will have proved your love of justice and rightness better than in writing twenty volumes of economics.'[22] But the most typical expression of this disenchantment is found with Flaubert, Taine or Renan, taking refuge in their writing and remaining silent on political events.

Among the factors that steered writers towards a reinforcement of autonomy with respect to external demands, a determining role was undoubtedly played by a hostility to politics and to those, like the proponents of social art, who wanted to reintroduce political stakes into the very heart of the field. Thus, by a strange reversal, it is by relying on the specific authority conquered in opposition to politics by pure writers and artists that Zola and the scholars produced by the development of higher education and research will be able to break with the political indifference of their predecessors in order to intervene, during the Dreyfus Affair, in the political field itself, but with weapons that are not those of politics.

The 'engaged', 'edifying', even 'missionary' Zola whom militant tradition, relayed by scholarly devotion, invented from start to finish conceals the fact that the defender of Dreyfus is the same person who defended Manet against the Académie, the Salon and bourgeois good taste, but also – and in the name of the same faith in the artist's autonomy – against Proudhon and his 'humanitarian', moralizing, and socializing readings of painting: 'I defended M. Manet as all my life I would defend any honest individuality that is under attack. I will always be on the side of the vanquished. There is an obvious struggle between indomitable temperaments and the crowd.' And a few pages later: 'I imagine that I am in the street and meet a troop of urchins throwing stones at Édouard Manet. Art critics – pardon me, policemen – do their job badly; they feed the tumult rather than calm it, and God forgive me, it even seems that they have enormous paving stones in their hands. There is already in this spectacle a certain crudeness that saddens me, as a disinterested, calm and free-stepping passer-by. I approach them, I question the urchins, and the policemen; I know what crime has been committed by this pariah who is being stoned. I return home, and I write, for the sake of honour and truth, a statement that will be read.'[23] It is such a statement that 'J'accuse' will make.

The exchanges between painters and writers

But, as the example of Zola alone suffices to remind us, here we must go back and take a larger view of the process of autonomization of the literary and artistic fields. One cannot in fact understand the collective conversion that led to the invention of the writer and artist through the establishment of relatively autonomous social universes where economic necessities are (partially) suspended unless we forsake the limits imposed by a division among specialties and competencies: the essential remains unintelligible as long as one remains confined within the limits of a single tradition, whether literary or artistic. Progress towards autonomy having been accomplished at different times in the two universes, because of different economic or morphological changes, and in relation to powers which also differed (such as the Académie or the market), the writers could benefit from the conquests of the painters to increase their independence, and vice versa.[24]

The social construction of autonomous fields of production goes hand-in-hand with the construction of specific principles of perception and appreciation of the natural and social world (and of the literary and artistic representations of that world); that is to say, it goes together with the elaboration of an intrinsically aesthetic mode of perception which situates the principle of 'creation' within the representation and not within the thing represented, and which is never so fully asserted as when it is able to constitute aesthetically the base or vulgar objects of the modern world.

If the innovations that led to the invention of the modern artist and art are only intelligible at the level of all the fields of cultural production together, this is because artists and writers were able to use the lags between the transformations occurring in the literary field and the artistic field to benefit, as in a relay race, from advances carried out at different moments by their respective avant-gardes. Thus the discoveries made possible by the specific logic of one or another of the two fields could have a cumulative effect and appear retrospectively as the complementary profiles of one and the same historic process.

I will analyse elsewhere the history of the way painters, and most especially Manet, had to struggle to conquer their autonomy from the Académie; and the process which led to the universe of artists ceasing to function as an *apparatus* hierarchized and controlled by a corps, and beginning to constitute itself little by little as a *field* of competition for the monopoly of artistic legitimacy: the process leading to the constitution of a field is a process of the *institutionalization of anomie*, after which no one can claim to be absolute master and possessor of the *nomos*, of the principle of vision and legitimate division. The symbolic revolution initiated by Manet abolishes the very possibility of reference to an ultimate authority, of a tribunal of last appeal, capable of ruling on litigation in matters of art: the monotheism of the central nomothete (incarnated, for a long time, in the Académie) gives way to competition among multiple uncertain gods. The challenge to the Académie reactivates the seemingly finished history of an artistic production entrenched within a closed world of predetermined possibles, and opens it to the exploration of an infinite universe of possibles. Manet wrecks the social foundation of the fixed and absolute point of view of artistic absolutism (just as he wrecks the idea of a privileged place for light, from now on appearing everywhere on the surface of things): he establishes the plurality of points of view, which is inscribed in the very existence of a field (and one may ask whether the oft-noticed abandonment of the sovereign, almost divine, point of view in the very writing of a novel does not also relate to the appearance in the field of a plurality of competing perspectives).

In invoking the revolutionary role of Manet (as well as that of Baudelaire and Flaubert), I would not want to encourage a naively discontinuous vision of the genesis of the field. Though it is true that one can locate the moment when the slow process of *emergence* (as Ian Hacking rightly says) of a structure undergoes the decisive transformation that seems to lead to the fulfilment of the structure, it is just as true that one may place at each of the moments in this continuous and collective process the emergence of a provisional form of that structure, already capable of influencing and controlling the phenomena that may be produced there, and thus of contributing to the more finished elaboration of the structure. But as an antidote to the illusion of first beginnings, I will borrow from Aristotle what might be seen as a (slightly ironic) formulation of the false problem which has given rise to so many sterile debates on the birth of the artist and the writer: how does a routed army stop its flight? At what moment can one say that it has stopped? Is it the moment when the first soldier stops, or the second, or the third? Or is it only when a sufficient number of soldiers have stopped fleeing, or even when the last of the runaways is arrested in his flight? In fact, one cannot say that it is with that person that the army has stopped; in effect it had begun to do so a long time before.

But, in their fight against the Académie, painters (in particular the 'refusés') could rely on all the work involved in the collective invention (begun with Romanticism) of the heroic figure of the struggling artist, a rebel whose originality is measured by how far he is the victim of incomprehension and how much scandal he arouses. But they also received the direct support of writers, long since emancipated from the academic authority that had assured them a recognized identity since the seventeenth century but only by assigning them a limited function and, in any case, one defined from the outside. The writers sent back to the painters an exalted image of the heroic rupture that they were in the process of accomplishing and, above all, they took into the discursive order the discoveries the painters were making in their practices, particularly with respect to the art of living.

After Chateaubriand, with his *Les Mémoires d'outre-tombe* where he exalted the endurance of misery, the spirit of devotion and the abnegation of the artist, the great Romantics – Hugo, Vigny and Musset – found in the defence of the martyrs to art many an occasion to express their contempt for the bourgeois or their pity for themselves. The very image of the ill-fated artist, a central element in the new vision of the world, borrows directly from the example of the generosity and self-denial which the painters lend to the whole intellectual universe: Gleyre refusing any remuneration from his students, Corot rescuing Daumier, Dupré renting a studio for Théodore Rousseau, and so on, not to mention all those who bore misery with heroism or sacrificed their lives for love of art, whose exalted but appalling existence is described in the *Scènes de la vie de bohème*, and in all novels in the same vein (those by Champfleury for example).

Disinterestedness against interest, nobility against baseness, largesse and audacity against pettiness and prudence, pure art and love against mercenary art and love – the opposition is everywhere affirmed, from the romantic epoch on, first in literature, with the innumerable contrasting portraits of the artist and the bourgeois (Chatterton and John Bell, the painter Théodore de Sommervieux and the old draper Guillaume of *La Maison du chat qui pelote*, etc.), but also and above all in fine art and caricature, with Philipon, Granville, Decamps, Henri Monnier or Daumier, who denounce the bourgeois upstart under the guise of Mayeux, of Robert Macaire or M. Prudhomme. And there is no doubt that no one did more than Baudelaire, whose first known writings are the *Salons* of 1845 and 1846, to build the image of the artist as solitary hero who, in the manner of Delacroix, leads the existence of an aristocrat indifferent to honours and wholly focused on posterity,[25] and also a saturnine person destined to bad luck and melancholy.

It is the theory of the remarkable economy of this world apart which writers develop when, as with Théophile Gautier in the preface to *Mademoiselle de Maupin*, or Baudelaire in the *Salon de 1846*, they produce, with respect to painting, the first systematic formulations of the theory of art for art's sake – this peculiar manner of living art that is rooted in an art of living which breaks with the bourgeois lifestyle, notably because it relies on the rejection of all social justification of art and the artist.

It is significant that the notion of art for art's sake appears in relation to *Roland furieux* by the sculptor Jean Duseigneur (or Jehan du Seigneur), exhibited at the Salon of 1831: it is in fact at this artist's house in the rue de Vaugirard that towards the end of 1830 gather those whom Nerval calls the 'petit cénacle' – Borel, Nerval, Gautier – and who, fleeing the extravagances of the 'Young France', will meet again, on more sober ground, at the rue de Doyenné. A painter turned writer (like Pétrus Borel and Delescluze), hence predisposed to play the role of intermediary between the two universes, Gautier, the most 'pictorial' of the writers and the 'impeccable master' of the young generation (according to the dedication of *Les Fleurs du mal*), will express the vision of art and the artist elaborated at the core of this group: to develop intellectual invention freely, however it shocks good taste, conventions and rules; to detest and reject all those whom the painters call 'grocers', 'philistines' or 'bourgeois'; to celebrate the pleasures of love and to sanctify art, considered as the second creator. Associating elitism and anti-utilitarianism, the artist mocks conventional morality, religion, duties and responsibilities, and despises anything that might evoke the idea that art could render service to society.

Like Tebaldeo of *Lorenzaccio* – someone who, as the only free being in a corrupt universe, can give meaning to the world, exorcise evil and change life by virtue of artistic contemplation and creation – so the painter who takes on the Académie (and whose stature can only be increased by the malevolence of official institutions) represents the incarnation *par excellence* of the 'creator', passionate and energetic by nature, impressive in his uncommon sensitivity and his unique power of transubstantiation. The very diverse world, polarized in itself, which is roughly designated as bohemia, is, as we have seen, the site of a formidable work of experimentation that Lamennais calls a 'spiritual libertinism', and through it a new art of living is invented.

The painters offer the writers, as a kind of 'exemplary prophecy' in Max Weber's sense, the model of the pure artist they are trying to invent and assert elsewhere; and pure painting, set up in opposition to the academic tradition and freed from the obligation to serve some purpose or simply to mean something, helps to bring into being the possibility of a 'pure' art. Artistic criticism, occupying such a large place in the activity of writers, is undoubtedly an opportunity for them to discover the truth of their practice and of their artistic project. What is effectively at stake is not only a redefinition of the functions of artistic activity, or even just the mental revolution needed to think through all the experiences excluded by the Academic order – 'emotion', 'impression', 'light', 'originality', 'spontaneity' – and to revise the most familiar words of the traditional lexicon of art criticism – 'effect', 'sketch', 'portrait', 'landscape'. It is a matter of creating the conditions of a new faith, capable of giving meaning to the art of living in this inverted world that is the artistic universe.

The painters breaking with the Académie and the bourgeois public could no doubt not have succeeded in the conversion that had to be accomplished without the assistance of the writers. Strong in their particular competence as professionals of precise explanation and sustained by a tradition of rupture with the 'bourgeois' order that was established in the literary field with Romanticism, the latter were predisposed to support the labour of ethical and aesthetic conversion performed by the avant-garde painters and to bring the symbolic revolution to its full realization by meeting, with the theory of 'art for art's sake', the requirements of the new economy of symbolic goods in terms of explicitly proposed and assumed principles.

But the writers also learned much for their own guidance from the defence of heretical painters. Thus the freedom that the painters – especially Manet – allowed themselves in asserting what Joseph Sloane[26] calls the 'neutrality of the subject', meaning the rejection of all hierarchy among objects and any didactic, moral or political function, was bound to exercise a reciprocal effect on the writers since, even if they had long been liberated from academic constraints, they were as users of language more directly subject to the exigencies of the 'message'.

The revolution that will lead to the constitution of separate artistic universes – shut, as it were, within the purity of the difference that defines them as such – was two-fold. It is first a matter of liberating painting from the obligation to fulfil a social function, to obey a command or a demand, to serve a cause. In this phase, the assistance of writers plays a determining role. Thus it is in the name of a painting freed, by comparison with written or spoken language, from delivering a message that Zola will denounce the didactic use that Proudhon wants to make of Courbet's paintings: 'What? You have writing, you have words, you can say everything you want, and you are going to use the art of lines and colours to teach and instruct? Ah! for pity's sake, remember that we are not just reason. If you are practical, leave to the philosopher the right to give us lessons, leave to the painter the right to give us emotions. I do not think you should require the artist to teach and, in any case, I absolutely deny the effect of a painting on the behaviour of the crowd.'[27]

Manet and all the Impressionists after him repudiate all obligation, not only to serve, but also to say something – so much so that in time, to take their enterprise of liberation to the limit, they will have to liberate themselves from the writer, since a writer, as Pissarro says of Huysmans, 'judges as a littérateur and most of the time sees only the subject matter.'[28] Even when, as with Zola, they defend them by affirming the specificity of the pictorial, the writers are, for the painters, alienating liberators. And even more so since, with the end of the academic monopoly on consecration, these *taste makers* become *artist makers* and, by their discourse, are in a position to 'make' a work of art as such. Moreover, barely liberated from the Academic institution, the painters – Pissarro and Gauguin first of all – have to achieve their freedom from the littérateurs who use the support of their work (as in the good old days of academic criticism) to exploit their taste and their sensibility, going as far as to super-impose or substitute their own commentary.

The assertion of an aesthetic that makes of the pictorial work (and any work of art) an intrinsically polysemic reality, hence irreducible to any gloss or exegesis, certainly owes much to the will of the painters to break the hold of the writers. But this does not mean that, in this effort to liberate themselves, they cannot find weapons and tools of thought in the literary field, notably among the Symbolists who, at more or less the same time, were rejecting any transcendence of the signified over the signifier, making music into the art *par excellence*.

The history of the relations between Odilon Redon and his critics, Huysmans especially, as described by Dario Gamboni,[29] is an exem-plary illustration of the last fight for liberation that the painters had to wage in order to achieve their autonomy and to assert the irreducibility of pictorial work to any kind of discourse (against the famous *ut pictura poesis*) or, which amounts to the same thing, its infinite availability for all possible discourses. Thus the long effort that led from Academic absolutism – which presupposes that there exists an ideal truth to which both the production and the contempla-tion of the work should conform – to subjectivism, which leaves each person free to create or re-create the work in a personal fashion, is accomplished.

But it is undoubtedly only with Duchamp that the painters will arrive at a suitable strategy to allow them to use the littérateur without being used in return, and thus to escape the position of structural inferiority in relation to the producers of metadiscourses where they are placed by their status as producers of necessarily mute objects, mute especially about their creators. It is a strategy which consists of denouncing and methodically thwarting – in the concep-tion and the very structure of the work, but also in an anticipated metadiscourse (the obscure and disconcerting title) or in a retrospec-tive commentary – any attempt at annexation of the work by discourse, this being achieved, obviously, without discouraging the exegesis – far from it – that is always so necessary to the fully accomplished social existence of the art object.

For form

The movement of the artistic field and the literary field towards a greater autonomy is accompanied by a process of differentiation of the modes of artistic expression and by a progressive discovery of the form which is suitable for each art or each genre, beyond the exterior signs, socially known or recognized, of its identity. Claiming the autonomy of the properly 'iconic' representation, as it will later be called, in relation to verbal enunciation, painters abandon literature – meaning the 'motif', the 'anecdote', anything that may evoke an intention to reproduce and to represent, in short, to *say* – holding that the painting should obey its own specifically pictorial laws, and be independent of the object represented. In the same way, writers eliminate the pictorial and the picturesque (in the manner of Gautier and the Parnassians, for example) in favour of the literary – invoking music, which does not serve as a vehicle for any meaning, in a stand against meaning and message – and, with Mallarmé, they exclude the brute speech of 'reportorial language', a purely denotative discourse, naively oriented to a referent.

It is significant that Gide explicitly evokes the lag of literature behind painting in order to exalt the 'pure' novel, devoid of meaning (the very novel that was invented by Joyce, Faulkner and Virginia Woolf): 'I have often wondered by what prodigious means painting was in the forefront, and how it has happened that literature could let itself be outdistanced? Into what discredit, these days, falls what we used to consider, in painting, the "motif"! A fine subject! That is funny. Painters only risk a portrait on condition that they avoid any resemblance.'[30]

All this is to say that from one purification to another the fights located in the different fields lead to the gradual isolating of the essential principle that properly defines each art and each genre, 'literariness' as the Russian Formalists say, or 'theatrality', with Copeau, Meyerhold or Artaud. Thus, for example, as free verse strips poetry of traits like rhyme and rhythm, the history of the field only allows the survival of a sort of highly concentrated extract (as with Francis Ponge) of the properties best designed to produce the poetic effect of a debanalization of words and things, the *ostranenie* of the Russian Formalists, without drawing on techniques socially designated as 'poetic'. Every time one of these relatively autonomous universes is instituted – whether an artistic field, a scientific field or one or another of their specifications – the historical process that is established there plays the same role of *abstractor of quintessence*. In this way, the analysis of the history of the field is undoubtedly, in itself, the only legitimate form of analysis of essence.[31]

The Formalists, and notably Jakobson, who was familiar with phenomenology, in their concern to respond as methodically and tellingly as possible to the old questions of criticism and the scholarly tradition about the nature of genres – theatre, novel or poetry – were content, as was the whole tradition of thought on 'pure poetry' or 'theatrality', to frame as a transhistoric essence what is a sort of *historical quintessence*, that is, the product of a long and slow work of historical alchemy which accompanies the process of autonomization of the fields of cultural production.

Thus the long struggle of painters to break free of commissions (even the most neutral and eclectic, that of state patronage) and to get rid of required subjects had revealed the possibility, and at the same time the necessity, of a cultural production free of any external instruction and injunction, capable of discovering within itself the principle of its own existence and its own necessity. In this way, it had helped to reveal to writers (who, in exalting or analysing it, had contributed to bringing it about) the possibility of a freedom henceforth offered to (and thereby imposed on) anyone wanting to enter into the role of painter or writer.

In view of the inevitable identification that a homology of position favours, how can we not assume that Zola in effect also claimed for himself the freedom he exacted for the painter? In suggesting that the artist is only responsible to himself, that he is perfectly free with respect to morality and society – and provoking, it has to be remembered, an enormous scandal, obliging him to leave the staff of *L'Événement* in 1866 – he asserts more radically than anyone had ever done in the past the right of the artist to personal impressions and subjective reactions: 'pure painting', relieved of the duty of signifying something, is an expression of the individual sensibility of the artist and of his originality of conception – in short, according to the famous phrase, 'a corner of creation seen through a temperament'. Zola admires the work of Manet not for his objective realism, as defended by Champfleury, but because the particular personality of the painter is revealed there. And in the same way, in the long plea that he writes in favour of *Germinie Lacerteux*, he celebrates not so much the naturalness and naturalism of the description as the 'free and high manifestation of a personality', 'the particular language of a soul' and 'the unique product of a mind', revoking any pretension to use ethical or aesthetic rules to measure a work that is situated 'above morality, above prudery and purities'.[32]

But beyond this, how can we not see that by such a reaffirmation –

unparalleled since Delacroix – of the power of the individual creator, and of the right to the free affirmation of the self, with its correlative of the right of the critic or spectator to an emotional understanding with no pre-existing conditions or presuppositions, he opens the way to that radical assertion of the writer's freedom represented by 'J'accuse' and the battles of the Dreyfus Affair? The right to subjective vision and the claim to the freedom to denounce and condemn, in the name of interior exigencies, the irreproachable violence of the reason of state are one and the same.

3

The Market for
Symbolic Goods

~∞~

In another domain, I had the honour, if not pleasure, of losing
money by getting the two monumental volumes of Carlos
Baker's biography of *Hemingway* translated.

ROBERT LAFFONT

The history which I have tried to reconstruct in its most decisive
phases by using a series of synchronic slices leads to the establishment
of this world apart – the artistic field or the literary field we know
today. This relatively autonomous universe (which is to say, of
course, that it is also relatively dependent, notably with respect to the
economic field and the political field) makes a place for an inverse
economy whose particular logic is based on the very nature of
symbolic goods – realities with two aspects, merchandise and signification, with the specifically symbolic values and the market values
remaining relatively independent of each other. At the end of a
process of specialization which has led to the appearance of a cultural
production specially destined for the market and, partly in reaction
against that, a production of 'pure' works destined for symbolic
appropriation, the fields of cultural production are organized, very
generally, in their current state.[1] The principle of differentiation is
none other than the objective and subjective distance of enterprises
of cultural production with respect to the market and to expressed or
tacit demand, with producers' strategies distributing themselves
between two extremes that are never, in fact, attained – either total

and cynical subordination to demand or absolute independence from the market and its exigencies.

Two economic logics

These fields are the site of the antagonistic coexistence of two modes of production and circulation obeying inverse logics. At one pole, there is the anti-'economic' economy of pure art. Founded on the obligatory recognition of the values of disinterestedness and on the denegation of the 'economy' (of the 'commercial') and of 'economic' profit (in the short term), it privileges production and its specific necessities, the outcome of an autonomous history. This production, which can acknowledge no other demand than one it can generate itself, but only in the long term, is oriented to the accumulation of symbolic capital, a kind of 'economic' capital denied but recognized, and hence legitimate – a veritable credit, and capable of assuring, under certain conditions and in the long term, 'economic' profits.[2] At the other pole, there is the 'economic' logic of the literary and artistic industries which, since they make the trade in cultural goods just another trade, confer priority on distribution, on immediate and temporary success, measured for example by the print run, and which are content to adjust themselves to the pre-existing demand of a clientèle. (However, the membership of these enterprises in the field is marked by the fact that the only way they can combine the economic profits of an ordinary economic enterprise with the symbolic profits assured to intellectual enterprises is by avoiding the crudest forms of mercantilism and by abstaining from fully revealing their self-interested goals.)

An enterprise moves closer to the 'commercial' pole the more directly or completely the products it offers on the market respond to a *pre-existing demand*, and *in pre-established forms*. Thus it follows that the length of the production cycle constitutes one of the best measures of the position of an enterprise of cultural production in the field. So one finds, on the one hand, enterprises with a *short production cycle*, aiming to minimize risks by an advance adjustment to predictable demand and benefiting from commercial networks and procedures for marketing (advertising, public relations, etc.) designed to ensure the accelerated return of profits by a rapid circulation of products which are fated to rapid obsolescence; and, on the other hand, enterprises with a *long production cycle*, founded on the acceptance of the risk inherent in cultural investments and above all on submission to the specific laws of the art trade: having no market in the present, this production (entirely turned towards the future) tends to constitute stocks of products which are always in danger of reverting to the state of material objects (and valued as such, that is, for example, by their weight in paper).[3]

Uncertainty has a great effect, and the chances of recovering expenses are meagre when one publishes a young writer. A novel that meets with no success has a life span (in the short term) which may be less than three weeks. In the case of medium success in the short term, once the manufacturing, copyright and distribution costs are subtracted, there remains about 20 per cent of the sales price for the publisher, who must recoup unsold copies, finance his stock and pay overheads and taxes. But when a book prolongs its career beyond the first year and enters into 'profit', it constitutes a financial 'flyer' which provides the basis for forecasting and a 'policy' of investments in the long term: once the first edition has recovered fixed costs, the book can be reprinted with its net costs considerably reduced and it thus assures regular returns (direct returns as well as auxiliary rights like translations, paperback editions, sales to television or cinema) which permit the financing of further more or less risky investments, of the sort which can assure in their turn the ultimate growth of 'assets'.

The uncertainty and risk that characterize the production of cultural goods can be read in the curves of the sales figures of three books published by Éditions de Minuit (Paris). A 'literary prize-winner' (curve A) has a strong initial sale (6,143 copies were distributed in 1959, of which 4,298 were sold in 1960, after deduction for unsold copies), then after this date achieves weak annual sales (of the order of 70 per year on average). *La Jalousie* (curve B), a novel by Alain Robbe-Grillet which appeared in 1957, sells 746 copies in its first year and does not achieve the level of initial sales of the prize-winning novel until four years later (in 1960), but thanks to a constant growth rate in annual sales from 1960 (20 per cent per year on average from 1960 to 1964, 19 per cent between 1964 and 1968), it attains in 1968 the cumulative figure of 29,462. *En Attendant Godot* (*Waiting for Godot*) (curve C), by Samuel Beckett, published in 1952, does not reach 10,000 copies until five years later: thanks to a growth-rate that remains more or less constant at 20 per cent from 1959 on (with the exception of the year 1963 – the curve also making an exponential jump at that date), this title attains in 1968 (when 14,298 copies are sold) a cumulative sales figure of 64,897 copies. (The case of a pure and simple failure would have to be added, that is to say, a *Godot* whose career would have been over at the end of 1952, leaving a balance sheet with a strong deficit.)

One could thus characterize the different publishing houses according to the share they give to risky, long-term investments and to sure, short-term investments and, by the same token, according to the proportion among their authors of writers for the long term and writers for the short term, the latter including journalists who extend their ordinary activity by 'topical' writings, 'personalities' who offer their 'testimony' in essays or autobiographical accounts

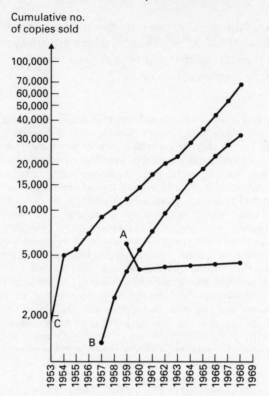

Figure 4 Comparative sales over time of three books published by Éditions de Minuit (*Source*: Éditions de Minuit)

and professional writers who bow to the canons of a tested aesthetic ('prize-winning' literature, successful novels, etc.).

Thus in 1975 the small avant-garde houses, such as Minuit (or, today, POL), confronted the 'major houses' like Laffont, Groupe de la Cité and Hachette; the intermediary positions were occupied by houses like Flammarion, Albin Michel, Calmann-Lévy – old 'traditional' firms acquired through inheritance, a patrimony containing both a force and a braking mechanism – especially Grasset, the old 'great house' today swallowed up by the Hachette empire, and Gallimard, the old avant-garde house long since arrived at the summit of consecration, which combines an enterprise geared to the management of assets (re-editions, paperback publications, etc.) with long-term enterprises ('Le Chemin', 'Bibliothèque des Sciences Humaines'), whose authors, as we shall see, are represented both in the list of bestsellers and the list of intellectual hits. As for the subfield of firms more oriented to long-term production, and hence to the 'intellectual' public, it polarizes around the opposition between Minuit (which represents the avant-garde in line for consecration) on the one hand and Gallimard, situated in the dominant position, on the other, with Le Seuil occupying the middle position.[4]

As representatives of these two opposite poles of the publishing field, Robert Laffont and Éditions de Minuit allow us to apprehend in their multiple aspects the oppositions that separate the two sectors of the field. On the one hand, Laffont is a vast enterprise (700 employees) publishing each year a considerable number of new titles (around 200) and openly oriented to the quest for success (for 1976 it announced seven printings of more than 100,000, fourteen at 50,000 and fifty at 20,000), which presupposes major promotional efforts, considerable advertising and public relations expenses (in particular those directed at bookstores) as well as an entire policy of choice guided by a sense of safe investment (until 1975 nearly half the books published consisted of translations of books that had proved themselves abroad) and by the search for the bestseller.[5] In the 'top-twenty list' with which the publisher counters those who 'still obstinately refuse to consider his firm literary', one finds names like Bernard Clavel, Max Gallo, Françoise Dorin, George-Emmanuel Clancier and Pierre Rey.

At the opposite end, Éditions de Minuit is a small artisanal firm, employing ten people or so, which publishes fewer than twenty titles per year (amounting in novels and plays to around forty authors over twenty-five years); devoting a tiny part of its budget to advertising (it even makes a strategic gambit of refusing to use the crudest forms of marketing), it has often, as in its beginnings, had sales of fewer than 500 copies ('The first book by P. which sold more than 500 copies was his ninth') and print runs of under 3,000 (according to a report in 1975, of seventeen new books published since 1971 – that is, over three years – fourteen had not reached the figure of 3,000, with the three others not having surpassed 5,000). In a state of deficit (in 1975) if one considers only new publications, the firm lives on its assets, that is, the profits guaranteed by those of its publications that have become famous (*Godot* for example).

A firm entering into the phase of exploiting accumulated symbolic capital has two different economies coexisting within it, one turned to production and research (at Gallimard's this means the series launched by Georges Lambrichs), the other oriented to the exploitation of assets and the distribution of consecrated products (with series like La Pléiade and especially Folio or Idées). One can easily conceive of the contradictions that result from the incompatibilities between the two economies:[6] an organization suitable for producing, distributing and realizing profits on one category of products is unadapted for the other; in addition, the weight that the demands of distribution and management loads on to the institution and on to the ways of thinking of its executives tends to exclude risky investments, even when the authors who might occasion them are not already diverted to other publishers. It goes without saying that the death of the founder cannot explain such a double process on its own, even though it might accelerate it, since it is inscribed in the logic of the development of enterprises of cultural production.

Without entering into a systematic analysis of the field of art galleries – which by virtue of its similarities with the field of publishing would lead to repetition – one may observe only that, here again, differences of antiquity (and notoriety), and hence of the degree of consecration and the market value of the works owned, follow very exactly differences in the relationship to the 'economy'. Lacking their own 'stable', the 'sales galleries' (Beaubourg, for example) exhibit a relatively eclectic choice (in 1977) of painters from very different epochs and schools and of different ages (abstractionists as well as post-surrealists, some

European hyper-realists, some new realists). That is to say, they show works that, being more accessible (because more canonized or because of their 'decorative' qualities), can find other buyers apart from professional and semi-professional collectors (who are recruited among the 'gilt-edged managers' and the 'fashion-industry magnates', as an informant puts it); they are thus in a situation to locate and attract a group of avant-garde painters who have already attracted notice, by offering them a slightly compromising form of consecration, that is, a market in which prices are much higher than in the avant-garde galleries.[7] By contrast, galleries like Sonnabend, Denise René or Durand-Ruel which represent important dates in the history of painting because, each in its own era, they knew how to assemble a 'school', are characterized by a *systematic gambit*.[8] Thus one can recognize in the succession of painters presented by the Sonnabend gallery the logic of an artistic development that leads from the 'New American Painting' and from Pop Art, with painters like Rauschenberg, Jasper Johns and Jim Dine, towards Oldenburg, Lichtenstein, Wesselman, Rosenquist and Warhol, sometimes classified under the label 'minimal art', and on to the more recent experimentation of 'poor art', conceptual art or art by correspondence. In the same way, the link is evident between the geometric abstraction that made a name for the Denise René gallery (founded in 1945 and launched with a Vasarely exhibition) and kinetic art, with artists like Max Bill and Vasarely making a kind of connection between the visual experimentation of the interwar period (especially that of the Bauhaus) and the optical and technological experimentation of the new generation.

Two modes of ageing

Thus the opposition between the two poles, and between the two visions of the 'economy' asserted there, takes the form of the opposition between two *life cycles of the enterprise of cultural production*, two *modes of ageing* by businesses, producers and products that completely exclude each other. The burden of over-heads and the corresponding concern for return on capital, obliging the huge joint-stock corporations (like Laffont) to turn their capital over very quickly, also very directly dictate their cultural policy, and in particular the selection of manuscripts.[9] In addition, these enterprises with short production cycles, in the manner of haute couture, are tightly meshed in with a whole set of agents and institutions of 'promotion' that must be constantly maintained and periodically mobilized.[10] By contrast, the small publisher may know personally, with the assistance of advisers who are also inhouse authors, the firm's whole set of published authors and books. The strategies he pursues in his relations with the press are perfectly suited to the demands of the most autonomous region of the field, which requires that opportunist compromises be avoided and which tends to pit success and intrinsic artistic value against each other. Symbolic and economic success in long-cycle production depends (at least in the beginning) on the moves of a few 'talent-spotters', that is, on authors and critics who make the firm's reputation by gaining it credit (by the fact of publishing there, bringing manuscripts there, speaking favourably of its authors, etc.) – and success also depends on the educational system, which alone is capable of offering, in time, a converted public.

While the reception of products called 'commercial' is more or less independent of the educational level of receivers, 'pure' works of art are not accessible except to consumers endowed with the disposition and the competence which are necessary for their appreciation. It follows that producers-for-producers depend very directly on the education system, even though they increasingly inveigh against it. The School occupies an homologous place to that of the Church which, according to Max Weber, must 'found and systematically delimit the new victorious doctrine and defend the old against prophetic attacks, establish what has and what does not have sacred value, and make it penetrate into the faith of the laity'. By means of the demarcation between what merits being transmitted and what does not, it reproduces continually the distinction between consecrated and illegitimate works and, by the same token, between the legitimate and the illegitimate ways of approaching legitimate works. In this function, it distinguishes itself from other authorities by the extremely slow tempo of its action. Devoted to their function of *discoverers*, avant-garde critics must enter into exchanges of attestation and charisma which often make them the spokespeople, sometimes the impresarios, of artists and their art, whereas authorities such as the academies or the corps of museum curators must combine tradition and tempered innovation in the degree to which their cultural jurisprudence is exercised on contemporaries. The education system, which claims a monopoly on the consecration of works of the past and on the production and consecration (by diploma) of conforming consumers, does not grant, except *post mortem*, and after a long process, the infallible sign of consecration that is constituted by the canonization of works as classics by inscribing them in curricula.

Thus the opposition is total between bestsellers with no tomorrow and the classics, lasting bestsellers which owe to the education system their consecration, hence their extended and durable market.[11] Inscribed in minds as the fundamental principle of division, it grounds two opposed representations of the activity of writer and even of publisher, as simple merchant or as audacious discoverer; and the latter can only succeed by fully acknowledging the specific laws and stakes of 'pure' production. At the more heteronomous pole of the field, that is to say, among the publishers and writers oriented to sales, as well as among their public, success is in itself a guarantee of value. This means that in this market success goes to success: announcing a print run contributes to making a bestseller; critics can do no better for a book or a play than to 'predict its success' ('This should be a big hit';[12] 'I would bet on the success of *Le Tournant* with my eyes closed'[13]). Failure, of course, is a condemnation without appeal: the person who has no audience has no talent (the same critic speaks of 'authors without talent and without an audience in the manner of Arrabal').

At the opposite pole, immediate success has something suspect about it, as if it reduced the symbolic offering of a priceless work to the simple 'give and take' of a commercial exchange. The vision that makes of asceticism in this world the condition of health in the hereafter finds its principle in the specific logic of symbolic alchemy that maintains that investments will not be recouped unless they are (or seem to be) operating at a loss, in the manner of a gift, which cannot assure itself of the most precious countergift, 'recognition', unless it sees itself as without return; and – as with the gift that it converts into pure generosity by occulting the countergift to come – it is the *interposed time interval* which forms a screen and which obscures the profit promised to the most disinterested investments.[14]

'Economic' capital cannot guarantee the specific profits offered by the field – and by the same token the 'economic' profits that they will often bring in time – unless it is reconverted into symbolic capital. The only legitimate accumulation, for the author as for the critic, for the art dealer as for the publisher or theatre director, consists in making a name for oneself, a name that is known and recognized, the capital of consecration – implying a power to consecrate objects (this is the effect of a signature or trademark) or people (by publication, exhibition, etc.), and hence of giving them value, and of making profits from this operation.

A commerce in things which are not commercial, the trade in 'pure' art belongs to the class of practices where the logic of pre-capitalist economy survives (like, in another sphere, the economy of exchanges between generations and, more generally, the economy of the family and all relations of *philia*).[15] Practical *denegations*, these *intrinsically double* and *ambiguous* behaviours lend themselves to two opposite but equally false readings, which undercut their essential duality and duplicity by reducing them either to denegation, or to what is denied, either to disinterestedness or to interest. The challenge that they offer to all kinds of economism resides precisely in the fact that they can be achieved in practice – and not merely in representations – only at the price of a constant and collective repression of the properly 'economic' interest and of the truth of the practice that 'economic' analysis uncovers.

The 'economic' enterprise denied by the art dealer or the publisher, in which art and business are conjugated, cannot succeed, even 'economically', if it is not governed by a practical mastery of the laws of the functioning of the field and of its specific requirements. The entrepreneur in cultural production must activate a very improbable combination (or in any case a very rare one) of realism, which implies minimal concessions to the denied (and not disowned) 'economic' necessities, and of the 'disinterested' conviction that excludes them. Therefore the tenacity with which Beethoven, the object *par excellence* of hagiographic exaltation of the 'pure' artist, defended his economic interests (especially the copyright on the sales of his scores) is perfectly understandable if one knows how to see a particular form of the entrepreneurial spirit in behaviour most apt to offend the economic angelicism of the romantic representation of the artist; at the risk of remaining at the level of a whim, the revolutionary intention must secure for itself the 'economic' means to realize an ambition irreducible to the 'economy' (for example, for Beethoven, the means to employ large-scale orchestras). In the same way, while the publisher or dealer who wants to act as 'discoverer' stands in stark contrast to the pure merchant, he contrasts just as much with those who employ the same inspired dispositions in both the commercial and the cultural dimensions of their enterprise (in the fashion of Arnoux): 'An error in the net cost or in the print run can unleash catastrophes, even if sales are excellent. When Jean-Jacques Pauvert undertook the reprinting of *Littré*, it seemed profitable by virtue of the unexpected number of subscribers. But, at its publication, it appeared that an error in estimating the net cost resulted in a loss of fifteen francs per volume. The publisher had to concede the operation to a colleague.'[16] The profound ambiguity of the universe of art means, on the one hand, that new entrants without capital can make an impression on the market by proclaiming the values in the name of which the dominants have accumulated their symbolic capital (more or less reconverted since into 'economic' capital); and, on the other, it means that only those who know how to reckon and deal with the 'economic' constraints inscribed in this denied economy are able fully to reap symbolic and even 'economic' profits on their symbolic investments.

The differences which separate the small avant-garde enterprises from the 'major enterprises' and the 'great firms' are superimposed on differences that can be observed among the products between the 'new', which is provisionally devoid of 'economic' value, the 'old', definitively devalued, and the 'ancient' or the 'classical', endowed with a constant or constantly growing 'economic' value. Similar differences are to be found among producers, between the avant-garde, which tends to recruit among the (biologically) young without being tied to a generation, authors or artists who are 'finished' or 'outdated' (who may be biologically young) and the consecrated avant-garde, the 'classics'.

To convince oneself of this it suffices to consider the relation between the biological age of painters and their *artistic age*, measured by the position that the field assigns them in space–time. The painters of avant-garde galleries can be contrasted just as well with painters of their own (biological) age who are exhibited in the Parisian galleries of the Right Bank as they can be with those painters who are much older (or already dead) and who are exhibited in the same galleries. The only thing they have in common with the former is biological age; with the latter – with whom they contrast in artistic age, measured in artistic generations (revolutions) – they have in common the similarity of the position they hold to that occupied by prestigious predecessors in the field at various stages in the past, and the strong chance of occupying homologous positions in its future states (as witnessed by indices of consecration such as catalogues, articles or books already associated with their work).

If one considers the pyramid of ages of the set of painters 'acquired'[17] by different galleries, one observes first a rather clear relation (also visible with writers) between the birthdate of painters and the position of galleries in the field of production: in the 1930–9 range at an avant-garde gallery like Sonnabend (and 1920–9 at Templon), in the 1900–9 range at a gallery of the consecrated avant-garde like Denise René (or at the Galerie de France), the modal age is situated in the period preceding 1900 at Drouant (or at Durand-Ruel), whereas galleries like Beaubourg (or Claude Bernard) that occupy intermediary positions between the avant-garde and the consecrated avant-garde, and also between the 'sales gallery' and the 'movement gallery', present a bimodal structure (with one mode before 1900 and another in the period 1920–9).

Coinciding in the case of avant-garde painters (exhibited by Sonnabend or Templon), biological age and artistic age (of which the best measure would undoubtedly be the era of the appearance of the corresponding style in the relatively autonomous history of painting) can clash in the case of academic followers in all the formerly canonic styles who are exhibited, alongside the most famous painters of the last century, in the galleries of the Right Bank (often situated in the vicinity of luxury stores) such as Drouant or Durand-Ruel, the 'Impressionist dealer'. Fossils of another age, these painters who do in the present what was done by the avant-garde of the past (just like *forgers*, but on their own account) make an art that is not, if one may say so, of their age.

Inversely to the avant-garde artists who are in some way 'young' twice over, in artistic age but also by their (provisional) refusal of money and the worldly importances by which artistic ageing occurs, fossilized artists are in some way old twice over, by the age of their art and their schemas of production but also by the whole lifestyle of which the style of their works is one dimension, and which implies

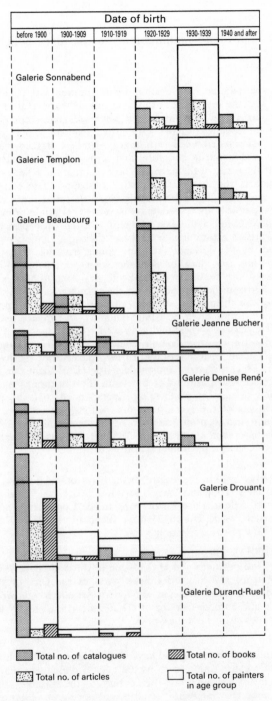

Date of birth					
before 1900	1900-1909	1910-1919	1920-1929	1930-1939	1940 and after

Galerie Sonnabend

Galerie Templon

Galerie Beaubourg

Galerie Jeanne Bucher

Galerie Denise René

Galerie Drouant

Galerie Durand-Ruel

Total no. of catalogues   Total no. of books

Total no. of articles   Total no. of painters in age group

Figure 5 Galleries and their painters (in 1977)

direct and immediate submission to secular obligations and rewards.[18]

The avant-garde painters have much more in common with the avant-garde of the past than with the rearguard of this avant-garde – above all, the absence of signs of extra-artistic or one might say *temporal consecration*, provided in abundance to the fossilized artists, established painters, often coming out of schools of the fine arts, crowned with prizes, members of academies, decorated with the Légion d'Honneur and furnished with official commissions. If one excludes the avant-garde of the past, one observes that the painters exhibited by the Drouant gallery mostly reveal characteristics opposed in every way to the image of the artist recognized by avant-garde artists and those who celebrate them. For these painters, quite frequently of provincial origin or even residence, the gallery 'discovering' a number of them is often their principal point of anchorage in Parisian artistic life. Several had their first exhibitions there and/or were 'launched' by the Drouant Prize for young painting. Undoubtedly more likely to have a fine arts education than the avant-garde painters (about a third of them attended the Beaux-Arts, the École des Arts Appliqués or the Arts Décoratifs, in Paris, in the provinces or in their country of origin), the Drouant painters readily call themselves 'students' of such-and-such and practise an art academic in style (most often post-Impressionist), in subjects (seascapes, portraits, allegories, peasant scenes, nudes, Provence landscapes, etc.) and in form (theatre sets, illustrations for de luxe editions, etc.). This uncomplicated art usually provides them with a veritable *career*, marked out by diverse rewards and promotions, such as prizes and medals (for 66 of them out of 133), and crowned with access to positions of power in the institutions of consecration and legitimation (a number of them are members of societies, presidents or committee members of the great traditional salons), or in the institutions of reproduction and legitimation (director of a provincial fine arts academy, professor in Paris, either at the Beaux-Arts or the Arts Décoratifs, museum curator, etc.). Two sample biographical notes:

> Born 23 May 1914 in Paris. Attends the École des Beaux-Arts. One-person shows in New York and Paris. Illustrates two books. Participates in the Paris Grand Salons. Prize for drawing in the Concours Général of 1932. Silver medal at the Fourth Menton Biennale in 1957. Works held by museums and private collections.

> Born in 1905. Studies at the École des Beaux-Arts in Paris. Member of the Salon des Indépendants and of the Salon d'Automne. Receives in 1958 the grand prize of the École des Beaux-Arts of the City of Paris. Works exhibited in the Paris Museum of Modern Art and in numerous museums in France and abroad. Curator of the Honfleur museum. Numerous one-person shows throughout the world.

Finally, a number of this rearguard have ultimately received the least equivocal marks of worldly consecration, such as the Légion d'Honneur, undoubtedly as counterpart to their integration into this century, by the intermediary of politico-administrative contacts who award 'commissions', or the connnections with high society implied by the function of 'official painter':

Born in 1909. Landscape and portrait painter. Executes the portrait of His Holiness Pope John XXIII as well as that of other famous people of our era (Cécile Sorel, Mauriac, etc.) displayed at the Drouant gallery in 1957 and 1959. Prix des Peintres Témoins de leur Temps (Prize for Painters as Witnesses of their Time). Participates at the Grand Salons of which he is an organizer. Participates at the Paris Salon organized by the Drouant gallery in Tokyo in 1961. His canvases figure in many museums in France and collections throughout the world.

Born in 1907. Had his start at the Salon d'Automne. His first trip to Spain influenced him strongly and the first Grand Prix de Rome (1930) decided his long stay in Italy. His work is especially associated with Mediterranean places: Spain, Italy, Provence. Author of illustrations for de luxe books and of set designs for the theatre. Member of the Institut. Exhibitions in Paris, London, New York, Geneva, Nice, Bordeaux, Madrid. Works exhibited in numerous museums of modern art and private collections in France and abroad. Officer of the Légion d'Honneur.[19]

The same regularities are observed among the writers. Thus 'authors with intellectual success' (that is to say, the set of authors mentioned in the 'selection' of the *Quinzaine Littéraire* for the years 1972 to 1974 inclusive) are younger than the authors of bestsellers (that is to say, the set of authors mentioned in the weekly listings of *L'Express* for the years 1972 to 1974) and above all less often awarded prizes by literary juries (31 per cent as against 63 per cent), and especially by the most 'compromising' juries in the eyes of 'intellectuals', and they are less often provided with decorations (4 per cent as against 22 per cent). While the bestsellers are published mostly by the large publishing firms specializing in books for quick sale (Grasset, Flammarion, Laffont and Stock), the 'authors with intellectual success' are, more than half of them, published by three publishers whose production is exclusively oriented to the 'intellectual' public (Gallimard, Le Seuil and the Éditions de Minuit).

These contrasts are even more marked if one compares more homogeneous populations, the writers of Laffont and of Minuit. Clearly younger, the latter are much more rarely awarded prizes and very much less often granted decorations.[20] In fact, the two categories of writers grouped by these two publishing houses are hardly comparable: on the one hand, the dominant model is that of the 'pure' writer, engaged in formal experimentation and estranged from his 'century'; on the other, the prime place goes to writer-journalists and journalist-writers who produce works 'halfway between history and journalism', 'belonging to biography and sociology, intimate journal and adventure story, screenplays and eye-witness testimony'.[21] 'If I look at the list of my authors, I see on the one hand those who came from journalism to books, such as Gaston Bonheur, Jacques Peuchmaurd, Henri-François Rey, Bernard Clavel, Olivier Todd, Dominique Lapierre, etc., and those former university professors, such as Jean-François Revel, Max Gallo and Georges Belmont, who made the reverse journey.' To this category of writers, very typical of 'commercial' publishing, we should add the authors of personal experiences and political, sporting or entertainment 'personalities' who often write to order, sometimes with the assistance of a journalist/ghost-writer.[22]

It is clear that the pre-eminence given to youth by the field of cultural production comes down, once again, to the spurning of power and of the 'economy' that is at its root: the reason why writers and artists always tend to place themselves on the side of 'youth' by the way they dress, and their corporal hexis especially, is because, in image as in reality, the opposition between age groups is homologous with the opposition between the serious 'bourgeois' and the 'intellectual' rejection of the spirit of seriousness. More precisely, distance from money and the authorities maintains a relation of circular causality with the status of dominant-dominated, definitively or temporarily alienated from money and power.

One may thus hypothesize that access to the social indices of maturity, which is both a condition for and an effect of access to positions of power, and the abandonment of practices associated with adolescent irresponsibility (including 'avant-gardist' cultural practices or even politics), must come earlier and earlier as one moves from artists to teachers, from teachers to members of the liberal professions, and from the latter to executives and bosses; and one may suggest that the members of the same biological age group, for example the whole cohort of students in the Grandes Écoles, have very different social ages, marked by different attributes and symbolic behaviours, as a function of the objective future they see lying before them. So the student at the Beaux-Arts feels obliged to 'look younger' than the student at the École Normale Supérieure, and that one to look younger than the student at the Polytechnique or the one at the École Nationale d'Administration or Hautes Études Commerciales.[23] By the same logic, one would have to analyse the relationship between the sexes inside the dominant region of the field of power, and more precisely the effects of the position of dominant-dominated which is incumbent on women of the 'bourgeoisie' and which brings them closer (structurally) to the young 'bourgeois' and the 'intellectuals', predisposing them to the role of mediator between the dominant and dominated sections (a role women have always played, in particular by means of the 'salons').

Leave a mark

However, the privilege accorded to 'youth', and to the associated values of change and originality, cannot be completely understood through the relationship between 'artists' and 'bourgeois' alone; it also expresses the specific law of change in the field of production, that is, the dialectic of distinction – whereby institutions, schools, works and artists which have 'left their mark' are destined to fall into

Bestselling authors and recognized authors

Date of birth	L'Express No.=92	Quinzaine Littéraire No.=106	Prizes	L'Express No.=92	Quinzaine Littéraire No.=106
Born before 1900	4	7	No	28	68
1900–9	10	27	Yes	48	31
1910–19	17	15	Renaudot	–	–
1920–9	33	28	Goncourt	25	6
1930–9	11	15	Interallié	–	–
1940 and after	5	5	Fémina	–	–
NR	12	9	Médicis	–	4
			Nobel	–	2
			NR	16	7

Stated profession	L'Express	Quinzaine Littéraire	Decorations and honours	L'Express	Quinzaine Littéraire
Man of letters	35	32	No	44	79
University professor	5	48	Yes	35	22
Journalist	26	6	Légion d'Honneur or		
Psychiatrist/analyst	–	2	Ordre du mérite	28	18
Other	10	7	NR	13	5
NR	16	11			

Place of residence	L'Express	Quinzaine Littéraire	Publishers*	L'Express	Quinzaine Littéraire
Provinces	5	13	Gallimard	8	34
outside Paris	2	5	Seuil	7	12
South	1	4	Denoël	3	6
other	2	4	Flammarion	11	5
Abroad	2	4	Grasset	14	8
Paris and suburbs	62	57	Stock	11	1
6/7th arrondissements	19	19	Laffont	18	3
8/16th/west	23	11	Plon	1	4
5/13/14/15th	11	11	Fayard	5	4
other arrondissements	7	9	Calmann-Lévy	1	2
suburbs (excl. west)	2	7	Albin Michel	5	–
NR	23	32	Others	11	33

*The number exceeds the total since a single author may publish with different publishing houses.
NR = Not reported.

To arrive at a population of authors recognized by the general intellectual public, we took those living French authors who were cited in the monthly feature 'La Quinzaine recommends' published by the *Quinzaine Littéraire* during the years 1972 to 1974. For the category of authors appealing to a wide public, we used those living French writers whose works had the largest print runs in 1972 and 1973; this list, based on information furnished by twenty-nine large bookstores in Paris and the provinces, is regularly published in *L'Express*. The selection made by the *Quinzaine Littéraire* gives a lot of attention to translations of foreign books (43 per cent of the cited titles) and to republications of canonical authors (e.g. Colette, Dostoevsky, Bakunin, Rosa Luxemburg), thus endeavouring to follow the very particular trends in the intellectual world; the list from *L'Express* gives a figure of only 12 per cent for foreign book translations, and these are generally international bestsellers (Desmond Morris, Mickey Spillane, Pearl Buck, etc.).

the past, to become *classic or outdated*, to see themselves thrown *outside* history or to 'pass into history', into the eternal present of consecrated *culture*, where trends and schools which were totally incompatible 'in their lifetime' may now peacefully coexist, because they have been canonized, academicized and neutralized.

Ageing occurs among enterprises and authors when they remain attached (actively or passively) to modes of production which – especially if they have left their mark – inevitably become dated; it occurs when they lock themselves into patterns of perception or appreciation that become converted into transcendent and eternal norms and so prohibit the acceptance or even the perception of novelty. Thus a dealer or publisher who once played the role of discoverer may let himself be locked within the *institutional concept* (such as the 'Nouveau Roman' or 'new American painting') that he himself helped to produce, according to the social definition applied among critics, readers and even younger authors, content to apply the schemas produced by the generation of initiators.

'I wanted the *new*, to get off the beaten track. This is why,' writes Denise René, 'my first exhibition was devoted to Vasarely. He was an *experimenter*. Then I displayed Atlan in 1945, because he too was *unprecedented, different*, new. One day, five unknowns – Hartung, Deyrolle, Dewasne, Schneider, Marie Raymond – came to show me their canvases. In an instant, in front of these *strict, austere* works, my path seemed revealed. Here there was enough *dynamite* to excite and *call into question* all artistic problems. So I organized the "Young Abstract Painting" exhibition (January 1946). For me, the *period of combat* was beginning: first, until 1950, *to impose* abstraction as a whole, *to overturn traditional positions* of figurative painting – *one is inclined to forget these days* that at one time it was widely prevalent. Then in 1954 there was the informal tidal wave: one witnessed the spontaneous generation of a number of artists who *were willingly swallowed up* in this cause. The gallery that, since 1948, *had fought for abstraction, avoided* the general infatuation and *stuck to* a *strict* choice. This choice was abstract constructivism, the outcome of *the great plastic revolutions* of the beginning of the century and developed by new experimenters today. A noble *austere* art, that continually asserts all its vitality. Why did I come gradually to *defend exclusively constructive art*? When I search within myself for the reason, it seems to me to be because no other art better expresses the artist's conquest of a world *threatened with decomposition*, a world in perpetual gestation. In a work by Herbin or Vasarely there is no place for *obscure forces, sinking, morbidity*. This art translates truthfully the total mastery of the creator. A helix, a skyscraper, a sculpture by Schoffer, a Mortensen, a Mondrian: these are works that reassure me; you may read in them, blindingly, the domination of human *reason*, the triumph of man over *chaos*. This for me is the role of art. There is plenty of room for emotion.'[24]

We see here how the commitment underlying the initial choices, the taste for 'strict' and 'austere' constructions, involves inevitable rejections; how – when the categories of perception and appreciation which made the initial 'discovery' possible are applied to it – every work coming out of the rupture with the old patterns of production and perception finds itself rejected as unformed and chaotic; how, finally, the nostalgic reference to fights waged to impose the canons once called heretical helps to legitimate the closing down of heretical contestation of what has become a new orthodoxy.

It is not enough to say that the history of the field is the history of the struggle for a monopoly of the imposition of legitimate categories of perception and appreciation; it is in the very *struggle* that the history of the field is made; it is through struggles that it is temporalized. The ageing of authors, works or schools is something quite different from a mechanical sliding into the past. It is engendered in the fight between those who have already left their mark and are trying to endure, and those who cannot make their own marks in their turn without consigning to the past those who have an interest in stopping time, in eternalizing the present state; between the dominants whose strategy is tied to continuity, identity and reproduction, and the dominated, the new entrants, whose interest is in discontinuity, rupture, difference and revolution. *Faire date* is at once *to make a new position exist* beyond established positions, *ahead [en avant]* of those positions, *en avant-garde*, and in introducing difference, to produce time itself.

In this struggle for life, for survival, one can understand the role given to *marks of distinction* which, in the best of cases, aim to pinpoint the most superficial and visible of the properties attached to a set of works or of producers. Words, names of schools or groups, proper names – they only have such importance because they make things into something: distinctive signs, they produce existence in a universe where to exist is to be different, 'to make oneself a name', a proper name or a name in common (that of a group). *False concepts, practical* instruments of classification which make resemblances and differences by naming them, the names of schools or groups which have flourished in recent painting – pop art, minimal art, process art, land art, body art, conceptual art, arte povera, Fluxus, new realism, new figuration, support-surface, poor art, op art – are products in the *struggle for recognition* by the artists themselves or by their appointed critics, and they fulfil the function of *signs of recognition* distinguishing galleries, groups and painters, and by the same token, the products that they fabricate or put on offer.[25]

The new entrants are bound to *continually banish to the past* – in the very process by which they achieve existence, that is, legitimate difference or even, for some shorter or longer period, exclusive legitimacy – those consecrated producers against whom they measure themselves and, consequently, their products and the taste of those who remain attached to them. Thus it is that galleries or publishing houses, like painters or writers, are distributed at any one time according to their artistic age, that is according to the antiquity of their mode of artistic production and according to the degree of canonization and the influence of that generative schema which is at one and the same time a schema of perception and appreciation. The field of galleries reproduces *in synchronic time* the history of artistic movements since the end of the nineteenth century: each of the major galleries was a gallery of the avant-garde at a more or less distant point in time, and it is all the more consecrated, like the works it consecrates (and which it can therefore sell more dearly), the more its apogee is distanced in time and the more its 'trademark' ('geometric abstraction' or 'American pop') is generally known and recognized – but the gallery is locked within this 'trademark' ('Durand-Ruel, the Impressionist dealer'), which is also a destiny.

At each moment in time, in any field of struggle whatsoever (the whole social field, field of power, field of cultural production, literary field, etc.), agents and institutions engaged in the game are simultaneously contemporaries and temporally discordant. The *field of the present* is merely another name for the field of struggle (as shown by the fact that an author of the past is present to the exact extent that he is still at stake). Contemporaneity as presence in the same present only exists in practice *in the struggle* that *synchronizes* discordant times or, rather, agents and institutions separated by time and in relation to time. For some, who are situated beyond the present, the only contemporaries they recognize and who recognize them are among other avant-garde producers, and the only audience they have is in the future; for others, traditionalists or conservatives, the only contemporaries they recognize are in the past (the dotted horizontal lines of the diagram in figure 6 show these hidden contemporaneities).

The temporal movement produced by the appearance of a group capable of leaving its mark by establishing an advanced position is rendered by a shifting of the structure of the field of the present, that is to say, of the temporally hierarchized positions confronting each other in a given field, each of the positions thus finding itself moved by one degree in a temporal hierarchy that is at the same time a social hierarchy (the diagonal lines of dashes link structurally equivalent positions – for example, the avant-garde – in the fields of different epochs). The avant-garde is at any one time separated by an *artistic generation* (understood as a gap between two modes of artistic production) from the consecrated avant-garde, itself separated by another artistic generation from the avant-garde already consecrated

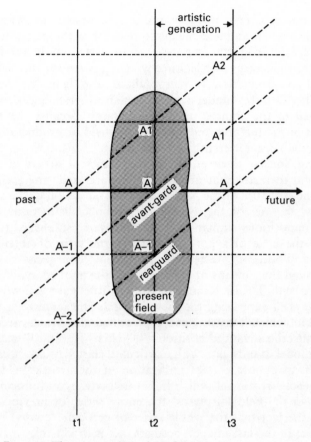

Figure 6 The temporality of the field of artistic production

when it made its entry into the field. It follows that, in the space of the artistic field as in social space, distances between styles or lifestyles are never better measured than in terms of time.

The logic of change

The consecrated authors dominating the field of production tend also to make gradual inroads into the market, becoming more and more readable and acceptable the more everyday they seem as a result of a more or less lengthy process of familiarization, whether or not associated with a specific apprenticeship. The strategies directed against their domination always aim at and, through them, reach the distinguished consumers of their distinctive products. To impose a new producer, a new product and a new system of taste on the market at a given moment means to relegate to the past a whole set of producers, products and systems of taste, all hierarchized in relation to their degree of legitimacy. The movement through which the field of production is temporalized also helps to define the temporality of tastes (understood as systems of preferences concretely manifested in the choices of consumption).[26] Because the different positions in the hierarchized space of the field of production (which are identifiable, indifferently, by the names of institutions, galleries, publishing houses, theatres, or by the names of artists or schools) correspond to tastes that are socially hierarchized, any transformation of the structure of the field involves a translation of the structure of tastes, that is, of the system of symbolic distinctions between groups: oppositions similar to those that were established (in 1975) between the taste of avant-garde artists, the taste of 'intellectuals', advanced 'bourgeois' taste and provincial 'bourgeois' taste, and which found their means of expression on the markets symbolized by the Sonnabend, Denise René, and Durand-Ruel galleries, would have found ways of expressing themselves just as efficaciously in 1945, in a space in which Denise René represented the avant-garde, or in 1875, when the advanced position was held by Durand-Ruel.

This model stands out with particular clarity today because, by virtue of an almost perfect unification of the artistic field and its history, each artistic act which leaves its mark by introducing a new position in the field 'displaces' the entire series of previous artistic acts. By the fact that the whole series of pertinent 'coups' is present in practice in the last one, an aesthetic act is irreducible to any other act situated in another position in the series and the series itself tends towards uniqueness and irreversibility.

This explains why, as Marcel Duchamp noted, the *returns* to past styles have never been so frequent: 'The characteristic of the century that is ending is to be like a double-barrelled gun: Kandinsky and Kupka invented abstraction. Then abstraction died. One wouldn't talk about it any more. It came back thirty-five years later with the American abstract expressionists. You could say that Cubism reappeared in an impoverished form with the postwar Paris school. Dada has similarly reappeared. Second shot, second wind. It is a phenomenon particular to this century. It did not exist in the eighteenth or nineteenth centuries. After Romanticism, there was Courbet. And Romanticism never came back. Even with the Pre-Raphaelites you do not have a resurrection of the Romantics.'[27]

In fact, these returns are always *seeming*, since they are separated from what they recover by the negative reference (when this is not by parodic intention) to something that was itself the negation (of the negation of the negation, etc.) of what they recover.[28] In the artistic or literary field at the current stage of its history, all acts, all gestures, all manifestations are, as a painter puts it so well, 'sorts of winks inside a milieu': these winks, silent and hidden references to other artists, present or past, affirm in and through the games of distinction a complicity that excludes a profane that is always fated to allow the essential to escape – that is, precisely the interrelations and inter-actions of which the work is just a silent trace. Never has the very structure of the field been as present in each act of production.

Homologies and the effect of pre-established harmony

Because they are all organized around the same fundamental oppo-sition as regards the relation to demand (that of the 'commercial' and the 'non-commercial'), the fields of production and distribution of different species of cultural goods – painting, theatre, literature, music – are structurally and functionally homologous among them-selves, and maintain, moreover, a relation of structural homology with the field of power, where the essential part of their clientele is recruited.

This structure is particularly marked in the theatre, where the opposition in Paris between the Right Bank and the Left Bank, inscribed in the objectivity of a spatial division, also works within minds as a principle of division. Thus the difference between 'bour-geois theatre' and 'avant-garde theatre', which functions as a prin-ciple of division permitting the practical classification of authors, plays, styles and subjects, is just as manifest in the social character-istics of the audiences of different Parisian theatres (age, profession, residence, frequency of attendance, preferred ticket price, etc.) as it is in the perfectly congruent characteristics of the authors performed (age, social origin, residence, lifestyle, etc.) and of the plays or the theatrical enterprises themselves.

It is indeed in a combination of all these respects that 'experimental theatre' is opposed to 'boulevard theatre'. On one side are the great subsidized theatres (Odéon, Théâtre de l'Est Parisien, Théâtre National Populaire) and the several small theatres of the Left Bank (Vieux Colombier, Montparnasse, etc.),[29] enterprises which are economically and culturally risky and which offer, at relatively low prices, plays that break with conventions (in the content or in the staging) and are destined for a young and 'intellectual' audience (students, teachers, etc.). On the other side are the 'bourgeois' theatres, ordinary commer-cial enterprises obliged by a concern for economic profitability to follow cultural strategies of an extreme prudence, avoiding risks and not making their clients take them. They offer spectacles that have proved themselves or that are designed for safe and certain box office receipts, to an older, 'bourgeois' audience (of administrators, members of the liberal professions and business executives), ready to pay high seat prices to attend shows of simple entertainment which obey, both in their tricks and in their staging, the canons of an aesthetic unchanged for a century: either French adaptations of foreign plays, distributed and in part commissioned by those responsible for the original show, following a formula borrowed from the film and music-hall industries, or revivals of the most tried and tested plays of the traditional boulevard.[30] Between the two, the classical theatres (Comédie-Française, Atelier) constitute neutral places which draw their audiences almost equally from all regions of the field of power and which offer neutral or eclectic programmes, 'the avant-garde boulevard' (in the words of a critic of *La Croix*), or consecrated avant-garde.

This structure, which is present in all artistic genres, and has been for a long time, tends to function today as a mental structure, organizing the production and perception of products:[31] the opposition between art and money (the 'commercial') is the generative principle of most of the judgements that, with respect to the theatre, cinema, painting and literature, claim to establish the frontier between what is art and what is not, between 'bourgeois' art and 'intellectual' art, between 'traditional' art and 'avant-garde' art.

Some examples among hundreds: 'I know a painter who has quality from the point of view of skill, subject matter, etc., but for me what he does is totally commercial; he fabricates a canvas as if he were making bread [. . .]. When artists become very well known, they often have a tendency to produce fabrications' (a gallery director in interview). Avant-gardism often offers no other guarantee of its conviction than its indifference to money and its spirit of contestation: 'Money doesn't matter to him: even beyond public service, he conceives of culture as an instrument of contestation.'[32]

The structural and functional homology between the space of authors and the space of consumers (and of critics) and the correspondence between the social structure of spaces of production and the mental structures which authors, critics and consumers apply to products (themselves organized according to these structures) is at the root of the *coincidence* that is established between the different categories of works offered and the expectations of different categories of the public. Indeed it is a coincidence so miraculous that it may appear as the product of a deliberate adjustment of the supply to the demand. While cynical calculation is obviously not absent, particularly at the 'commercial' pole, it is neither necessary nor sufficient in order to produce the harmony observed between producers and consumers of cultural products. Thus critics serve their public so well only because the homology between their position in the intellectual field and the position of their public in the field of power is at the foundation of an objective connivance (based on the same principles as the ones theatre demands), which means that critics never defend the interests of their clientele as sincerely and hence as effectively as when they defend their own interests against their adversaries, the critics occupying opposite positions to theirs in the field of production.[33]

The critics who have the greatest reputation for conformity to the expectations of their audience can be believed when they assure us that they never espouse the opinion of their readers, and that the root of the efficacy of their criticism resides not in a demagogic adjustment to public taste but in an objective agreement, which justifies a perfect sincerity – indispensable for being believed, and hence efficacious.[34] The critic for *Le Figaro* never reacts simply to a show; he reacts to the reaction of the 'intellectual' critique which he is prepared to anticipate even before it has been formulated, since he also masters the generative opposition on the basis of which it is engendered. The 'bourgeois' aesthetic, which is in the dominated position, rarely expresses itself without reserve or prudence, and the praise of the 'boulevard' almost always takes the defensive form of a denuncia-tion of the values of those who refuse to value it. Thus, in a review of the play by Herb Gardner, *A Thousand Clowns*, which he concludes with an encomium saturated with keywords ('What naturalness, what elegance, what ease, what human warmth, what suppleness, what finesse, what vigour and what tact, what poetry too, what art'), Jean-Jacques Gautier writes: 'He makes us laugh, he amuses us, he has wit, the gift of repartee, a sense of farce; he cheers, he relieves, he enlightens, he enchants; he does not stand for that seriousness that is a form of emptiness, the gravity which is the absence of grace [. . .]; he clings to humour as the last weapon against conformity; he overflows with vitality and health, he is fantasy incarnate and, under the sign of laughter, would give to those around him a lesson in human dignity and virility; above all, he wants people who surround him *not to be ashamed of laughing in a world in which a laugh is the object of suspicion.*'[35]

It is a matter of overturning the dominant representation (in the artistic field) and of demonstrating that conformity lies on the side of the avant-garde and its denunciation of 'bourgeois' conformity: the true daring belongs to those who have the courage to defy the conformity of anti-conformity, even though they run the risk of thereby winning 'bourgeois' applause . . .[36] This reversal from a 'pro' to a 'con', which is not within the reach of the first 'bourgeois' to come along, is what allows the 'intellectual of the right' to experience the double turnaround that brings him back to the point of departure, but by distinguishing it (at least subjectively) from the 'bourgeois' as the supreme testimony of intellec-tual boldness and courage. When he tries to turn the adversary's own weapons against him, or at least to dissociate himself from the image that the latter imputes to him ('pushing comedy to plain vaudeville but in the subtlest manner possible'), be this by resolutely assuming the image instead of simply enduring it ('courageously lightweight'), the 'bourgeois' intellectual betrays the fact that, at the risk of denying himself as an intellectual, he must recognize 'intellectual' values in his combat against those very values. Strategies long reserved for the polemics of political essayists (who are more directly confronted with an objec-tifying critique) made their appearance – after the revolutionary events of May '68 – on the stage of boulevard theatres, locations *par excellence* of bourgeois assurance and reassurance. 'Renowned as neutral terrain and a depoliticized zone, boulevard theatre arms itself to defend its integrity. Most of the plays presented at the beginning of this season evoke political or social themes apparently exploited as so many plot springs (adultery and others) in the immutable mechanism of this comic formula: unionized servants for Félicien Marceau, strikers for Anouilh, the rebellious younger generation for everybody.'[37]

Because their own interests as 'intellectuals' are at stake, those critics who are primarily there to reassure the 'bourgeois' public cannot simply play on the stereotyped image the latter has of the 'intellectual': undoubtedly, they let themselves suggest to the public that a number of the attempts to make it doubt its aesthetic competence or the shocks intended to shake its ethical or political convictions are in fact inspired by a taste for scandal and a spirit of provocation or mystification – that is, when they are not done quite simply out of the resentment felt by a failed writer who has a tendency to bring about a strategic inversion of his powerlessness and incompetence.[38] After all, they cannot completely fulfil their function unless they show themselves capable of speaking *as intellectuals* who do not allow themselves to be counted as such, who would be the first to understand if there were anything to understand,[39] and who do not fear confronting avant-garde authors and their critics on their own ground. From whence comes the value they grant to those institutional signs and insignia of intellectual authority which are especially recognized by non-intellectuals, such as belonging to academies; and also, among theatre critics, the stylistic and conceptual coquettishness designed to testify that one knows what one is talking about, or, among political essayists, the outdoing of the other in marxological erudition.[40]

'Sincerity' (which is one of the preconditions of symbolic efficacy) is only possible – and effective – in the case of a perfect, immediate harmony between the expectations inscribed in the position occupied and the dispositions of the occupant. One cannot understand how this agreement, for example between most journalists and their newspaper (and by the same token the readership and the newspaper), is established without taking into account the fact that the objective structures of the field of production are the basis of the categories of perception and appreciation which structure the perception and appreciation of the different positions offered by the field and its products. Thus it is that the antithetical pairs of persons or institutions – of newspapers (*Figaro/Nouvel Observateur* or, on another level, with reference to another practical context, *Nouvel Observateur/Libération*, etc.), of theatres (Right Bank/Left Bank), galleries, publishing houses, magazines, fashion designers – may all function as classificatory schemas, allowing one to give labels and to take one's bearings.

As we see particularly well in the case of avant-garde art, this sense of social orientation allows one to move in a hierarchized space where the *places* – galleries, theatres, publishing houses – which mark positions in this space by the same token mark the cultural products that are associated with them, among other reasons because through them a public is designated which (on the basis of the homology between field of production and field of consumption) qualifies the product consumed, helping to make it either rare or on the other hand vulgar (the price of being widespread). It is this practical mastery which allows the most informed of innovators to feel and to foresee, *beyond all cynical calculation*, 'what is to be done' – where, when, how and with whom to do it, given everything that has been done, everything that is done, all those who do it, and where, when and how they do it.[41]

The choice of a place of publication (in the largest sense) – publisher, magazine, gallery, newspaper – is only so important because to each author, each form of production and each product there corresponds a *natural place* (already existing or to be created) in the field of production, and because producers or products not in their right place – 'displaced' as we say – are more or less condemned to failure. All the affinities that guarantee a sympathetic public, critics who understand, etc., for those who have found their places in the structure, on the contrary play against those who have gone astray from their natural places. Just as publishers of the avant-garde and producers of bestsellers agree in saying that they would inevitably run into trouble if they ventured to publish works objectively designed for the opposite pole of the publishing space, so critics cannot exercise 'influence' on their readers unless the readers grant them that power because they are structurally attuned in their vision of the social world, their tastes and their whole habitus.

Jean-Jacques Gautier, for a long time literary critic of *Le Figaro*, gives a good account of this elective affinity between a journalist and his paper and, through it, his readers: a good *Figaro* editor, who has himself been chosen according to the same mechanisms, chooses a literary critic because 'he has the right tone for addressing the readers of the paper', because, *without needing to want to do so*, 'he naturally speaks the language of *Le Figaro*' and might be this paper's 'ideal reader'. 'If tomorrow, in *Le Figaro*, I started speaking the language of *Les Temps Modernes* for example, or *Saintes Chapelles des Lettres*, people would no longer read me or understand me, and so they would not listen to me, because I would be assuming a certain number of ideas or arguments which our readers don't give a damn about.'[42] Every position has corresponding *presuppositions*, a *doxa*, and the homology between the positions occupied by producers and those of their clients is the condition of this complicity. This is particularly necessary when, as in the theatre, what is involved is more essential, closer to the ultimate source of revenue.

Thus, even though the specific interests which are attached to a position in a specialized field (and which are relatively autonomous in relation to interests linked to a social position) can only be satisfied legitimately, and thus efficaciously, at the cost of a perfect submission to the specific laws of the field – that is to say, in this particular case, at the cost of a denial of interest in its ordinary form – nevertheless the relationship of homology established between the field of cultural production and the field of power (or the social field in its entirety) means that works which are produced with reference to purely 'internal' ends are always predisposed to fulfil external functions as an added bonus – and all the more efficaciously because their adjustment to demand is not the product of a conscious search but the result of a structural correspondence.

Even if they are totally opposed in their principles, the two modes of cultural production, 'pure' art and 'commercial' art, are linked by their very opposition, which acts both objectively, in the form of a space of antagonistic positions, and within minds, in the form of schemas of perception and appreciation which organize all perception in the space of producers and products. And the struggles between holders of antagonistic definitions of both artistic production and the very identity of the artist contribute to determining the production and reproduction of the belief which is both a fundamental condition and an effect of the functioning of the field. No doubt 'pure' producers can more easily ignore the opposed positions – even if, as a foil and reversion to an 'outmoded' state, the latter still orient their 'research' negatively; these producers still draw an important part of their energy, if not their inspiration, from the rejection of all temporal compromises, sometimes embracing in the same condemnation those who import on to the terrain of the sacred some 'commercial' practices and interests, and those who make temporal profits from the symbolic capital which they have accumulated at the price of an exemplary submission to the exigencies of 'pure' production. As for those who are called 'successful authors', they must expect disciplinary calls from the new entrants whose only capital is their conviction and their intransigence, and who have the greatest interest in the denial of interest. It is thus that, whatever one's position in the field, no one can completely ignore the fundamental law of the universe:[43] the imperative imposed by disavowal of the 'economy' is presented with all the appearance of transcendence, even if it is only the product of cross-cutting censorships – which we may suppose weigh on each of those who help to make them felt by all the rest.

The production of belief

It is a very general property of fields that the competition for what is at stake conceals the collusion regarding the very principles of the game. The struggle for the monopoly of legitimacy helps to reinforce the legitimacy in the name of which it is waged. Ultimate conflicts over the legitimate reading of Racine, of Heidegger or of Marx preempt the question of the interest and the legitimacy of these conflicts and, at the same time, the truly incongruous question of the social conditions which made them possible. Though apparently merciless, these conflicts safeguard what is essential: the conviction invested in them by the protagonists. Participation in the interests which are constitutive of membership of the field (which presupposes them and produces them by its very functioning) implies the acceptance of a set of presuppositions and postulates which, being the incontestable condition of discussions, are by definition sheltered from debate.

Having thus brought to light the best concealed effect of this invisible collusion – that is, the permanent production and reproduction of the *illusio*, the collective adhesion to the game that is both cause and effect of the existence of the game – one may suspend the charismatic ideology of 'creation', which is the visible expression of this tacit belief and undoubtedly constitutes the principal obstacle to a rigorous science of the production of the value of cultural goods. It is this charismatic ideology, in effect, which directs the gaze towards the apparent producer – painter, composer, writer – and prevents us asking who has created this 'creator' and the magic power of transubstantiation with which the 'creator' is endowed. It also steers the gaze towards the most visible aspect of the process of production, that is, the material *fabrication* of the product, transfigured into 'creation', thereby avoiding any enquiry beyond the artist and the artist's own activity into the conditons of this demiurgic capability.

It is enough to pose the forbidden question to perceive that the artist who makes the work is himself made, at the core of the field of production, by the whole ensemble of those who help to 'discover' him and to consecrate him as an artist who is 'known' and recognized – critics, writers of prefaces, dealers, etc. Thus, for example, the merchant in art (dealer in paintings, publisher, etc.) is inseparably both the one who exploits the work of the artist by making commerce of his products and the one who, in putting it on the market of symbolic goods through exhibition, publication or staging, ensures that the product of artistic fabrication will receive a *consecration* – and the consecration will be greater the more consecrated the merchant himself is. He contributes to 'making' the value of the author he supports by the sole fact of bringing him or her into a known and renowned existence, so that the author is assured of publication (under his imprint, in his gallery or his theatre, etc.) and offered as a guarantee all the symbolic capital the merchant has accumulated.[44] By this means, the author is drawn into the cycle of consecration and is introduced into more and more select company and into more and more rare and exotic places (for example, in the case of a painter, group exhibitions, one-person exhibitions, prestigious collections, museums).

The charismatic image of 'great' dealers or great publishers as inspired discoverers who, guided by their disinterestedness and irrational passion for a work, have 'made' the painter or writer, or permitted him to 'make' himself by sustaining him in difficult times by the faith they have placed in him and by relieving him of material worries, transfigures the real functions. The publisher or the dealer can only organize and rationalize the distribution of the work, which (especially perhaps for painting) is a considerable enterprise, presupposing information (on the 'interesting' places to exhibit, especially abroad) and material means; only a dealer, acting as intermediary and screen, can allow a producer to project an inspired and 'disinterested' picture of himself and his activity by enabling him to avoid contact with the market, relieving him of the tasks, both ridiculous and demoralizing, associated with the marketing of his work. (It is probable that the job of writer or painter, and their correlative images, would be totally different if the producers had to market their products for themselves and if they depended directly for their way of life on the sanctions of the market or on institutions which did not know or recognize anything except these sanctions, like the 'commercial' publishing firms.)

However, in moving backwards from the 'creator' to the 'discoverer' as 'creator of the creator', we have only displaced the initial question, and we would still have to determine where the person who trades in art gets that power to consecrate which has been recognized in him. The same question may be posed about the avant-garde critic or the consecrated 'creator' who discovers an unknown or who 'rediscovers' a little-known predecessor. It is not enough to recall that the 'discoverer' never discovers anything that is not already discovered, at least by some people: painters already known to a small number of painters or connoisseurs, or authors 'introduced' by other authors (we know, for example, that manuscripts almost always arrive via recognized intermediaries). The discoverer's symbolic capital is inscribed in the relationship with the writers and the artists he or she supports ('a publisher', says one of them, 'is his catalogue'), their own value being defined in the set of objective relationships uniting them with each other and opposing them to other writers and artists; in the relationship with other dealers and other publishers, of unity or rivalry depending on the competition between them, notably for the appropriation of authors and artists; and in the relationship, finally, with critics, whose verdicts depend on the relation between the position they occupy in their own space and the position of the author and the publisher in their respective spaces.

If we want to avoid going endlessly backwards in the causal chain, perhaps we ought to stop thinking within the theological logic of 'first beginnings' which leads inevitably to faith in the 'creator'. The principle of the effectiveness of acts of consecration resides in the field itself and nothing would be more futile than to search for the origin of 'creative' power (that sort of *mana* or ineffable *charisma* untiringly celebrated by tradition) anywhere else than in this space of play as it was progressively established, that is to say, in the system of objective relations which constitute this space, in the struggle for which it provides the arena and in the specific form of belief engendered there.

In matters of magic it is not so much a question of knowing what the specific properties of the magician are, or those of instruments, operations and magical representations, but of determining the foundation of the collective belief, or, better, of the *collective misrecognition*, collectively produced and maintained, which is at the source of the power that the magician appropriates. If, as Mauss indicates, it is 'impossible to understand magic without the magic group', it is because the power of the magician is a *legitimate imposture*, collectively misrecognized, and hence recognized. The artist who, in attaching his name to a *ready-made*, confers on it a market price which is not measured on the same scale as its cost of fabrication, owes his magic efficacy to a whole logic of the field that recognizes and authorizes him; his act would be nothing but a crazy or insignificant gesture without the universe of celebrants and believers who are ready to produce it as endowed with meaning and value by reference to the entire tradition which produced their categories of perception and appreciation.

There is undoubtedly no better verification of these analyses than the fate of the attempts which multiplied around the 1960s, in the art milieu itself, to break the circle of belief. There was Manzoni, for example, with his tins of 'artist's shit', his magical pedestals capable of transforming the things deposited there into a work of art, his affixing of signatures to living people (who were thereby converted into works of art). Or there was Ben, exhibiting a piece of cardboard with the label 'unique copy', or a canvas bearing the inscription 'canvas 45 cm long'. Because their gestures apply to the artistic act an intention to provoke or deride – something annexed to artistic tradition since Duchamp – they are immediately converted into artistic 'actions', registered as such, and thus consecrated by the apparatuses of celebration. Art cannot deliver the truth about art without concealment, by turning this unveiling into an artistic manifestation. And it is significant, *a contrario*, that all the attempts to question the field of artistic production itself, the logic of its functioning and the functions it fulfils, whether by the highly sublimated and ambiguous routes of discourse or by artistic 'actions', as with Maciunas or Flynt, attract unanimous condemnation. By refusing to play the game, to contest art *according to the rules of art*, their authors are not questioning a way of playing the game, but challenging the game itself and the belief underlying it, and that is the only unforgivable transgression.[45]

So it can be seen that it is both true and false to say (with Marx, for example) that the market value of the work of art has no common measure with its cost of production: true, if one takes into account only the fabrication of the material object, the responsibility of the artist (or at least the painter) alone; false, if one means the production of the work of art as a sacred and consecrated object, product of an immense enterprise of *symbolic alchemy* involving the collaboration, with the same conviction but very unequal profits, of a whole set of agents engaged in the field of production. They include obscure artists and writers just as much as consecrated 'masters', critics and publishers as much as authors, enthusiastic clients no less than convinced vendors. The contributions ignored by the partial materialism of economism are so many that it suffices to take them into account to see that the production of a work of art, that is of the artist, is no exception to the law of the conservation of social energy. The irreducibility of the work of symbolic production to the act of material fabrication performed by the artist has undoubtedly never been as visible as it is today. Artistic work in its new definition makes artists more than ever tributaries to the whole accompaniment of commentaries and commentators who contribute directly to the production of the work of art by their reflection on an art which often itself contains a reflection on art, and on artistic effort which always encompasses an artist's work on himself.

The appearance of this new definition of art and of the role of the artist cannot be understood independently of the transformations in the field of artistic production. The constitution of an unprecedented ensemble of institutions for recording, conserving and analysing works (reproductions, catalogues, art magazines, museums acquiring the most recent works, etc.), the growth in personnel (full-time or part-time) dedicated to the *celebration* of the work of art, the intensification of the circulation of works and of artists, with the great international exhibitions and the multiplication of galleries with many branches in various countries, etc. – everything combines to favour the establishment of an unprecedented relationship between the interpreters and the work of art. The discourse on the work is not a simple side-effect, designed to encourage its apprehension and appreciation, but a moment which is part of the production of the work, of its meaning and its value.

We need only cite Marcel Duchamp once more:

> Q: To come back to your ready-mades, I thought that R. Mutt, the signature on *The Fountain*, was the manufacturer's name. But in the article by Rosalind Krauss, I read: *R. Mutt, a pun on the German, Armut, or poverty*. Poverty would completely change the meaning of *The Fountain*.
> A: Rosalind Krauss? The redhead? It isn't that at all. You can deny it. Mutt comes from Mott Works, the name of a big firm that makes sanitary equipment. But Mott was too close, so I made it Mutt, because there was a comic strip in the papers in those days, Mutt and Jeff, everyone knew it. So right from the start there was a resonance. Mutt was a fat little guy, and Jeff was tall and thin ... I wanted a different name. And I added Richard ... Richard is a good name for a loo! You see, it's the opposite of poverty ... But not even that, just R.: R. Mutt.
> Q: What possible interpretation is there of the *Bicycle Wheel*? Should one see it as the integration of movement into the work of art? Or as a fundamental point of departure, like the Chinese who invented the wheel?
> A: That machine has no intention, except to get rid of the appearance of a work of art. It was a whim. I didn't call it a 'work of art'. I wanted to throw off the desire to create works of art [. . .]
> Q: What about the geometry book left out in the weather? Can one say that it is the idea of integrating time and space? And with a pun on 'géometrie dans l'espace' and 'temps', the rain and sun that transforms the book?
> A: No, no more than the idea of integrating movement into sculpture. It was a joke. A pure joke. To denigrate the solemnity of a book of principles.

One grasps here, directly exposed, the injection of meaning and value performed by the commentator (himself inscribed in a field) and the commentary, and the commentary on the commentary – and in its turn the naive but cunning exposure of the falseness of the commentary will also make a contribution. The ideology of the inexhaustible work of art, or of 'reading' as re-creation, masks – by the quasi-exposure which is often observed in matters of ·faith – the fact that the work is in fact made not twice, but hundreds of times, thousands of times, by all those who have an interest in it, who find a material or symbolic profit in reading it, classifying it, decoding it, commenting on it, reproducing it, criticizing it, combating it, knowing it, possessing it.

Artistic production, notably in the 'pure' form in which it appears at the core of a field of production which has achieved a high degree of autonomy, represents one of the limits of the possible forms of productive activity. The proportion of material, physical or chemical transformation (that performed for example by a metallurgical worker or an artisan) gets reduced to a minimum in relation to the proportion of essentially symbolic transformation, that performed by the attaching of a painter's signature or a couturier's label (or, at another level, the attribution by an expert). In contrast to fabricated objects with a weak or nugatory symbolic import (undoubtedly increasingly rare in the era of *design*), the work of art, like religious goods or services, amulets or various sacraments, receives value only from collective belief as collective misrecognition, collectively produced and reproduced.

What this reminds us is that, at least at this extreme end of the continuum which goes from the simple fabricated object, tool or piece of clothing to the consecrated work of art, the work of material fabrication is nothing without the labour of production of the value of the fabricated object. The 'court cloak' evoked by the old economists is valid only for a court which, in producing itself and in reproducing itself as such, reproduces everything making for the life of the court, that is to say, the whole system of agents and institutions charged with producing and reproducing the habitus and the 'habits' of the court, with both satisfying and producing the 'desire' for a court cloak (which the economist assumes to be given). As a quasi-experimental verification, the value of court dress disappears with the court and the associated habitus, once the fallen aristocrats no longer have any choice but to become, in Marx's words, the 'dancing masters of Europe' . . . But is it not thus, to different degrees, with all objects, and even those which seem for all the world to contain within themselves the principle of their 'utility'? Which would signify that utility is perhaps a 'dormant virtue' and that there is room for an *economics of the social production of utility and value* aiming to determine how those 'subjective scales of value' which determine the objective value of exchange are constituted, and what the logic is – mechanical aggregation, or symbolic domination and the effect of the imposition of authority, etc.? – behind the way the synthesis of these 'individual scales' operates.

The 'subjective' dispositions which are at the source of value have, as products of a historical process of institution, the objectivity of something established in a collective order which transcends consciousnesses and individual wills. It is a quality of social logic that it can *institute* in the form of fields and of habituses an essentially social libido which varies with the social universes where it is engendered and which it sustains (*libido dominandi* in the field of power, *libido sciendi* in the scientific field, etc.). It is in the relationship between the habituses and the fields to which they are adjusted to a greater or lesser degree (according to the degree to which they are produced by them) that the foundation of all the scales of utility is generated: that is to say, the fundamental adhesion to the game, the *illusio*, recognition of the game and of the utility of the game, belief in the value of the game and in its stakes – the basis of all the allocations of meaning and of value. The economy known by the economists, who endeavour to ground it in reason by founding it on a 'rational nature', relies like all other economies on a form of fetishism, but one that is better masked than others by the fact that the libido at its root presents all the appearances of nature, for the time being anyway, to minds – that is, habitus – fashioned by its structures.

PART II

Foundations of a Science of Works of Art

～∞～

When for a certain time the human soul has been treated with that impartiality invested by the physical sciences in the study of matter, then an immense step will have been taken. It is the only way for humanity to rise a little above itself. It will then consider itself candidly and purely in the mirror of its works of art. It will be god-like, judging itself from on high. Well, I consider this feasible. It is perhaps, as for mathematics, just a matter of finding a method.

GUSTAVE FLAUBERT

I

Questions of Method

~∞~

Forschung is die Kunst, den nächsten Schritt zu tun.

KURT LEWIN

I have never had much taste for 'grand theory', and when I read works which might enter into that category, I cannot stop myself from feeling a certain irritation before a typically scholastic combination of false audacity and true carefulness. I could reproduce here dozens of those pompous and almost empty sentences, which often finish with a disparate enumeration of proper names followed by dates, a humble procession of the ethnologists, sociologists or historians who have furnished the 'grand theoretician' with the substance of his meditation, and who bring him, as a tribute, the proofs of 'positivity' indispensable to the new academic respectability. I will give only one example of this, a quite ordinary one, but out of charity omit citing its author: 'As a number of ethnological reports have taught us, there exists in this type of society a sort of institutionalized obligation to exchange gifts, which prevents the accumulation of capital disposable for purely economic ends: economic surplus, in the form of presents, feasts and emergency aid, is transformed into non-specified obligations, into political power, into respect and social status (Goodfellow, 1954; Schott, 1956; Belshaw, 1965, esp. pp. 46ff.; Sigrist, 1967, pp. 176ff.).'

And when it happens that the implacable mechanics of academic demand oblige me to contemplate for a moment writing one of these so-called synthetic texts on some aspect of my previous work, I find myself suddenly reminded of the most sombre evenings of my adolescence when, obliged to expound on the subjects required by scholastic routine, among fellow students harnessed to the same task, I felt I was chained to the bench of an eternal galley where copyists and compilers interminably reproduce the instruments of scholastic repetition – courses, theses or instruction manuals.

A new scientific spirit

To the same degree as I dislike those pretentious professions of faith by pretenders eager to sit down at the table of 'founding fathers', so do I delight in those books in which theory, because it is the air one breathes, is everywhere and nowhere – in the detour of a note, in the commentary on an old text, or in the very structure of interpretative discourse. I feel completely at home with those authors who know how to infuse the most decisive theoretical questions into a meticulously conducted empirical study, and who give concepts a usage that is both more modest and more aristocratic, sometimes going as far as to conceal their own contribution within a creative reinterpretation of theories which are immanent in their object.

To expect a solution to such and such a canonic problem from case studies – for example as I did in order to try to understand fetishism by equipping myself not with classic texts by Marx or Lévi-Strauss, but with an analysis of high fashion and the couturier's 'label'[1] – means to inflict a transformation on the tacit hierarchy of genres and objects which is not unlike that performed, according to Erich Auerbach, by the inventors of the modern novel, notably Virginia Woolf: 'The great exterior turning points and blows of fate are granted less importance; they are credited with less power of yielding decisive information concerning the subject; on the other hand there is confidence that, in any random fragment plucked from the course of a life, at any time, the totality of its fate is contained and can be portrayed.'[2] It is a similar transformation that must be effected in order to succeed in establishing a new scientific spirit within the social sciences: theories which are nourished less by purely theoretical confrontation with other theories than by confrontation with fresh empirical objects, and concepts which have above all the function of designating, in stenographic fashion, ensembles of generative schemas of scientific practices which are epistemologically controlled.

The notion of habitus, for example, expresses above all a rejection of a whole series of alternatives into which social science (and, more generally, all anthropological theory) was locked, that of the conscious (or the subject) and the unconscious, that of finality and mechanism, etc. At the moment when I introduced it, via the publication in French of two articles by Panofsky which had never been brought together, one on Gothic architecture, where the word was employed (as an 'indigenous' concept) to account for the effect of scholastic thought on the terrain of architecture, and the other on the Abbé Suger, where it could also have a role to play,[3] 'habitus' permitted me to break with the structuralist paradigm without falling back into the old philosophy of the subject or of consciousness, that of classical economy and its *homo economicus*, returning these days under the name of 'methodological individualism'. In taking up the Aristotelian notion of *hexis*, converted by scholastic tradition into *habitus*, I wanted to react against structuralism and its strange philosophy of action which, implicitly in the Lévi-Straussian notion of the unconscious and avowedly among the Althusserians, made the agent disappear by reducing it to the role of supporter or bearer (*Träger*) of the structure. I wanted to do this while slightly taking advantage of the use (unique in his work) which Panofsky made of the notion of habitus, in order to avoid reintroducing the pure knowing subject of the neo-Kantian philosophy of 'symbolic forms' to which the author of *Perspective as Symbolic Form* had remained wedded. On this point I was close to Chomsky, who proposed at around the same time the notion of *generative grammar*. I wanted to demonstrate the active, inventive and 'creative' capacities of the habitus and the agent (which are not expressed by the term 'habit').[4] But I intended to indicate that this generative power is not that of a universal nature or of reason, as it is with Chomsky (the habitus – the word says it – is acquired and it is also a possession which may, in certain cases, function as a form of capital), nor is it that of a transcendental subject in the idealist tradition.

To take back from idealism, as Marx suggested in the *Theses on Feuerbach*, the 'active aspect' of practical knowledge which the materialist tradition had left to it, notably with the theory of 'reflection', it was necessary to break with the canonical opposition between theory and practice, so profoundly inscribed in the structures of the division of labour (through the very existence of professionals of intellectual labour) and even in the structures of the division of intellectual labour, and hence in the mental structures of intellectuals, preventing them from even conceiving of a practical knowledge or a knowledgeable practice. It was necessary to unveil and describe a cognitive activity of the constructing of social reality which is not, either in its instruments or in its approaches (I am thinking in particular of its activities of classification), the pure and purely intellectual operation of a calculating and rational consciousness.

It seemed to me that the concept of habitus – long outmoded, despite a number of occasional usages[5] – was the best one to signify that desire to escape from the philosophy of consciousness without annulling the agent in its true role of practical operator of constructions of the real. The intention in taking up a word from tradition and reactivating it – diametrically opposed to the strategy of trying to associate one's name with a neologism or, on the model of the natural sciences, with an 'effect', even a minor one – is inspired by the conviction that work on concepts may also be cumulative. What a search for originality at all costs (often facilitated by ignorance) and a religious fidelity to such and such a canonic author (which inclines one to ritual repetition) have in common is a forbidding of what appears to me the only possible attitude to theoretical tradition: an inseparable assertion of both continuity and rupture, through a critical systematization of acquisitions from all quarters.

The social sciences are in a situation that is hardly favourable to the establishment of such a realist relation to theoretical heritage: judgements continue to be guided by the values of originality, which are those of the literary, artistic or philosophical fields. Discrediting as servile or merely fashionable the desire to acquire the specific instruments of production by inscribing oneself within a tradition and thereby within a collective enterprise, the social sciences favour those short-lived bluffs used by small entrepreneurs without capital to try to associate their name with a hallmark – as we see in the domain of literary analysis today, where there is no critic who does not give himself or herself a *nom de guerre* ending in -ism, -ique, or -ology. Moreover, the position the social sciences occupy, halfway between scientific disciplines and literary disciplines, is not made to favour the development of modes of production and the transmission of knowledge of a sort to foster cumulativity: even if an active appropriation and an accomplished mastery of a mode of scientific thought are as difficult and as precious (and not only for the scientific effects they produce) as was its initial invention (more difficult and more precious, in any case, than the false, nugatory or negative innovations engendered by the search for distinction at all costs), they are often mocked and discredited as a servile imitation of an epigone, or as a mechanical application of an already invented art of inventing. But, just as music may be made not to be rather passively listened to, or even played, but to open the way to composition, so scientific works, in contrast to theoretical texts, call not for contemplation or dissertation, but for practical confrontation with experience; to truly understand them means to activate in relation to a different object the mode of thought they express, to reactivate it in a new act of production, just as inventive and original as the initial one, and completely opposed to the de-realizing *commentary* of the *lector*, an impotent and sterilizing metadiscourse.

The same dispositions were the impetus for the use of a concept such as field. Here again, the notion first of all served to designate a theoretical posture, generative of choices of method (negative just as much as positive) in the construction of objects: I am thinking for example of the work on institutions of higher education, and in particular the Grandes Écoles, where it served to remind us that each of these institutions could not deliver its singular truth unless, paradoxically, it was set in the system of objective relationships constitutive of the space of competition that it forms along with all the others.[6] But it has also allowed us to escape the alternatives of internal interpretation and external explanation (alternatives which face all sciences of cultural works, social history and the sociology of religion, of law, of science, of art and literature) by reminding us of the existence of social microcosms, separate and autonomous spaces, in which works are generated. In all these areas, the opposition between a formalism born of the codification of artistic practices which have achieved a high degree of autonomy, and a reductionism bent on bringing artistic forms directly back to social formations, had obscured the fact that what the two currents had in common was a lack of recognition of the *field of production* as a space of objective relations. It follows that a genealogical investigation – which would lead to authors as distant from each other as Trier or Lewin – would have no interest, here again, except in so far as it would permit us to better characterize the theoretical choice (and the topic, to speak in Joëlle Proust's terms,[7] in which it is inscribed) and to situate it more clearly in the space of positions in relation to which it defines itself.

The *relational* (rather than the structuralist) mode of thinking (which, as Cassirer has shown,[8] is that of the whole of modern science and which has found some applications, with the Russian Formalists especially,[9] in the analysis of symbolic systems, myths or literary works) can only be applied to social realities at the cost of a radical rupture with the usual representation of the social world. The tendency to a mode of thought which Cassirer calls 'substantialist', and which leads to privileging the different social realities, considered in themselves and for themselves, to the detriment of the objective relations, often invisible, which bind them, is never as powerful as when these realities – individuals, groups or institutions – entrench themselves with all the force of social sanction.

It is thus that a first effort to analyse the 'intellectual field'[10] stopped at the immediately visible relations between agents engaged in intellectual life: the interactions between authors and critics or between authors and publishers had disguised from my eyes the objective relationships between the relative positions that one and the other occupy in the field, that is to say, the structure that determines the form of those interactions. And the first rigorous formulation of the notion was elaborated on the occasion of an interpretation of a chapter of Weber's *Wirtschaft und Gesellschaft* on religious sociology, an interpretation which (haunted as it was by reference to the problems posed by the study of the literary field of the nineteenth century) was nothing like a scholarly commentary. Instead of a critique of the interactionist vision of relations among religious agents proposed by Weber, which implied a retrospective criticism of my first representation of the intellectual field, I proposed a construction of the religious field as a *structure of objective relations*, allowing us to account for the concrete form of the *interactions* that Weber tried desperately to enclose in a *realist typology*, one breached by innumerable exceptions.[11]

It only remained to activate the system of general questions thus elaborated in order to discover, in applying it to different terrains, the properties specific to each field, and the constants revealed by the comparison of different universes treated as so many 'particular cases of the possible'. Far from functioning as simple metaphors guided by rhetorical intentions of persuasion, the methodical transfer of general problems and concepts, each time made specific by their very application, relies on the hypothesis that structural and functional homologies exist between all the fields. This is a hypothesis which finds its confirmation in the heuristic effects these transfers produce, and finds its corrective in the difficulties to which they give rise. The patience of repeated translation into practice is one of the possible avenues of 'semantic ascension' (in Quine's sense) which allows us to take to a higher level of generality and formalization those theoretical principles engaged in the empirical study of different universes and of the constant laws of the structure and history of different fields. By virtue of the particularities of its functions and of its functioning (or, more simply, the sources of information concerning it), each field delivers more or less clearly the properties it shares with all the others. Thus, undoubtedly because the 'economic' aspect of practices is less censored there and because, culturally less legitimate, it is less protected against objectification (which always involves a form of desacralization), the field of high fashion introduced me more directly than any other universe to one of the most fundamental properties of all fields of cultural production, namely the essentially magical logic of the production of the producer and of the product as fetishes.

The theory of fields which was thus gradually elaborated[12] nevertheless owes nothing, contrary to appearances, to a transfer of the economic mode of thought – even though, in rethinking from a structuralist perspective Weber's analysis, which applied to religion a certain number of concepts borrowed from economics (like competition, monopoly, supply and demand, etc.), I found myself introduced at the outset to general properties, applicable to different fields, which economic theory had brought to light without appreciating their true theoretical foundation. Far from the transfer being at the root of the construction of the object – as when one borrows from another universe (preferably prestigious, such as ethnology, linguistics or economics) a decontextualized notion, a simple metaphor with a purely emblematic function – it is rather the construction of the object which calls for the transfer and grounds it.[13] And, as I hope to be able one day to demonstrate,[14] everything leads us to suppose that, far from being the founding model, the economic theory of the field is a particular case of the general theory of fields which is gradually being constructed by a sort of theoretical induction that is empirically validated, and which, while allowing us to understand the fecundity and the limits of the validity of transfers such as the one Weber effected, obliges us to rethink the presuppositions of economic theory, especially in the light of what is learned from the analysis of fields of cultural production.

The general theory of the economy of practices as it is progressively disentangled from the analysis of different fields ought thus to escape all forms of reductionism, beginning with the most common and also the best known, which is economism. To analyse the different fields (religious field, scientific field, etc.) in the different configurations in which they may appear according to the era and to national traditions, treating each of them as a *particular case* in the true sense, that is, as a case which figures among other possible configurations, is to give the comparative method its full effectiveness. By this route, it is possible to gain an understanding of each case in its most concrete singularity without falling back complacently on an ideographic description (of a determined state of a determined field); and to try to grasp, in the very same process, the invariant properties of all fields and the specific form taken by the general mechanism in each field, as well as the system of concepts – capital, investment, interest, etc. – utilized to describe them. In other words, constructing the particular case as such obliges us in practice to bypass one of those unfortunate alternatives which the routine of lazy thought and the division of 'intellectual temperaments' reproduces indefinitely, pitting the uncertain and hollow generalities of a discourse proceeding by the unconscious and uncontrolled universalization of a singular case against the infinite minutiae of an erroneously exhaustive study of a particular case which, for lack of being apprehended as such, cannot deliver either what it has of the singular or what it has of the universal.

One sees, however, what might make such a project excessive. To enter, for each case, into the particularity of the historically considered configuration, one must each time master the literature devoted to a universe which is artificially isolated by premature specialization. One must also launch an empirical analysis of a methodically elaborated case, knowing that the necessities of theoretical construction will impose on the empirical procedures all sorts of supplementary requirements, to the point of leading sometimes to methodological choices or to technical operations which, in the view of a positivist submission to the data as given, always risk appearing, by a strange inversion, as gratuitous freedoms, even unjustifiable liberties.[15] The impression of heuristic strength often gained by the application of theoretical schemas expressing the very movement of reality has its counterpart in the permanent feeling of dissatisfaction aroused by the immensity of the work necessary to obtain the full return on the theory in each of the cases considered – which explains the innumerable restartings and reshuffles – and to try to export it farther and farther from its region of origin, so as to generalize it by the integration of observed traits in cases as diverse as possible. This labour could be prolonged indefinitely if one did not have to put a stop to it, a rather arbitrary one, in the hope that the first results, provisional and revisable, will have done enough to indicate the direction which should be taken by a social science concerned with converting into a really integrated and cumulative programme of empirical research that legitimate ambition for systematicity which is imprisoned by the totalizing pretensions of 'grand theory'.

Literary *doxa* and resistance to objectification

Probably because they are protected by the veneration of all those who were raised, often from their earliest youth, to perform sacramental rites of cultural devotion (the sociologist being no exception), the fields of literature, art and philosophy pose formidable obstacles, both objective and subjective, to scientific objectification. In this case more than any other, the conduct of the research and the presentation of its results have run the risk of letting themselves be imprisoned within the alternatives of an enchanted cult or a disabused denigration – each of them being present, under diverse guises, inside each of the fields. The very intention to write a science of the sacred has something of the sacrilegious about it, and the feeling of *transgression* – particularly scandalous, this, for those who continually pay lip service to the latter word – may incline those who risk performing it to increase the injuries which they must inevitably inflict (and self-inflict) by futile excesses – expressing not so much the desire to make the reader suffer (as one might have thought) as the temptation to 'twist the stick in the other direction', to overcome resistances.[16]

The rupture that must be effected in order to ground a rigorous science of cultural works is hence more than and different from a simple methodological overturning:[17] it implies a veritable *conversion* of the most common manner of thinking and living the intellectual life, a sort of *épochè* of the *belief* commonly granted to cultural things and to the legitimate ways of approaching them.[18] I did not think it necessary to specify that suspending support for the *doxa* in this way is a methodical *épochè* which does not in any way imply a reversal of the scale of cultural values, and even less a practical conversion to the counterculture, or even, as some pretend to believe, a cult of the lack of culture. This at least was true until the new Pharisees tried to confer on themselves a certificate of cultural virtue by denouncing loudly, in these days of restoration, the threats made against art (or philosophy) by analyses whose iconological intention looks to them like iconoclastic violence.

It remains true that scientific analysis finds a quasi-experimental validation in those kinds of spontaneous experiences which iconoclastic acts are, whether or not they are conceived as artistic acts (that is to say, performed by artists or by the simply uninitiated). As a practical suspension of the ordinary belief in the work of art or in the intellectual values of disinterestedness, such an act gives evidence of the collective belief which is at the basis of both the artistic order and the intellectual order, a belief which is left intact by criticisms which appear to be the most radical.[19]

This methodical suspension is all the more difficult in that the adhesion to the cultural sacred has not, allowing for exceptions, had to enunciate itself in the form of explicit theses, still less to ground itself rationally. There is nothing more certain, for those taking part in it, than the cultural order. Cultivated people are in culture as in the air they breathe, and it takes a major crisis (and the criticism that accompanies it) for them to feel obliged to transform the *doxa* into *orthodoxy* or into *dogma*, and to justify the sacred and the consecrated ways of cultivating it. It follows that it is not easy to find a systematic expression of the cultural *doxa*, but it nevertheless always crops up here and there. So when, for example, in their very classic *Theory of Literature*, René Wellek and Austin Warren extol the very banal 'explanation in terms of the personality and the life of the writer',[20] it is belief in the 'creative genius' that they are tacitly admitting that they take for granted (and no doubt most of their readers along with them), thus dedicating themselves, in their own terms, to 'one of the oldest and best-established methods of literary study', one that consists of searching for the explanatory principle of a work inside an author taken in isolation (uniqueness and singularity being central properties of a 'creator'). In the same way, when Sartre gives himself the project of recapturing the mediations through which social determinisms had fashioned the singular individuality of Flaubert, he condemns himself to imputing to the only factors capable of being apprehended from the viewpoint thus adopted – that is to say, the social class of origin as refracted through the family structure – both the effects of generic factors brought to bear on any writer by virtue of the fact that the writer is included in an artistic field occupying a dominated position in the field of power, and also the effects of the specific factors acting on the whole ensemble of writers occupying the same position as he does in the artistic field.

The statistical analysis which is sometimes used to reinforce external analysis, and which is commonly perceived by the defenders of the 'personalist' vision of 'creation' as the manifestation *par excellence* of 'reductive sociology', in no way escapes the dominant vision. Because it tends to reduce each author to a set of properties which may be grasped at the level of the individual taken in an isolated state, it runs every risk, unless special care is taken, of ignoring or annulling the *structural properties* linked to the position occupied in a field. These properties – as, for example, with the structural inferiority of the vaudevillean or the illustrator – are not generally evident except through generic characteristics such as membership of groups or institutions, reviews, movements, genres, etc, that traditional historiography ignores or accepts as self-evident without putting them into an explanatory model. To which may be added the fact that most of the analysts merely apply to *preconstructed populations* – just like most of the corpus worked on by practitioners of structuralist hermeneutics – *principles of classification* which are themselves *preconstructed*. They often skip the analysis of the process of the constitution of the lists they work on, which are in fact prize lists – that is, they miss the history of the process of canonization and hierarchization that leads to the delimitation of the population of canonic authors. They also dispense with reconstructing the genesis of the systems of classification (names of groups, schools, genres, movements, etc.) which are the instruments and the stakes in the struggle over classification, and which contribute thereby to establishing groups. For want of proceeding to a historical critique of this sort of the instruments of historical analysis, one runs the risk of unwittingly cutting out what is at issue and at play in reality itself – for example, the definition and delimitation of the population of writers, meaning those and only those who, among 'those writing', have the right to call themselves writers.

The 'original project', founding myth

But it is with his theory of the 'projet originel' that Sartre elucidated one of the fundamental presuppositions of literary analysis in all its forms, one inscribed in the expressions of ordinary language, and in particular in phrases like 'already', 'since then', 'from his earliest days' so dear to biographers.[21] It maintains that each life is a whole, a coherent and directed ensemble, and that it cannot be apprehended except as the unitary expression of an intention, both subjective and objective, which is made manifest in every experience, especially the earliest. Thanks to the retrospective illusion which leads to the interpretation of recent events as the end result of initial experiences or ways of behaving, and thanks to the ideology of the gift or predestination, which seems to feature very particularly in the case of exceptional people who are willingly credited with a prophetic clairvoyance, it is tacitly acknowledged that life follows the pattern of a story and unfolds from an origin, understood both as a point of departure and also as a first cause or, better, a generative principle, up till a final point which is also a goal.[22] It is this tacit philosophy that Sartre brings to an explicit state with the 'original project', by placing as a fundamental of a whole existence an explicit awareness of the determinations implied in a social position.

Regarding a critical period in Flaubert's life, the years 1837 to 1840, which he analyses at length in terms of a first beginning pregnant with the whole later development, or a sort of sociological *cogito* ('I think as a bourgeois, therefore I am a bourgeois'), Sartre writes: 'From 1837 and into the 1840s, Gustave has an experience which is crucial for the direction of his life and the meaning of his work: he *feels*, inside and outside himself, the bourgeoisie as his class of origin [. . .]. We must now trace the course of this *discovery* so pregnant with consequences.'[23] The research decision itself, in its double movement, expresses the philosophy of the biographer who makes a life into a succession of events which are definitively discernible – since they are all there in a potential state – in the crisis which serves him as point of departure: 'We must, in order to see clearly, run through this life once more from adolescence to death. We will then come back to the years of crisis – 1838 to 1844 – which potentially contain all the force lines of this destiny.'[24]

Analysing essentialist philosophy (of which Leibnizian monadology seemed to him to be the exemplary form), Sartre observed in *Being and Nothingness* that it abolished chronological order by reducing it to logical order. Paradoxically, his philosophy of biography produces an effect of the same type, but starting from an absolute beginning which consists in this case of the 'discovery' accomplished by an original act of awareness: 'Between these different conceptions, there is no chronological order: from the moment of its appearance in him, the notion of bourgeois enters into permanent disaggregation and all the avatars of the Flaubertian bourgeois are given simultaneously: circumstances call forth one or another of them, but only for an instant and against the dark background of this contradictory indistinction. At seventeen as at fifty, he is against all of humanity [...]. At twenty-four as at forty-five, he blames the bourgeois for not establishing itself as the privileged order.'[25]

It is worth rereading the pages in *Being and Nothingness* which Sartre devotes to 'Flaubert's psychology' and where he tries, against Freud and Marx combined, to tear the 'being' of the 'creator' away from every kind of 'reduction' in general – from genre, from class – and to assert the transcendence of the ego against the aggressions of genetic thought, incarnated by psychology or by sociology, according to the period, and also against 'what Auguste Comte called *materialism*, that is, explaining the higher by the lower'.[26] It is at the end of this long 'demonstration', where he mainly shows that any means will serve him to safeguard his final convictions, that Sartre introduces this sort of conceptual monster that is the autodestructive notion of 'original project', a free and conscious act of autocreation by which the creator assigns himself his life's project. With the founding myth of the belief in the uncreated 'creator' (which is to the notion of habitus what the Book of Genesis is to the theory of evolution), Sartre inscribes in the origin of each human existence a sort of free and conscious act of autodetermination, an original project without origin which encompasses all subsequent acts in the inaugural choice of a pure freedom, tearing these acts definitively away, by this transcendental negation, from the hands of science.

This myth of origin which aims to challenge any explanation by origin has the merit of giving an explicit form, and the appearance of a systematic justification, to the belief in the irreducibility of consciousness to external determinations, the foundation of the resistance provoked by the social sciences and their will to 'reductive' 'objectification': the 'determinist' threat they always pose never seems more menacing than when the social sciences push scientistic arrogance to the point of taking intellectuals themselves as their object.

If the assertion of the irreducibility of consciousness is one of the most constant features of the philosophy of the professors of philosophy, it is undoubtedly because it constitutes a way of defining and defending the frontier between what rightly belongs to philosophy and what it may relinquish to the sciences of nature and society. Thus Caro, in the opening lecture he gave to the Sorbonne in 1864, agreed to concede to the positive sciences all *exterior* phenomena, provided it was granted to him in return that phenomena of consciousness reveal a 'higher order of facts, realities and causes which escape, not only the present grasp, but the possible grasp of scientific determinism.'[27] This is an illuminating text, which makes it apparent that nothing is very new under the sun of philosophy and that, in beating back materialism or determinism, our modern defenders of liberty, the individual and the 'subject' aim (without always knowing it) to defend a hierarchy and a difference in nature or essence which separates philosophers from all other thinkers – with the latter often characterized as 'scientists' or 'positivists' who are not content with making a profession out of 'reducing the higher to the lower' and so snatching its object from the higher discipline, but push their impudence, with the sociology of philosophy, to the point of taking the sovereign discipline as their object, by an intolerable reversal of the established intellectual order.

God is dead, but the uncreated creator has taken his place. The same person who announced the death of God seizes all of his properties.[28] If it is true, as Sartre himself saw clearly, that the modern novelist – Joyce, Faulkner or Virginia Woolf – has abandoned the divine point of view, the thinker does not resign himself so easily to forsaking the sovereign position. Replaying in another register the Husserlian denial of any genesis of the absolute subject, logical in contingent and historical subjects, he submits 'creators' in the person of Flaubert to a supposedly radical interrogation, designed to mark once and for all the limits of all objectification. Instead of objectifying Flaubert by objectifying the social universe which was expressed through him, and of which Flaubert himself sketched the objectification (notably in the *Sentimental Education*), Sartre is satisfied with projecting on to Flaubert, in a non-analysed state, a 'comprehensive' representation of the anxieties generically attached to the position of writer, thus bestowing on himself that form of narcissism by proxy which is routinely taken for the supreme form of 'comprehension'.

How could it have escaped Sartre that the writer whom he describes, in terms of youngest son, as the idiot of the Flaubert family is also, in terms of writer, the idiot of the bourgeois family? What prevents him from understanding is, paradoxically, the thing through which he takes part in what he pretends to understand, the unthought which is inscribed in his own position as writer and from which he flees, in some way, into an auto-analysis functioning as the supreme form of *denegation*. In other words, the obstacle that inhibits Sartre from seeing and knowing what is really at stake in his analysis – to wit, the paradoxical position of the writer in the social world, and, more precisely, in the field of power, and in the intellectual field as a universe of belief where the fetishism of the 'creator' is progressively generated – is precisely everything that *attaches* him to this position of writer and which he has in common with Flaubert, and with all other writers, major and minor, of the past and the present, and in addition with the majority of his readers who are predisposed in advance to grant him what he grants himself, and which he grants them at the same time, at least in appearance.

The illusion of the all-powerfulness of a thought capable of being the sole foundation for itself undoubtedly belongs to the same disposition as the ambition for unequivocal domination over the intellectual field. And the realization of this desire for omnipotence and ubiquity which defines the total intellectual – one who is capable of triumphing in all genres and in that supreme genre which is the philosophical critique of other genres – can only foster the expansion of the *hubris of the absolute thinker*, having no other limits than the ones his freedom freely assigns to itself, and who is thus predisposed to produce an exemplary expression of the myth of the immaculate conception.[29] Victim of his triumph, the absolute thinker cannot resign himself to searching within the relativity of a generic destiny – and even less within the specific factors capable of explaining the singularities of his experience of that common fate – for the veritable principle of his practice and, in particular, for the very special intensity with which, carried along by his hegemonic dream, he lives and speaks the common illusions.

Sartre belongs to those who, in Luther's phrase, 'sin bravely': one may be grateful to him for having brought out, by giving it an explicit formulation, the (tacit) presupposition of the literary *doxa* which supports methodologies as diverse as university monographs in the style of Lanson ('the man and his work'), or the analyses of texts applied to a single fragment of an individual oeuvre (Baudelaire's 'Les Chats' in the case of Jakobson or Lévi-Strauss) or to the oeuvre of a single author, or even undertakings in the social history of art or literature which, in trying to account for an oeuvre on the basis of psychological or social variables attached to a singular author, are doomed to allow the essential to escape. As is well demonstrated by a biography conceived as a retrospective integration of the whole personal history of the 'creator' into a purely aesthetic project, the labour necessary to destroy the obstacles to an adequate construction of the object (that is, reconstructing the genesis of the unconscious categories of perception through which primary experience receives the object) is part and parcel of that labour which is indispensable to the reconstruction of the genesis of the field of production in which this representation is produced. It is clear, in fact, that the interest in the personage of the writer or the artist grows in parallel with the autonomization of the field of production and with the correlative elevation of the status of producers.

The charismatic representation of the writer as 'creator' leads to bracketing out everything which is found inscribed in the position of author at the heart of the field of production and in the social trajectory which led her there: on the one hand, the genesis and structure of the totally specific social space in which the 'creator' is inserted and constituted as such, and where her 'creative project' itself is formed; and on the other hand, the genesis of the simultaneously generic and specific dispositions, common and singular, which she has imported into this position. It is only by submitting (without complacency) the author and the work under study to such an objectification (and, by the same token, the author of the objectification), and also by eliminating all vestiges of narcissism linking the analyst to the analysand, limiting the scope of the analysis, that one may found a science of cultural works and of their authors.

Thersites' viewpoint and the false rupture

But the intellectual world also produces less enchanted images of itself and of its vocation. And one might be tempted – as a counterbalance to that unreal aspect of the sovereign image used by the total intellectual to project the illusion and the reality of his sovereignty – to give the floor to all the ordinary citizens of the Republic of Letters, to the obscure ones and to the foot-soldiers who, in the fashion of Thersites (the simple, surly soldier of the *Iliad* dramatized by Shakespeare in *Troilus and Cressida*) denounce the hidden vices of the great. Undoubtedly, a journalist concerned with 'objectivity' would proceed in this way, in one of those enquiries into the intellectual world designed to demonstrate, as is much done these days, the 'end of intellectuals'. Observing professional honour by being equally challenging to the foremost and the least, to those 'one absolutely must have' and those who absolutely want to be there, this journalist would infallibly produce, without even needing to look for it, a levelling of the differences which would be in perfect harmony with the journalist's positional interests, which are inclined to relativism.

There is no great intellectual in the eyes of the lesser ones, and this applies especially perhaps to those who, while occupying a dominated position in the universe, come to exercise a power there of another order. Owing part of their power over the consecrated producers to their art of maintaining or sparking competition among them, and being able to approach and observe them, sometimes with the right and duty of judging them (notably on committees and commissions arranged for this purpose), they are well placed to discover the contradictions, weaknesses or pettinesses which go unnoticed by a more distanced reverence.

This means that the dominated regions of the fields of cultural production are permanently inhabited by a sort of rampant anti-intellectualism. This contained violence explodes into the light of day when there are great crises in the field (as with the 1848 revolution, so aptly described by Flaubert), or when regimes bent on taming free thought reach power (Nazism and Stalinism being at the extreme end); but anti-intellectualism also emerges at times in topical pamphlets where the most brutally reductive sociologism is often used as a weapon by the resentment of disappointed ambitions and lost illusions, or the impatience of arriviste pretensions, in order to destroy or cut down to size the most improbable conquests of free thought.

But the objectifications of the intellectual game inspired by these intellectual passions remain necessarily partial and blind to themselves: the resentment of disappointed love leads to a reversal of the dominant vision, demonizing what it once made divine. Since those who produce them are not able to comprehend the game as such or the position they occupy in it, the 'revelations' of a denunciation have a blind spot, which is simply the point (of view) from which they are taken; not being able to reveal anything of the reasons and the *raisons d'être* of the targeted behaviours, which are only evident in a global view of the game, they merely betray their own *raisons d'être*.

And, in fact, one could show that the different categories of 'critiques' of the intellectual world which are generated in the very heart of this microcosm could be easily related to the major classes of positions and trajectories at the core of this world: the disenchanted and haughty critique of polite society's anti-intellectualism (the paradigm undoubtedly being Raymond Aron's *L'Opium des intellectuels*) is opposed to the peevish polemic of populist anti-intellectualism in its diverse variants, just as the aristocratic distance of conservative intellectuals who come from the grande bourgeoisie and are recognized by it, and who are also endowed with a form of internal consecration, contrasts with the marginality of 'proletaroid intellectuals' who come from the petite bourgeoisie.[30]

The partial objectifications of the polemic or the pamphlet are just as formidable an obstacle as the narcissistic complacency of projective criticism. Those who produce these instruments of combat posing as instruments of analysis forget that they ought first to apply them to that part of themselves which belongs to the objectified category. This would presuppose that they were able to situate themselves and situate their adversaries in the space of the game where their stakes are engendered, and thus to discover the point of view which is the basis of their insights and their oversights, of their lucidity and their blindness. 'Error is privation,' and in order to have at one's disposal a true *instrument of rupture* with all partial objectifications, or, rather, an instrument of objectification of *all* spontaneous objectifications, along with the blind spots they imply and the interests they engage (not excluding the 'knowledge of the first kind' which is the lot of researchers themselves so long as they are engaged in the field as empirical subjects), it is necessary to construct as such this site of the coexistence of all the points from which the definitions of so many different and competing points of view stem – which is simply the field (artistic, literary, philosophical, etc.).

The space of points of view

This means that one cannot hope to get out of the circle of relativizations which mutually relativize each other, like so many reflections indefinitely reflecting each other, without putting into practice the maxim of reflexivity, trying to construct methodically the space of possible points of view on the literary (or artistic) act in relation to which the method of analysis to be proposed is defined.[31] The history of criticism which I would like to sketch here in a preliminary way has the sole purpose of trying to bring to the consciousness of the one who writes it (and of his readers) the principles of vision and division which are the basis of the problems they pose and the solutions they bring to them. It demonstrates at the outset that position-takings on art and literature, like the positions where they are generated, are organized around pairs of oppositions, often inherited from past polemics, and conceived as insurmountable antinomies, absolute alternatives, in terms of all or nothing, and while these structure thought, they also imprison it in a series of false dilemmas. A first division is the one which pits internal readings (in the sense of Saussure speaking of 'internal linguistics'), that is to say, formal or formalist readings, against external readings calling on explanatory and interpretative principles, such as economic and social factors, which are external to the work itself.

I request indulgence for this evocation of the universe of position-takings with respect to literature. Concerned to stay with what seems to me essential, that is, explicit or implicit founding principles, I have not deployed the whole arsenal of references and quotations which would have given full force to my argument. Above all, I have reduced to what seems to me to be their inner truth those 'theories' which, like that of French semiologists, do not err on the side of excessive coherence and logic, with the result that one could always find in them, given a close search, something to use to challenge me. Moreover, the proposed method of analysis of works is constructed in relation to both the literary field and the artistic field (and also the juridical and scientific fields) in such a way that, to be truly complete, my 'picture' of possible methodologies would also have to encompass the prevailing traditions in the study of painting, namely Erwin Panofsky, Frédéric Antal or Ernst Gombrich as well as Roman Jakobson, Lucien Goldmann and Léo Spitzer.

The first tradition, in its most widespread form, is simply the literary *doxa* already evoked; it is rooted in the job and ethos of the professional commentator on texts (literary or philosophical and, in other times, religious), which a certain medieval taxonomy contrasted, under the name of *lector*, with the producer of texts, the *auctor*. Encouraged by the authority and routines of the scholarly institution to which it is perfectly harmonized, the 'philosophy' of reading inherent in the practice of the *lector* does not have to constitute itself as a doctrine; except for some rare exceptions (such as New Criticism in the American tradition or the 'hermeneutical' in the German tradition), it most often remains in an implicit state and is perpetuated subterraneously beyond (and through) apparent renovations of the academic liturgy such as 'structural' or 'deconstructionist' readings of texts treated as perfectly self-sufficient.[32] But it may also rely on the commentary on canons of 'pure' reading which are enunciated at the very core of the literary field, for example by T. S. Eliot in *The Sacred Wood* (which describes the literary world as 'autotelic') or by the writers of the *NRF* (*Nouvelle Revue Française*) and especially Paul Valéry, or again, it may rely on a soft eclectic combination of discourses on art derived from Kant, from Roman Imgarden, the Russian Formalists and the structuralists of the Prague School, such as in the *Theory of Literature* by René Wellek and Austin Warren, which claims to separate out the essence of literary language (connotative, expressive, etc.) and to define the necessary conditions of the aesthetic experience.

These approaches to literature owe their apparent universality only to the fact that they are upheld almost everywhere by the scholastic institution of the teaching of literature, that is to say, they are rooted in manuals or *textbooks* (such as the collection by Cleanth Brooks and Robert Penn Warren entitled *Understanding Poetry* which reigned in American colleges well beyond the year of its first publication in 1938), and also in habits of thought among the professors who find in them a justification for their practice of reading decontextualized texts. Proof of this relationship of cause and effect may be seen in the resemblances to be observed between the practices and 'theories' which crop up, like simultaneous inventions, in the scholarly institutions of different nations. I am thinking of detailed 'explication' or the 'close reading' of poems understood as 'logic structure' and 'local texture', which is extolled by John Crowe Ransom,[33] and, more generally, of those professions of literary faith, as innumerable as they are indistinguishable, which assert that the only purpose of a poem is the poem itself as a self-sufficient structure of significations. One would have to cite here, pell-mell, the defenders of New Criticism – John Crowe Ransom, already mentioned, Cleanth Brooks, Allen Tate, etc., and the 'Chicago Critics', who see a poem as an 'artistic whole', the depository of a 'power' whose causes the critic must seek in the interrelations and the structure of the poem, independently of all reference to external factors (the biography of the author, the public addressed, etc.) – and the English critic F. R. Leavis, very close to his American contemporaries in his practices and his premises and also in the immense hold he exercised on universities, British ones in this case. It would be necessary also to cite, for the German tradition, the whole litany of expositions of the hermeneutic 'method' (of which one can get an idea by reading the historical account offered by Peter Szondi[34]). Finally, one would have to mention, for the French tradition, all the professorial (and other) professions of formalist (or internalist) faith, without overlooking the modernized versions of the famous 'explication de textes' brought about by the structuralist *aggiornamento*. But nothing is more liable to convince us of the ritual character of all these practices, and all these discourses designed to regulate and justify them, than the extraordinary tolerance of repetition, redundancy and the monotony of the liturgical litany manifest in all these interpreters, who are nevertheless totally devoted to the cult of originality.

If one wishes to ground this tradition in theory, it seems to me that one could look in two directions: on the one hand, to the neo-Kantian philosophy of symbolic forms, and more generally all the traditions which assert the existence of universal anthropological structures, such as the comparative mythology of Mircea Eliade or Jungian psychoanalysis (or, in France, Bachelardian psychoanalysis); and on the other, to the structuralist tradition. In the first case, literature is conceived of as a 'form of knowledge' (W. K. Wimsatt) different from the scientific form, and the purpose of internal and moral reading is to regrasp the universal forms of literary reason, of 'literarity' in its different species, poetic especially – that is to say, the ahistoric structuring structures which are at the root of the literary or poetic construction of the world, or, more banally, something like the 'essences' of the 'literary', of the 'poetic' or of figures like the metaphor.

The structuralist solution is much more powerful, intellectually and socially. Socially, it has often taken over from the internalist *doxa* and conferred an aura of scientificity on professorial commentary as a formal taking apart of decontextualized and detemporalized texts. Breaking with universalism, Saussurean theory apprehends cultural works (languages, myths, structured structures without a structuring subject, and also, by extension, works of art) as historical products whose specific structure must be brought out by analysis, but without making reference to the economic or social conditions of the production of the work or of its producers. But even if it vaunts its connection with structural linguistics, structural semiology only retains the second presupposition: it tends to bracket the historicity of cultural works and, from Jakobson to Genette, it treats the literary object as an autonomous entity, subject to its own laws and owing its 'literariness' or 'poeticity' to the particular treatment given to its linguistic material, that is to say, to the techniques and procedures which are responsible for the predominance of the aesthetic function of language – techniques such as parallels, oppositions and equivalencies between the phonetic, morphological, syntactic and even semantic levels of the poem.

From the same perspective, the Russian Formalists establish a fundamental opposition between literary (or poetic) language and ordinary language. While the latter, 'practical' and 'referential', communicates by references to the external world, literary language takes advantage of diverse procedures to foreground the enunciated itself, in order to distance ordinary discourse and to turn attention away from external referents and towards its 'formal' structures. In the same way, the French structuralists treat the work of art as a mode of writing which, like the linguistic system that it utilizes, is an auto-referential structure of interrelations constituted by a play of specific literary conventions and 'codes'. And Genette points out the postulate involved in these analyses of *essence* (the outcome, in Jakobson, of the combined influence of Saussure and Husserl and *fundamentally anti-genetic*) when he suggests that everything that is constitutive of a discourse is manifest in the linguistic properties of the text and that the work itself furnishes information on the manner in which it ought to be read. The *absolutization* of the text could not be pushed any farther.

By a strange turn of events, 'creative' criticism today seeks a solution to the crisis of the profoundly anti-genetic formalism of structuralist semiology by returning to the positivism of the most traditional literary historiography, with a form of criticism labelled, by a misnomer, 'literary genetics', 'a scientific approach possessing its own techniques (the analysis of manuscripts) and project of elucidation (the genesis of the work)'.[35] Jumping without other form of proof from the *post hoc* to the *propter hoc*, this 'methodology' searches in what Gérard Genette calls the 'avant-texte' for the genesis of the text. The rough draft, the outline, the sketch – in short anything that can be lifted from notebooks and jotting books – is constituted as the unique and ultimate object of the search for the scientific explanation.[36] Thus it is difficult to see what differentiates those such as Durry, Bruneau, Gothot-Mersch, Sherrington, as authors of minute analyses of Flaubert's plans, projects or scenarios, from the new 'genetic critics' who do the same thing (they ask very seriously whether 'Flaubert had begun to prepare *Sentimental Education* in 1862 or in 1863') but with the feeling of effecting 'a sort of revolution in literary studies'.[37] The gap between the programme of a true genetic analysis of the author and of the work such as it is defined here (and partially put into operation in this book) and the analysis, founded on the comparison of successive states and stages of the work, of the manner in which the work is fabricated ought to suggest (better, it seems to me, than all critical discourse) the *limits* of a *textual genetics*, justified in itself but risking presenting a new obstacle to a rigorous science of literature. (I could also, at the risk of seeming unjust, invoke the disproportion between the immensity of the work of erudition involved and the slightness of the results obtained.) In fact, if one brings this project back to the truth of it, one may see in the rigorous and methodical edition of preparatory texts a precious material for the analysis of the *work of writing* (one gains nothing except confusion by calling it 'editorial genesis'). And it is in just this fashion that Pierre-Marc de Biasi treats the notebooks of the *Education* when he observes, for example, how Flaubert develops an entirely neutral observation on the trade in knives and blades in the streets of Paris shortly before the uprising of June 1848 in order to make of it, by the effect of suggestion in the writing, the mysterious sign of a general plot, designed to nourish the anxieties of Dambreuse and of Martinon.[38]

But the analysis of the successive versions of a text could not take on its full explanatory force unless it tried to *reconstruct* (no doubt a little artificially) the logic of the labour of writing understood as a search accomplished under the structural constraint of the field and the space of possibles it offers. One could better understand the hesitations, the regrets, the returns by knowing that the writing, a perilous navigation in a universe of threats and dangers, is also guided, in its negative dimension, by an anticipated knowledge of probable reception, inscribed in a state of potentiality in the field; and that, similar to the *pirate, peiratès*, someone who tries for a coup, who attempts something new (*peirao*), the writer as conceived of by Flaubert is one who adventures outside the channels marked out by buoys for routine use and one who is expert in the art of finding a passage through the perils consisting of the *common places*, the 'accepted ideas', the conventional forms.

In fact, it is probably in Michel Foucault that one finds the most rigorous formulation of the foundations of the structural analysis of cultural works. Conscious that no cultural work exists by itself, that is, outside the relations of interdependence that unite it to other works, he gives the name 'field of strategic possibilities' to the 'regulated system of differences and dispersions' within which each individual work defines itself.[39] But, very close to the semiologists such as Trier and the uses they have made of the idea of 'semantic field', he explicitly refuses to search outside the 'field of discourse' for the principle which would elucidate each of the discourses within it: 'If the Physiocrats' analysis belongs to the same discourses as that of the Utilitarians, this is not because they lived in the same period, nor because they confronted one another within the same society, nor because their interests interlocked within the same economy; but because their two options sprang from one and the same distribution of the points of choice, from one and the same strategic field.'

Thus, faithful in this respect to the Saussurean tradition and to the rupture it effects between internal linguistics and external linguistics, Foucault asserts the absolute autonomy of the 'field of strategic possibilities'. He rejects as a 'doxological illusion' the endeavour to find in 'the field of polemics' or in 'the divergences of interests or mental habits of individuals' (all of what I put, more or less at the same time, into the notions of field and of habitus) the explanatory principle of what happens in the 'field of strategic possibilities'. That appears to him to be determined solely by the 'strategic possibilities of the conceptual games', according to him the sole reality which a science of works can seek to know. In this way, he transfers to the firmament of ideas oppositions and antagonisms that are rooted (without being reduced to them) in the relations between producers and he rejects any relating of works to the social conditions of their production (as he will later continue to do in a critical discourse on knowledge and power which – for want of taking into account agents and their interests, and especially violence in its symbolic dimension – remains abstract and idealist).

Of course, it is not a matter of denying the determination exercised by the space of possibles and the specific logic of the sequences in and through which novelties (artistic, literary or scientific) are engendered, since it is one of the functions of the notion of a relatively autonomous field, one endowed with its own history, to take account of them. Nevertheless, it is not possible, even in the case of the scientific field, to treat the cultural order (the *épistèmè*) as totally independent of the agents and institutions which actualize it and bring it into existence, and to ignore the socio-logical connections which accompany or underwrite logical sequences; this would be at the very least to prevent oneself from taking into account changes which happen to occur in this arbitrarily separated (and therefore dehistoricized and de-realized) universe – unless one grants the cultural order an immanent propensity to transform itself by a mysterious form of *Selbstbewegung* which finds its principle only in its internal contradictions, as did Hegel (who is also present in that other presupposition of the notion of *épistèmè*, the belief in the cultural unity of an era and a society).

One must resign oneself to admitting that there is a history of reason which does not have reason as its (sole) principle. In order to account for the fact that art – or science – seems to find within itself the principle and the form of its changing, and that everything happens as if history were interior to the system and as if the coming-into-being of forms of representation or expression merely expressed the internal logic of the system, it is not necessary to hypostasize (as has often been done) the laws of this evolution. 'The action of works upon works' of which Brunetière spoke is only ever exercised by the intermediary of authors whose strategies are also guided by the interests linked to their position in the structure of the field.

To think of each of the spaces of cultural production as a field is to preclude any form of reductionism, any *flattening projection* of one space on to another which leads to thinking of the different fields and their products in terms of foreign categories (in the manner of those who make philosophy a 'reflection' of science, deducing, for example, the metaphysics from the physics, etc.).[40] And one must in the same way scientifically put to the test that 'cultural unity' of an epoch and a society which the history of art and of literature accepts as a tacit assumption, through a sort of diluted Hegelianism[41] or (but is this not the same thing?) in the name of a more or less renovated form of culturalism, even if it be the kind for which Foucault found the theoretical guarantee in the notion of *épistèmè*, a sort of *Wissenschaftswollen*, very close to the old notion of *Kunstwollen*.[42] It would be a matter of examining, for each of the historical configurations considered, on the one hand the structural homologies between different fields which may underlie encounters or correspondences with no borrowing involved; and on the other hand those direct exchanges which depend, in their form and very existence, on the positions occupied in their respective fields by the agents or institutions concerned, and hence on the structure of those fields, and also on the relative positions of the fields in the hierarchy established among them at the moment under consideration, determining all sorts of effects of symbolic domination.[43]

By choosing to dissect and construct the subject on the basis of either a geographical unity (Basle, Berlin, Paris or Vienna) or a political one, there is the risk of returning to a definition of unity in terms of *Zeitgeist*. In effect, one tacitly assumes that the members of a single 'intellectual community' have in common certain problems linked to a common situation – for example, an interrogation of the relations between appearance and reality – and also that the members mutually 'influence each other'. If one realizes that each field – music, painting, poetry, or in another order, economy, linguistics, biology, etc. – has its autonomous history, which determines its specific rules and stakes, one sees that the interpretation by reference to the history unique to the field (or to the discipline) is the preliminary for an interpretation with respect to the contemporary context, whether one is dealing with other fields of cultural production or with political and economic production. The fundamental question then becomes to know whether the *social effects of chronological contemporaneity, or even spatial unity* – like the fact of sharing the same specific meeting places (literary cafés, magazines, cultural associations, salons, etc.) or of being exposed to the same cultural messages, common works of reference, obligatory issues, key events, etc. – are strong enough to determine, over and above the autonomy of different fields, a common problematic, understood not as a *Zeitgeist* or a community of spirit or lifestyle, but rather as a space of possibles, a system of different position-takings in relation to which each must be defined. This brings up in a direct way the question of national traditions linked to the pre-eminence of state structures (notably scholastic) which lend themselves to the promotion to a greater or lesser degree of the pre-eminence of a central cultural site, of a cultural capital, and to encouraging more or less adequately the specialization within it (of genres, disciplines, etc.), or which, on the contrary, lend themselves to an interaction between members of different fields, or to consecrating a particular configuration of the hierarchical structure of the arts (with a predominance permanently or temporarily given to one of them – music, painting or literature) or of the scientific disciplines.

These disparities between hierarchies may be the basis of dissonances often imputed to the 'national character' and they help to explain the different forms taken by the international circulation of ideas, fashions and intellectual models. An example is the primacy accorded in France, at least until the middle of the twentieth century, to literature and to the figure of the writer (in contrast to criticism and erudition, which are often treated as pedantic), a primacy which time and again goes right to the heart of the school system in the shape of a series of oppositions between literature (*agrégation de lettres*) and philology (*agrégation de grammaire*), between discourse and erudition, between 'brilliance' and 'seriousness', between bourgeoisie and petite bourgeoisie, and one which governs all the relations throughout the nineteenth century which individual agents manage to maintain with the German model. The hierarchy among disciplines (literature/philology) is so strongly identified with the hierarchy among nations (France/Germany) that those who would like to invert such a relation, one which is politically overdetermined, are suspected of a sort of treason (one thinks of the nationalist polemics of Agathon against the Nouvelle Sorbonne).

The same critique applies to the Russian Formalists.[44] Refusing to consider anything other than the system of works, that is, the 'network of relationships established between texts' (and secondarily, the relationships, incidentally very abstractly defined, between this network and other 'systems' functioning in the 'system-of-systems' constituting society – not so far from Talcott Parsons), these theoreticians are also forced to find in the 'literary system' itself the principle of its dynamics. Thus, even if it does not escape their notice that this 'literary system' (far from being a balanced and harmonious structure in the manner of Saussurean language) is the site, at any one time, of tensions between opposed literary schools, the canonized and the non-canonized, and presents itself as an unstable equilibrium between opposed tendencies, they continue (especially Tynianov) to believe in the immanent development of this system and, like Michel Foucault, they remain very close to the Saussurean philosophy of history when they assert that everything which is literary (or, with Foucault, scientific) can be determined only by previous states of the 'literary (or scientific) system'.[45]

Refusing to seek, like Weber, the principle of change in the struggles between the orthodox which 'routinizes' and heresy which 'de-banalizes', they are obliged to turn the process of 'automatization' and 'de-automatization' (or 'de-banalization' – *ostranenie*) into a sort of natural law of poetic change and, more generally, of all cultural change – as if 'de-automatization' would automatically result in 'automatization', which is itself born of a wear-and-tear linked to a repetitive use of the means of literary expression (destined to become 'as scarcely perceptible as the grammatical forms of language'). 'Evolution', writes Tynianov, 'is caused by the need for ceaseless dynamics. Every dynamic system inevitably becomes automatized and an opposite constructive principle dialectically arises.'[46] The almost tautological character of these propositions, couched in terms of a dormant virtue, inevitably flows from the confusion of two planes, the plane of works which, by a generalization of the theory of parody, are described as *referring themselves* back to one another (which is effectively one of the properties of works produced within a field), and the plane of objective positions in the field of production and the antagonistic interests based on them. (This confusion, exactly the same as that of Foucault when he speaks of the 'strategic field' with regard to the field of works, is found symbolized and condensed in the ambiguity of the concept of *ustanovka*, which could be translated both as position and position-taking, understood as the act of 'positioning oneself with reference to some given data'.[47])

While there is no doubt that the orientation and the form of change depend on the 'state of the system', that is, on the repertory of actual and virtual possibilities that are offered at a given moment by the space of cultural position-takings (works, schools, exemplary figures, available genres and forms, etc.), they depend also and above all on the relations of symbolic force between agents and institutions. Having totally vital interests in the possibilities offered as instruments and stakes in the struggle, these agents and institutions use all the powers at their disposal to activate those which seem the most in accord with their specific intentions and interests.

As for external analysis, whether it treats cultural works as simple reflection or as 'symbolic expression' of the social world (in the phrase used by Engels with respect to the law), it relates them directly to the social characteristics of the authors, or of the groups to whom they were addressed or were assumed to be addressed, and regards them as expressing those social characteristics. To reintroduce the field of cultural production as an autonomous social universe is to get away from the *reduction* effected by all forms, whether more or less refined, of the 'reflection' theory which subtends Marxist analyses of cultural works, and in particular those of Lukács and Goldmann, and which is never completely spelt out, perhaps because it would not withstand the test of being made explicit.

It is presupposed, in effect, that understanding the work of art would mean understanding the vision of the world belonging to a social group which has figured either as starting point or as intended recipient for the artist in composing the work. This group, whether patron or recipient, cause or end, or both at the same time, would be in some way expressed through the artist, who would be able to make explicit (without being aware of it) truths and values of which the group being expressed is not necessarily conscious. But what group are we speaking of? The one from which the artist comes – and which might not coincide with the group from which his or her public is recruited – or the group which is the principal or privileged recipient of the work – which supposes that there is always a single and only one? Nothing permits us to suppose that the declared recipient, when one exists, whether patron or one to whom the work is dedicated, would be the true addressee of the work, or in any case that that person acts as an efficient cause or as a final cause in the production of the work. At the very most, this person could be the circumstantial cause of a labour which finds its basis in the whole structure and history of the field of production, and *through it* in the whole structure and history of the social world under consideration.

To thus bracket out the specific logic and history of the field in order to relate the work directly to the group to which it is objectively destined, and to make the artist the unconscious spokesperson of a social group to which the work of art would reveal what it unwittingly thought or felt, is to force oneself back on assertions to which metaphysics would not object: 'Between such an art and such a social situation, could there be anything but a fortuitous encounter? Of course, Fauré did not wish it so, but his *Madrigal* manifestly created a diversion in the year when unionization was recognized, the year in which 42,000 workers at Anzin launched a 46-day strike. He offers individual love as if to curb class warfare. In the final analysis, one might say that the grande bourgeoisie required of its musicians that their dream factories furnish the dreams it needed politically and socially.'[48] To understand the social significations of a piece by Fauré or a poem by Mallarmé without reducing them to the function of compensatory escapism, of denial of social reality, of a flight into lost paradises (which they share with many other forms of expression) would mean first of all to determine everything which is inscribed within the position from which they are produced. This means their position in poetry as it is defined around the 1880s, at the end of a continual movement of purification and sublimation which was begun in the 1830s with Théophile Gautier and the preface to *Mademoiselle de Maupin*, extended by Baudelaire and Parnassus, and brought right up to its most evanescent limit with Mallarmé. It would mean determining as well what this position owes to the negative relation which sets it against the naturalist novel, and what conversely brings it closer to all the manifestations of reaction against naturalism, scientism and positivism: for example, the psychological novel (obviously in the forefront), the denunciation of positivism in philosophy with Fouillée, Lachelier and Boutroux, the revelation of the Russian novel and its mysticism with Melchior de Vogüé, the conversions to Catholicism, etc. Finally, it would mean determining what in the familial and personal trajectory of Mallarmé or Fauré predisposed them to occupy, in fulfilling it, that social role progressively fashioned by its successive occupants, and in particular the relationship, examined by Rémy Ponton,[49] between a declining social trajectory which condemns the poet to the 'hideous work of a pedagogue' and his pessimism, or hermetic (meaning anti-pedagogic) use of language, itself a manner of breaking with a rejected social reality. We would still have to explain the 'coincidence' between the product of that ensemble of specific factors and the diffuse demands of a declining aristocracy and a threatened bourgeoisie, and in particular their nostalgia for former pomp which is equally expressed in the taste for the things of the eighteenth century and in the flight into mysticism and irrationalism. In any case, the convergence of independent causal series and the appearance it gives of a pre-established harmony between the properties of the work and the social experience of privileged consumers appear like a trap waiting for those who want to avoid the internal reading of the work or the internal history of the artistic life, and so proceed to put the epoch and the work into direct relationship with each other, with both reduced to a few schematic properties selected for the purpose at hand.

Exclusive attention to functions (which the internalist tradition, and in particular structuralism, were undoubtedly wrong to neglect) tends to ignore the question of the internal logic of cultural objects, their structure as language, to which the structuralist tradition gives exclusive attention. More profoundly, it leads to an omission of the agents and institutions which produce these objects – priests, jurists, writers or artists – and for whom they also fulfil functions which are defined, essentially, within the universe of producers. Max Weber has the merit of illuminating, in the particular case of religion, the role of specialists and their own interests; however, he always remains enclosed in the Marxist logic of research into functions which (even when precisely formulated) do not teach us very much about the structure of the religious message itself. But, above all, Weber does not perceive that the universes of specialists function like relatively autonomous microcosms, structured spaces (hence spaces amenable to structural analysis, but of another type) of objective relations between positions – that of the prophet and that of the priest or that of the consecrated artist and that of the avant-garde artist, for example. These relations are the true principle of the position-takings of different producers, of the competition which pits them against each other, of the alliances they form, of the works they produce or defend.

The efficacy of external factors, economic crises, technical transformations, political revolutions, or quite simply social demand on the part of a particular category of patrons, of which traditional social history seeks the direct manifestation in the works, can only be exercised by the intermediary of the transformations of the structure of the field which these factors may determine.

One may, by way of an illuminating analogy, evoke the notion of 'the Republic of Letters' and recognize in the description offered by Bayle several of the fundamental properties of the literary field (the war of all against all, the closing in of the field upon itself, etc.): 'Liberty is what reigns in the Republic of Letters. This Republic is an extremely free state. In it the only empire is that of truth and reason; and under their auspices, war is naively waged against just about anybody. Friends must be on their guard against friends, fathers against children, fathers-in-law against sons-in-law: it is a century of iron [. . .]. In it everyone is both sovereign and accountable to everyone else.'[50] But, as the half-positive, half-normative tone of this literary evocation of the literary milieu shows, this is a notion of spontaneous sociology and in no way a constructed concept and it has never provided a foundation for a rigorous analysis of the functioning of the literary world or for the methodical interpretation of the production and circulation of works (as those who rediscover it today would have us believe). In addition, this image (useful only because it spots a true structural homology, as ordinary intuition often does) can become dangerous if it leads to ignoring everything, beyond the analogies within difference, separating the literary field from the political field (the same evasiveness burdens the notion of the avant-garde). In effect, even if one finds in the literary field all the traits characteristic of the functioning of political and economic fields, and more generally of all fields – relationships of force, capital, strategies, interests – there is not a single one of the phenomena designated by these concepts which does not appear in a completely specific form, completely irreducible to the corresponding traits in the political field, for example.

Even further away, the notion of *art world*, which is in use in the United States in sociological and philosophical fields, is inspired by a social philosophy completely opposed to that which informs the idea of the Republic of Letters as Bayle presents it, and marks a regression in relation to the theory of the field as I proposed it. Suggesting that 'works of art can be understood by viewing them as the result of the coordinated activities of all the people whose cooperation is necessary in order that the work should occur as it does,' Howard S. Becker concludes that the enquiry must extend to all those who contribute to this result, meaning 'people who conceive the idea of the work (e.g. composers or playwrights); people who execute it (musicians or actors); people who provide the necessary equipment (e.g. musical instrument makers); and people who make up the audience for the work (playgoers, critics, and so on).'[51] Without entering into a methodical exposé of everything that separates this vision of the 'world of art' from the theory of the literary or artistic field, I will merely remark that the latter is not reducible to a *population*, that is to say, to the sum of individual agents linked by simple relations of *interaction* or, more precisely, of *cooperation*: what is lacking, among other things, from this purely descriptive and enumerative evocation are the *objective relations* which are constitutive of the structure of the field and which orient the struggles aiming to conserve or transform it.

Bypassing the alternatives

The notion of field allows us to bypass the opposition between internal reading and external analysis without losing any of the benefits and exigencies of these two approaches which are traditionally perceived as irreconcilable. Keeping what is inscribed in the notion of intertextuality, meaning the fact that the space of works always appears as a field of position-takings which can only be understood in terms of relationships, as a system of differential variations, one may offer the hypothesis (confirmed by empirical analysis) of a homology between the space of works defined by their essentially symbolic content, and in particular by their *form*, and the space of positions in the field of production. For example, free verse defines itself against the alexandrine and everything it implies aesthetically, but also socially and even politically. In effect, the interplay of homologies between the literary field and the field of power or the social field in its entirety means that most literary strategies are overdetermined and a number of 'choices' hit two targets at once, aesthetic and political, internal and external.

Thus the opposition (often described as an insurmountable antinomy) between structure, which is apprehended synchronically, and history is at last overcome. The motor of change or, more precisely, the motor of the properly literary process of automatization and de-automatization described by the Russian Formalists is not inscribed in the works themselves but in the opposition – which is constitutive of all fields of cultural production, even if it appears in its paradigmatic form in the religious field – between orthodoxy and heresy. It is significant that in speaking of the priesthood and prophets, Weber also refers to *Veralltäglichung* and *Ausseralltäglichung*, meaning banalization and de-banalization, routinization and de-routinization. The process in which works are caught up is the product of the struggle between those who espouse conservatism because of the dominant position they temporarily occupy in the field (by virtue of their specific capital), that is to say, they defend routine and routinization, the banal and banalization, in a word, they defend the established symbolic order, and those who are inclined to a heretical rupture, to the critique of established forms, to the subversion of the prevailing models and to a return to the purity of origins. In fact, only knowledge of the structure can provide the tools of a true knowledge of the processes which lead to a new state of the structure and which thereby also comprise the means of comprehending this new structure.

It is certain that, as symbolic structuralism (such as Michel Foucault defines it in the case of science) reminds us, the direction of change depends on the state of the system of possibilities (conceptual, stylistic, etc.) inherited from history. It is these possibilities which define what it is possible or not possible to think or do at a given moment in any determined field. But it is no less certain that the direction of change also depends on the interests (often completely disinterested according to the canons of ordinary existence) guiding agents, as a function of their position in the social structure of the field of production, towards this one or that one among the offered possibles or, more exactly, towards a region of the space of possibles which is comparable to the one they occupy in the space of artistic positions.

In short, the strategies of agents and institutions engaged in literary or artistic struggles are not defined by a pure confrontation with pure possibles. Rather, they depend on the position these agents occupy in the structure of the field (that is to say, in the structure of the distribution of specific capital) or the recognition, institutionalized or not, which is granted to them by their competitor-peers and by the public as a whole, and which influences their perception of the possibles offered by the field and their 'choice' of those they will try to make into reality or produce. But, conversely, the stakes of the struggle between dominants and pretenders, the issues they dispute, the very theses and antitheses they throw at each other, depend on the state of the legitimate problematic, that is, the space of the possibilities bequeathed by previous struggles, a space which tends to give direction to the search for solutions and, consequently, influences the present and future of production.

To objectify the subject of objectification

At the end of this effort to apply the principle of reflexivity by trying to objectify (retrospectively) the space of possibles in relation to which a method of analysis of cultural works has been constituted which brings to light, precisely, the decisive function of that space of possibles in the construction of any cultural work, it is hoped that a convincing case has been made that the *instrument of rupture* with all partial visions is indeed the idea of the field. It is this (or, more precisely, the labour of constructing the object whose programme it defines) that offers the real possibility of taking a point of view on the ensemble of viewpoints which come into being through it. This labour of objectification, when it applies, as it does here, to the very field in which the subject of the objectification is situated, allows us to achieve a scientific point of view on the empirical viewpoint of the scholar – which, being thus objectivized in the same way as other points of view, with all its determinations and limits, finds itself opened up to methodical criticism.

It is by giving oneself the scientific means to take one's own naive viewpoint as object that the scientific subject truly effects the break with the empirical subject, and simultaneously with other agents who (whether professionals or not) remain enclosed within a point of view of which they are unaware. The reason it is sometimes so difficult to communicate the results of truly reflexive research is because readers must be persuaded not to see as an 'attack' or a 'criticism' (in the ordinary sense) what is intended to be an analysis; they must accept that they have to turn on to their own viewpoints that objectifying point of view which is fundamental to the analysis, and associate themselves, notably by submitting to a critique founded on the acceptance of its premises, with a liberating effort to objectify all objectifications, instead of challenging its fundamentals by reducing them to an attempt to give the appearance of scientific universality to a particular point of view.

To adopt the viewpoint of reflexivity is not to renounce objectivity, but to question the privilege of the knowing subject, which the anti-genetic vision arbitrarily frees, as purely noetic, from the labour of objectification. To adopt this viewpoint is to strive to account for the empirical 'subject' in the very terms of the objectivity constructed by the scientific subject (notably by situating it in a determined place in social space–time) and thereby to give oneself awareness and (possible) mastery of the constraints which may be exercised on the scientific subject via all the ties which attach it to the empirical 'subject', to its interests, motives, assumptions, beliefs, its *doxa*, and which it must break in order to constitute itself. It is not sufficient to seek within the subject, as the classical philosophy of knowledge teaches us, for the preconditions of possibility (and also the limits) of the objective knowledge that the subject establishes. One must also search within the object constructed by science for the *social conditions of possibility of the scholarly subject* (for example, the *skholè* and the whole heritage of problems, concepts, methods, etc., which render its activity possible) and the possible limits of its acts of objectification.

This totally unprecedented form of reflection leads to repudiating the absolutist pretensions of classical objectivity, but without being then condemned to relativism. In effect, the conditions of possibility of the scientific subject and those of its object are one and the same; to any progress in the knowledge of the social conditions of production of scientific subjects corresponds progress in the knowledge of the scientific object, and vice versa. This is never as well observed as when research takes as its object the scientific field itself, that is to say, the veritable *subject* of scientific knowledge.

Appendix

The Total Intellectual and
the Illusion of the Omnipotence
of Thought

The illusion of limitless thought is never as visible as in the analysis that Sartre devotes to Flaubert's work, where he reveals the limits of the comprehension that he can have of another intellectual, that is, of himself as an intellectual. This dream of omnipotence is rooted in the unprecedented social position that Sartre constructed by concentrating within a single person an ensemble of intellectual and social powers which had until then been split up.[52] Transgressing the invisible, but almost unbridgeable, frontier which separated professors, philosophers and critics from writers, petit-bourgeois 'speculators' from bourgeois 'inheritors', academic prudence from artistic audacity, erudition from inspiration, the heaviness of the concept from the elegance of the writing, but also reflexivity from naiveté, Sartre truly invented and incarnated the figure of the *total intellectual*, the thinker-writer, metaphysician-novelist and artist-philosopher who brings to the political struggles of the time all the authority and abilities combined in his person. This has the effect, among other things, of authorizing him to establish an asymmetric relationship as much with the philosophers as with the writers, present or past, setting out to think them through more ably than they could themselves, by making the experience of the intellectual and of his social status the privileged object of an analysis which he believes is perfectly lucid.

The philosophical 'revolution' against philosophies of knowledge (symbolized by Léon Brunschwicg) goes hand in hand with the 'revolution' in the writing of philosophy. The operation of the Husserlian theory of intentionality – which leads to substituting for the closed world of consciousness knowing itself the open world of the consciousness which 'bursts upon' things, upon the world and others – involves the eruption into philosophical discourse of a whole universe of new objects (such as the celebrated café waiter) which had been excluded from the rather confined atmosphere of 'academic' philosophy and reserved until then for writers. It also calls for a new, openly literary manner of speaking about unexpected objects. And also for a new lifestyle: the philosopher writes, in the tradition of the writer, at café tables. As is manifest in his choice of Gallimard, the bastion of pure literature, to publish the philosophical writings previously entrusted to Alcan, ancestor of the Presses Universitaires de France, Sartre abolishes the frontier between literary philosophy and philosophical literature, between the effects of 'literariness' authorized by phenomenological analysis and the effects of depth guaranteed by existential analyses within a metaphysical novel such as *La Nausée* or *Le Mur*. By dramatizing and vulgarizing philosophical themes, plays with a thesis like *Huit clos* or *Le Diable et le Bon Dieu* were predisposed to enter into both bourgeois conversation and philosophy courses.

Traditionally entrusted to university people, criticism is the indispensable accompaniment of that profound transformation of the structure of the division of intellectual work. In the course of years of apprenticeship, Sartre finds in the analysis of his chosen authors, all foreign to the scholarly pantheon, an opportunity (if a slightly academic one) to stake out and assimilate the techniques constitutive of the 'calling' of avant-garde writer, integrating the influences of Céline, Joyce, Kafka and Faulkner in a literary form which is immediately, and justly, recognized as very 'classical'. Therefore, Sartre did not effect in the novel the revolution of forms called for in his critiques in *Situations* any more than he did in the theatre, where he remains closer to Giraudoux (another writer bred in the École Normale Supérieure) or, in a strict sense, to Brecht – for *Les Séquestrés d'Altona* – than to Ionesco or to Beckett. However, critical discourse allows him to give the flavour of an analyst's report to his imposition of a new definition of the writer and of the novelistic form. In writing in an article about Faulkner that a novelistic technique implies a metaphysics, he sets himself up as the holder of a monopoly of legitimacy with respect to the novel, against people like Gide, Mauriac and Malraux, since he is the only one who has credentials as a metaphysician. The auto-legitimating function of criticism is clearly seen when, skirting polemic, it is applied to his most immediate rivals, such as Camus, Blanchot or Bataille, claimants to the dominant position, where there is only room for one, and to the correlative emblems and attributes that go with it, such as the right to claim the heritage of Kafka, the metaphysical novelist *par excellence*.

The strategies of distinction made possible by criticism owe their particular effectiveness to the fact that they rely on a 'total' oeuvre which gives its author the right to import into each domain the totality of the technical and symbolic capital acquired in others, metaphysics into the novel or philosophy into the theatre, simultaneously defining rivals as partial intellectuals, or even truncated ones: Merleau-Ponty, despite several excursions into criticism, is only a philosopher; Camus, having naively betrayed in *Le Mythe de*

Sisyphe and *L'Homme révolté* that he had nothing much of the professional philosopher about him, is only a novelist; Blanchot is only a critic and Bataille an essayist; not to mention Aron, disqualified in any case for not having taken up that other obligatory component of the figure of the total intellectual – political engagement (on the Left).

With the ground prepared by critical essays and philosophical manifestos before the Second World War, and also by the great success of *La Nausée*, which was immediately recognized as a 'magisterial' synthesis of literature and philosophy, the concentration of all the kinds of intellectual capital characterizing the figure of the total intellectual reaches completion in the immediate postwar period with the creation of *Les Temps Modernes*. The 'intellectual review', as the composition of the editorial board shows, gathers under Sartre's banner the living representatives of all the intellectual traditions integrated in the oeuvre and person of the founder, and allows the Sartrean project of thinking through all aspects of existence to be established in a collective programme ('we should miss nothing of our era,' as the 'editorial presentation' put it) and all intellectual production to be thus given an orientation, as much in its form as in its themes.

But the reconciliation of all genres of production performed by Sartre remains a particular form of philosophical ambition, growing out of the intersection of two phenomenologies, that of Hegel, read by Kojève, and that of Husserl, revised by Heidegger. Through the philosopher-writer, a philosophy which (with Kant notably) had been asserted against 'worldly' compromises obtains in the intellectual field as a whole the hegemonic position it had always claimed – without ever truly winning it except in the university field. One realizes that the will to totalization, the form which the ambition for absolute power takes in the intellectual field, is never asserted more clearly than in philosophical works, and first of all in *L'Être et le Néant*, the first affirmation of the claim to unsurpassable thought (which will find its absolute weapon in the omnivorous dialectic of *La Critique de la raison dialectique*, the ultimate effort to maintain a threatened intellectual power). The very size of the book, similar to that of compendiums or treatises,. the amplitude of the field of vision and the universe of objects taken up (in appearance coextensive with life itself, in fact very classical and very near to a broadened scholarly tradition), the supreme loftiness (marked among other signs by the absence of references) of the confrontation with authors of the highest rank (Hegel, Husserl, or Heidegger) and especially perhaps the pretension to surpass everything and conserve everything, starting with competing systems of thought such as psychoanalysis or the social sciences – everything in this book attests to the will to institute philosophy as the founding authority, founded to reign without competition over all terrains of existence and of thought, to instal itself as transcendent authority, capable of delivering to any person, institution or system of thought to which it is applied a truth about itself of which it has been dispossessed.

Having become the incarnation of the total intellectual, Sartre could not avoid encountering the demands of political involvement inscribed in the personage of the intellectual since Zola together with the vocation to moral magisterium which was so completely constitutive of the figure of the dominant intellectual that it had once imposed itself on Gide himself. Thrown into politics – this means, in the quasi-revolutionary period after the end of the Second World War, into the Communist Party – he finds once again, in the typically philosophical strategy of a radical superseding of what went before by a critical questioning of fundamentals (which he will employ once again with respect to Marxism and the human sciences), a method of giving a theoretically acceptable form to the relationship of mutual legitimation that he endeavours to establish with the party (in the fashion of the prewar Surrealists, but in a very different intellectual atmosphere and in a very different state of the Communist Party). The free assent of the high-flying 'fellow traveller' is not at all the unconditional handing over of self (fine for the proletariat, in line with the equation: 'The Party *is* the proletariat' . . .) that some have occasionally wanted to see in it: it is in fact what permits the intellectual to establish himself as the founding conscience of the party, and to place himself with respect to the party and the 'people' in a relationship which is that of the For-oneself (*Pour-soi*) to the In-oneself (*En-soi*), and thus be assured of a certificate of revolutionary virtue while safeguarding the full freedom of an elective adherence, the only kind seen as capable of grounding itself in reason. This distance from all established positions and from those who occupy them, whether communists of the *Nouvelle Critique* or Catholics of *Esprit*, is what defines the 'free intellectual', and its ontological transfiguration, the For-oneself.

One might in effect show that the fundamental categories of Sartrean ontology, the Pour-soi and En-soi, are a sublimated form of the antithesis (which haunts Sartre's whole work) between the 'intellectual' and the 'bourgeois' or the people. As a 'bastard' without justification, a thin film of nothingness and freedom between the bourgeois (the 'skunks' of *La Nausée*) and the people, who have in common that they are fully what they are and no more than that, the intellectual is always distant from himself, separated from his being – hence from all those who are only what they are – by the tiny and unbridgeable gap which makes for his misery and his grandeur.[53] His misery, hence his grandeur: this reversal is at the heart of the ideological transfiguration which, from Flaubert to Sartre (and beyond), allows the intellectual to found his point of spiritual honour on the transmutation into free choice of his exclusion from temporal powers and privileges. And the 'desire to be God', the imaginary union of the En-soi and Pour-soi that Sartre inscribes in the universality of the human condition, could after all only be a transfigured form of the ambition to reconcile the satisfied plenitude of the bourgeois and the critical disquiet of the intellectual, a mandarin's dream which is more naively expressed with Flaubert: 'to live as a bourgeois and think as a demi-God.'

Sartre converts into an ontological structure, constitutive of human existence in its universality, the social experience of the intellectual, a privileged pariah, doomed to the (blessed) malediction of an awareness which puts him at a distance from his condition and his conditionings. The malaise that he expresses is the pain of being [*mal d'être*] an intellectual and not a maladjustment [*mal-être*] within the intellectual world – where he is, at the end of the day, as at ease as a fish in the sea.[54]

2

The Author's Point of View

Some General Properties of Fields of Cultural Production

~∞~

> The goal of a true critic should be to discover which problem
> the author posed himself (knowingly or not) and to find
> whether he solved it or not.
>
> PAUL VALÉRY

The science of cultural works presupposes three operations which are
as necessary and necessarily linked as the three levels of social reality
that they apprehend. First, one must analyse the position of the
literary (etc.) field within the field of power, and its evolution in time.
Second, one must analyse the internal structure of the literary (etc.)
field, a universe obeying its own laws of functioning and transformation, meaning the structure of objective relations between positions
occupied by individuals and groups placed in a situation of competition for legitimacy. And finally, the analysis involves the genesis of
the habitus of occupants of these positions, that is, the systems of
dispositions which, being the product of a social trajectory and of a
position within the literary (etc.) field, find in this position a more or
less favourable opportunity to be realized (the construction of the
field is the logical preamble for the construction of the social
trajectory as a series of positions successively occupied in this field).[1]

Readers may, throughout this chapter, replace *writer* with *painter, philosopher, scholar*, etc., and *literary* with *artistic, philosophical, scientific*, etc. (As a
reminder when necessary, meaning those times when recourse is not made to the

generic description of *cultural producer* - a term chosen, with no particular pleasure, to mark the break with the charismatic ideology of 'creator' - we will follow the word *writer* with *etc.*).[2] This does not mean that differences among fields are being ignored. Thus, for example, there is no doubt that the intensity of the struggle varies according to genres, and to the rarity of the specific abilities they require at any particular time, that is, according to the probability of 'disloyal competition' or 'illegal practice' (which is undoubtedly why the intellectual field, continuously threatened by heteronomy and by heteronomous producers, is one of the strategic places for perceiving the logic of the struggles which haunt all fields).

Thus the real hierarchy of explanatory factors requires a reversal of the approach ordinarily adopted by analysts. On no account do we ask how such and such a writer came to be what he was - at the risk of falling into the retrospective illusion of a reconstructed coherence. Rather we must ask how, given his social origin and the socially constituted properties he derived from it, that writer has managed to occupy or, in certain cases, produce the positions which the determined state of the literary (etc.) field offered (already there or still to be made), and thus how that writer managed to give a more or less complete and coherent expression to the position-takings inscribed in a potential state within these positions (for example, in the case of Flaubert, the contradictions inherent in art for art's sake and, more generally, in the condition of the artist).

The literary field in the field of power

A number of the practices and representations of artists and writers (for example, their ambivalence as much towards the 'people' as towards the 'bourgeois') can only be explained by reference to the field of power, inside of which the literary (etc.) field is itself in a dominated position. The field of power is the space of relations of force between agents or between institutions having in common the possession of the capital necessary to occupy the dominant positions in different fields (notably economic or cultural). It is the site of struggles between holders of different powers (or kinds of capital) which, like the symbolic struggles between artists and the 'bourgeois' in the nineteenth century, have at stake the transformation or conservation of the relative value of different kinds of capital, which itself determines, at any moment, the forces liable to be engaged in these struggles.[3]

A real challenge to all forms of economism, the literary order (etc.) which was progressively instituted in the course of a long and slow process of autonomization presents itself as an inverted economic world: those who enter it have an interest in disinterestedness. Like *prophecy*, and especially the prophecy of doom, which according to Weber proves its authenticity by the fact that it secures no remuneration,[4] the heretical rupture with current artistic traditions finds its criterion of authenticity in disinterestedness. This does not mean that there is no economic logic in this charismatic economy founded on the sort of social miracle which is an act free of any determination other than the intrinsically aesthetic intention. We shall see that there are economic conditions for the economic challenge which leads to its being oriented towards the most risky positions of the intellectual and artistic avant-garde, and for the aptitude to maintain oneself there in a lasting way in the absence of any financial counterpart; and there are also economic conditions of access to symbolic profits – which are themselves capable of being converted, in the more or less long term, into economic profits.

It would be necessary to analyse, by this logic, the relations between writers or artists and publishers or gallery directors. These *double* personages (of which Flaubert sketched the paradigmatic figure in the character of Arnoux) are those through whom the logic of the 'economy' penetrates to the heart of the universe of production for producers. They must therefore combine completely contradictory dispositions: economic dispositions which, in certain sectors of the field, are totally foreign to producers, and intellectual dispositions near to those of the producers whose work they can exploit only in so far as they know how to appreciate it and give it value. In fact, the logic of the structural homologies between the field of publishers or galleries and the field of corresponding artists or writers means that each of the 'merchants in the temple' of art presents properties near to those of 'his' artists or 'her' writers, which favours the relationship of confidence and belief on which exploitation is founded (merchants may be content with taking on writers or artists at their own game, that of *statutory disinterestedness*, in order to obtain from them the renunciation which makes their profits possible).

Because of the hierarchy established in the relations among the different kinds of capital and among their holders, the fields of cultural production occupy a dominated position, temporally, within the field of power. As liberated as they may be from external constraints and demands, they are traversed by the necessity of the fields which encompass them: the need for profit, whether economic or political. It follows that they are at any one time the site of a struggle between two principles of hierarchization: the heteronomous principle, which favours those who dominate the field economically and politically (for example, 'bourgeois art'), and the autonomous principle (for example, 'art for art's sake'), which leads its most radical defenders to make of temporal failure a sign of election and of success a sign of compromise with the times.[5] The state of relations of forces in this struggle depends on the autonomy which the field *globally* disposes of, meaning the degree to which its own norms and sanctions manage to impose themselves on the ensemble of producers of cultural goods and on those who – occupying the temporally (and temporarily) dominant position in the field of cultural production (successful playwrights or novelists) or aspiring to occupy it (dominated producers available for mercenary tasks) – are the nearest to the occupants of the homologous position in the field of power, and hence the most sensitive to external demands and the most heteronomous.

The degree of autonomy of a field of cultural production is revealed to the extent that the principle of external hierarchization there is subordinated to the principle of internal hierarchization: the greater the autonomy, the more the symbolic relationship of forces is favourable to producers who are the most independent of demand, and the more the break tends to be noticeable between the two poles of the field, that is, between the *subfield of restricted production*, where producers have only other producers for clients (who are also their direct competitors), and the *subfield of large-scale production*, which finds itself *symbolically* excluded and discredited. In the former, whose fundamental faith is independence with respect to external demands, the economy of practices is founded, as in the game of *loser takes all*, on an inversion of the fundamental principles of the field of power and of the economic field. It excludes the quest for profit and it guarantees no correspondence of any kind between monetary investments and revenues; it condemns the pursuit of honours and temporal standing.[6]

According to the *principle of external hierarchization* in force in the temporally dominant regions of the field of power (and also in the economic field) – that is, according to the criterion of *temporal success* measured by indices of commercial success (such as print runs, the number of performances of plays, etc.) or social notoriety (such as decorations, commissions, etc.) – pre-eminence belongs to artists (etc.) who are known and recognized by the 'general public'. On the other hand, the *principle of internal hierarchization*, that is, the degree of specific consecration, favours artists (etc.) who are known and recognized by their peers and only by them (at least in the initial phase of their enterprise) and who owe their prestige, at least negatively, to the fact that they make no concessions to the demand of the 'general public'.

Because it provides a good measure of the degree of independence ('pure art', 'pure research', etc.) or of subordination ('commercial art', 'applied research', etc.) with respect to the demands of the 'general public' and the constraints of the market, hence of the presumed adhesion to the values of disinterestedness, the size of the audience (which implies its social quality) undoubtedly constitutes the surest and clearest indicator of the position occupied in the field. Heteronomy occurs in effect through demand, which may take the form of the personalized commission formulated by a 'patron', a sponsor or client, or the anonymous expectation and sanction of a market. It follows that nothing divides cultural producers more clearly than the relationship they maintain with worldly or *commercial success* (and the means of obtaining it, as for example, these days, submission to the press or to the means of modern communication): recognized and accepted, even expressly sought out by some, success is rejected by the defenders of an autonomous principle of hierarchization as evidence of a mercenary interest in economic and political profits. And for the most resolute defenders of autonomy, the opposition between works made for the public and works which must make their own public is elevated into a fundamental criterion of evaluation.

These opposed visions of temporal success and the economic sanction mean that there are few fields, except the field of power itself, where the antagonism is as total (in the boundaries of interests linked to membership in the field) between occupants of polar positions: writers or artists from opposite sides may, at the limit, have nothing in common except their participation in the struggle for the imposition of opposite definitions of literary or artistic production. Perfect illustrations of the distinction between relations of interaction and structural relations which are constitutive of a field, they may never meet each other, or may even methodically ignore each other, and yet remain profoundly determined, in their practice, by the relation of opposition which unites them.

Thus, in the second half of the nineteenth century, a period when the literary field achieved a degree of autonomy which it has never since surpassed, one has a first hierarchy according to the degree of real or presumed dependence on the audience, on success, on the economy. This principal hierarchy finds itself intersected by another, which is established (in the second vertical dimension of space) according to the *social and 'cultural' quality* of the public concerned (measured by its presumed distance from the seat of specific values) and according to the symbolic capital which it guarantees to producers in granting them its recognition. It is thus that, at the core of the *subfield of restricted production* (which, being dedicated in an exclusive manner to production for producers, recognizes only the principle of specific legitimation), those who are assured of recognition by their peers, a presumed index of a durable consecration (the consecrated avant-garde), are opposed to those who have not reached the same degree of recognition from the standpoint of specific criteria. This inferior position assembles artists or writers of different ages and artistic generations who may contest the consecrated avant-garde, whether in the name of a new principle of legitimation, according to the model of heresy, or in the name of a return to the old principle of legitimation (see the diagram on p. 124).

Non-success is in itself ambiguous since it may be perceived either as chosen or as endured, and since the indices of recognition by peers (which separates 'cursed artists' from 'failed artists') are always uncertain and ambiguous, as much for observers as for the artists themselves. The most *unfortunate* authors find in this objective indetermination the means of maintaining an uncertainty about their own destiny, aided in this by all the institutional supports which collective bad faith provides for them. In addition, the institutionalization of permanent revolution as the legitimate mode of transformation of fields of cultural production means that the literary and artistic avant-garde has benefited, since the end of the nineteenth century, from a favourable prejudice founded on the memory of 'errors' of perception and appreciation by the critics and publics of the past. Failure may thus always find justifications in the institutions resulting from a whole historical labour – for example, the notion of the 'cursed artist' [*artiste maudit*] confers a recognized existence on the real or presumed gap between temporal success and artistic value. More widely, because the agents and authorities who are designated (or designate themselves) for judging and consecrating are themselves involved in a struggle for consecration (and so always capable of being relativized and contested), the world of bad faith gains an objective support; thanks to this, painters without clientele, actors without roles, writers without publications or even without a public may disguise from themselves their failure, and meanwhile play on the ambiguity of the criteria of success which allows them to confuse the elected and provisional failure of the 'cursed artist' with the naked failure of the simply unsuccessful. This is an effort which becomes more and more strained as, with time and ageing, the contraction of possibles signalled by the repetition of negative sanctions makes the voluntarist prolongation of adolescent indetermination more and more untenable.

Even if the logic of competition for the rediscovery, rehabilitation or canonization of works of the past leads in the end to a form of 'literary survival' for a number of writers whom their contemporaries would have unhesitatingly classified in the category of 'failures', it is rare to find a case as extraordinary as that of Alphonse Rabbe, the author of the *Album d'un pessimiste* (recently reissued), who is described by Pascale Casanova as follows: 'A failed writer, forgotten, passed over in silence by his contemporaries, a mediocre poet, who was born in 1788 in Provence and failed in every one of his endeavours. A disappointed painter, an art critic without great talent, an amateur musician, an actor whose southern accent condemned him to comedy, a second-rate historian, provincial politician, anonymous pamphleteer, marginal journalist, he died in 1828, leaving a moving posthumous book, an apologia for suicide, logically entitled *The Album of a Pessimist*. He was promoted as a "surrealist of death" a century later by André Breton.'[7]

In the same way, at the other pole of the field, that of the subfield of large-scale production, dedicated and devoted to the market and profit, a similar opposition to the one separating the consecrated avant-garde from the avant-garde is established. Through the intermediary of the size and social quality of the audience (partially responsible for the volume of profits), and hence via the financial value of the consecration which it brings by its approbation, it is an opposition between bourgeois art, provided with all the rights of the bourgeoisie, and 'commercial' art in its pure state, doubly devalued as mercantile and 'popular'. Authors who manage to assure themselves of worldly success and bourgeois consecration (especially the Academy) are distinguished as much by their social origin and their trajectory as by their lifestyle and literary affinities from those who are condemned to so-called popular success, such as the authors of rural novels, vaudeville writers or songwriters.

The degree of autonomy of the field may be measured by the importance of the effect of translation or of *refraction* which its specific logic imposes on external influences or commissions, and by the transforming, even transfiguring, effect it has on religious or political representations and the constraints of temporal powers. (The mechanical metaphor of refraction, obviously very inexact, is valid here only negatively, in order to banish from the mind the even more inappropriate model of reflection.) The degree of autonomy may also be measured by the strength of the negative sanctions (discredit, excommunication, etc.) inflicted on heteronomous practices such as direct subjugation to political directives, for instance, or even to aesthetic and ethical demands, and especially by the strength of the positive incitements to resistance and even open struggle against those in power (the same drive to autonomy being capable of producing opposed position-takings according to the nature of the powers they contest).

The degree of autonomy of the field (and thereby, the state of relations of force established there) varies considerably according to periods and national traditions.[8] It is related to the degree of symbolic capital which has been accumulated over the course of time by the action of successive generations (the value accorded to the name of a writer or philosopher, the statutory and almost institutionalized licence to contest powers, etc.). It is in the name of this collective capital that cultural producers feel the right and the duty to ignore the demands or requirements of temporal powers, and even to combat them by invoking against them their own principles and norms. When they are inscribed in a state of objective potentiality, or even exigency, within the *specific rationale* of the field, liberties and daring gestures which would be unreasonable or quite simply unthinkable in another state of the field (or in another field) become normal, if not everyday.[9]

The symbolic power acquired in the observance of the rules of the functioning of the field is opposed to all forms of heteronomous power which certain artists or writers and more widely all holders of cultural capital – experts, administrators, engineers, journalists – may find themselves granted as a counterpart to the technical or symbolic services they render to the dominants (notably in the reproduction of the established symbolic order). This heteronomous power may be present at the very heart of the field, and producers who are the most wholeheartedly devoted to internal truths and values are considerably weakened by that sort of 'Trojan horse' represented by writers and artists who accept and bend to external demand.

That said, the submission is never as total as the polemic vision would have us believe when it treats all conservative writers as simple *spokespeople*. Nothing illustrates better – because it allows us to reason *a fortiori* – the effect of refraction exercised by the field than the case of writers who are the most visibly subject to external necessities – those exercised by political powers, whether conservative or progressive, or exercised by economic powers, which may be brought to bear directly or through the mediation of critical or public success, etc. The logic of political polemic still haunting a number of would-be scientific analyses thus results in ignoring the difference between the representations these writers offer and those which are produced by the dominants themselves – bankers, captains of industry, businessmen or their representatives in the political order – when they act as occasional producers of cultural goods.

In the exemplary case of the conservative 'philosophies' which appear in Germany in the first half of the nineteenth century, that is, at a moment when the traditional bases of the aristocracy and its confidence in its own legitimacy are shaken (especially as a result of reforms tending to abolish privileges and bondage), the works produced by professional ideologues are immediately distinguished by the fact that they bear numerous markers of their authors' membership of the intellectual field. Thus, even though he appeals to aristocrats who are foreign to the field, a writer such as Adam Müller, author of articles and essays in a turgid and quasi-philosophical style, manifests his membership of the field by the fact that he feels obliged to speak violently against Fichte and against the dominant intellectual traditions (Kant and natural law, the physiocrats and rational agriculture, Adam Smith and the ideology of the market) before proposing a true 'theory', founded on the 'idea' (which he distinguishes from the 'concept') of 'natural richness'. In this way, he separates himself from simple amateurs, politicians or great aristocrats, who are not troubled by these 'theoretical' preoccupations – a Friedrich August von der Marwitz, for example, with his letters and essays directed at his peers, displaying the innocent assurance of ignorance as he exalts the earth, birth, nature and tradition, denounces reforms, the centralization of administration, and the generalization of the market economy, and addresses himself very directly to aristocrats who ensure their conversion by entering the army or by playing the game of economic modernization.[10]

The same opposition is found again in the technocratic literature which flourished in France between 1950 and 1970, separating authors who, even if they develop thoughts almost interchangeable in their thematic (which allows us to analyse them as a group), distinguish themselves very profoundly by their discursive strategies and especially by the direction in which their references are oriented.[11] Professionals are more likely to refer – at least negatively – to the intellectual field, its debates and problems, its conventions and presuppositions, the greater their recognition within it and the more strongly they recognize its norms (distributing themselves into a hierarchy which, to cite only a few key points, goes from Jean Fourastié to Bertrand de Jouvenel and to Raymond Aron); whereas the amateurs, whether politicians (Michel Poniatowski, Valéry Giscard d'Estaing), captains of industry (François Dalle) or senior civil servants (François Bloch-Lainé or Pierre Massé), are content with reproducing school discourses which stem more or less directly from professional texts or courses, without bothering with the problems which concern intellectuals, and often not even being aware of their existence.

Being objectively and subjectively foreign to the field of cultural production, producers whom we may call *naive*, by analogy with the field of painting, may express their conviction at the first level, without paying the least attention to other producers (except, in the case of politicians, to those who are situated like them in the political field), as witnessed by the simplicity of their style, the wholesome assurance of their arguments and especially the naiveté of their references.

By contrast, for fear of being excluded from the field, people classified by indigenous taxonomies as 'right-wing intellectuals' have lost the right to this robust innocence, and their concern to affirm their statutory franchises as intellectuals makes them distance themselves from the first truths of primary conservatism, but only to discover them again in the course of the polemic against 'left-wing intellectuals': the simplicity or the very clarity they affect poses as a deliberate rejection of the vain complexity of the people they designate, *from the outside*, as 'intellectuals', meaning 'left-wing intellectuals'. The generative formula of their discourse is completely summed up in the famous title of the book by Raymond Aron, *L'Opium des intellectuels*, a play on words which turns the Marxist slogan about religion as the 'opiate of the masses' against intellectuals dedicated to the Marxist religion of the 'people', and against their claim to the status of awakeners of minds.[12]

The *nomos* and the question of boundaries

Internal struggles, notably those setting the proponents of 'pure art' against the proponents of 'bourgeois art' or 'commercial art' and leading the former to refuse to regard the latter as writers, inevitably take the form of conflicts over *definition*, in the proper sense of the term. Each is trying to impose the *boundaries* of the field most favourable to its interests or – which amounts to the same thing – the best definition of conditions of true membership of the field (or of titles conferring the right to the status of writer, artist or scholar) for justifying its existence as it stands. Thus, when the defenders of the most 'pure', the most rigorous and the narrowest definition of belonging declare that a certain number of artists (etc.) are not *really* artists, or that they are not *true* artists, they deny them existence *as* artists – from the *point of view*, that is, which as 'true' artists they wish to impose within the field as the legitimate view on the field, the fundamental law of the field, the principle of vision and division (*nomos*) defining the artistic field (etc.) *as such*, meaning as the site of art as art.

This 'seeing from the standpoint of' (following Wittgenstein's expression) which 'pure' artists seek to impose against ordinary vision is quite simply, at least in this case, the founding point of view by which the field is constituted as such and which, accordingly, defines the right of entry into the field: 'that none enter here' unless endowed with a point of view which accords or coincides with the founding point of view of the field. Someone who refuses to play the game of art as art, which defines itself against ordinary vision and against the mercantile or mercenary ends of those who put themselves into its service, wants to reduce the business of art to the business of money (according to the founding principle of the economic field, 'business is business'). The strictest and most restricted definition of the writer (etc.), which we accept these days as going without saying, is the product of a long series of exclusions and excommunications trying to deny existence as writers worthy of the name to all sorts of producers who could live as writers in the name of a larger and looser definition of the profession.

One of the central stakes in literary (etc.) rivalries is the monopoly of literary legitimacy, that is, among other things, the monopoly of the power to say with authority who is authorized to call himself writer (etc.) or even to say who is a writer and who has the authority to say who is a writer; or, if you prefer, the monopoly of the *power of consecration* of producers and products. More precisely, the struggle between occupants of the two opposite poles of the field of cultural production has at stake the monopoly on the imposition of the legitimate definition of the writer, and it is comprehensibly organized around the opposition between autonomy and heteronomy. As a consequence, if the literary field (etc.) is universally the site of a struggle over the definition of writer (etc.), then there is no universal definition of the writer, and analysis never encounters anything but definitions corresponding to a state of the struggle for the imposition of the legitimate definition of the writer.

This means that the problems of sampling which confront all specialists cannot be resolved by one of those arbitrary decrees of ignorance which are known as 'operational definitions' (and which are very likely to be simply the unconscious application of a historical definition, and so, when it concerns distant epochs, to be anachronistic): the semantic flux of notions like writer or artist is both the product and the condition of struggles aiming to impose the definition. In this way, it belongs to the very reality which it is concerned to interpret. To decide on paper and in a more or less arbitrary fashion debates which are not settled in reality, such as the question of whether this or that pretender to the title of writer (etc.) belongs to the population of writers, is to forget that the field of cultural production is the site of struggles which, through the imposition of the dominant definition of the writer, aim to delimit the population of those who possess the right to participate in the struggle over the definition of the writer.

This struggle about the boundaries of the group and conditions of membership is by no means abstract: the reality of all cultural production, and the very idea of the writer, may find themselves radically transformed by the sole fact of an enlargement of the ensemble of people who have their say on literary things. It follows that any enquiry aiming, for example, to establish the properties of writers and artists at a given moment predetermines its result in the inaugural decision delimiting the populations to be subjected to statistical analysis.[13]

There is no way of getting out of the circularity unless it is addressed as such. It is up to the study itself to collect the definitions confronting each other, together with the vagueness inherent in their social uses, and to furnish the means of describing their social bases. For example, by analysing statistically how diverse indices of recognition as a writer (such as presence in book selection or literary prize lists) awarded by different instances of consecration (academies, the education system, the authors of lists, etc.) are distributed among producers of books (socially characterized), and also by examining how the authors of book selection and literary prize lists and of definitions of the writer are themselves distributed in the space thus constructed, one could succeed in determining the factors which control access to different forms of the status of writer, and hence the implicit and explicit content of the definitions at work.

But one may also break the circle by constructing a model of the *process of canonization which leads to the establishment of writers*, through an analysis of the different forms embraced by the literary pantheon, at different periods, in the different selections made both in documents – textbooks, anthologies, miscellanies and so forth – and in monuments – portraits, statues, busts or medallions of 'great men' (one thinks of the amount Francis Haskell draws out of Delaroche's picture, painted in 1837 in the semicircle of the École des Beaux-Arts and depicting the pantheon of the artists consecrated at the time).[14] One might, in combining different methods, try to follow the process of consecration in the diversity of its forms and its manifestations (inauguration of statues or commemorative plaques, attribution of street names, creation of commemorative societies, introduction into university courses and so forth), to observe the fluctuations in the stock of different authors (through the sales figures of books or through the articles written about them), to untangle the logic of struggles for their rehabilitation, etc. And not the least contribution of such a labour would be to make explicit the process of conscious or unconscious inculcation which leads us to accept the established hierarchy as self-evident.[15]

The struggles over definition (or classification) have *boundaries* at stake (between genres and disciplines, or between modes of production inside the same genre) and, therefore, hierarchies. To define boundaries, defend them and control entries is to defend the established order in the field. In effect, the growth in the volume of the population of producers is one of the principal mediations through which external changes affect the relations of force at the heart of the field. The great upheavals arise from the eruption of newcomers who, by the sole effect of their number and their social quality, import innovation regarding products or techniques of production, and try or claim to impose on the field of production, which is itself its own market, a new mode of evaluation of products.

To produce effects is already to exist in a field, even if these effects are mere reactions of resistance or exclusion. It follows that the dominants have trouble defending themselves against the threat contained in any redefinition of the right of entry, explicit or implicit, since they are granting existence, by fighting against them, to those they want to exclude. The Théâtre-Libre has a real existence in the theatrical subfield from the moment it becomes the object of attacks from the official defenders of bourgeois theatre – who moreover have effectively helped to hasten its recognition. And there is an infinite number of examples of situations where, as in affairs of honour and all symbolic struggles, fully fledged members of the field are condemned to oscillate between the contemptuous gesture, which carries the risk of being misunderstood or looking like shameful impotence or cowardice, and condemnation or denunciation, which, regardless of what one does, contains a form of recognition.

One of the most characteristic properties of a field is the degree to which its dynamic limits, which extend as far as the power of its effects, are converted into a juridical frontier, protected by a right of entry which is explicitly codified, such as the possession of scholarly titles, success in a competition, etc., or by measures of exclusion and discrimination, such as laws intended to assure a *numerus clausus*. A high degree of codification of entry into the game goes along with the existence of explicit rules of the game and a minimum consensus on these rules; by contrast, a weak degree of codification conveys states of the field in which the rules of the game are being played for in the playing of the game. The literary or artistic fields are characterized, particularly compared with the university field, by a weak degree of codification, and, by the same token, by the extreme permeability of their boundaries and the extreme diversity of the definition of the *posts* they offer and the principles of legitimacy which confront each other there. The analysis of the properties of agents attests to the fact that they require neither inherited economic capital to the same degree as the economic field, nor educational capital to the same degree as the university field or even sectors of the field of power such as the senior civil service.[16]

But because it is one of the *uncertain sites* in the social space which offer poorly defined posts – to be made rather than already made and, to this very degree, extremely elastic and undemanding – and also futures which are very uncertain and extremely dispersed (in contrast, for example, with public service or the university), the literary and artistic field attracts and welcomes agents who are very different from each other in their properties and their dispositions, and hence in their ambitions, and who are often rather self-assured and endowed with sufficient security to refuse to settle for a career in the university or civil service and to face the risks of this profession which is not really one.

The 'profession' of writer or artist is, in effect, one of the least codified there is; one of the least capable, too, of completely defining (and nourishing) those who claim it, and who, quite often, cannot assume the function they take as their principal one unless they have a secondary profession to provide them with their main income. But one can see the subjective profits offered by this double status, with the proclaimed identity allowing one, for example, to be satisfied with all the small jobs described as being just to pay the bills, which are offered by the profession itself (such as that of reader or proofreader in publishing houses) or by related institutions (such as journalism, television, radio and so forth). These jobs (for which the art professions have equivalents, not to mention the cinema) have the virtue of placing their occupants at the heart of the 'milieu', where the information circulates which is part of the specific competence of the writer or artist, where relationships are forged and protection is acquired which is useful to gaining publication, and where sometimes positions of specific power are conquered – the status of publisher, editor of a review, of collections of essays – which may contribute to the growth of specific capital, through the recognition and the homage obtained from new entrants in exchange for publication, sponsorship, advice and so forth.

It is for the same reasons that the literary field is so attractive and so welcoming to all those who possess all the characteristics of the dominants *minus one*: to 'poor relations' of the great bourgeois dynasties,[17] aristocrats ruined or in decline, members of minorities stigmatized or rejected from other dominant positions, and in particular from high public service, and those whose uncertain and contradictory social identity predisposes them in some way to occupy the contradictory position of dominated among the dominants. Thus, for example, if one excepts the 'bourgeois' theatre which requires an immediate connection between author and audience, racial discrimination is generally less strong in the intellectual and artistic field than in other fields; and in any case, because of the significance of style and lifestyle in the personage of the writer or artist, it is undoubtedly not as strong as purely social discrimination (against provincials especially) – witness the innumerable manifestations of class contempt in polemics.

The *illusio* and the work of art as fetish

The struggles for the monopoly of the definition of the mode of legitimate cultural production contribute to a continual reproduction of belief in the game, interest in the game and its stakes, the *illusio* – of which the struggles are also the product. Each field produces its specific form of the *illusio*, in the sense of an investment in the game which pulls agents out of their indifference and inclines and predisposes them to put into operation the distinctions which are pertinent from the viewpoint of the logic of the field, to distinguish what is *important* ('what matters to me', is of *interest*, in contrast to 'what is all the same to me', or *in-different*). But it is just as true that a certain form of adherence to the game, of belief in the game and the value of its stakes, which makes the game worth the trouble of playing it is the basis of the functioning of the game, and that the *collusion* of agents in the *illusio* is the root of the competition which pits them against each other and which makes the game itself. In short, the *illusio* is the condition for the functioning of a game of which it is also, at least partially, the product.

This interested participation in the game is established in the conjunctural relationship between a habitus and a field, two historical institutions which have in common the fact that they are both inhabited (but for a few details) by the same fundamental law; it *is* precisely this relationship. Therefore it has nothing in common with that emanation of some *human nature* which is ordinarily assigned to the notion of interest.

As is shown by comparative history and sociology, and notably the analysis of precapitalist societies – or the fields of cultural production of our societies – the particular form of the *illusio* presumed by the economic field, that is to say, economic interest in the sense of utilitarianism, and its form of economics, is merely a particular case among a world of forms of interest which are observed in reality. It is simultaneously the precondition and the product of the emergence of the economic field which is constituted by instituting the quest for the maximization of monetary profit as a fundamental law. Even if it is a historical institution in the same way as the artistic *illusio*, the economic *illusio*, as interest in the game founded on economic interest in the restricted sense, presents itself with all the appearances of logical universality. We must be thankful to Pareto for expressing with consummate clarity this illusion of universality which subtends all of economic theory when he contrasts conduct which is 'determined by usage', such as the act of removing one's hat when coming into a living room, with conduct which is the culmination of 'logical reasoning' based on experience, such as the act of buying a large quantity of wheat.[18]

Each field (religious, artistic, scientific, economic, etc.), through the particular form of regulation of practices and the representations that it imposes, offers to agents a legitimate form of realizing their desires, based on a particular form of the *illusio*. It is in the relation between the system of dispositions produced in whole or in part by the structure and functioning of the field and the system of objective potentialities offered by the field that the system of satisfactions which are (really) desirable is defined in each case, and that the reasonable strategies called for by the immanent logic of the game are engendered (which may be accompanied or not by an explicit representation of the game).[19]

The producer of the *value of the work of art* is not the artist but the field of production as a universe of belief which produces the value of the work of art as a *fetish* by producing the belief in the creative power of the artist. Given that the work of art does not exist as a symbolic object endowed with value unless it is known and recognized – that is to say, socially instituted as a work of art by spectators endowed with the aesthetic disposition and competence necessary to know it and recognize it as such – the science of works takes as object not only the material production of the work but also the production of the value of the work or, what amounts to the same thing, of the belief in the value of the work.

It must therefore take into account not only the direct producers of the work in its materiality (artist, writer, etc.), but also the ensemble of agents and institutions which participate in the production of the value of the work via the production of the belief in the value of art in general and in the distinctive value of this or that work of art. We may include critics, art historians, publishers, gallery directors, dealers, museum curators, patrons, collectors, members of instances of consecration like academies, salons, juries, etc., and the whole ensemble of political and administrative authorities competent in matters of art (various ministries, according to the period, such as the Direction des Musées Nationaux, the Direction des Beaux-Arts, etc.) who may act on the art market, either by verdicts of consecration, whether accompanied or not by economic benefits (purchases, subsidies, prizes, scholarships, etc.), or by regulatory measures (tax breaks granted to sponsors or to collectors, etc.), not to mention the members of institutions which work towards the production of producers (schools of fine arts, etc.) and towards the production of consumers capable of recognizing the work of art as such, that is, as a value, starting with teachers and parents, in charge of the initial inculcation of artistic dispositions.[20]

This means that the science of art cannot be given its own object of study unless there is a break not only with traditional art history, which succumbs without a fight to the 'fetishism of the name of the master' described by Walter Benjamin, but also with the social history of art, which only seemed to break with the presuppositions of the most traditional construction of the object. Indeed, by limiting itself to an analysis of the social conditions of production of an individual artist (grasped most often through his social origin and education), the latter gives in to the whole traditional model of artistic 'creation' which makes the artist the exclusive producer of the work of art and its value. Despite its interest in recipients or patrons of the work, it never poses the question of their contribution to the creation of the value of the work and its creator.

The collective belief in the game (*illusio*) and in the sacred value of its stakes is simultaneously the precondition and the product of the very functioning of the game; it is fundamental to the power of consecration, permitting consecrated artists to constitute certain products, by the miracle of their signature (or brand name), as *sacred* objects. To give an idea of the collective labour which goes to produce this belief, it would be necessary to reconstitute the circulation of the innumerable acts of credit which are exchanged among all the agents engaged in the artistic field: among artists, obviously, with group exhibitions or prefaces by which consecrated authors consecrate the younger ones, who consecrate them in return as masters or heads of schools; between artists and patrons or collectors; between artists and critics, and in particular avant-garde critics, who consecrate themselves by obtaining the consecration of the artists they champion or by rediscovering or re-evaluating minor artists and thus activating and giving proof of their power of consecration, and so forth.

What is certain is that it would be foolish to search for an ultimate guarantor or guarantee of this fiduciary currency that is the power of consecration outside of the network of relations of exchange through which it is both produced and circulates, that is, in a sort of central bank which would be the ultimate bond of all acts of credit. This role of central bank was held until the middle of the nineteenth century by the Académie, monopoly holder of the legitimate definition of art and the artist, of the *nomos*, principle of legitimate vision and division permitting the separation between art and non-art, between the 'true' artists, worthy of being publicly and officially exhibited, and the others, condemned to oblivion by the rejection of the jury. The institutionalization of anomie which resulted from the establishment of a field of institutions placed in a situation of competition for artistic legitimacy caused the disappearance of the very possibility of a verdict from a court of final appeal, and it doomed artists to an endless struggle for a power of consecration which can no longer be acquired and consecrated except in and through the struggle itself.

It follows that one cannot found a genuine science of the work of art without tearing oneself out of the *illusio*, and suspending the relationship of complicity and connivance which ties every cultivated person to the cultural game, in order to constitute the game as object. But nevertheless it must not be forgotten that this *illusio* is part of the very reality we are concerned to comprehend, and that one must put it into the model designed to account for it, along with everything which combines to produce it and maintain it, such as critical discourses which contribute to the production of the value of the work of art which they seem to record. While it is necessary to break with the discourse of celebration which thinks of itself as an act of 're-creation' re-editing the original 'creation',[21] one must be careful not to forget that this discourse and the representation of cultural production that it helps to accredit are part of the complete definition of this very particular process of production, as preconditions of the social creation of the 'creator' as fetish.

Position, disposition and position-taking

The field is a network of objective relations (of domination or subordination, of complementarity or antagonism, etc.) between positions – for example, the position corresponding to a genre like the novel or to a subcategory like the society novel, or from another point of view, the position locating a review, a salon, or a circle as the gathering place of a group of producers. Each position is objectively defined by its objective relationship with other positions, or, in other terms, by the system of relevant (meaning efficient) properties which allow it to be situated in relation to all others in the structure of the global distribution of properties. All positions depend, in their very existence, and in the determinations they impose on their occupants, on their actual and potential situation in the structure of the field – that is to say, in the structure and distribution of those kinds of capital (or of power) whose possession governs the obtaining of specific profits (such as literary prestige) put into play in the field. To different *positions* (which, in a universe as little institutionalized as the literary or artistic field,[22] can only be apprehended through the properties of their occupants) correspond homologous *position-takings*, including literary or artistic works, obviously, but also political acts and discourses, manifestos or polemics, etc. – and this obliges us to challenge the alternative between an internal reading of the work and an explanation based on the social conditions of its production or consumption.

In the phase of equilibrium, the *space of positions* tends to govern the *space of position-takings*. It is to the specific 'interests' associated with different positions in the literary field that one must look for the principle of literary (etc.) position-takings, and even the political position-takings outside the field. Historians, who had the habit of going in the other direction, ended up discovering, with Robert Darnton, what a political revolution might owe to the contradictions and conflicts of the 'Republic of Letters'.[23] Artists do not really *feel* their relationship to the 'bourgeois' except through their relationship to 'bourgeois art', or, more generally, to the agents or institutions which express or incarnate the 'bourgeois' necessity at the very heart of the field, such as the 'bourgeois artist'. In short, the only way external determinations are exercised is through the intermediary of specific forces and forms of the field, that is, after having undergone a *restructuration*, and this restructuration is all the more major the more autonomous the field and the more capable it is of imposing its specific logic, which only represents the objectification of its whole history in institutions and mechanisms.[24]

It is thus only by taking into account the specific logic of the field as a space of positions and position-takings, actual and potential (the space of possibles or the problematic), that one may adequately understand the form that these external forms may take in the course of their translation according to this logic. This is so whether it is a matter of social determinations operating through the habitus of producers who have been durably fashioned by them, or the determinations exercised on the field at the actual moment of the work's production, such as an economic crisis or an expansionist movement, a revolution or an epidemic.[25] In other words, economic or morphological determinations are only exercised through the specific structure of the field and they may take completely unexpected routes – with economic expansion, for example, liable to exercise its most important effects through mediations such as a growth in the volume of producers or in the audience of readers and spectators.

The literary (etc.) field is a force-field acting on all those who enter it, and acting in a differential manner according to the position they occupy there (whether, to take the points furthest removed from each other, that of a writer of hit plays or that of an avant-garde poet), and at the same time it is a field of competitive struggles which tend to conserve or transform this force-field. And the position-takings (works, political manifestos or demonstrations, and so on), which one may and should treat for analytical purposes as a 'system' of oppositions, are not the result of some kind of objective collusion, but rather the product and the stake of a permanent conflict. In other words, the generative and unifying principle of this 'system' is the struggle itself.

The correspondence between this or that position and this or that position-taking is not established directly, but only through the mediation of two systems of differences, of differential distances, of relevant oppositions into which they are inserted (and so different genres, styles, forms, manners and so forth are each to the others what the corresponding authors are, as we shall see). Each position-taking (thematic, stylistic and so on) is defined (objectively and sometimes intentionally) in relation to the universe of position-takings and in relation to the *problematic* as a *space of possibles* indicated or suggested there. It receives its distinctive *value* from the negative relationship which unites it to the coexisting position-takings to which it is objectively referred and which determine it by circumscribing it. It follows, for example, that the meaning and value of a position-taking (artistic genre, particular work and so on) change automatically, even while the adopted stance remains identical, when the universe of substitutable options simultaneously offered to producers and consumers is changed.

This effect is exercised above all on works called classics, which ceaselessly change in line with changes in the universe of coexisting works. This can be clearly seen when the simple *repetition* of a past work in a profoundly transformed field produces a completely automatic *effect of parody* (in the theatre, for example, this effect may make it necessary to mark a slight distance from a text which can no longer be defended as it is). It is understandable why writers' efforts to control the reception of their own work are always partially doomed to failure: the very effect of their work may transform the conditions of its reception; they would not have had to write a number of things they wrote, or write them *as* they wrote them (for example, resorting to rhetorical strategies that try to 'twist the stick in the other direction' by going to the other extreme), if they had been granted from the start what they are granted retrospectively.

One thus escapes from the eternalization and absolutism wielded by literary theory when it turns into the transhistorical essence of a *genre* all the properties the latter owes to its historical position in a (hierarchized) structure of differences. But one is not thereby condemned to a historicist immersion in the singularity of a particular situation. In fact, only comparative analysis of variations in relational properties can lead to the true constants, such as the fact that a hierarchy of genres (or, in another universe, of disciplines) seems always and everywhere to be one of the principal determining factors of the practices of production and reception of works.

The science of the work of art thus takes as its very own object the *relationship between two structures*, the structure of objective relations between positions in the field of production (and among the producers who occupy them), and the structure of objective relations among the position-takings in the space of works. Equipped with the hypothesis of a homology between the two structures, research – by setting up a to-and-fro between the two spaces and between identical data offered there under different guises – may accumulate the information which gives us *at one and the same time* works read in their interrelations, and the properties of agents, or their positions, also apprehended in their objective relations. A stylistic strategy of this sort may thus furnish the starting point for a search for its author's trajectory, or some piece of biographical information may incite us to read differently a formal particularity of the work or some property of its structure.

The principle of change in works resides in the field of cultural production and, more precisely, in the struggles among agents and institutions whose strategies depend on the interest they have – as a function of the position they occupy in the distribution of specific capital (institutionalized or not) – in conserving or in transforming the structure of that distribution, hence either in perpetuating the current conventions or in subverting them. But the stakes of the struggle among the dominants and the pretenders, between orthodoxy and heresy, and the very content of the strategies they can put into effect to advance their interests, depend on the space of position-takings already brought about, and this, functioning as a problematic, tends to define the space of possible position-takings, and thus to shape the search for solutions and, consequently, the evolution of production. And on the other hand, however great the autonomy of the field, the chances of success of strategies of conservation and subversion always depend in part on the reinforcement that one or another camp can find in external forces (for example, in new clienteles).

Radical transformations of the space of position-takings (literary or artistic revolutions) can only result from the transformations of relations of force constitutive of the space of positions which are themselves made possible by the intersection between the subversive intentions of a section of producers and the expectations of a section of the public (internal and external), hence by a transformation of the relations between the intellectual field and the field of power. When a new literary or artistic group imposes itself on the field, the whole space of positions and the space of corresponding possibilities, hence the whole problematic, find themselves transformed because of it: with its accession to existence, that is, to difference, the universe of possible options finds itself modified, with formerly dominant productions, for example, being downgraded to the status of an outmoded or classical product.

The space of possibles

The relationship among positions and position-takings is by no means a relationship of mechanical determination. Between one and the other, in some fashion, the space of possibles interposes itself, that is to say, the space of position-takings actually realized, as it appears when it is perceived through the categories of perception constitutive of a certain habitus, that is, as an oriented space, pregnant with position-takings identifiable as objective potentialities, things 'to be done', 'movements' to launch, reviews to create, adversaries to combat, established position-takings to be 'overtaken' and so forth.

To grasp the effect of the space of possibles, which acts as a discloser of dispositions, it suffices – proceeding in the fashion of logicians who admit that each individual has 'counterparts' in other possible worlds in the form of the ensemble of people each could have been if the world had been different – to imagine what people such as Barcos, Flaubert or Zola might have been if they had found in another state of the field a different opportunity to deploy their dispositions.[26] One does this spontaneously with respect to a work of ancient music when one wonders whether it makes more sense to play it on the harpsichord, the instrument for which it was conceived, or to substitute the piano because the author's 'counterpart' who composed in a world containing this instrument would have used the piano – knowing full well that, in writing for this instrument, this possible composer would undoubtedly not have realized his intentions in the same manner, and that those intentions would themselves have been different.

Thus the heritage accumulated by collective work presents itself to each agent as a space of possibles, that is, as an ensemble of probable *constraints* which are the condition and the counterpart of a set of *possible uses*. Those who think in simple alternatives need to be reminded that in these matters absolute freedom, exalted by the defenders of creative spontaneity, belongs only to the naive and the ignorant. It is one and the same thing to enter into a field of cultural production, by settling an entrance fee which consists essentially of the acquisition of a *specific code* of conduct and expression, and to discover the finite universe of *freedom under constraints* and *objective potentialities* which it offers: problems to resolve, stylistic or thematic possibilities to exploit, contradictions to overcome, even revolutionary ruptures to effect.[27]

For bold strokes of innovation or revolutionary research to have some chance of even being conceived, it is necessary for them to exist in a potential state at the heart of the system of already realized possibles, like *structural lacunae* which appear to wait for and call for fulfilment, like potential directions of development, possible avenues of research. Moreover, they must have some chance of being received,[28] meaning accepted and recognized as 'reasonable', at least by a small number of people, the same ones who would no doubt have been able to conceive of them.[29] Just as the (realized) tastes of consumers are in part determined by the state of what is on offer (so that, as Haskell has shown, any important change in the nature and number of works offered helps to determine a change in preferences shown), any act of production depends, too, in part on the state of the space of possible productions which presents itself in a concrete way in the form of practical alternatives between projects which are concurrent and more or less incompatible (proper names or concepts ending in -ism), each of these projects constituting for this reason a challenge to the defenders of all the others.

This space of possibles impresses itself on all those who have interiorized the logic and necessity of the field as a sort of *historical transcendental*, a system of (social) categories of perception and appreciation, of social conditions of possibility and legitimacy which, like the concepts of genres, schools, manners and forms, define and delimit the universe of the thinkable and the unthinkable, that is to say, both the finite universe of potentialities capable of being thought and realized at a given moment – freedom – and the system of constraints inside which is determined what is to be done and to be thought – necessity. A veritable *ars obligatoria*, as the Scholastics put it, it acts like a grammar in defining the space of what is possible or conceivable within the limits of a certain field, constituting each of the 'choices' taken (in matters of *mise en scène*, for example) as a grammatically consistent *option* (in contrast to choices which lead one to say the author 'will do anything'); but it is also an *ars inveniendi* which allows the invention of a diversity of acceptable solutions within the limits of grammaticality (the possibilities inscribed in the grammar of the *mise en scène* invented by Antoine have not yet been exhausted). In this way, this is undoubtedly how any cultural producer is irremediably placed and dated in so far as he or she participates in the same *problematic* as the ensemble of his or her contemporaries (in the sociological sense). There is no Nouveau Roman for Diderot, even if Robbe-Grillet can, by an anachronistic projection of his space of possibles, find a prefiguration of it in *Jacques le Fataliste*.

Because the system of schemata of thought which results in part from the interiorization of oppositions constitutive of the structure of the field is shared by the ensemble of participants and also by a greater or lesser portion of the public (notably in the form of oppositions functioning as principles of vision and division, of marking, carving up, framing), it secures a form of objectivity endowed with the transcendent necessity of shared proof, that is to say, it is universally admitted (within the limits of the field) as self-evident.[30]

It is certain that (at least in the sector of production for producers, and undoubtedly beyond it) the properly stylistic or thematic interest of this or that choice, and all pure stakes (meaning purely internal ones) of properly aesthetic experimentation (or, elsewhere, scientific research), *mask*, even in the eyes of those who make these choices, the material or symbolic profits which are associated with them (at least for a while) and which only present themselves exceptionally as such, in the logic of cynical calculation. The specific schemas of perception and appreciation structuring the perception of the game and its stakes and reproducing according to their own logic the fundamental divisions of the space of positions (for example, 'pure' art versus 'commercial' art, 'bohemian' versus 'bourgeois', 'Left Bank' versus 'Right Bank', and so on), or again the division into genres,[31] determine the positions which seem acceptable or attractive (in the logic of the vocation) or, on the contrary, impossible, inaccessible or unacceptable (it is more or less the same with university 'disciplines' or scientific 'specialties').

It is impossible to explain completely the astonishingly tight correspondence established at a given moment between the space of positions and the space of dispositions of those who occupy them without taking into account at one and the same time the space of possibilities prevailing at this moment, and also at different critical turning points in each artistic (etc.) career – that is to say, different genres, schools, styles, forms, manners, subjects and so on – considered as much in their internal logic as in the social value attached to each of them because of its position in the corresponding space, and also the socially constituted categories of perception and appreciation which the different agents or classes of agents apply to it.

Thus poetry as it presents itself to a young pretender of the 1880s is not what it was in 1830, or even in 1848, and even less what it will be in 1980. Poetry is, first of all, an elevated position in the hierarchy of literary occupations, securing for its occupants, by a sort of *caste effect*, the assurance, at least subjective, of an essential superiority to all other writers, with the least of the poets (especially Symbolists) perceiving themselves as superior to the best of the novelists (naturalists).[32] It is also an ensemble of exemplary figures – Lamartine, Hugo, Gautier, etc. – who have helped to compose and impose the personage and the role, and whose works and their premises (the romantic identification of poetry with lyricism, for example) define the *landmarks* in relation to which all poets must locate themselves. These are the normative representations – that of the 'pure' artist, indifferent to success and the verdicts of the market – and the mechanisms which, by their sanctions, sustain them and give them a real efficacy. Finally, this poetry is the state of stylistic possibilities, the worn state of the

alexandrine, overfamiliarity with the metric boldnesses of the romantic generation, etc., which orient the search for new forms.

It would be totally unjust and futile to try to challenge this requirement to
reconstruct things because of the almost indisputable fact that it is difficult to
realize in practice. Scientific progress can consist, in certain cases, of identifying
the presuppositions and the theorems which are implicitly contained in the
labours (irreproachable because unreflected upon) of 'normal science', and of
proposing programmes to try to resolve questions that ordinary research takes
as resolved for simple lack of having posed them. In fact, by being attentive, one
finds frequent evidence of representations of the space of the possibles. It lies,
for example, in the image of the great precursors in relation to whom people
think of themselves and against whom they define themselves, like the complementary figures of Taine and Renan for that generation of novelists and scholars,
or the antagonistic personages of Mallarmé and Verlaine for a whole generation
of poets. It is, more simply, the exalted representation of the occupation of the
writer or artist which may orient the aspirations of an entire period: 'The new
literary generation grew up completely permeated with the spirit of 1830. The
verse of Hugo and Musset, the plays of Alexandre Dumas and Alfred de Vigny
circulated in schools despite the hostility of the university; an infinite number of
novels on the Middle Ages, lyrical confessions and despairing verses were
secretly written in the lecture halls.'[33] And one should cite again the passage
from *Manette Salomon* where the Goncourts suggest that what attracts and
fascinates in the profession of the artist is less the art itself than the life of the
artist (the same logic which is observed these days in the differential diffusion of
the figure of the intellectual): 'At heart, Anatole was not so much summoned by
art as attracted by the life of the artist. He dreamt of a studio. He aspired to it
with a schoolboy's imaginings and the appetites of his nature. What he saw
there were the horizons of bohemia enchanting when viewed from afar: the
novel of Misery; the shedding of bonds and rules; the freedom, indiscipline and
disorder, with every day filled with chance, adventure and the unexpected; the
escape from the orderly and ordering household, from the family's doings and
its tedious Sundays, the bourgeois jokes; the voluptuous mystery of the female
model; work that entails no pain; the right to dress up all year round, a sort of
eternal carnival – these were the images and temptations conjured up for him by
a rigorous and austere career in art.'[34] If these sources of information, and so
many other similar examples filling the texts, are not usually read as such, it is
because the *literary disposition* tends to derealize and dehistoricize everything
which evokes social realities. This neutralizing treatment reduces this authentic
testimony about the experience of a milieu and an era or about historical
institutions – salons, circles, bohemia, and so on – to the status of obligatory
anecdotes of a literary childhood and adolescence, and inhibits the astonishment
they ought to arouse.

Thus the field of possible position-takings is open to the *sense of
placement* (in the double sense, incorporating the meaning of *investment*) in the guise of a certain structure of probabilities, probable
profits or losses, as much on the material plane as on the symbolic
plane. But this structure always includes a share of indetermination,
linked in particular to the fact that, above all in a field as little
institutionalized as this one, agents, no matter how strict the necessi-

ties inscribed in their position, always dispose of an objective margin of freedom (which they may seize or not according to their 'subjective' dispositions), and that these freedoms augment each other in the billiard game of structured interactions, thus opening a place, especially in periods of crisis, for strategies capable of subverting the established distribution of chances and profits in favour of the available margin of manoeuvre.

This means that the structural lacunae of a system of possibles, which is undoubtedly never given *as such* to the subjective experience of agents (contrary to what the *ex post* reconstruction might have us believe), cannot be filled by the magic virtue of a sort of tendency of the system to complete itself. The summons contained in these gaps is only understood by those who, as a result of their position in the field and their habitus, and of the (often discordant) relationship between the two, are free enough from the constraints inscribed in the structure to be able to recognize as applying to them a virtuality which, in a sense, only exists for them. This gives their enterprise, after the event, the appearance of predestination.

Structure and change: internal struggles and permanent revolution

Arising out of the very structure of the field, that is, from the synchronic oppositions between antagonistic positions (dominant/dominated, consecrated/novice, orthodox/heretic, old/young, etc.), the changes continually taking place at the centre of the field of restricted production are largely independent in their source from the external changes which may seem to determine them because they accompany them chronologically (and this is so even if these changes owe part of their ultimate success to this 'miraculous' intersection of causal series which are – highly – independent).

Any change taking place in a space of positions which are objectively defined by the distance separating them determines a generalized change. This means that it is no use looking for a privileged place of change. It is true that the initiative for change can be traced back, almost by definition, to new (meaning younger) entrants. These are the ones who are also the most deprived of specific capital, and who (in a universe where to exist is to be different, meaning to occupy a distinct and distinctive position) only exist in so far as – without needing to want to – they manage to assert their identity (that is, their difference) and get it known and recognized ('make a name for oneself') by imposing new modes of thought and expression which break with current modes of thought and hence are destined to disconcert by their 'obscurity' and their 'gratuitousness'.

Because the position-takings define themselves, to a large extent, negatively, in relation to others, they often remain almost empty, reduced to a stance of defiance, rejection, rupture. The 'youngest' writers structurally (who may be almost as old biologically as the 'old ones' they intend to outmode) – that is, the least advanced in the process of legitimation – reject what their most consecrated precursors are and do, everything which in their eyes defines the 'old-fashioned' poetics or whatever (and which they sometimes *parody*), and the youngest also affect to spurn any mark of *social ageing*, starting with the signs of consecration, either internal (academy, etc.) or external (success). For their part, the consecrated authors see in the voluntarist and forced character of certain of the intentions to outmode them the indisputable signs of a 'gigantic and hollow pretension', as Zola put it. And in fact, the more one moves through history, that is, through the process of autonomization of the field, the more the manifestos (it suffices to think of the *Surrealist Manifesto*) tend to be reduced to pure manifestations of difference (though one should not draw the conclusion that they are inspired by the cynical search for distinction).[35]

The effect of a need to demarcate oneself in order to exist is surely recognizable in the fact that Breton – but one could provide multiple examples – prefers a break with the *Nouvelle Revue Française* of Gide and Valéry to annexation, which is the counterpart of sponsorship and protection, and in the way he pitilessly asserts his difference in his relationships with competing groups such as Tzara's or Goll and Dermée's – who also claim the title of surrealism for their movement.[36] As soon as it manages to occupy a distinct and recognizable position in the historically constituted space of coexisting (and therefore competing) works which designate by their mutual relationships the space of possible position-takings – prolongations, outmodings, ruptures – the known and recognized work situates the others, by an active evaluation which determines the evolution of their *distinctive value*.

One would have to rewrite, from this perspective, the history of the poetic movements directed in turn against the successive incarnations of the exemplary figure of the poet – Lamartine, Hugo, Baudelaire or Mallarmé; to use major constitutive and legislative texts such as prefaces, programmes or manifestos to try to rediscover the objective configuration of the space of possible or impossible forms and figures as it presented itself to each of the great innovators;

to find how each of them pictured his or her revolutionary mission, whether it concerned forms to destroy (sonnets, alexandrines, 'poetic droning'), rhetorical devices to demolish (comparison, metaphor) or content and sentiments to banish (lyricism, effusion, psychology). Everything happens as if, in expelling from the universe of legitimate poetry those procedures whose conventional character dooms itself by overuse, each of these revolutions has contributed to a sort of historical analysis of poetic language, tending to isolate its most specific procedures and effects, such as the rupture with phonosemantic parallelism.[37]

The history of the novel, at least since Flaubert, may also be described as a long effort to 'kill the novelistic',[38] in Edmond de Goncourt's phrase, that is to say, to purify the novel of everything that seems to define it – plot, action, hero. The line goes from Flaubert and the 'novel about nothing' or the Goncourts and the ambition for a 'novel without events, plot, or low amusements'[39] to the 'Nouveau Roman' and the dissolution of the linear story and, with Claude Simon, the search for an almost pictorial (or musical) composition, founded on periodic returns and internal correspondences of a limited number of narrative elements, situations, characters, locations, actions, repeated several times with modifications or modulations.

This 'pure' novel gives all the signs of requiring a new reading of the sort hitherto reserved for poetry, whose 'ideal' limit is the scholastic exercise of decoding or re-creation based on repeated reading. In fact, the writing can only incorporate an expectation of such an exigent reading because it is produced in a field where the felicitous conditions of this demand are realized. The 'pure' novel is the product of a field where the boundary between the critic and the writer tends to disappear, the writer being such an expert on the theory behind his novels because he puts a reflexive and critical thought about the novel and its history into his novels, constantly recalling their status as fiction.[40] Without infinitely increasing the number of examples of this reflexive doubling, one could, by going farther back in time, discern it again at the heart of the *Dada Manifesto*, a paradoxical discourse which wants to be both what it is, a manifesto, and a critical reflection on what it is, an anti-manifesto, an autodestructive manifesto.[41]

In the same way, René Leibowitz describes the revolutionary work of Schoenberg, Berg and Webern as the outcome of a new realization and a systematic and (in his expression) 'ultra-consequential' application of the principles inscribed in an implicit state in the whole musical tradition, a tradition still present in its entirety in works which surpass it by achieving it on another plane. So he observes that Schoenberg, seizing hold of the ninth interval which romantic musicians still used only rarely, and in a fundamental position, 'consciously decides to draw all the consequences' and to use it in all possible inversions. And he notes: 'Now it is the total realization of the fundamental compositional principle which, while implicit in the whole previous evolution of polyphony, becomes explicit for the first time in Schoenberg's work: it is the principle of *perpetual development*.'[42] Finally, summing up Schoenberg's principal achievements, he concludes: 'All this, in summary, merely consecrated in a more straightforward and systematic fashion a state of affairs which, less straightforwardly and systematically, already existed in the final tonal works by Schoenberg himself, and up to a certain point, in certain works by Wagner.'[43] How can we not recognize here a logic which has found its most exemplary expression in the case of mathematics? This is the logic which (as Daval and Guilbaud have shown with regard to reasoning by recurrence), as 'a sort of reasoning on reasoning or reasoning raised to the second degree',[44] leads the mathematician to work ceaselessly on the outcome of the work of previous mathematicians, objectivizing the operations which were already present in their work, though in an implicit state.

Reflexivity and 'naiveté'

The evolution of the field of cultural production towards a greater autonomy is thus accompanied by a greater *reflexivity*, which leads each of the 'genres' to a sort of critical turning in on itself, on its own principle, on its own premises: and it becomes more and more frequent that the work of art, a *vanitas* which betrays itself as such, includes a sort of autoderision. In effect, to the extent that the field closes in on itself, a practical mastery of the specific attainments of the whole history of the genre which are objectified in past works and recorded, codified and canonized by the whole corpus of professionals of conservation and celebration – historians of art and literature, exegetes, analysts – becomes part of the conditions of entry into the field of restricted production. The history of the field is truly irreversible; and the products of this relatively autonomous history present a kind of *cumulativity*.

Paradoxically, the presence of the specific past is most visible of all among the avant-garde producers who are controlled by the past when it comes to their intention to surpass it, an intention itself linked to a state of the history of the field. The reason the field has a directed and cumulative history is because the very intention of *surpassing* which properly defines the avant-garde is itself the result of a whole history, and because it is inevitably situated in relation to what it aims to surpass, that is, in relation to all the activities of surpassing which have occurred in the very structure of the field and in the space of possibles it imposes on new entrants. This means that what happens in the field is more and more linked to a specific history of the field, and hence it becomes more and more difficult to *deduce* it directly from the state of the social world at the moment under consideration. It is the very logic of the field which tends to select and consecrate all legitimate ruptures with the history objectified in the structure of the field, that is, those ruptures which are the product of a disposition formed by the history of the field and informed by that history, and hence inscribed in the continuity of the field.

Thus the whole history of the field is immanent in each of its states and to be equal to its objective requirements, as a producer but also as a consumer, one must *possess* a practical or theoretical mastery of this history and the space of possibles in which it occurs. The entrance fee to be acquitted by any new entrant is none other than the mastery of the set of achievements which underly the *current problematic*. Any interrogation arises from a tradition, from a practical or theoretical mastery of the *heritage* which is inscribed in the very structure of the field, as a *state of things*, dissimulated by its own evidence, which delimits the thinkable and the unthinkable and which opens the space of possible questions and answers. This is seen particularly well in the case of the most advanced sciences, where the mastery of theories, methods and techniques is the condition of access to a universe of problems which professionals agree to consider as interesting or important.

Paradoxically, communication between professionals and lay people is never as difficult as in the case of the social sciences, where the barrier to entry is socially less visible. Ignorance of the specific problematic which is historically constituted in the field and which gives the solutions offered by the specialist their meaning leads to scientific analyses being treated as answers to questions of common sense, and results in practical interrogations, ethical or political, which are like *opinions*, and most often 'attacks' (because of the effect of disclosure they produce). This structural *allodoxia* is encouraged by the fact that one always finds, at the very heart of the field, 'naifs' (not necessarily innocents) who, for want of the theoretical and technical means to master the current problematic, import into the field certain social problems in a crude state, without subjecting them to the necessary transmutation in order to constitute them as sociological problems. In this way, they confer an apparent ratification on an endoxic problem – usually political – which lay people project on to scientific productions.

In the artistic field in its advanced state of evolution, there is no place for those who do not know the history of the field and everything it has engendered, starting with a certain totally paradoxical relationship with history's legacy. Once again, it is the field which constructs and consecrates as such those designated as 'naifs' by their ignorance of the logic of the game. To be convinced of this, it is enough to compare methodically le Douanier Rousseau, as a 'painter object' entirely 'made' by the field and the field's plaything, with the person who might well have 'discovered' him (he was the inventor of Brisset, whom he called the 'le Douanier Rousseau of philology'), Marcel Duchamp, creator of an art of 'painting' involving not only the art of producing a work, but the art of *producing oneself* as a painter. Nor should we forget that these two personages, endowed with properties so antithetical that no biographer would dream of relating them to each other, at least have in common the fact that they only exist as painters for posterity as a result of the entirely particular logic of a field which has reached a high degree of autonomy and is inhabited by a tradition of permanent rupture with aesthetic tradition.

Le Douanier Rousseau has no 'biography' in the sense of a life story worthy of being recounted and transcribed;[45] a minor civil servant, steady, in love with Eugénie Léonie V., a saleswoman in 'household goods', he has for clients only 'modest folk who lend little value to his paintings' – all these traits have an air of parody and turn this character from a Courteline or Labiche comedy into the intended victim of cruel scenes of burlesque consecration which are mounted by his 'friends', painters (like Picasso) and poets (like Apollinaire), and whose parodic character undoubtedly did not completely escape him.[46] Without a history, he is also deprived of culture and occupation: he makes his start at age forty-two, and in fact he owes the basic essentials of his aesthetic education to the Exposition Universelle of 1889. The choices he makes, in subject as well as in manner, appear as the realization of a popular or petit-bourgeois 'aesthetic' – that expressed in ordinary photographic production – but oriented by the deeply allodoxical intention of an admirer of academic painters, Clément, Bonnat, Gérôme, whose mythological and allegorical scenes like *Lioness Meeting a Jaguar*, *Love in the Wild Animal Cage*, and *Saint Jerome Sleeping on a Lion* he thought he was imitating. (These academic admirations are doubtless not unconnected with the secondary studies begun, that is to say, prematurely *interrupted*, by le Douanier.)[47]

It has often been said that Rousseau 'copied' his works, or that he used a pantograph to produce the sketches which he then set about 'colouring' like the images in a child's colouring book. A number of 'originals' of his 'copies' have also been located in popular publications, illustrated magazines and illustrations for *feuilletons* – especially for *La Guerre* (1894) – as well as children's albums and photographs – originals for *Les Artilleurs* (1895) which is at the Guggenheim Museum, *Une Noce à la Campagne* (1905) and *La Carriole du Père Juniet* (1908).[48] But it has been less noticed that the most characteristic thematic and stylistic traits of his work correspond to that 'aesthetic' expressed in the practical photography of the popular classes or the petite-bourgeoisie: often placed at the centre of the image, according to a rigid and sometimes brutal frontality (*Jeune Fille en Rose*, in Philadelphia), the figures are given all the emblems and symbols of their estate, which, along with the caption (almost always present), are meant to provide the rationale for the painting. Thus, as in popular photography which consecrates the meeting between an emblematic site and a figure, in a painting naively entitled *Moi-même* the painter is provided with all the attributes of his function – palette, brushes, beret – and Paris is designated by all the symbols proper for its identification – bridges over the Seine, the Eiffel Tower. The moments he records are the Sundays of petit-bourgeois life, and his figures, provided with all the inevitable accessories of the fête (impeccably stiff collars, moustaches gleaming with brilliantine, black waistcoats) pose before the photographer charged with solemnizing those solemn moments when social relations are confirmed or created – relationships which are made visible by symbolizing them: in *Une Noce à la Campagne*, the hands (difficult to treat) are hidden, except the bride's which grasps the groom's. Even when he copies a model borrowed from scholarly tradition, le Douanier reintroduces his 'functionalist' vision. Thus in *Heureux Quatuor* (1902) Rousseau imposes a change of functional status on the different elements – the man, the woman, the cherub, the animal – that he has taken, as Dora Vallier shows, from Gérôme's *Innocence* (1852): the cherub participates in the scene and the bitch has become a dog, a symbol of fidelity which enters into this allegory of love.[49] And these furtive borrowings are those of a plagiarist-*bricoleur* who is unaware of all the discreetly parodic and subtly distanced appropriations deliberately practised by the most refined of his contemporaries.

That said, these products of an artistic intention typical of the popular 'aesthetic' introduce, by the very fact of their 'naiveté', a *distance* of a sort the most advanced artists find seductive: 'What I liked', said Rimbaud, 'were absurd paintings, pictures over doorways, stage sets, carnival backdrops, bright-coloured prints, old-fashioned literature, church Latin, erotic books full of misspellings, the kind of novels our grandmothers read, fairy tales, little children's books, old operas, silly old songs, the native rhythm of country rimes.'[50] And, in fact, following the logic which will be taken to its limit with the productions assembled under the name of outsider art, a sort of *natural art* which only exists as such by an *arbitrary* decree of the most refined, le Douanier Rousseau, like all 'naive artists' – Sunday painters born of state pensions and paid holidays – is literally *created* by the artistic field. A creature-creator who has to be produced as a legitimate creator, taking the shape of the personage of le Douanier Rousseau, in order to legitimate his product,[51] he offers the field, without knowing it, an opportunity to realize certain of the possibilities which were objectively inscribed there: 'if he had lived twenty-five years earlier, meaning that if, instead of dying in 1910 he had died in 1884, before the foundation of the Salon des Indépendants, we would never have heard of him.'[52] Critics and artists can only give pictorial existence to this 'painter' who owes nothing to the history of painting – and who, as Dora Vallier puts it, 'benefits from an aesthetic revolt that he doesn't even see' – if they view him historically and so situate him in the space of artistic possibles, citing in relation to him works and authors no doubt unknown to him and, in any case, profoundly alien to his intentions – popular engravings, the Bayeux tapestry, Paolo Uccello or the Dutch. In the same way, the 'theoreticians' of outsider art can only constitute the artistic productions of children or of schizophrenics as an extreme form of art for art's sake, in a sort of absolute misinterpretation, because they overlook the fact that they cannot appear as such except to an *eye* produced, as theirs is, by the artistic field, one invested with the history of this field.[53] It is the whole history of the artistic field which determines (or makes possible) the essentially contradictory approach, one necessarily doomed to failure, by which they aim to constitute artists against the historical definition of the artist. This *art brut*, meaning natural and uncultivated, only exercises such a fascination in so far as the creative act of the highly cultivated 'discoverer' who makes it exist as such manages to forget itself and make itself forgotten (meanwhile asserting itself as one of the supreme forms of 'creative' freedom): thus constituted as art without an artist, a natural art, arising from a gift of nature, it procures the feeling of a miraculous necessity, in the manner of an *Iliad* written by a monkey at a typewriter, thus furnishing the supreme justification for the charismatic ideology of the uncreated creator. It is significant that the most consequential, therefore the most inconsequential, of these theoreticians of natural culture (Roger Cardinal for example) make the absence of any relationship with the artistic field, and especially any apprenticeship, the most decisive criterion of belonging to *art brut* (the only ones who fit this criterion completely are schizophrenic painters and some extraordinary individuals, like Scottie Wilson (born in 1890), a travelling salesman who late in life discovered a vocation as an illustrator and who, hung in the galleries and modern art museums of New York, London and Paris, and sought after by experts, wanted to stay on the margins and went on to the streets to sell paintings which the galleries were selling two hundred times dearer).

It is not by chance that the history of the artistic field offers both (and almost simultaneously) the paradigm of the 'naive' painter and its total converse (just as paradigmatic), the roué painter *par excellence*, Marcel Duchamp. Born of a family of artists – his maternal grandfather, Émile-Frédéric Nicolle, is a painter and engraver, his elder brother is the painter Jacques Villon, his other brother Raymond Duchamp-Villon is a Cubist sculptor, the eldest of his sisters is a painter – Marcel Duchamp moves in the artistic field like a fish in water. In 1904, after having obtained his baccalauréat – a rare title among painters of the period – he turns up in Paris at his brother Jacques's, frequents the Académie Julian, haunts the gatherings of avant-garde painters and writers happening at Raymond's, and by the age of twenty he has tried all possible styles. Continually breaking with conventions, whether those of the avant-garde, such as the rejection of the nude among Cubists (with his *Nude Descending a Staircase*), he does not cease to assert his will 'to go further', to surpass all past and present experimentation in a sort of permanent revolution.

But it is a matter, in his case, of a conscious and well-equipped intention – since it is founded on direct knowledge of all past and present experimentation – to rehabilitate painting by getting rid of the 'physical aspect', the 'strictly retinal', in order to 'recreate ideas' (from whence the importance of titles). 'I am fed up', he says, 'with the expression "stupid as a painter",' and to escape 'the platitudes of the café and the studio' he often invokes four-dimensional space and non-Euclidean geometry. Knowing the game to his finger-tips, he produces objects whose production as works of art presupposes the production of the producer as artist: he invents the *ready-made*, that manufactured object promoted to the dignity of an art object by the artist's symbolic stroke, often signified by a play on words. For someone familiar with Brisset and de Roussel, the pun, a sort of verbal *ready-made*, reveals unexpected relationships of meaning between ordinary words, just as the *ready-made* reveals hidden aspects of objects by isolating them from the familiar context which gives them their customary meaning and function.

It is significant that at the very moment when Duchamp makes an artistic game of it, the pun, one of the most typical traits of bohemian culture (the philosopher Colline emits a continual flow of them in *Scenes of Bohemian Life*), becomes one of the foundations of the art of *cabaret* which is developed around Montmartre, at the Lapin Agile (the 'Agile Rabbit'), a pun on the name of André Gil, who painted its sign) and at the Chat Noir. With figures such as Willy, Maurice Donnay and Alphonse Allais, cabaret exploits the slightly sulphurous prestige of the artistic milieu by popularizing the humour of the studio for the mass public and bringing them the traditions of parody and caricature characteristic of the artistic spirit (a little like, in another era, the theatre of Jules Romain will offer the then prestigious traditions of the 'esprit normalien' ['wit of the École Normale Supérieure'] to the bourgeois public). (In recent times, the newspaper *Libération*, born in the aftermath of the 1968 student movement, has taken the intellectual play on words, to be found in its legitimate form among the noblest authors of the day – such as Jacques Lacan – and popularized it for a wide audience with intellectual pretensions and aspirations, while offering at the same time a marked-down designer-label form of intellectual lifestyle.)

By virtue of the somewhat provocative freedom with which it asserts the discretionary power of the creator, as well as by the distance the producer thereby proclaims with respect to his own production, the *ready-made* situates itself at the opposite pole from the shameful 'assisted *ready-mades*' of le Douanier Rousseau, who hides his sources. But above all, just as a good chess player, master of the immanent necessity of the game, may inscribe in each move the anticipation of the subsequent moves he will make, Duchamp foresees interpretations in order to undermine or thwart them; and when, as in *La Mariée Mise à Nu par ses Célibataires (The Bride Stripped Bare by Her Bachelors)*, he uses mythical or sexual symbols, he knowingly refers to esoteric, alchemical, mythological or psychoanalytic culture. A virtuoso of the art of playing with all the possibilities offered by the game, he gives the appearance of coming back to simple common sense in order to denounce the convoluted interpretations which the most zealous commentators have given his works; or else he leaves hanging in doubt, by irony or humour, the meaning of a work which is *deliberately polysemic*. By thus reinforcing the ambiguity which makes the work transcendent over all interpretations, including those of the author himself, he methodically draws on the possibilities of a willed polysemy which, with the appearance of a corps of professional interpreters – meaning professionally determined to find meaning and necessity, however much work of interpretation or overinterpretation is involved – is found inscribed in the field itself, and therefore in the creative intention of producers. It is understandable that one could say of Duchamp that he is 'the only painter to have made himself a place in the world of art as much for what he did not do as for what he did';[54] the refusal to paint (marked by retirement after the unfinished *Grand Verre* in 1923) thus becomes, as an actualization of the Dada refusal to separate art from life, an artistic act, even the supreme artistic act, similar in its order of contemplative silence to the shepherd of Heidegger's Being.

Thus the relative autonomy of the field is asserted more and more in works whose formal properties and value are derived only from the structure, hence the history, of the field, increasingly barring the 'short circuit', meaning the possibility of passing directly from what is produced in the social world to what is produced in the field. The perception called for by the work produced within the logic of the field is a *differential* perception, distinctive, drawing into the perceiving of each singular work the space of compossible works, and hence attentive and sensitive to the *deviations* in relation to other works, contemporary but also past. The spectator deprived of this historic competence is doomed to the indifference of one who does not have the means to make differentiations. It follows, paradoxically, that adequate perception and appreciation of an art produced by a permanent rupture with history tends to become historical through and through: it is increasingly rare that delectation does not have as a precondition the consciousness and the knowledge of the historical games and stakes of which the work is the product, of the 'impact', as people are fond of saying, that it has and which clearly cannot be grasped without historical comparison and references.[55]

The independence with respect to historical conditions has its foundations in the historical process which led to the *emergence* of a social game (relatively) free of the determinations and constraints of the historical conjuncture. Since everything produced there draws its existence and meaning, essentially, from the specific logic and history of the game itself, this game is kept afloat by virtue of its own *consistency*, meaning the specific regularities which define it and the mechanisms – such as the dialectic of positions, dispositions and position-takings – which confer on it its own *conatus*.

This is true, too, of social science itself, which cannot assert itself as such, meaning as liberated (as much as possible at the moment under consideration) from social determinations, except in so far as the social conditions of autonomy with respect to social demand are instituted. It cannot break the circle of relativism brought about by its very existence unless it brings to light the social conditions containing the possibility of a thought liberated from all social conditionings and fights to establish such conditions, meanwhile equipping itself with the means, especially theoretical ones, to fight within itself the epistemological effects of epistemological ruptures which always involve social ruptures.

Only the social history of the process of autonomization enables us to take proper account of the freedom with regard to 'social context' which is lost through a direct engagement with current social conditions and as a result of the very effort to explain. It is within history that the principle of freedom from history resides. This by no means implies that the most 'pure' products, 'pure' art or 'pure' science, cannot fulfil totally 'impure' social functions – such as the functions of distinction and social discrimination or, more subtly, the function of a disavowal of the social world which is inscribed, like a subtly repressed renunciation, in freedoms and ruptures strictly confined to the order of pure forms.

Supply and demand

The homology between the space of producers and the space of consumers, meaning between the literary (etc.) field and the field of power, grounds the unintentional adjustment between supply and demand: at the temporally dominated and symbolically dominant pole of the field, writers produce for their peers (meaning for the field itself or even for the most autonomous section of this field); and at the other extreme, writers produce for the dominant regions of the field of power, for example the 'bourgeois theatre'. Contrary to what Max Weber suggests in the particular case of religion, adjustment to demand is never completely the result of a *conscious transaction* between producers and consumers, and still less of a deliberate search for adjustment, except perhaps in the case of the most heteronomous enterprises of cultural production (which, for this very reason, are correctly called 'commercial').

It is as a function of the necessities inscribed in their position within the field of production as a space of objectively distinct positions (different theatres, publishers, newspapers, fashion houses, galleries, etc.) with which different interests are associated that different enterprises of cultural production are led to offer objectively differentiated products; and these receive their distinctive meaning and value from their position in a system of distances differentiated and adjusted, without really looking for adjustment, according to the expectations of the occupants of homologous positions in the field of power (among whom the majority of consumers are recruited). When a work 'finds', as the saying goes, an audience which understands and appreciates it, this is almost always the effect of a *coincidence*, of a meeting between causal series which are partially independent, and is almost never – and, in any case, never completely – the result of a conscious search for adjustment to the expectations of customers, or to the constraints of command or demand.

The homology established today between the space of production and the space of consumption is the basis of a permanent dialectic which means that the most diverse tastes find that they can be satisfied by works on offer, which appear as if they were their objectification, while the fields of production find the conditions of their constitution and of their functioning in the tastes which ensure – immediately or in due course – a market for their different products.

If the accord between supply and demand presents all the appearances of a pre-established harmony, it is because the relationship between the field of cultural production and the field of power takes on the form of an almost perfect homology between two structures in chiasmus. In effect, in the same way that in the field of power economic power increases as one goes from temporally dominated positions to temporally dominant ones, while cultural capital varies in the inverse direction, so in the field of cultural production, economic profits increase as one goes from the 'autonomous' pole to the 'heteronomous' pole, or, if you will, from 'pure' art to 'bourgeois' or 'commercial' art, whereas specific profits vary inversely.

The effect of homology, which might be called automatic, also sustains the action of all institutions aiming to foster contacts, interactions, even transactions, between different categories of writers or artists and the different categories of their bourgeois clients, especially academies, clubs and perhaps above all salons – the latter are undoubtedly the most important of the institutional mediations between the field of power and the intellectual field. In effect, salons themselves constitute a field of competition for the accumulation of social capital and symbolic capital: the number and quality of habitués – politicians, artists, writers, journalists and so on – are a good measure of the power of attraction of each of these meeting places for members of different sections and, by the same token, of the power which may be exercised through it, and thanks to homologies, over the field of cultural production and over all instances of consecration such as the academies. (This is well illustrated, for example, in the analysis offered by Christophe Charle of the role of Madame de Loynes and Madame Caillavet in the rivalry between Jules Lemaitre and Anatole France.[56]) Designated by the opposition between work and leisure, money and art, the useful and the futile to concern themselves with art and taste, and with the domestic cult of moral and aesthetic refinement (which was, moreover, the major condition of success in the matrimonial market), at the same time as they take responsibility for the maintenance of social relations within the family group (as 'mistresses of the house'), women of the aristocracy and bourgeoisie occupy in the field of domestic power a position homologous to that held by writers and artists, dominated among the dominants, at the heart of the field of power. This undoubtedly helps to predispose them to play the role of intermediaries between the world of art and the world of money, between the artist and the 'bourgeois' (this is how we should interpret the existence and effects of *liaisons*, notably those established between women of the aristocracy and the Parisian grande bourgeoisie and writers or artists issuing from the dominated classes).

It seems that, historically, the constitution of a relatively autonomous field of artistic production offering *stylistically diversified* products might go hand in hand with the appearance of two or more groups of patrons of the arts having different artistic expectations.[57] It is acknowledged in a general way that the initial diversification which is the basis for the functioning of a space of production as a field is only possible thanks to the diversity of publics, which it evidently helps to constitute as such: just as one does not think today of 'experimental' cinema without an audience of students and of aspiring intellectuals and artists, so one cannot conceive of the appearance and development of an artistic and literary avant-garde in the course of the nineteenth century without the public guaranteed it by the literary and artistic bohemia concentrated in Paris. Although too destitute to buy, bohemia provides a justification for the development of points of distribution and specific consecration of a suitable sort to secure a form of symbolic patronage for the innovators, whether through polemic or scandal.

The homology between positions in the literary (etc.) field and positions in the global social field is never as perfect as the one established between the literary field and the field of power from which the bulk of its clientele is usually recruited. Writers and artists situated at the economically dominated (and symbolically dominant) pole of the literary field, itself temporally dominated, can doubtless feel a solidarity (at least in their rejections and rebellions) with the occupants of economically and culturally dominated positions in social space. Nevertheless, since the homologies of position on which these alliances of act or thought are built are also associated with profound differences in economic and social conditions, they are not exempt from misunderstanding, or even a sort of structural bad faith. The structural affinity between the literary avant-garde and the political vanguard is the source of *rapprochements* – for example, between intellectual anarchism and the Symbolist movement – and flaunted convergences (Mallarmé speaking of the book as an 'attentat' – a terrorist act) which retain their fair share of prudent distancing.[58]

Discrepancy and misunderstanding are even clearer between the dominants in the field of power and their homologues at the core of the field of cultural production. When they think of themselves in relation to cultural producers – and in particular to 'pure' artists – the dominants may feel themselves on the side of nature, instinct, life, action, virility, and also common sense, order and reason (in opposition to culture, intelligence, thought, femininity, etc.). Yet they can no longer arm themselves with certain of these oppositions when they think of their relationship with the dominated classes with whom they also contrast themselves – oppositions such as theory to practice, thought to action, culture to nature, reason to instinct, intelligence to life. And they have need of certain of the properties offered them by writers and especially artists in order to think of and justify themselves, in their own eyes in the first instance, as existing as they do: the cult of art tends to become a more and more necessary element of the bourgeois art of living, with the 'disinterestedness' of 'pure' consumption being indispensable, thanks to the 'supplement of soul' it brings, for marking the distance from the primary necessities of 'nature' and from those subjected to them.

It remains true that cultural producers may use the power conferred on them, above all in periods of crisis, by their capacity to produce a systematic and critical representation of the social world in order to mobilize the virtual force of the dominated and to help to subvert the established order in the field of power. And the particular role that 'proletaroid intellectuals' have been able to play in a number of subversive movements, religious or political, undoubtedly results from the fact that the effect of the homology of position which brings these dominated intellectuals to feel solidarity with the dominated is often reinforced (notably in the case of the leaders of the French Revolution studied by Robert Darnton) with an identity or at least with a similitude of condition; and so everything inclines them to put their capacities for systematization and explication at the service of popular indignation and revolt.

Internal struggles and external sanctions

Internal struggles are to an extent arbitrated by external sanctions. In effect, even if they are largely independent *in their principle* (meaning in the causes and reasons determining them), the clashes which unfold inside the literary (etc.) field always depend, *in their outcome*, happy or unhappy, on the correspondence they have with external clashes (those which unfold at the core of the field of power or the social field as a whole) and the support that one group or another may find there. Thus it is that changes as decisive as an upheaval in the internal hierarchy of different genres, or a transformation in the hierarchy within genres themselves, affecting the structure of the field as a whole, are made possible by the *correspondence between internal changes* (themselves directly determined by the transformation in the chances of access to the literary field) *and external changes* which offer to new categories of producers (successively, the Romantics, Naturalists, Symbolists, etc.) and to their products consumers who occupy positions in social space which are homologous to their own position in the field, and hence consumers endowed with dispositions and tastes in harmony with the products these producers offer them.

A successful revolution in literature or in painting (we will demonstrate this with respect to Manet) is the product of the meeting between two processes, relatively independent, which occur in the field and outside it. The new heretical entrants who refuse to enter into the cycle of simple reproduction, based on the mutual recognition of the 'old' and the 'new', and break with the current norms of production in defiance of the expectations of the field can usually only succeed in imposing recognition of their products by virtue of external changes. The most decisive of these changes are the political ruptures, such as revolutionary crises, which change the power relations at the heart of the field (thus, the 1848 revolution reinforces the dominated pole, determining a provisional shift of writers towards 'social art'), or the appearance of new categories of consumers who, having an affinity with the new producers, guarantee the success of their products.

The subversive action of the avant-garde, discrediting current conventions, meaning the norms of production and evaluation of the aesthetic orthodoxy, and making the products realized according to these norms seem superseded and outmoded, gets objective support from the *wearing out of the effect* of consecrated works. This wearing out has nothing mechanical about it. It is primarily the result of the routinization of production associated with the impact of epigones and academicism, which even avant-garde movements do not escape, and arises from the repeated and repetitive application of proved procedures and the uninventive use of an art of inventing already invented. Furthermore, the most innovative works tend, *with time*, to produce their own audience by imposing their own structures, through the effect of familiarization, as categories of perception legitimate for any possible work (so that one comes to see the works of art of the past – and, as Proust noticed, the natural world itself – through categories derived from an art of the past that has become natural). The spreading of the norms of perception and appreciation they were tending to impose is accompanied by a *banalization* of the effect of debanalization that they were once able to exercise. This sort of *erosion of the effect of rupture* undoubtedly varies according to the recipients, and in particular depends on how long they have been exposed to the innovative work and, by the same token, on how close they are to the centre of avant-garde values: the best-informed consumers (and, foremost, competitors, and usually those among them who are the most direct disciples) are naturally the most inclined to experience a feeling of weariness and to seek out the procedures and tricks, even the tics, which made for the initial originality of the movement. Of course, banalization can only be intensified or accelerated if there is also snobbery, the deliberate search for distinction as against common taste which introduces into consumption a logic analogous to the distinctive overstatement of the avant-garde (providing another example of the homology between production and consumption).[59]

It can be seen that the relative rarity, hence the value, of cultural products tends to decrease with the advance of a process of consecration, since this is almost inevitably accompanied by a banalization designed to encourage dissemination, the latter determining in turn a devaluation entailed by the increase in the number of consumers and by a corresponding weakening of the distinctive rarity of goods and of the act of consuming them. The devaluation of products offered by the avant-garde in the course of consecration happens even faster if the newcomers can invoke purity of origins and the charismatic rupture between art and money (or success) and use these to denounce the compromises with the times evidenced by the diffusion of products in the process of canonization among a more and more extended clientele, a clientele enlarged beyond the sacred limits of the field of production, extending even so far as simple lay people, whose very admiration is always suspected of profaning sacred work.

The case of André Gide can be seen as a typical example of the representation which the avant-garde (here 'young literature') makes of an avant-garde in the process of consecration and the moral reprobation with which it undermines successes when they are considered compromises: 'What disturbs Gide is *not the success of hacks whom he despises, or of established writers* like Anatole France, or Paul Bourget, or Pierre Loti, who evolve in zones too different from his own, but rather comparison with certain of his own kind and stature, even if they are his elders, who have broken through the wall of the ghetto at the cost of what he takes as *unpardonable concessions*: Maeterlinck, who has become a sage in current consumption; Barrès, who took a short-cut through politics; Henri de Régnier, whose *La Double Maîtresse* has stamped him as a novelist who writes too many newspaper articles; and shortly Francis Jammes, whose fine sentiments are going to bring him a readership which was cool towards his fine poetry; not to mention the hundred thousand copies notched up by the Aphrodite of the former *alter ego*, Pierre Louÿs.'[60]

Thus the social ageing of a work of art, the imperceptible transformation pushing it towards the *déclassé* or the classic, is the result of a meeting between an internal movement, linked to struggles within the field provoking the production of different works, and an external movement, linked to social change in the audience, which sanctions and reinforces (by making it visible to all) the loss of rarity. Just as the great brand names in perfume, when they have let their clientele grow excessively, have lost a share of their first customers in a direct relationship to their acquisition of new publics (wide distribution of products at low prices being accompanied by a drop in sales), and just as, like Carven in the 1960s, they have little by little brought together a composite clientele made up of elegant but ageing women who remain faithful to the perfumes of their yesteryears and of young but less wealthy women who discover these outmoded products when they are out of fashion,[61] so in the same way (because differences in the matter of economic and cultural capital are translated into temporal differences in access to rare goods), a formerly highly distinctive product which is disseminated (hence making itself less select) and simultaneously loses the new clients who are the most concerned about distinction will witness its initial clientele age and the social quality of its public decline. Thus one knows from a recent study that composers devalued by the effect of dissemination, such as Albinoni, Vivaldi or Chopin, are more and more savoured as one goes towards the higher age groups and towards lower levels of education.

In the literary or artistic field, those last to arrive in the avant-garde may take advantage of the correlation which people tend to establish spontaneously between the quality of the work and the social quality of its public in order to try to discredit the work of the avant-garde already in the course of consecration, by attributing the lowering of the social quality of its audience to a renunciation or slackening of subversive intention. And the new heretical rupture with forms which have now become canonical may rely on a *potential audience* which expects of the new product what the initial audience expected of the product previously consecrated. The new avant-garde occupying the position (or, in the language of marketing, the niche) abandoned by the consecrated avant-garde will find it all the easier if it justifies its iconoclastic ruptures by invoking a return to the initial and ideal definition of the practice, that is to say, to purity, obscurity and to the poverty of its beginnings; literary or artistic heresy is made against orthodoxy, but also with it, in the name of what it once was.

Here we are apparently dealing with a *very general model*, which is valid for all enterprises founded on the renunciation of temporal profit and the disavowal of the economy. The inherent contradiction in enterprises which, like those of religion or art, spurn material profit while assuring, *in more or less the long term*, profits of all kinds to those who have the most ardently rejected them is undoubtedly the basis of the *life-cycle* characterizing them. The initial phase, full of asceticism and renunciation, which consists of the accumulation of symbolic capital, is succeeded by a phase of exploitation of this capital, which ensures temporal profits and, through them, a transformation of lifestyles which brings in its wake the loss of symbolic capital and favours the success of rival heresies. In the literary or artistic field, this cycle is bound to set in because by the time success comes (often very late), the founder cannot, if only as a result of the inertia of the habitus, completely break initial commitments, and because in any case the enterprise dies with the founder. However, the cycle finds its full development in certain religious enterprises where the heirs and successors may gather the profits of the ascetic enterprise without ever having manifested the virtues which secured them.

The meeting of two histories

In the order of consumption, cultural practices and consumptions which may be observed at a given moment in time are the product of the meeting between two histories, the history of the fields of production, which have their own laws of change, and the history of the social space as a whole, which determines tastes by the intermediary of the properties inscribed in a position, and notably through the social conditionings associated with particular material conditions of existence and a particular rank in the social structure. Similarly, in the order of production, the practices of writers and artists, starting with their works, are the product of the meeting of two histories, the history of the production of the position occupied and the history of the production of the dispositions of its occupants. Even if the position contributes to making dispositions, the latter – to the extent that they are partially the product of independent circumstances, exterior to the field properly speaking – have an autonomous existence and effectiveness, and they may help to *make* the positions.

In no field is the clash between positions and dispositions more constant and more uncertain than in the literary and artistic field. While it is true that the space of available positions helps to determine the expected, even required, properties of possible candidates, and hence the categories of agents they may attract and more especially *retain*, it remains true that the perception of the space of possible positions and trajectories and the appreciation of the value that each one of them receives from its place in this space depend on the dispositions of agents. However, since the positions it offers are not very institutionalized, never legally guaranteed, and thus are very vulnerable to symbolic contestation, and are non-hereditary (although some specific forms of transmission do exist), the field of cultural production constitutes the terrain *par excellence* of struggles for the redefinition of the 'post'.

However great the effect of the field, it is never exercised in a mechanical fashion, and the relationship between positions and position-takings (notably works of art) is always mediated by the dispositions of agents and by the space of possibles which they constitute as such through the perception of the space of position-takings they structure. Social origin is not, as is sometimes believed, the basis of a linear series of mechanical determinations, with the profession of the father determining the position occupied, and that in turn determining the position-takings. Account must be taken of the effects which are exercised through the structure of the field, and in particular through the space of possibles offered, and which depend principally on the intensity of the competition, itself linked to quantitative and qualitative characteristics of the flow of new entrants.

The posts of 'pure' writer and artist, like that of 'intellectual', are institutions of freedom, which are constructed against the 'bourgeoisie' (in the artists' terms) and, more concretely, against the market and against state bureaucracies (academies, salons, etc.) through a series of ruptures, partially cumulative, which are often made possible only by a diversion of the resources of the market – hence of the 'bourgeoisie' – and even of state bureaucracies.[62] These posts are the end point of all the *collective work* which has led to the constitution of the field of cultural production as a space independent of the economy and politics; but, in return, this work of emancipation cannot be carried out or extended unless the post finds an agent endowed with the required dispositions, such as an indifference to profit and a propensity to make risky investments, as well as the properties which, like income, constitute the (external) conditions of these dispositions. In this sense, the collective invention which produces the job of writer and artist is always to be begun again.

However, the institutionalization of past inventions and the recognition increasingly granted to an activity of cultural production which is its own purpose, and the will to emancipation which it involves, tend to reduce progressively the cost of this permanent reinvention. The further the process of autonomization advances, the more possible it becomes to occupy the position of 'pure' producer without having the properties – or at least without having them all or to the same degree – that had to be possessed to *produce* the position; the more, in other words, the new entrants who orient themselves to the most 'autonomous' positions may skip over the more or less heroic sacrifices and ruptures of the past (while securing their symbolic profits for themselves by turning them into a cult).

Trying to establish a direct correlation between producers and the social group from which they draw their economic support (collectors, spectators, patrons, etc.) is to forget that the logic of the field means that one can make use of the resources offered by a group or an institution to produce products which are more or less independent of the interests and values of this group or that institution. The posts of a totally extraordinary kind offered by the literary (etc.) field once it has achieved a high degree of autonomy owe it to their objectively contradictory objective intention to exist only at the lowest degree of institutionalization: in the first place in the form of words – 'avant-garde' for example, or names of exemplary figures, the cursed artist and his heroic legend – which are constitutive of a tradition of liberty and critique; then, and above all, in the form of *anti-institutional institutions*, of which the paradigm might be the 'Salon des Refusés' or the small avant-garde journal, and mechanisms of competition able to provide the kinds of incentives and rewards that make efforts at emancipation and subversion conceivable. Thus, for example, acts of prophetic denunciation, of which 'J'accuse' is the paradigm, are so profoundly constitutive, after Zola, and especially perhaps after Sartre, of the figure of the intellectual that they are incumbent on all who aspire to a position – especially a dominant one – in the intellectual field. This is a paradoxical universe in which freedom from institutions is found inscribed *in* those institutions.

The constructed trajectory

One understands why the constructed biography can only be the last step in the scientific approach: in effect, the *social trajectory* is defined as the *series of positions* successively occupied by the same agent or the same group of agents in successive spaces. (The same thing is true for an institution, which has only a structural history: the illusion of the constancy of the nominal depends on ignoring the fact that the social value of positions which are nominally unchanged may differ at different moments in the field's own history.) It is in relation to the corresponding states of the structure of the field that *the meaning* and the social value of biographical events are determined at each moment, events understood as *placements/investments* and *displacements/disinvestments* in this space or, more precisely, in the successive states of the structure and distribution of different kinds of capital in play in the field, economic capital as well as symbolic capital like the specific capital of consecration. Trying to understand a career or a life as a unique and self-sufficient series of successive events without any other link than association with a 'subject' (whose consistency is perhaps only that of a socially recognized proper name) is almost as absurd as trying to make sense of a trip on the metro without taking the structure of the network into account, meaning the matrix of objective relations between the different stations.

Any social trajectory must be understood as a unique manner of travelling through social space, where the dispositions of the habitus are expressed; each displacement towards a new position (in so far as it implies the exclusion of a more or less vast set of substitutable positions and, thereby, an irreversible narrowing of the range of initially compatible possibles) marks a stage in a process of *social ageing* which could be measured by the number of these decisive alternatives, bifurcations of a tree with innumerable dead branches which stands for the story of a life.

Thus numberless individual histories can be replaced by *families of intragenerational trajectories* at the core of the field of cultural production (or, if you like, typical forms of specific ageing). On the one hand, there are those displacements which are circumscribed within a single sector of the field of cultural production and which correspond to a larger or smaller accumulation of capital – capital of recognition for artists situated in the symbolically dominant sector, and economic capital for those who are situated in the heteronomous sector. On the other hand, there are those displacements which imply a change of sector and the conversion of one kind of specific capital into another – for example, the Symbolist poets who turn towards the psychological novel – or even the conversion of symbolic capital into economic capital – in the case of a move from poetry to the novel of manners or to the theatre, or, still more sharply, to cabaret or the serial.

And in the same fashion, one may distinguish inside the field of cultural production among several major classes of *intergenerational* trajectories. On the one hand, there are *ascending* trajectories, which may be *direct* (those of writers coming out of the working class or salaried sections of the middle classes) or *crossed* (those of writers from the commercial or artisanal petite-bourgeoisie, or even the peasantry, generally because of a critical rupture in the collective trajectory of the lineage, due to bankruptcy or the death of the father, for example). On the other, there are *transversal* trajectories – horizontal but, in a sense, declining – at the heart of the field of power, which lead to a field of cultural production based on positions which are temporally dominant and culturally dominated (the industrial grande bourgeoisie) or based on median positions, almost equally rich in

economic capital and cultural capital (the liberal professions like
doctors, lawyers and so on); to which should be added *nil displacements*. (To be completely precise, one would still have to differentiate
among trajectories according to their point of arrival at the heart of
the field of cultural production, meaning at a position temporally
dominated and culturally dominant or the reverse, or yet, at a neutral
position; the apparently nil movements of intellectuals of the second
generation, for example, may include a displacement from one pole
to another of the field of cultural production.)

It is only then that one may isolate, within an overall picture of the
possible links between intergenerational trajectories and intragenerational trajectories, those which are the most probable, such as the
one which leads certain ascending intergenerational trajectories,
especially the crossed ones, to extend into intragenerational trajectories, leading from the symbolically dominant pole to the symbolically
dominated pole, meaning to inferior genres or inferior forms of major
genres (the regionalist or working-class novel, etc.).

Biographical analysis thus understood can lead us to the principles
of the evolution of the work of art in the course of time. Positive or
negative sanctions, success or failure, encouragements or warnings,
consecration or exclusion, all indicating to each writer (etc.) – and the
ensemble of his rivals – the objective truth of the position he occupies
and his probable future, are effectively one set of the major mediations
through which the incessant redefinition of the 'creative project' is
shaped, with failure encouraging reconversion or retreat from the
field, and consecration reinforcing and liberating initial ambitions.

Social identity carries a determinate right to the possibles. According to the symbolic capital recognized in her as a function of her
position, each writer (etc.) sees herself accorded a determinate set of
legitimate possibles, meaning, in a determinate field, a determinate
share of possibles objectively offered at each given moment in time.
The social definition of what is permitted to someone, what she may
reasonably allow herself without appearing pretentious or demented,
is set out through all sorts of licences and requirements, calls to order
both negative and positive (noblesse oblige), which may be public
and official, like all forms of *nominations* or verdicts guaranteed by
the state, or, on the contrary, officious, tacit, and even almost
imperceptible. And we know that through the intrinsically magical
effect of consecration or stigmatization, the verdicts of institutions of
authority tend to produce their own verification.

Forming the basis of aspirations which are lived as natural because
they are immediately recognized as legitimate, this right to the
possible grounds the almost corporeal sentiment of *importance*,

which determines for example the *place* that one may be granted within a group – meaning the sites, central or marginal, elevated or humble, conspicuous or obscure, etc., which one has the right to occupy, the amount of the space that one may decently hold and the time that one may take up (from others) there. The subjective relationship that a writer (etc.) maintains, at each moment, with the space of possibles depends very strongly on the possibles which are statutorally granted her at this moment, and also on her habitus which is originally constituted within a position itself carrying a certain right to possibles. All forms of social consecration or statutory assignment – whether conferred by an elevated social origin, a major scholastic success or, for writers, the recognition of peers – have the effect of increasing the right to the rarest possibles, and, through this *assurance*, of increasing the subjective capacity to realize them in practical terms.

The habitus and the possibles

The propensity to orient oneself towards the most risky positions, and especially the capacity to hold on to them in the absence of any economic profit in the short term, seems to depend in large part on the possession of significant economic and symbolic capital. In the first place, this is because economic capital ensures the conditions of freedom from economic necessity, private income being one of the best substitutes for sales. In fact, those who manage to maintain themselves in the most adventurous positions long enough to obtain the symbolic profits which may be provided there are recruited essentially from among the most affluent, who also have the advantage of not being obliged to devote themselves to secondary jobs for subsistence. This contrasts with so many poets coming from the petite-bourgeoisie who have been forced to abandon poetry sooner or later for the sake of literary activities which are better remunerated, such as writing novels of manners, or else have been obliged to devote a major share of their time to the theatre or novels (such as François Coppée, Catulle Mendès or Jean Aicard).[63] In the same way, when ageing (which resolves ambiguities) converts the elective and provisional rejections of the adolescent bohemian life into a failure without remission, writers of humble origins are more willing to resign themselves to 'industrial literature', which makes writing an activity like any other; except when anti-intellectualist rebellion pushes the bitterest of them to the reversals and repudiations which reduce them to the ugliest aspects of political polemics.

But above all, the conditions of existence associated with high birth favour dispositions like audacity and indifference to material profit, or a sense of social orientation and the art of foreseeing new hierarchies, which incline a person to head for the most exposed outposts of the avant-garde and towards investments which are the riskiest because they are ahead of demand, but which are very often also the most viable symbolically and in the long run, at least for the first investors. The *sense of placement/investment* seems to be one of the dispositions most closely linked to social and geographical origin, and consequently, through the social capital which is its correlative, one of the mediations through which the effects of a contrast in social origins, and especially between Parisian and provincial roots, manifest themselves in the logic of the field.[64]

In a general manner, it is the people who are richest in economic capital, cultural capital and social capital who are the first to head for new positions (a proposition which seems to be confirmed in all fields, in the economy as well as in sciences). This is the case with the writers surrounding Paul Bourget, who abandon Symbolist poetry for a new form of the novel, one breaking with the naturalist tradition and better adapted to the expectations of the cultivated public. Conversely, it is a bad sense of placement/investment, linked with social or geographic distance, which sends writers from the working class or the petite-bourgeoisie, provincials or foreigners, in the direction of the dominant positions at a time when the profits they provide tend to be diminishing, due to the very attraction they exercise (thanks, for example, to the economic profits they return, in the case of the naturalist novel, or the symbolic profits they promise, in the case of Symbolist poetry) and due to the intensified competition focused on them. It is this same characteristic which encourages these writers to stay in positions which are either declining or threatened at a time when the best informed are abandoning them; or else to let themselves be drawn by the attraction of the dominant sites towards positions antinomic to the dispositions they import into them, only to discover their 'natural place' too late, meaning after much wasted time, under the impact of the forces of the field and in the mode of relegation.

The classic case of this is Léon Cladel (1835-1892), son of a master saddler of Montauban, an 'artisan turning into a bourgeois', journeyman of a craft guild and also a landowner who, concerned to 'make his only heir a gentleman', places him in the Montauban seminary at the age of nine. After law studies in Toulouse, Cladel is admitted to the bar in Montauban, discovering with horror the peasantry and their subjection to monetary interests; he then leaves for Paris, where he lives the bohemian life; he returns to Quercy, 'tired of struggling, obscure and isolated, tired of fighting'; but he cannot 'give Paris up', so he instals himself there again; he links himself with the Parnassian movement, writes a novel, finds a publisher with the help of his mother, and for the 300 francs she has given him, secures a preface from Baudelaire; then, after seven years of a rather miserable bohemian life, he returns to his native Quercy and devotes himself to the regionalist novel.[65] Every work by this eternally *displaced person* bears the mark of the antinomy between the dispositions associated with the point of departure, which will also be the point of arrival, and the positions aimed for and provisionally occupied: 'The wager consisted of illustrating his Quercy, territory of latinity and home of rustic Hercules, with a sort of antique and barbarous "geste". In portraying the fierce scuffles of louts as the arrogant posturing of village champions, Cladel hoped to be counted among the number of the modest rivals of Hugo and Leconte de Lisle. Thus were born *Ompdrailles*, *La Fête votive de Bartholoné-Porte-Glaive* – bizarre tales, pastiches of the *Iliad* and the *Odyssey* in turgid or Rabelaisian language.'[66]

Those who accede to positions where their presence is totally improbable are subject to a *structural double bind* which, as in Cladel's case, may survive their more or less rapid expulsion from an impossible post. This double contradictory constraint often condemns the momentarily 'miraculous ones' to projects of a pathetic incoherence, sorts of autodestructive homages to the values of a universe which denies them any value (such as this project of describing the Quercy peasants in the language of Leconte de Lisle, which oscillates between parody and slavish adherence). And Léon Cladel himself, in the preface to his novel *Celui-de-la-Croix-aux-Boeufs* (1871), speaks of the contradiction that tears him apart with a desperate lucidity – but with no practical effect – which is the privilege of all victims of similar contradictions: 'Instinctively carried to the study of plebeian types and milieux, and on the other hand a fervent lover of the beauties of style, it was almost fated that there should sooner or later be a contest between the brutal and the refined.'[67] Always in a double bind, Cladel is a peasant among the Parnassians (who dismiss him as belonging to the people, along with his friend Courbet) and a petit-bourgeois among the peasants of his native province. It is not surprising that the form and content of the rustic novel to which he resigns himself, where the intention to rehabilitate gives way to a complacent portraying of peasant savagery and bleakness, express in themselves the contradictory truth of an incoherent trajectory: he writes that 'this beggar-dreamer, child of beggars, had an innate love of popular manners, as well as of rustic activities. So if from the beginning, without any tergiversation, he had tried to render them frankly with that wholesome roughness of touch which distinguishes the early style of master painters, he might perhaps have succeeded right away in creating a place for himself among the brightest stars of the young generation he belonged to.'[68] One could not put it better . . .

It is in confrontation with Parisian and bourgeois artists and writers, which pushes them back towards the people, that writers and artists from the working class or the provincial petite-bourgeoisie come to discover what distinguishes them negatively, and even, exceptionally, to accept and proclaim this, in the manner of Courbet, who makes much of his provincial accent, his patois and 'people's' style. 'According to the description by Champfleury [realist novelist, friend of Courbet and Cladel], the German Brasserie in Paris, where realism was hatched as a movement, was like a Protestant village where rustic manners and a plain gaiety reigned. Its leader Courbet was a "companion", he shook hands, ate and spoke a lot, was strong and obstinate as a peasant, exactly the opposite of the dandy of the thirties and forties. His behaviour in Paris was *deliberately working class*; *he spoke patois conspicuously*, he smoked, sang and joked like a man of the people. Observers were impressed with his plebeian and rustically free technique [. . .]. Du Camp wrote that he painted his canvases "like one shines boots".'[69]

These unassimilable *parvenus* throw themselves into this effort of dissimilation with all the more conviction the less successful their initial attempts to *be assimilated* have been. It is thus that Champfleury, himself born into the humblest provincial petite-bourgeoisie, long 'torn between two tendencies, realism in the manner of Monnier and a German-style poetry, romantic and sentimental,'[70] finds himself pushed towards militant realism by the failure of his first efforts and perhaps especially by the discovery of his difference, which thrusts him back towards the 'popular', that is, towards objects excluded by the legitimate art of the time and in the manner then considered 'realist' of treating them. And this forced return to the 'people' is no less ambiguous and doubtful than the withdrawal by regionalist writers to the 'soil': hostility to the libertarian audacities and the deliberate populism of bourgeois intellectuals may encourage an anti-intellectualist populism, more or less conservative, which is just a phantasmagoric projection of relationships internal to the intellectual field.

One may find a typical example of this field effect in the trajectory of the same Champfleury who, after having been the leader of the young realist writers of 1850 and the 'theoretician' of the realist movement in literature and painting, was progressively eclipsed by Flaubert, then by the Goncourts and Zola. Having become an executive in the national manufactory of Sèvres, he made himself the historian of popular imagery and literature, to end his career under the Second Empire, after a series of twists and turns, as the official theoretician (he receives the Legion d'Honneur in 1867) of a conservatism based on the exaltation of popular wisdom – and especially of a resignation to hierarchies expressed in the cult of popular arts and traditions.[71]

The dialectic of positions and dispositions

Thus the dispositions associated with a certain social origin cannot be fulfilled unless they are responsive in the shape they take to, on the one hand, the structure of possibles opened up by the different positions and position-takings of their occupants, and, on the other hand, to the position occupied in the field, which (through the attitude to this position as a feeling of success or failure, itself linked to dispositions, hence to the trajectory) governs the way these possibles are perceived and appreciated. The same dispositions may thus lead to aesthetic or political position-takings which are very different according to the state of the field in relation to which they have to be determined.[72] This shows the inanity of attempts to connect realism in literature or in painting directly to the characteristics of social groups – especially the peasantry – from which its inventors or defenders come, Champfleury or Courbet for example. It is only inside a determinate state of the artistic field, and in relation to other artistic positions and their occupants, themselves socially characterized, that the dispositions of realist painters and writers are determined; dispositions which elsewhere and in another time might have been manifested were otherwise expressed in a form of art which, in this structure, appeared as the most accomplished manner of expressing an inseparably aesthetic and political revolt against 'bourgeois' art and artists (or the 'spiritualist' critique which supported them) and, through them, against the 'bourgeois'.[73]

The interaction between positions and dispositions is clearly reciprocal. Any habitus, as a system of dispositions, is only effectively realized in relation to a determinate structure of socially marked positions (marked among other things by the social properties of its occupants, through which it allows itself to be perceived); but, conversely, it is through dispositions, which are themselves more or less completely adjusted to those positions, that one or another potentiality lying inscribed in the positions is realized. Thus, for example, if it appears impossible to understand the differences separating the Théâtre de l'Oeuvre and the Théâtre-Libre on the basis merely of the differences in habitus between their founders – Lugné-Poe, son of a Parisian bourgeois and relatively educated, and Antoine, a provincial petit-bourgeois and autodidact – it seems no less impossible to account for them on the sole basis of the structural positions of the two institutions. If, at least originally, they seem to reproduce the opposition between their founders, it is because they are the realization of it in a state of the field marked by the opposition between Symbolism, more bourgeois – firstly by virtue of the characteristics of its defenders – and naturalism, more petit-bourgeois. Antoine, who defined himself, like the naturalists and with their theoretical support, against the bourgeois theatre, proposes a systematic transformation of the staging, a *specific* revolution, founded on a coherent gambit: privileging the setting over the characters, the determining context over the determined text, he makes the set 'a coherent and complete universe in itself over which reigns, alone, the director'.[74] At the other extreme, the 'muddled and fecund' directing of Lugné-Poe, who situates himself in relation to the bourgeois theatre but also in relation to Antoine's innovations, leads to productions which are described as a 'mixture of refined invention and come-what-may' and which, issuing from a 'sometimes demagogic, sometimes elitist' project, attracts an audience in which anarchists and mystics rub shoulders.[75]

In short, it is in a particular space that the opposition between dispositions receives its complete definition, namely its full historical particularity. There it takes the shape of a system of oppositions to be found everywhere – between newspapers or critics favourable to one or the other, between the authors staged and between the contents of works, with on the one side the 'slice of life', which in some ways resembles vaudeville, and on the other, subtle experiments inspired by the concept of several levels of meaning within the same work, as enunciated by Mallarmé. Everything allows us to suppose that, as this case suggests, the bearing of dispositions – hence the explanatory force of 'social origin' – is particularly great when one is dealing with a *position being born*, still to be made, rather than one already made or established and hence capable of imposing its own norms on its occupants; and to suppose, more generally, that the freedom which is left to dispositions varies according to the state of the field (and in particular to its autonomy), according to the position occupied in the field, as well as according to the degree of institution-alization of the corresponding post.

If one cannot deduce position-takings from dispositions, neither can one relate them directly back to positions. Thus, *a similarity of position*, especially a negative one, is not sufficient for founding a literary or artistic group, even if it tends to favour alliances and exchanges. This is clearly seen in the case of supporters of art for art's sake who, as shown by Cassagne,[76] are linked by relations of mutual esteem and sympathy: Gautier invites Flaubert, Théodore de Banville, the Goncourts and Baudelaire to his Thursday dinners; between Flaubert and Baudelaire the affinity is linked to the quasi-simultaneity of their starts and their trials; the Goncourts and Flaubert appreciate each other very much and it is at Flaubert's that the two brothers discovered Bouilhet; Théodore de Banville and Baudelaire are very old friends; Louis Ménard, who is an intimate of Baudelaire, of Banville and of Leconte de Lisle, becomes part of

Renan's circle; Barbey d'Aurevilly is one of the most fervent defenders of Baudelaire. The field effect tends to create conditions favourable for the rapprochement of occupants of identical or neighbouring positions in objective space, but it is not sufficient to determine the gathering together of a corps, a precondition for the appearance of the *corporative effect* from which the most famous literary and artistic groups have drawn immense symbolic profits, even up to and as a result of the more or less resounding ruptures which have put an end to them.

Formation and dissolution of groups

Whereas the occupants of the dominant positions (especially in economic terms, such as the bourgeois theatre) are very homogeneous, the avant-garde positions, which are defined mainly negatively, in opposition to the dominant positions, bring together for a while (in the phase of the *initial accumulation of symbolic capital*) writers and artists who are very different in their origins and their dispositions and whose interests, momentarily coming together, will later start to diverge.[77] As small isolated sects whose negative cohesion is reinforced by an intense affective solidarity, often concentrated in the attachment to a leader, these dominated groups tend to enter into crisis, by an apparent paradox, when they achieve recognition – the symbolic profits of that recognition frequently going only to a few, or even only one of them – and when the negative forces of cohesion are weakened. Differences of position at the heart of the group, and especially social and educational differences which the oppositional unity of the group's beginnings allowed to be surmounted and sublimated, are translated into an unequal participation in the profits of the accumulated symbolic capital. This experience is all the more painful for the first unrecognized founders if the consecration and the success attract a second generation of followers, who are very different from the first in their dispositions but who share, sometimes more generously than the first shareholders, in the dividends.

This model of the process of constitution and dissolution of avant-garde groups which have achieved consecration finds an exemplary illustration in the history of the Impressionists,[78] and also in the progressive separation of the Symbolists and Decadents. Starting from the same barely marked position within the field, and defined by the same opposition to naturalism and Parnassus – from which Verlaine and Mallarmé, their leaders, were each excluded – the

Decadents and the Symbolists diverge as they attain full social existence. Drawn from the most favoured milieux (namely from the middle or grande bourgeoisie and the nobility) and provided with substantial educational capital, the Symbolists are pitted against the Decadents, who often come from families of artisans and are virtually devoid of educational capital, in the same way that the salon (Mallarmé's 'Tuesdays') contrasts with the café, the Right Bank with the Left Bank and bohemia and, on the aesthetic plane, that hermeticism resting on an explicit theory and a resolute break with all the old forms contrasts with a 'clearness' and 'simplicity' founded on 'common sense' and 'naiveté'; in politics the Symbolists affect indifference and pessimism, but without excluding some bursts of anarchist radicalism, while the Decadents are progressives and more reformist.[79]

It is clear that the effect of opposition between the two schools, which intensifies with the advance of the process of institutionalization necessary to constitute a fully fledged literary group – that is, an instrument for accumulating and concentrating symbolic capital (with the adoption of a name, the drawing up of manifestos and programmes and the setting up of aggregation rites, such as regular meetings) – tends to multiply those initial differences by consecrating them: Verlaine celebrates naiveté (just as Champfleury countered art for art's sake with 'sincerity in art'), while the Verlainean taste for sincerity and simplicity doubtless helps to push Mallarmé towards the hermeticism of 'the enigma in poetry'. And, as if to provide the crucial proof of the effect of dispositions, it is those Decadents with the most privileged social origins who join the Symbolists (Albert Aurier) or else rally to them (Ernest Raynaud), whereas those of the Symbolists who are the nearest to the Decadents in terms of social origin, René Ghil and Ajalbert, are excluded from the Symbolist group, the former because of his faith in progress, and the latter, who will end up as a realist novelist, because his books are judged insufficiently obscure.[80]

The opposition between Mallarmé and Verlaine is the paradigmatic form of a division being gradually established and more and more sharply asserted in the course of the nineteenth century, the one between the professional writer, forced by his enterprise to lead a dutiful, regular, almost bourgeois life, and the amateur writer, either a bourgeois dilettante for whom writing is a pastime or a hobby, or an eccentric and miserable bohemian living from all the odd jobs offered by journalism, publishing or teaching. The contrast in their works is based on a contrast in lifestyles, which it expresses and symbolically reinforces. At odds with the bourgeois world and its values, professional writers, with the upholders of art for art's sake in the first rank, are also cut off in a thousand ways from bohemia, its pretension, its incoherences, its very disorder so incompatible with methodical production. We must quote the Goncourts: 'Literature is conceived in silence, and as it were, in sleep away from the activities and things around one. Emotions are contrary to the gestation of the imagination. One needs regular, calm days, a bourgeois state of being, the tranquillity of a grocer, in order to bring forth greatness, torment, poignancy, the pathetic ... Those who spend themselves in passion, in nervous agitation, will never write a passionate book.'[81] This contrast between the two categories of writers is undoubtedly the source of the strictly political antagonisms (*and not vice versa*) which are particularly manifest at the time of the Commune.[82]

A whole life's confrontation between positions and dispositions, between the effort to make the 'post' and the necessity to make oneself suitable for the 'post', with the successive adjustments which tend to bring displaced individuals back to their 'natural place' as the outcome of a series of calls to order, explains the correspondence which is regularly observed, no matter how far one pushes the analysis, between positions and the properties of their occupants. For example, within the popular novel which (more often than any other category of novel) is abandoned to writers coming from the dominated classes and to the feminine gender, the different manners, more or less distanced, of treating this genre – in short, the positions within the position – are themselves linked to social and educational differences, with the most distanciated, semi-parodic treatments (of which the prime example is *Fantomas*, celebrated by Apollinaire) being the prerogative of the most privileged writers.[83] By the same logic, Rémy Ponton observes that among boulevard authors, who are directly subject to the financial sanction of bourgeois taste, writers coming from the working class or petite-bourgeoisie are very strongly underrepresented, whereas they are more strongly represented in vaudeville, which, as a comic genre, allows a greater role for facile effects or funny and scabrous scenes as well as permitting a sort of half-critical freedom. The playwrights who write both for the boulevard and vaudeville present characteristics intermediate between those of the authors of these two subgenres.[84] In short, the concordance – surprising in a world which would have itself free of any determination and constraint – is perfect between the inclinations of agents and the exigencies inscribed in the positions they occupy. This harmony established in social terms aptly favours the illusion of the absence of any social determination.

A transcendence of institution

If the history of art or literature, like the history of philosophy, and in another sense the history of the sciences themselves, may assume the appearance of a strictly internal evolution, with each of these systems of autonomous representations seeming to develop according to its own dynamic, independently of the action of artists, writers, philosophers or scholars, it is because each new entrant must reckon with the established order in the field, with the rule of the game immanent in the game, and knowledge and recognition (*illusio*) of the game are tacitly imposed on all those who take part in it. The expressive drive or impulse which gives experimentation its intention or direction (often negatively) must take account of the space of possibles, a sort of *specific code*, simultaneously juridical and communicative, whose cognition and recognition constitute the veritable right of entry into the field. Like a language, this code acts both as a *censor*, by the possibles it excludes in fact or by right, and a *means of expression* enclosing within defined limits the possibilities of infinite invention it provides; it functions as a historically situated and dated system of schemas of perception, appreciation and expression which define the social conditions of possibility – and, by the same token, the limits – of the production and circulation of cultural works, and which exist both in an *objectified state*, in the structures constitutive of the field, and in an *incorporated state*, in the mental structures and dispositions constitutive of the habitus.

It is in the relationship between the expressive drive, where the dispositions and interests inherent in the position are expressed, and this specific code – and especially the universe of things to say and do, of problems imposed as if for a test – that specific interests (intrinsically musical, philosophical, scientific and so on) are defined. What one sometimes attributes to the effects of 'fashion', namely to the deliberate will to be part of it – *interesse* – is in fact the result of the competitive logic which leads those who are part of it and those who want to be to compete against each other, consciously or unconsciously, towards the same objectives and over the same objects.

This order, established both within things (documents, instruments, scores, paintings, etc.) and within bodies (skills, techniques, abilities), is presented as a reality *transcending* any private and circumstantial act aimed at it. It thus seems to give foundation to the declared or latent Platonism of those like Husserl or Meinong who try to base properly philosophical activity on the irreducibility of the contents of consciousness (*noèmes*) to conscious acts (*noèses*), of

number to (psychological) operations of calculation, or those like
Popper and many others who assert that the world of ideas, its
functioning and its becoming, is autonomous in relation to knowing
subjects.[85] In fact, although it has its own laws, transcendent of
consciousness and of individual wills, cultural heritage, which exists
in a materialized and in an incorporated state (in the form of a
habitus functioning as a sort of historical transcendental), only exists
and effectively persists (meaning *actively*) in and through the struggles
located in fields of cultural production; that is, cultural heritage exists
by and for the agents disposed and able to assure its continued
reactivation.

Thus, this 'third world', neither physical nor psychic, in which
Husserl and others after him thought to find the proper object of
philosophy, owes its existence and persistence, beyond all individual
appropriations, to the very competition for its appropriation. It is in
and through the competition among agents who cannot participate
in this collective capital without having (more or less completely)
incorporated it in the form of the cognitive and evaluative dispositions of a specific habitus (the one they put to work in their own
production and in the appreciation of the production of other agents)
that this product of collective history, transcending each person
because immanent in all of them, finds itself established as the norm
of all practices which refer to it. Through the criss-crossing constraints and controls which each person who is appropriated by it
brings to bear on all the others, this *opus operatum*, otherwise fated
to the insignificance of a dead letter, is continually asserted as a
collective *modus operandi*, as the mode of cultural production whose
norm is impressed, at each moment, on all producers.

The transcendent world of cultural works does not encompass
within itself the principle of its transcendence; neither does it contain
the principle of its becoming, even if it helps to *structure* the thoughts
and acts which are the source of its transformation. Its structures
(logics, aesthetics, etc.) may impress themselves on all those who
enter into the game of which it is at once the product, the instrument
and the stakes, without nevertheless escaping the transformative
action which the very acts and thoughts they govern cannot fail to
produce, be it only by the effect of being *put to work*, never reducible
to pure execution.

This means that when it comes to understanding the functioning
of a field of cultural production and what may be produced in it, one
cannot separate the expressive drive (which has its source in the very
functioning of the field and in the fundamental *illusio* which makes it
possible) from the specific logic of the field, pregnant with objective

potentialities, and from everything which will simultaneously constrain and authorize the expressive drive to convert itself into a *specific solution*. It is in this intersection between a 'problem situation', as Popper says, and an agent disposed to *recognize* this 'objective' problem and make it his own (one thinks of the example analysed by Panofsky of the problem of the rose window of a cathedral's west façade, bequeathed by Suger to the architects who will invent Gothic art) that the specific solution is determined, produced either by starting from an art of inventing already invented or thanks to the invention of a new art of inventing. The probable future of a field is inscribed, at each moment, in the structure of the field, but each agent makes his own future – thereby helping to make the future of the field – by realizing the objective potentialities which are determined in the relation between his powers and the possibles objectively inscribed in the field.

A final unavoidable question remains: what part is played by conscious calculation in the objective strategies that observation brings to light? It suffices to read literary memoirs, correspondence, personal diaries and perhaps especially the explicit position-takings on the literary world as such (like those collected by Huret) in order to be convinced that there is no simple answer and that self-awareness, always partial, is yet again a matter of position and trajectory within the field, and that it thus varies according to agents and historical periods. If it is nevertheless necessary to deal with it, when all is said and done, this is above all to exorcise the alternatives of innocence or cynicism which carry the risk of introducing into the analysis – and especially *into the reading* made of it – antagonist visions of the daily struggle at the heart of the intellectual field, that of exalted celebrants, usually applied to the great of the past, and that of a Thersites who arms himself with all the resources of a second-rate 'sociology' in order to discredit rivals by reducing their intentions to their presumed interests.

The entire effort I have deployed here has been aimed at destroying, at their roots, these mirror visions. 'Do not laugh, do not deplore, do not detest,' said Spinoza, 'just understand' – or better, make it necessary, give it reason. Knowledge of the *model* permits us to understand how it happens that agents (hence the author and reader of this text) may be what they are and do what they do. Having recalled this, I can now answer the question about conscious calculation with an example, while asking the reader to mobilize all the resources of the method of analysis I have endeavoured to present, in order to be able to put into practice the Spinozan maxim and thus to substitute the often rather melancholic joys of the necessitating vision for the perverse pleasures (always ambivalent and often alternating) of celebration and denigration.

In 1909 at the time of founding of the *Nouvelle Revue Française*, which was to occupy a dominant place in the intellectual field, it was necessary for André Gide, endowed as he was, according to his biographer, 'with antennae to detect channels, networks, or better yet, zones where "micro-climates" reigned', to 'put all his diplomacy to work' and administer well-judged 'doses' in order to 'make the NRF the centre of attraction, round a secure nucleus, for values which are diverse but indisputable and promising', and to make it the 'locus of tangential zones which were unaware of or misinterpreted each other'. A journal's table of contents is both an exhibition of the symbolic capital available to the enterprise and a politico-religious position-taking. One must therefore 'secure' a few major shareholders (Paul Claudel, Henri de Régnier, Francis Carco, and even Paul Valéry) together with a range of contributors as widely distributed as possible over the 'politico-literary chessboard' (this is still the biographer talking) in order to avoid lapsing into an overly marked, and therefore compromising, orientation. Three hymns by Claudel are published with 'joy' and judged 'very welcome' because the *Revue* 'ran the risk of over-indulging in criticism, *Normalisme* and intellectualism'; since Michel Arnaud offered 'an image gently oriented "to the left"' of Péguy, a necessary counterweight will be supplied by Francis Jammes, and so forth.[86]

The gathering together of the authors and, secondarily, of the texts which make up a literary review has as its genuine principle, as we see, social strategies close to those governing the constitution of a salon or a movement – even though they take into account, among other criteria, the strictly literary capital of the assembled authors. And what these strategies themselves have as a unifying and generative principle is not something akin to the cynical calculation of a banker with symbolic capital (even if André Gide is also that, objectively), but rather a common habitus, or, better still, an ethos which is one dimension of it and which unites the members of what one calls 'the nucleus'. Once this group or network has been established, it co-opts more or less regular contributors, deciding in particular on the contents of the first issues, and this summary is itself designed to function by 'what it represents' – namely a certain specifically literary prestige, and also a certain politico-religious line – as a rallying point for some and a deterrent for others, or in any case as a *marker* in the classification struggles located in any field. In the case of the NRF, this unifying principle is none other than dispositions which are predisposed to occupy a median, and central, position between the 'salons' and the university, meaning between 'probity' (which is just as separate from the 'salon mentality' as from the 'successful writers') and the sense of bourgeois distinction (which is distanced both from intellectualism and from a humanism savouring of 'communalism' belonging to those writers excessively marked by their school – meaning the Normaliens).[87]

Declining to draw a moral from this story, which does not really have one, I will merely observe once more how artificial, sterile, even misleading are all attempts to extract from texts and only from texts the unifying principle of the groups of works and authors thus constituted or, worse, to extract theoretical coherence from the intentions inscribed in the social label – a concept ending in -ism, of course – attached to them by history.

'The impious dismantling of the fiction'

As for becoming aware of the logic of the game as such, and of the *illusio* which is its bedrock, I long believed that this was somehow precluded, by definition, by the fact that this lucidity would turn the literary or artistic enterprise into a cynical mystification or a conscious trickery. This remained true until I came to read carefully a text by Mallarmé which expresses well, even if in a very obscure manner, both the objective truth of literature as a fiction founded on collective belief, and the right we have to salvage, in face of and against all kinds of objectification, literary pleasure:

> We know, captives of an absolute formula that, indeed, there is only that which is. Forthwith to dismiss the cheat, however, on a pretext, would indict our inconsequence, denying the very pleasure we want to take: for that *beyond* is its agent, and even its engine, as I might say were I not loath to perform, in public, the impious dismantling of the fiction and consequently the literary mechanism, to display the principal part or nothing. But I venerate how, by a trick, we project to some forbidden – and thunderous! – height the conscious lack in us of what is bursting up there.
> Why should we do this?
> It is a game.[88]

Thus beauty is nothing but a fiction, condemned to be dealt with as such, against the Platonic belief in the beautiful as eternal essence, a pure fetishism by which the creator bows down before the projection of an illusory transcendence of what is lacking in literary life here below, and perhaps also in life itself. In the case of a poetry which has achieved self-awareness, this fiction is not satisfied with reproducing nature, and the seasonal cycle, like the (Wagnerian) music which, through the alternation of the light and the dark, mimics in its alternating breaths the mystery of the original tragedy of the death and resurrection of nature.[89] Breaking with musical *mimesis*, still very near to myth or rites, poetry leaves the natural order so as to situate itself, consciously, in the intrinsically human order of convention, of the 'arbitrariness of the sign', as Saussure will say, of 'human artifice', as Mallarmé says.[90]

The renunciation of musical magic is a decisive moment in that sort of ultimate attempt, so many times deferred, by which the poet sets out, 'late in life' but with a Cartesian boldness, 'to acknowledge through and through the crisis of the ideal and equally the social' which 'tests'[91] him, and to cast radical doubts on his belief in the existence of writing: 'Does literature exist?'[92] At the end of 'this kind of investigation which might have been peacefully avoided as dangerous' and this radical 'clearance' of all literary beliefs, what remains? 'Reverence for twenty-four letters' inherited from the indefinitely repeated 'dice throws' of an individual history, and a 'métier', a *sense of the game of letters*, of their symmetries, which must not be confused with the *sense of the literary game* ('Nor does a personage feel a great taste for the instituted and special honours of letters').[93] As for the poet, it is vain to ask whether he is the agent or the one acted upon ('action, reflection') and whether 'the supernatural term', the poetic telos, that outcome outside of nature[94] or against nature (in contrast to music) which is verse, is the product of 'his initiative or the virtual force of divine characters', 'a means (what else!), a principle'.

A truly negative theology, the reflexive critique used by the poet to assign himself his doctrine and his territory wrecks the poetic sacral and the self-mystifying myth of the creation of a transcendent, 'escaping'[95] object modelled after nature. But the abolished *beyond* remains the 'engine' of the 'pleasure we *want* to take', by a sort of deliberate fetishism (if the terms can be used together). It is in the name of literary pleasure, this 'ideal joy',[96] sublime product of sublimation, that one is *entitled* to save the game of letters, and even, as we shall see, the literary game itself: 'Faced with a superior attraction as a vacuum [that of the beyond which continues to act as a lack, as a 'nothingness'], we are entitled, drawing it out of us by our boredom with things when they make themselves solid and preponderant[97] – frantically to detach them in order to fill ourselves up[98] and also give them brilliance, across the vacant space, in celebrations held at will and alone.' And Mallarmé himself comments, in an added note: 'My point of view is pyrotechnic as well as metaphysical. For when fireworks reach the height and nature of thought they can illuminate pure joy.'[99]

A reader of Max Muller, Mallarmé knows that the gods are often born of a forgotten error of language; he is not trying to restore to the poet a divine right and prophetic wizardry outside human language, established on the basis of a new transcendence. Even though he poses as a postulate (he uses the word) with respect to the new poetic doctrine that 'a throw of the dice never abolishes chance' and even though 'challenging the titles of an acknowledged function',[100] he refuses to 'garland the altar' of the poetic cult and to perpetuate the metaphysical dreams of the great aesthetic tradition, he cannot resist devoting himself to the Pyrrhonic games of linguistic pyrotechnics; and this with no other purpose than to produce, for his own pleasure, the illuminations of verbal fireworks capable of masking by their splendour the emptiness of the skies in which they burst. Thus he can only tear himself away from 'that subtle invasion, like a sort of indefinable defiance', which led him to question the existence of literature and of the writer, and the very meaning of his 'vocation', by countering an 'extraordinary summons' with the immediate evidence of this aesthetic equivalent of a *cogito*: yes, literature exists, since I *rejoice* in it. But can one be completely satisfied with this proof by pleasure, *jouissance* (*aisthèsis*), even if one understands that poetry gives itself meaning by giving a meaning, even if imaginary, to the world?[101] And is not the pleasure aroused by the voluntarist fiction of 'solitary festivities' doomed to appear as fictive, since it is clearly linked to the will to lose oneself in this game of words, to 'pay oneself in the fake currency of one's dream'?

The invocation of the famous phrase of Marcel Mauss is not as out of place as it seems. In effect, Mallarmé does not forget as his commentators do that, as he says at the beginning, the crisis is also 'social'; he knows that the solitary and vaguely narcissistic pleasure that he wants to do everything to save is doomed to be perceived as an illusion if it is not rooted in the *illusio*, the collective belief in the game, and the value of its stakes, which is both the condition and the product of the functioning of the 'literary mechanism'. And he concludes that, to save this pleasure which we only take because we 'want to take it' as well as the Platonic illusion which is its 'agent', he has no other choice than to take the course of 'revering', by another deliberate fiction, the authorless trickery which puts the fragile fetish outside the grasp of critical lucidity. Refusing to 'perform, in public, the impious dismantling of the fiction and consequently of the literary mechanism, to display the principal part or nothing', he chooses to enunciate this seminal nothingness only in the mode of denegation, that is, in the very forms he does not deliver, since he has almost no chance of being truly heard.[102]

The solution which Mallarmé brings to the question of knowing whether the mechanisms constitutive of those social games which are the most surrounded with prestige and mystery, like those of art, literature, science, law or philosophy (those depositories of values communally held as the most sacred, the most universal), should be enunciated (which, in fact, comes down to denouncing them) is less satisfying than his way of posing the question. Adopting the course of keeping secret the 'literary mechanism' – or not revealing it except in the most strictly shrouded form – is to prejudge that only a few great initiates are capable of the heroic lucidity and the deliberate generosity which are necessary to confront in their truth the 'legitimate impostures', as Austin says, and to perpetuate, against the illusory expectation of a transcendent guarantee, that faith in those values to which the great humanist trickeries render at least the homage of their hypocrisy.

Appendix

Field Effect and Forms of Conservatism

The entire output of conservative intellectuals bears the mark of the objective relationship uniting them to other positions in the field and imposed on them via the *specific problematic*, inscribed in the very structure of the field, of which they represent the passive (or, as one says in physics, the resistant) moment. They never have the initiative in problems in a world about which they would have nothing to say, finding nothing there to object to, were it not for the challenges offered by the critical thought they never cease to criticize. In fact, their most typical discursive strategies are the direct translation of a contradictory position of double exclusion, itself associated, in most cases, with a *crossed trajectory*. Often originating in the dominant positions in the field of power, it is only at the price of a double reversal that those 'intellectuals on the right' such as Joseph Schumpeter and Raymond Aron who are recognized as 'intellectuals' by 'intellectuals on the left' have arrived in the field of cultural production and, more precisely, at temporally dominant positions in this field which, as we know, occupies a dominated position at the core of the field of power. Always exposed to seeing themselves rejected both by the dominants as too 'intellectual' and by 'intellectuals' as too subservient to the 'bourgeois' order, they are obliged to fight ceaselessly on two fronts and to counter each of the two camps with what they share with the other. To the dominants they present themselves as 'intellectuals' and, in their concern to distinguish themselves from all forms of conservatism in the first degree, they must engage in argumentation instead of making assertions or thrusts – thereby threatening to introduce a suspect distance from an immediate and indisputable adherence to the established order; and it even happens that they take advantage of their familiarity with intellectual critique to criticize the pre-critical ideology of spontaneous conservatism and to give political lessons to politicians in the name of political science.[103]

But on the other hand, to convince an already converted bourgeois public that they have no reason to envy the bearers of cultural legitimacy and that they may easily triumph over these not-so-clever ones, at least in the domains where the dominants (in the field of power) and their homologues in the intellectual field agree to deny them access, such as economics and politics, the conservatives must, furthermore, resort to strategies which almost always consist of turning against 'intellectuals' their own weapons – those of logic and social critique, for example; they say what the latter should say if they knew what speaking really meant, and reduce to the absurd, by an aggressively consequent explanation of ultimate consequences, the theses under attack. They also tend to justify themselves by making a final reversal and returning again to the original ground of simple verities – intellectual and stylistic – and giving lessons in political realism and common sense.[104]

Being defined by a double rejection, conservative intellectuals must fall back simultaneously or successively on two contradictory strategies: they must combat the 'intellectual' critique by reducing it to its simplest expression, which constantly exposes them to the simplistic limpidity of the vulgarizer; yet, at the risk of losing all specific force, they must also demonstrate that they are capable of fighting back 'intellectually' against the critiques of 'intellectuals', and that their taste for clarity and simplicity, even if it is inspired by a form of anti-intellectualism, is the effect of a free intellectual choice. Being themselves, by their position and by their trajectory, the site of opposed and contradictory political intentions, they may take a position on each political position-taking by starting from another position, reproaching the left for not having the rigour of the right, the right for lacking the generous intelligence of the left.

By virtue of their propensity and their ability to vary the point of observation according to the object observed, of adopting *successively and separately* all the points of view from which each of the viewpoints actually expressed may be objectified, hence apprehended as such (with the exception of that scattered viewpoint which is their own), they excel at a polemical use of the appearance of objectivity, identified with a sort of neutralism which pretends to line the right and the left up against each other by reflecting back to each the image the other has of it, or ought to have of it.[105] They thus exhaust themselves in trying to combine the intellectual and the man of action, the scholar and the politician, at the peril of never being one or the other, and of being and feeling themselves strangers, and suspect, to both the one group and the other.

Even if it encompasses the same contradictory exigencies, the position of political essayist is a much more difficult one to hold than that of literary or art critic. The dominants have, in effect, in issues of economics and politics, a claim to expertise which they do not have in matters of art and literature and these days they assert this claim all the more strongly because, as a result of transformations in the methods of education and selection, the dominants now have the scholastically guaranteed conviction of being able to make themselves their own spokesmen, including on the terrain of 'theory'.

Often convinced that they owe their position to their educational merits and their technical competence alone, and that they can thus situate themselves above the divisions and conflicts of the field of power, the new mandarins of the great state bureaucracy feel themselves legitimated in arbitrating conflicts (in their eyes illusory ones) between particular interests, taking as their basis the vision derived from a global knowledge of economic mechanisms. Against the uselessly sophisticated analyses of the 'intellectual of the right', still too oriented towards intellectuals, and against the naive and archaic professions of faith of private employers, the nobility of state – an educationally selected and guaranteed bureaucratic 'elite' thinking of itself as a sort of *referee* capable of having a dialogue with both intellectuals and employers and of negotiating with the dominated classes or their representatives (and hence capable of holding itself at an equal distance from the dominant pole and the dominated pole of the field of power – works more and more vigorously to impose an unmarked discourse whose robust platitudes have an affinity with the exigencies of the political field and the journalistic field.

Distinguished defenders of a genteel conservatism have almost nothing in common, except in belonging to the same political camp, with the proponents of a populist conservatism with an anti-intellectual basis which haunts, in an endemic state, the lower categories of the intelligentsia, the 'conservative revolutionaries' of pre-Nazi and Nazi Germany, the workerist Zhdanovites of Russia or China and all communist parties of all countries at all times, American McCarthyites of the 1950s, not to mention all the minor pamphleteers who make a scandalous hit by denouncing intellectuals. Instead, this internal anti-intellectualism is often produced by dominated intellectuals, those of the first generation, whose ethical dispositions and *lifestyle* (accent, manners, bearing, etc.) lead them to feel ill at ease and displaced, as it were, notably in their confrontation with the bourgeois elegance and liberties of born intellectuals. When relative failure comes along to destroy their initial aspirations to a culture from which they expected everything, they willingly turn to resentment and moral indignation (notably, with the denunciation of what Pareto called the 'pornocracy') against the contradiction they perceive between the cosmopolitan, liberated, aesthetic, even disenchanted and cynical lifestyle of high-flying intellectuals and their advanced position-takings, notably in politics.

The dominants have always found their best guard dogs, the fiercest anyway, among intellectuals disappointed and often *scandalized* by the casualness of those heirs who have the luxury of repudiating their heritage. The horror inspired in them by the games of the bourgeois intellectual, whether conservative or revolutionary, throws the petit-bourgeois intellectuals, who have had such great difficulty in reaching the outer margins of an intelligentsia they idealized from afar, into an anti-intellectualism which has the violence of disappointed love.[106] Driven by the ardour of the renegade, they sell out and change camps, delivering to the 'bourgeois' the secrets of a world whose underside and dark corners they know better than anyone – their views of the social universe predisposing them to it. Thus it often happens that they come to fulfil the expectations of the dominants and to satisfy their need to be reassured against the disquieting audacities, even if merely symbolic ones, which are encouraged among certain dominant intellectuals by their dominated position in the field of power.

Hence one cannot completely explain the taking of a *position* by these 'proletaroid intellectuals', who have given their orientation and colouration to political formations as different as fascist and Stalinist regimes, without taking into account, in addition to the effects of dispositions associated with their trajectory, the less visible effects of a diminished position in the intellectual field. One may in effect propose as a general law that cultural producers are all the more likely to submit to the solicitations of external powers (whether the state, parties, economic powers or, as today, journalism) and to use resources imported from the exterior to regulate internal conflicts, the lower their positions in the internal hierarchies of the field and the more deprived they are of specific capital. It is through the dominated (according to specific criteria) that heteronomy occurs.

The paradigm of this attempt by dominated intellectuals to overturn relations of force by arming themselves with non-specific power (in the fashion of members of the literary bohemia during the French revolution) is without any doubt the Zhdanovism which, in the USSR but also in China and in all historical situations when the transfiguration of internal interest into external 'missions' turns out to be viable, leads second-rate writers and artists to call upon the 'people' and to invoke the imperatives of 'social art' or 'popular art' to prevail over the holders of a specific authority in the field (especially when the latter, as was the case in China, protest against the gap between the revolutionary ideal and reality, that is, against the rule of civil servants devoted to the party).[107]

The terrorist violence given an opportunity by these extraordinary situations to be fully carried out is merely the extreme limit of the ordinary violence of disappointed ambition which is exercised every day, in the irreproachable guise of the bad-tempered critique or the inspired denunciation of scandals and conspiracies, or, more slyly, through the more elusive collective decisions of commissions and committees, administrations and administrators, whether scientific or artistic.

To give its full impact to the critique of the gentle forms of tyranny exercised within the Republic of Letters, it would be necessary to go beyond the overly facile condemnation of the extreme forms of Zhdanovism and to inventory the innumerable manifestations of the repressive violence exercised by all agents of the maintenance of symbolic order whose portrait was sketched by Flaubert in the character of Hussonnet, the former revolutionary of the literary café converted into a bureaucrat responsible for literary matters. This task is all the more urgent, scientifically and politically, in that the more or less unexpected upheavals which are observed everywhere in the political world give disappointed intellectuals so often today a chance to express twice over, at the cost of a few *apparent* renunciations, the same repressive drives of resentment, the first time in the declared violence of denunciation or 'revolutionary' repression, and the second time in the latent and irreproachable violence of bureaucratic or journalistic power, thanks to which they try to impose exogenous principles of vision and division.[108]

PART III

To Understand Understanding

~∞~

Artists write for their peers, or at least for those who understand them.

BARBEY D'AUREVILLY

I

The Historical Genesis of the Pure Aesthetic

~∞~

> I have had to struggle here with my dearest aesthetic impressions, endeavouring to push intellectual honesty to its ultimate, cruellest limits.
>
> MARCEL PROUST

The multiple responses that philosophers, linguists, semiologists and art historians have given to the question of the specificity of literature ('literariness'), poetry ('poeticity') or the work of art in general, and to the question of the properly aesthetic perception they call for, all concur in stressing the properties of gratuity, the absence of function, the primacy of form over function, disinterestedness and so on. Here I will not evoke all those definitions that are merely variants of Kantian analysis, such as Strawson's, according to which the work of art has as its function not to have a function, or that of T. E. Hulme, for whom artistic contemplation is a 'detached interest'.[1] Instead I will be content with giving an ideal-typical example of these efforts to constitute as a universal essence — at the price of a *double dehistoricization*, of both the work and the gaze at the work — what is in fact a very particular experience of the work of art, one very evidently situated in social space and in historical time. According to Harold Osborne, the aesthetic attitude is characterized by the concentration of attention (it *'frames apart'* the perceived object from its environment), by the suspension of discursive and analytic activities (it ignores the sociological and historical context), by disinterestedness and detachment (it sets aside past and future preoccupations) and, finally, by indifference to the existence of the object.[2]

Analysis of essence and illusion of the absolute

If these analyses of essence agree on what is the essential, it is because what they have in common is to take as object – whether tacitly or explicitly (such as those analyses claiming to derive from phenomenology) – the subjective experience of the work of art which is that of the analyst, meaning of a cultivated person of a certain society, but they do so without paying attention to the *historicity* of this experience or of the object to which it is applied. This means that they effect, unwittingly, a *universalization of the particular case*, and in the same way constitute a particular experience, situated and dated, of the work of art as a transhistoric *norm* of all artistic perception. Concomitantly they pass over in silence the question of the *historical and social conditions of possibility* of this experience; they exclude, in effect, the analysis of the conditions under which works considered as worthy of the aesthetic gaze were produced and constituted as such; and equally, they ignore the question of the conditions under which the aesthetic disposition they call for is produced (phylogenesis) and continually reproduced in the course of time (ontogenesis). But only this double analysis could take account both of the nature of aesthetic experience and of that illusion of universality which accompanies it, and which such analyses of essence naively register.

It would be necessary, to be perfectly convincing, to submit to detailed examination some examples of the efforts made by modern abstractors of quintessence to disengage the pure essence of the work of art, to define for example, with Jakobson, what makes a verbal message a literary work. And also to show how they enclose themselves within the alternative (or vicious circle) of subjectivism or realism (for which the lover provides the formula: 'Is she pretty because I love her, or do I love her because she is pretty?'): must we say that it is the aesthetic point of view which creates the artistic object, or rather that it is the specific and intrinsic properties of the work of art which give rise to aesthetic experience – a literary one for example – in the reader capable of reading them adequately, that is, aesthetically, or, in more precise terms, capable of considering the message in and for itself?[3] This vicious circle is evident with Wellek and Warren, who define literature by the intrinsic properties of the message, while elsewhere specifying the properties which the 'competent reader' must possess to satisfy the requirements of the work in apprehending it aesthetically.[4] As for Panofsky, he apparently manages to get off the hook because he accompanies his analyses of essence with historical references. If the work of art is indeed, as he says, 'what demands to be perceived aesthetically', and if any object, natural as well as artificial, may be apprehended according to an aesthetic intention, meaning in its form rather than its function, then how may we avoid the conclusion that it is the aesthetic intention which makes the aesthetic object? And how can we make such a definition operational? Do we not observe that it is almost impossible to determine at what moment the worked-on-object becomes a work of art, when exactly, for example, a letter becomes 'literary', that is, at what moment form prevails over function? Does this mean that the difference inheres in the intention of the author? But this intention, like the intention of the reader or the spectator, moreover, is itself the object of socialization conventions which converge to define the always uncertain and historically changing boundary between the simple utensil and the work of art: 'Classic taste demanded that private letters, legal speeches and the shields of heroes should be *artistic* [...] while modern taste demands that architecture and ashtrays should be "functional" ...'[5]

There is undoubtedly no better confirmation of the almost universal acceptance – at least among the bearers of university titles – of the assumptions underlying the aesthetic *doxa* than the fact that the Wittgensteinian philosophers who are the quickest to flush out the *essentialist fallacy* in classical definitions of the poetic or of the literary will nevertheless invoke here and there, as if inadvertently, the 'gratuitousness of the work of art' and its absence of function, or the 'disinterested perception of things', among the most universally endorsed formalist commonplaces (within the confines of cultivated circles, of course).[6]

But, to escape this aporia, is it sufficient to assert, with Arthur Danto,[7] that the basis of the difference between works of art and ordinary objects is none other than an institution, to wit, the 'art world' which confers on them the status of candidates for aesthetic appreciation? This is a terse assertion, and if a sociologist may be permitted such a judgement, rather 'sociological'; born once again out of a singular experience which is too quickly universalized, it only designates the fact of the *institution* (in the active sense) of the work of art. It overlooks the historical and sociological analysis of the genesis and structure of the institution (the artistic field) which is capable of accomplishing such an act of institution, that is, of imposing the *recognition* of the work of art as such among all those (*and only those*) who (like the philosopher visiting a museum) have been constituted (through the effort of socialization, which also has to be analysed in terms of its social conditions and logic) in such a fashion that (as their entry into a museum attests) they are disposed to recognize as artistic and to apprehend as such the works socially designated as artistic (notably by their exhibition in a museum). (I have put between parentheses, for the fun of it, some of those things philosophers put between parentheses without realizing it ...)

All this means that one cannot divide a science of works into two parts, one devoted to production, the other to perception. The principle of reflexivity automatically asserts itself here: the science of the production of the work of art, that is, of the progressive emergence of a relatively autonomous field of production providing itself with its own market, and of a production which, being its own end, asserts the absolute primacy of form over function, is also for that very reason the science of the emergence of the pure aesthetic disposition, capable of privileging in the works thus produced (and potentially, in everything in the world) the form over the function.

What the analysis of essence forgets are the social conditions of the production (or the invention) and of the reproduction (or the inculcation) of dispositions and classificatory schemas which are activated in artistic perception – the social conditions of that kind of *historical transcendental* which is the condition of the aesthetic experience which naively describes it. The understanding of the particular relationship with the work of art which consists of an immediate comprehension born of familiarity relies on the analyst using himself to gain an understanding which is inaccessible to a simple phenomenological analysis of the lived experience of the work, to the extent that this experience relies on the active forgetting of the history which has produced it. It is only by mobilizing all the resources of the social sciences that one can bring to fruition that historicist form of the transcendental project which consists of reappropriating, by historical anamnesis, the historical forms and categories of artistic experience.

Although it appears to itself like a gift of nature, the eye of the nineteenth-century art-lover is the product of history. From the angle of phylogenesis, the pure gaze capable of apprehending the work of art as it demands to be apprehended (in itself and for itself, as form and not as function) is inseparable from the appearance of producers motivated by a pure artistic intention, itself indissociable from the emergence of an autonomous artistic field capable of posing and imposing its own goals in the face of external demands; and it is also inseparable from the corresponding appearance of a population of 'amateurs' or 'connoisseurs' capable of applying to the works thus produced the 'pure' gaze which they call for. And from the angle of ontogenesis, it is associated with very particular conditions of training, such as the precocious frequenting of museums and the prolonged exposure to school teaching and especially to the *skholè* as a form of leisure, and the distance with respect to the constraints and urgencies of necessity which such training presupposes. This means, it must be said in passing, that an analysis of essence which passes these conditions over in silence tacitly elevates into a universal norm of all practice claiming to be aesthetic these particular properties of an experience which is in fact the product of privilege.

What the ahistorical analysis of the work of art and of aesthetic experience really describes is an *institution* which, as such, enjoys a kind of twofold existence, in things and in minds. In things, it exists in the form of an artistic field, a relatively autonomous social universe which is the result of a slow process of emergence. In minds, it exists in the form of dispositions which invent themselves through the very movement of self-invention of the field to which they are adjusted. When things and dispositions are directly in accord with each other, meaning when the eye is the product of the field to which it relates, then everything appears to be immediately endowed with meaning and value. This is so clearly the case that in order for a totally extraordinary question to be posed about the foundation of the meaning and value of the work of art, something usually taken for granted by all those who swim like fish in the water of the cultural world, an experience has to arise which a cultivated person finds totally exceptional – even though it is, on the contrary, totally ordinary, as empirical observation shows,[8] for those who have not had the occasion or the chance to acquire the dispositions objectively required by the work of art. An example is Arthur Danto's visit to the exhibition of Warhol's Brillo boxes at the Stable Gallery, when he discovered the arbitrary (*ex instituto*, as Leibniz would have said) character of the imposition of value carried out by the field through exhibition in a place both consecrated and capable of consecrating.[9]

The experience of the work of art as immediately endowed with meaning and value is an effect of the harmony between the two aspects of the same historical institution, the cultivated *habitus* and the artistic field, which mutually ground each other. Given that the work of art does not exist as such, meaning as an object symbolically endowed with meaning and value, unless it is apprehended by spectators possessing the aesthetic disposition and competence which it tacitly requires, one could say that it is the eye of the aesthete which constitutes the work of art – but only if one immediately remembers that it can only do so to the extent that it is itself the product of a long collective history, that is, of the progressive invention of the 'connoisseur', and of a long individual history, that is, of prolonged exposure to the work of art. This relation of circular causality, that of belief and the sacred, characterizes any institution which can only function if it is established simultaneously within the objectivity of a social game and within dispositions ready to enter into the game and participate in it. Museums could say at their gates – but they do not need to, since it so goes without saying – 'Let no one enter here unless they are lovers of art.' The game makes up the *illusio*, the investment in the game by the informed player who, possessing a sense of the game because made by the game, plays the game, and thereby makes it exist.

It is clear that one does not need to choose between, on the one hand, the subjectivism of theories of the 'aesthetic consciousness' which reduce the aesthetic quality of a natural thing or a human work to a simple correlate of a purely contemplative attitude of consciousness, neither theoretical nor practical, and on the other hand an ontology of the work of art such as that proposed by Gadamer in *Truth and Method*. Questions of the meaning and value of the work of art, like the question of the specificity of aesthetic judgement, can only find solutions in a social history of the field, linked to a sociology of the conditions of the constitution of the particular disposition which the field calls for in each of its states.

Historical anamnesis and the return of the repressed

What makes a work of art a work of art and not a mundane thing or a simple utensil? What makes an artist an artist, as opposed to a craftsman or a Sunday painter? What makes a urinal or a bottle rack that is exhibited in a museum into a work of art? Is it the fact that it is signed by Duchamp, a recognized artist (and recognized first and foremost *as* an artist) and not by a wine merchant or a plumber? But is that not simply replacing the work-of-art-as-fetish with the 'fetish of the name of the master' of which Benjamin spoke? Who, in other words, has created the 'creator' as a recognized producer of fetishes? And what confers its magic efficacy on his name, whose celebrity is the measure of his pretension to exist as an artist? What makes the affixing of his name, like the label of a famous designer, multiply the value of the object (which helps to raise the stakes in attribution disputes and to establish the power of experts)? Where does the ultimate principle reside of the effect of nomination or of theory (a particularly appropriate word since it is a matter of seeing, *theorein*, and of giving to be seen) – that ultimate principle which, by introducing difference, division and separation, produces the sacred?

Such questions are analogous in type to those raised by Mauss in his *Theory of Magic*, when he pondered on the principle of magic's effectiveness and found himself moving back from the instruments employed by the sorcerer to the sorcerer himself, and from there to the belief of his clients, and little by little back to the whole social universe amidst which magic is evolved and practised. But in the infinite regress towards the primary cause and the ultimate foundation of the work of art's value, one must stop somewhere. And in order to explain this sort of miracle of transubstantiation which is the source of the work of art's existence – and which, though commonly forgotten, is brutally recalled through moves à la Duchamp – one must replace the ontological question with the historical question of the genesis of the universe in which the value of the work of art is ceaselessly produced and reproduced in a veritable continuous creation – that is, the artistic field.

The analysis of essence merely records the outcome of the analysis which history itself has performed objectively through the process of autonomization of the field and through the progressive invention by agents (artists, critics, historians, curators, experts, etc.) of techniques and concepts (genres, mannerisms, periods, styles, etc.) which are characteristic of this universe. The science of works will not free itself completely from an 'essentialist' vision unless it successfully carries out a historical analysis of the genesis of those central figures in the artistic game, the artist and the expert, and of the dispositions they put to work in the production and reception of works of art. Notions which have become obvious and banal such as those of the artist or 'creator', like the very words which designate and constitute them, are the products of a long historical process.

This is often forgotten by art historians themselves when they ponder the emergence of the artist in the modern sense of the term, still without avoiding completely the trap of 'essentialist thought' inscribed in the use (always haunted by anachronism) of historically invented, and therefore dated, words. Unable to question everything implicitly involved in the modern notion of the artist, and in particular the professional ideology of the uncreated 'creator' which evolved throughout the nineteenth century, they stop at the apparent object, meaning the artist (or, elsewhere, the writer, the philosopher, the scholar), instead of constructing and analysing the field of production of which the artist, socially instituted as a 'creator', is the product. They do not see that the ritual inquiry concerning the place and time of the appearance of the figure of the artist (as opposed to the craftsman) in fact leads back to the question of the economic and social conditions of the gradual constitution of an artistic field capable of grounding belief in the quasi-magical powers attributed to the artist.

It is not merely a matter of exorcizing the 'fetish of the name of the master' by a simple sacrilegious and slightly childish inversion – whether one wishes it or not, the name of the master is indeed a fetish. Rather, it is a matter of describing the gradual emergence of the entire set of social mechanisms which make possible the figure of the artist as producer of that fetish which is the work of art – in other words, the constitution of the artistic field (in which analysts and art historians themselves are included) as the locus where belief in the value of art – and in that power to create value which belongs to the artist – is constantly produced and reproduced. This leads to surveying not only the indices of the artist's autonomy (such as those revealed through the analysis of contracts, like the appearance of the signature, affirmations of the artist's specific competence, recourse in cases of dispute to arbitration by peers, etc.), but also the indices of the field's autonomy, such as the emergence of a set of specific institutions which are required for the functioning of the economy of cultural goods – places of exhibition (galleries, museums, etc.), institutions of consecration (academies, salons, etc.), institutions for the reproduction of producers (art schools, etc.), and specialized agents (dealers, critics, art historians, collectors, etc.), endowed with the *dispositions* objectively required by the field and with *specific categories of perception and appreciation* which are irreducible to those in common use and which are capable of imposing a specific measure on the value of artists and their products.

As long as painting is measured by surface covered or by length of labour, or by the quantity and price of the raw materials used (gold or ultramarine paints), the artist-painter is not radically different from a house painter. This is why, among all the inventions which accompany the emergence of the field of production, one of the most important is undoubtedly the elaboration of a properly artistic language: first a way of naming painters and of speaking about them and about the nature and the mode of remunerating their work, and through this elaborating an autonomous definition of properly artistic value, irreducible as such to strictly economic value; and also, in the same way, a way of speaking about painting itself, using appropriate words, often pairs of adjectives, which enable one to talk about the specificity of pictorial technique, the *manifattura*, even the particular manner of a painter, which it helps to make exist socially by naming it. By the same logic, the discourse of celebration, especially the biography, plays a determining role, probably less by what it says about painters and their work than by the fact of establishing the painter as a memorable figure, one worthy of a historical account, like a statesman or poet (we know that the ennobling comparison – *ut pictura poesis* – contributes (at least for a while, until it becomes a hindrance) to the affirmation of the irreducibility of pictorial art).

A genetic sociology should also include in its model the action of producers themselves, their claim to the right to be the sole judges of pictorial production, to make their own criteria for the perception and appreciation of their products. It should take into account the effect exercised on them and on the image they have of themselves and their production (and thereby, the effect exercised on their actual production) by the images of painters and their production which comes back to them from other agents engaged in the field – other artists but also critics, clients, patrons, collectors, etc. (One may assume, for example, that the interest which certain collectors started to take in sketches and cartoons from the quattrocento on could only have helped to exalt the impression the artist had of his own dignity.)

The history of the specific institutions which are indispensable to artistic production should be backed up with a history of the institutions which are indispensable to consumption, and hence to the production of consumers and in particular, of *taste*, as disposition and as competence. The inclination of the 'expert' to consecrate a part of his or her time to the contemplation of works of art for the sole purpose of the pleasure to be enjoyed from them cannot become an essential dimension of the lifestyle of the gentleman or the aristocrat (increasingly identified, at least in England and France, with the person of taste) without the whole collective labour necessary to produce the instruments of the cult of the work of art: one thinks of notions such as 'good taste', undergoing constant elaboration, or of designations like *virtuoso*, borrowed from the Italian, or *connoisseur*, taken from the French, characterizing and producing figures in seventeenth- and eighteenth-century England who are able to boast an art of living freed from the utilitarian and basely material ends to which 'vulgar' people sacrifice themselves. But one must also take into account practices as highly ritualized as the 'Grand Tour', a cultural pilgrimage lasting several years and culminating in a visit to Italy and Rome, which constitutes the almost obligatory crowning achievement of their studies for the children of the great aristocracy of England and elsewhere; we must consider as well the institutions offering, usually for payment, cultural products to a broader and broader public, the specialized periodical publications, magazines and works of criticism, literary and artistic newspapers and weeklies, private galleries (gradually converted into museums), annual exhibitions, guidebooks aimed at visitors to the painting and sculpture collections of aristocratic palaces or museums, public concerts and so forth.

Besides the fact they foster the growth of a *public* for cultural works, which is thereby given the means (and required) to acquire a cultivated disposition, *public* institutions like museums, which have no other purpose than to offer for contemplation works often produced with quite other destinations in mind (such as religious paintings, dance or ceremonial music, etc.), have the effect of bringing about a social rupture which, by tearing works out of their original context, strips them of their diverse religious or political functions and thus reduces them, by a sort of active *épochè*, to their properly artistic function. The museum, as it isolates and separates (*frames apart*), is undoubtedly the site *par excellence* of that act of *constitution*, continually repeated with the untiring constancy of things, through which both the status of the sacred conferred on works of art and the sacralizing disposition they call for are affirmed and continually reproduced.[10] The experience of the pictorial work as it has been asserted by this site in its exclusive devotion to pure contemplation tends to become the norm for the experience of all objects belonging to the very category which has been constituted by the fact of their being exhibited.

Everything inclines us to think that the history of aesthetic theory and of the philosophy of art is closely linked (without being its direct reflection, since it, too, develops in a field) to the history of the institutions suited to fostering access to pure delectation and disinterested contemplation, such as museums or those practical manuals of visual gymnastics called tourist guides or writings on art (among which must be included innumerable travel writings). In fact, it is clear that the theoretical writings which the history of traditional philosophy treats as contributions to the knowledge of the object are also (and more especially) contributions to the *social construction of the very reality* of this object, and hence of the theoretical and practical conditions of its existence (the same thing may be said about treatises on political theory by Machiavelli, Bodin or Montesquieu).

It would be necessary to rewrite the history of pure aesthetics *from this perspective*, showing, for example, how professional philosophers have imported into the domain of art certain concepts originally developed in the *theological* tradition, especially a conception of the artist as a 'creator' endowed with an almost divine faculty called 'imagination' and capable of producing a 'second nature', a 'second world', *sui generis* and autonomous; how Alexandre Baumgarten, in his *Philosophical Reflections on Poetry* of 1735, transposed into the aesthetic order a Leibnizian cosmogony according to which God, in the creation of the best of all possible worlds, chose ours among an infinity of worlds, all formed of compossible elements and governed by specific internal laws, making of the poet a creator and of the poem a world subject to its own laws, whose truth does not reside in its correspondence with the real, but in its internal coherence; how Karl Philipp Moritz tried to prove that the work of art is a microcosm whose beauty 'has no need of being useful' because it has 'within itself the purpose of its existence'; how, following another theoretical line (which must also be considered in its social dimension, by situating each thinker in his field), the idea that supreme good consists of the contemplation of the Beautiful (with its different theoretical foundations, Platonic and Plotinian, but also Leibnizian) was developed by different writers, and in particular Shaftesbury, Karl Philipp Moritz and Kant (who adopts the viewpoint of the receiver rather than the producer of the work of art, meaning the stance of contemplation), and then Schiller, Schlegel, Schopenhauer and many others; and how this predominantly German philosophical tradition was connected through the intermediary of Victor Cousin with French writers of art for art's sake, especially Baudelaire or Flaubert, who reinvented in their own fashion the theory of the 'creator', of the 'other world' and of pure contemplation.[11]

It would be necessary also to reveal in each case, as I have tried to do with respect to Kant, the indices of a social relation which is always implicated in the relationship to the work of art (for example in pairs of adjectives such as pure and impure, intelligible and sensory, refined and vulgar, etc.), and to put this hidden but fundamental relationship in turn into relation with the position and trajectory of the author in the field (philosophical, artistic, etc.) and in social space. This genealogy, which would probably rather irksomely record returns and repetitions which are linked, often in an indiscernible manner, to conscious or unconscious borrowings or to reinventions, would constitute the surest and most radical exploration of that unconscious which all cultivated people, because they have it in common, are ready to uphold as a universal (a priori) form of knowledge.

Historical categories of artistic perception

Thus the more established the field becomes, the less can the production of the work of art, of its value but also of its meaning, be reduced to the sole labour of an artist – who, paradoxically, increasingly becomes the focus of attention. Production of the work brings into play all the producers of works classified as artistic, whether great or small, famous (celebrated) or unknown, as well as critics, themselves constituted as a field, not to mention collectors, middlemen, curators – in short, all those who have ties to art and who, living for art and living off art, confront each other in the competitive struggle over the definition of the meaning and value of the work of art, and hence the delimitation of the world of art and (true) artists, and who collaborate through these very struggles in the production of the value of art and the artist.

If the science of works of art is still today in its infancy, it is probably because those in charge of it, and in particular art historians and theoreticians of the aesthetic, are engaged unwittingly (or without in any case drawing out all the consequences) in the struggles which yield the meaning and value of the work of art: in other words, they are caught up in the object they would take as their object. To be convinced of this it is enough to observe that the concepts used to think about works of art, and in particular to judge and classify them, are characterized, as Wittgenstein has noted, by the most extreme indeterminacy, and this is so whether one looks at genres (poetry, tragedy, comedy, drama or novel), forms (ballad, rondeau, sonnet or sonata, alexandrine or free verse), periods or styles (Gothic, baroque, classical), or movements (Impressionists, Symbolists, realists, naturalists). And the confusion is just as present in concepts used to characterize the work of art itself, to perceive it and appreciate it, such as the adjectival pairs which structure artistic experience.

Because they are inscribed in common language and are applied for the most part beyond the properly aesthetic sphere, these categories of judgement of taste are shared by all speakers of the same language and so permit an apparent form of communication. Nevertheless they always remain marked, even in the use made of them by professionals, by an extreme vagueness and flexibility which, as Wittgenstein again has observed, makes them completely resistant to essentialist definition.[12] This is probably because the use made of these terms and the meaning given to them depend on the particular points of view, situated socially and historically, of their users – points of view which are quite often completely irreconcilable.

The analyst conscious of the fact that his or her analysis of the game is always threatened with being itself caught up in the game can expect almost insurmountable difficulties in presenting findings. In particular, this is because the most methodically controlled language is certain to appear, once a naive reading brings it back into the social game, as the taking of a position in the very debate it is trying to objectify. Thus, for example, just when one has substituted a more neutral term, like 'periphery', for a more indigenous word such as 'province' which is overly charged with pejorative connotations, it remains the case that the opposition between centre and periphery which one might resort to in order to analyse certain effects of symbolic domination exercised in the literary or artistic world, at the national or international level, is itself a stake in the struggles of the field under analysis, and that each of the terms used to name it may have, according to the receiver's point of view, diametrically opposite connotations. So, for example, we have the desire of the 'central' ones, meaning the dominants, to describe the position-takings of those on the 'peripheries' as an effect of lag or of 'provincialism', and on the other hand the resistance of those on the 'peripheries' to the loss of standing implicit in this classification, and their efforts to convert a peripheral position into a central position or at least into a chosen distance.

In short, although one can always argue about taste (and, as everyone knows, the confrontation over preferences plays an important part in daily conversations), it is certainly true that communication in these matters takes place only with a very high degree of misunderstanding: in effect, the classificatory schemes which render it possible also help to render it practically ineffective. Thus it is possible for individuals occupying different positions in social space to give completely different meanings and values – and often opposed ones – to the adjectives commonly used to characterize works of art or mundane objects.[13] And one would never finish a survey of the notions, starting with the idea of beauty, which in different periods have taken on different, even radically opposite, meanings, notably in the wake of artistic revolutions. One example is the notion of 'finish' which, after having condensed the inseparably ethical and aesthetic ideal of academic painting, found itself banished from art by Manet and the Impressionists.

Thus the categories engaged in the perception and appreciation of the work of art are doubly linked to historical context: associated with a social universe which is situated and dated, they are also the object of usages which are themselves socially marked by the social position of their users. The majority of notions which artists and critics employ to define themselves or to define their adversaries are weapons and stakes in struggles, and a number of the categories which art historians deploy in order to treat their topic are nothing more than classificatory schemes issuing from these struggles and then more or less skilfully disguised or transfigured. Initially conceived, most often, as insults or condemnations (our term 'category' stems from the Greek *katègorein*, meaning to accuse publicly), these combative concepts gradually become the technical categorems on to which, thanks to genesis amnesia, critical dissections and academic theses or dissertations confer an air of eternity.

If there is a truth, it is that truth is a stake in the struggle; and, even though the divergent or antagonist classifications or judgements made by agents engaged in the artistic field are indisputably determined or oriented by specific dispositions and interests linked to positions in the field and to points of view, they are nevertheless formulated in the name of a pretension to universality, to absolute judgement, which is the very negation of the relativity of points of view.[14] 'Essentialist thought' is at work in all social universes and most especially in fields of cultural production – the religious field, the scientific field, the literary field, the artistic field, the legal field, etc. – where games which have the universal at stake are played out. But it is quite clear in that case that 'essences' are norms. This is what Austin was recalling when he analysed the implications of the adjective 'real' [*vrai*] in expressions such as 'real' man, 'real' courage, or in the case here, 'real' artist or 'real' masterpiece: in all these examples, the word 'real' implicitly contrasts the case under consideration with all cases in the same class which have also been given this predicate by other speakers (although in a manner which is not 'really' justified), this predicate being symbolically very powerful, like any claim to the universal.

The only thing science can do is to try to establish the truth of these struggles over truth and to grasp the objective logic behind the way the stakes and camps, the strategies and victories, are determined; to relate representations and instruments of thought, which feel as if they are unconditioned, back to the social conditions of their production and use, that is, to the historical structure of the field where they are generated and where they operate. By following the methodological postulate, constantly supported by empirical analysis, of the homology between the space of position-takings (literary or artistic forms, concepts and instruments of analysis, etc.) and the space of positions occupied in the field, one is led to historicize those cultural products which all share a pretension to universality. But historicizing them is not only (as some think) to relativize them, recalling that they have meaning only with reference to a determined state of the field of struggles; it also means giving them back their necessity by tearing them out of the indeterminacy which stems from a false eternalization and relating them back to the social conditions of their genesis – a truly generative definition.

This holds true, too, for 'reception'. Contrary to the common representation which maintains that sociological analysis, by relating each form of taste to its social conditions of production, reduces and relativizes the practices and representations concerned, one can see it as tearing them out of the arbitrary and making them absolute, by making them both necessary and incomparable, hence justified in existing as they do. One may, in effect, suggest that two persons possessing each a different *habitus*, not being exposed to the same situation and to the same stimulations, do not hear the same music and do not see the same paintings since they construe them differently, and so they are bound to bring forth different value judgements.

The oppositions structuring aesthetic perception are not given a priori, but are historically produced and reproduced; they are indissociable from the historical conditions of their being put into operation. By the same token, the aesthetic disposition, which constitutes as works of art the objects socially designated for its application (at the same stroke extending its activity to aesthetic expertise, with its categories, concepts, taxonomies), is a product of the whole history of the field which must be reproduced, in each potential consumer of the work of art, by a specific apprenticeship. It is sufficient to observe the distribution of the aesthetic disposition in history (one thinks, for example, of those critics who until the end of the nineteenth century defended an art subordinated to moral values and didactic functions), or else observe the aesthetic disposition at the core of a society today, in order to be convinced that nothing is less natural than the ability to adopt towards a work of art (and even more so towards any ordinary object) the aesthetic posture such as essentialist analysis describes it.

The invention of the pure gaze is brought about in the very movement of the field towards autonomy. In effect, as we have seen, the assertion of the autonomy of the principles of production and evaluation of the work of art is inseparable from the assertion of the autonomy of the producer, that is, of the field of production. The pure gaze – like pure painting to which it necessarily corresponds and which is made to be beheld in itself and for itself, as painting, as a play with form, values and colours, meaning independently of any reference to transcendent meanings – is the result of a process of purification. It is the product of a veritable essentialist analysis carried out by history in the course of successive revolutions which, as in the religious field, always lead the new avant-garde to challenge orthodoxy, in the name of a return to the rigour of beginnings and a purer definition of genre.

In more general terms, the evolution of different fields of cultural production towards a greater autonomy is accompanied, as we have seen, by a sort of reflexive and critical turning back by producers upon their own production, which leads them to distinguish its own principle and its specific assumptions. In so far as it manifests a rupture with external demands and a desire to exclude artists suspected of obeying them, the affirmation of the primacy of form over function, of mode of representation over the object of representation, is the most specific expression of the claim to the autonomy of the field and of its pretension to produce and to impose the principles of a specific legitimacy as much in the order of production as in the order of reception of the work of art. To make the manner of saying it triumph over the thing said, to sacrifice the 'subject', heretofore directly subject to demand, to the manner of treating it, to the pure play of colours, values and forms, to constrain the language in order to constrain the attention paid to language – all this finally comes down to affirming the specificity and unsubstitutability of the product and the producer by putting the stress on the most specific and most irreplaceable aspect of the act of production. The artist challenges any external constraint or demand and affirms his or her mastery over what defines him or her and what belongs to him or her by right, that is, the manner, form, style – *art* in short, thus established as the exclusive purpose of art. One must quote Delacroix: 'All subjects become good through the worthiness of the author. Oh, young artist, do you seek a subject? Everything is a subject, the subject is you yourself, your impressions, your emotions before nature. You must look within yourself, not around you.'[15] The true subject of the work of art is none other than the properly artistic manner of apprehending the world, that is, the artists themselves, their manners and styles, those infallible marks of the mastery to which they owe their art. Baudelaire and Flaubert in the domain of writing, and Manet in the domain of painting, pushed to its ultimate consequences, at the cost of extraordinary subjective and objective difficulties, the conscious affirmation of the all-powerfulness of the artistic gaze. By showing an ability to apply it not only to base and vulgar objects as was the aim of the realism of Champfleury and Courbet, but also to insignificant objects, the 'creator' can assert an almost divine power of transmutation and can posit the autonomy of form over the subject, at the same time assigning to cultivated perception its fundamental norm.

The second reason for the reflexive and critical return of art upon itself is the fact that the closing of the field of production creates the conditions for a circularity and an almost perfect reversibility of the relations of production and consumption. In becoming the principal object of the position-takings and contentions among producers, stylistic principles are embodied in a more and more rigorous and accomplished manner in works of art at the same time as they are asserted, always more explicitly and systematically, in the confrontation between the producer and the critical judgements brought to bear on the work, or in confronting the works of other producers and in the theoretical discourse produced by and for that encounter. In addition, the practical mastery of the specific achievements inscribed in past and recorded works, codified and canonized by a whole corpus of professionals of conservation and celebration – historians of art and literature, exegetes, analysts, critics – is part of the conditions of entry into the field of production. From this it follows, contrary to what a naive relativism teaches, that 'time' in the history of art is really irreversible, and that it presents a form of *cumulativity*. Absolutely nothing is more connected to the proper tradition of the field, including the intention to subvert it, than avant-garde artists who, at the risk of appearing as naifs, must inevitably situate themselves in relation to all previous efforts at overtaking which have occurred in the history of the field and in the space of possibles which it imposes on new entrants.

What survives in the field is more and more linked to the specific history of the field, and to it alone, and hence is more and more difficult to deduce from the state of the social world at any given moment (as a certain 'sociology' which ignores the specific logic of the field claims to do). Adequate perception of works which – like Warhol's Brillo boxes or Klein's monochrome paintings – obviously owe their existence, their value and their formal properties to the structure of the field, and so to its history, can only be differential and diacritical, meaning attentive to the deviations with respect to other works, contemporary but also past. As with production, the consumption of works which have come out of a long tradition of ruptures with tradition tends to become historical through and through, and yet more and more totally dehistoricized: in effect, the history brought into play by decoding and appreciation is increasingly reduced to the pure history of forms, completely eclipsing the social history of struggles over forms which is the life and the movement of the artistic field.

This counters the challenge made by formalist aesthetics, only interested in the form (in reception as much as in production), to sociological analysis. In effect, works that stem from purely formal research seem made to consecrate the exclusive validity of internal reading, a reading which is attentive solely to the properties of form, and to frustrate or discredit all attempts to reduce these works to a social context against which they were constituted.[16] However, in order to reverse the situation, it suffices to observe that the formalist ambition's objection to any kind of historicization rests on a lack of awareness of its own social conditions of possibility, as does the aesthetic philosophy, moreover, which records and ratifies this ambition ... What is forgotten in both cases is the historical process in the course of which the social conditions of freedom from external determinations emerge, that is, the relatively autonomous field of production and the pure aesthetic it makes possible.

The conditions of pure reading

Like the 'pure' perception of pictorial or musical works, the 'pure' reading that the most advanced works of the avant-garde imperatively require and that critics and other professional readers tend to apply to any legitimate work is a *social institution* which is the end result of a whole history of the field of cultural production, a history of the production of the pure writer – and the pure consumer whom the field helps to produce by producing for that person. Being the product of social conditions of a particular type, the text postulates the existence of a reader capable of adopting the posture corresponding to these conditions: since it is the expression of a field which has achieved a high degree of autonomy, it contains within itself an injunction, a summons – actually the one recorded and ratified, without knowing it, by most theories of reception and of reading. In effect, by grounding themselves in an apparently phenomenological analysis of the lived experience of a cultivated reader, these theories are compelled to extract, from this embodied norm, naively normative theses.

What is baptized as the 'implicit' reader by reception theory (and Wolfgang Iser), the 'archilecteur' by Michael Riffaterre,[17] or the 'informed reader' by Stanley Fish[18] – the reader of whom analysis really speaks (for example, in the description of the experience of reading as retention and protension with Wolfgang Iser[19]) – is none other than the theoretician himself, who, by following a very common inclination among *lectores*, takes as object his own experience (not analysed sociologically) as a cultivated reader. He does not need to push empirical observation very far to discover that the reader called for by pure works is the product of exceptional social conditions which reproduce (*mutatis mutandis*) the social conditions of their production (in this sense, the author and legitimate reader are interchangeable).[20]

This once again means that the break with intuitionism and the narcissistic complacency of the hermeneutic tradition can only be achieved in and through a reappropriation of the whole history of the field of production which has produced the producers, the consumers and the products, and hence produced the analysts themselves – that is, in and through a historical and sociological labour which constitutes the only effective form of knowledge of self. It is in this sense, diametrically opposed to that offered by the 'hermeneutic' tradition, that one may assert than 'in the end, all understanding is an understanding of oneself.'[21]

To understand is to grasp a necessity, a *raison d'être*, by reconstructing, in the particular case of a particular author, a generative formula whose knowledge allows one to reproduce in another mode the very production of the work, to feel necessity accomplish itself, even outside any empathic experience. The gap between necessitating reconstruction and participating comprehension is never as manifest as when interpreters are led by their labour to experience as necessary the practices of agents who occupy certain positions in the intellectual field or in social space which are totally alien to their own, and hence likely to appear to them profoundly 'antipathetic'.[22] The labour needed to reconstruct the generative formula at the source of a work has nothing to do with that sort of direct and immediate identification between the unique ego of the reader and the unique ego of the creator evoked in the romantic vision of the 'living reading', understood (especially by Herder) as a sort of divining intuition of the author's soul. Moreover, the practice of reading as it can be observed with Georges Poulet himself (I am thinking of his analysis of a page of *Madame Bovary*) has no connection with what he says about it in his *Phenomenology of Reading*, that is, with an effort to put oneself in the place of the author, in order to re-live in some way an immanent experience of the work, and to arrive at that state of empathic fusion in which the reader's 'consciousness' 'acts as if it were the consciousness' of the author.

If the romantic representation of reading remains so strong within the scholarly tradition, both literary and philosophical, it is because it undoubtedly offers the best justification for the propensity of the *lector* to identify with the *auctor* and thus to participate, by procuration, in the 'creation' – an identification which certain inspired exegetes have grounded in theory, by defining interpretation as a 'creative' activity.[23] In the manner of Bachelard, who spoke of 'cosmic narcissism' with respect to an aesthetic experience of nature founded on the relationship 'I am beautiful because nature is beautiful and nature is beautiful because I am beautiful,'[24] one could call *hermeneutic narcissism* that form of encounter with works and authors in which the hermeneutic scholar affirms his intelligence and grandeur by his empathic insight into great authors. The social history of interpretations which ought to accompany (or precede) any new interpretation would never come to the end of an inventory of the errors committed by many interpreters for the sole reason that they felt themselves authorized to see 'their' authors in their own image, thus lending them thoughts and feelings which are in fact rigorously situated and dated. We can all remember the pedantic and ridiculous annotations of school classics; but a number of sophisticated readings with no other foundation than projective identification and a more or less conscious transference are only better received because the ethical dispositions expressed in them are less rebarbative. In short, one cannot re-live or help someone else re-live the lived experience of others, and it is not sympathy which leads to true understanding, but true understanding which leads to sympathy, or better, to that sort of *amor intellectualis* which, based on the renunciation of narcissism, accompanies the discovery of necessity.[25]

Only a sociological critique of pure reading, conceived as an analysis of the social conditions of possibility of this singular activity, can allow us to break with the assumptions that it tacitly engages, and perhaps also to escape the constraints and limitations which ignorance of these conditions and assumptions makes acceptable in the activity of pure reading.[26] Paradoxically, formalist criticism, which sees itself as free of any reference to institutions, tacitly accepts all the 'theses' inscribed in the existence of the institution from which it derives its authority. It tends to exclude any real questioning of the institution of reading, that is, any challenge to the delimitation of the corpus of texts consecrated by the institution as much as to a definition of the legitimate mode of reading which apprehends (according to more or less codified interpretative frameworks) texts constituted as self-sufficient realities, concealing within themselves their reason for being.

One cannot get out of the enchanted circle of *legenda* producing the *modus legendi* which reproduces them as objects worthy of being read, and read as timeless objects of a purely aesthetic delectation, without taking that circle as object within two sorts of inquiry: on the one hand, a history of the progressive invention of pure reading, a mode of apprehending works which is partly linked with the autonomization of the field of literary production and the corresponding appearance of works demanding to be read (or reread) in themselves and for themselves; on the other hand, a history of the process of canonization which has led to the constitution of a corpus of canonic works whose value the education system tends continually to reproduce by producing aware consumers (which means converted ones) as well as sacralizing commentaries. The analysis of critical discourse on works is in effect both a critical preliminary to a science of works and a contribution to a science of the production of works as objects of belief.

Without even contemplating sketching out this programme here (it is, moreover, partly achieved in the work of historians),[27] I just want to stress the affinity between the position of *lector* and the dehistoricized and dehistoricizing reading of a corpus of canonic works which are themselves dehistoricized. We know that until the beginning of the nineteenth century the idea (which did not need to be explained because it was so self-evident) of a time-immemorial 'humanity' underlies the selection of what one calls the 'humanities':[28] this 'culture' is made up essentially from the great texts of Greek and Roman antiquity which, through the commentaries and grammatical and rhetorical exercises focused on them, were thought to furnish the entire sum of eternal topics indispensable to thought about the fundamental problems of politics, morality and metaphysics.[29] As Durkheim observed, 'everything should maintain youth in that conviction that man is always and everywhere similar to himself; that the only changes which he presents in history are reduced to exterior and superficial modifications [. . .]. Therefore one could not, upon leaving school, conceive of human nature other than as a sort of eternal reality, immutable and invariable, independent of time and space, since the diversity of places and conditions do not affect it.'[30] Throughout the nineteenth century, ancient languages and literatures continued to dominate curricula and, despite the effort of a minority current which wanted, in the Encyclopedic spirit, to train observation and experimentation, pedagogy remained oriented towards the acquisition of rhetoric (through Latin or French discourse) and moral education or, more precisely, the 'elevation of thought'.[31] The combination of a universalistic humanism and a formalist reading of texts reaches its apogee under the Third Republic, in the secularized spiritualism of the university cult of the text treated as pure form (with the scholastic genre of 'explication de textes') and suitable for admission into the pantheon of canonic authors, there to serve as the basis for a sort of republican and national consensus, founded on the neutralization through derealization and eclecticism of any conflict which might divide the different sections of the dominants (faith and reason, conservatism and progressivism, etc.). As Lionel Gossman notes, we observe that after 1870, in England and the United States as well as in France, the teaching of literature, which had been geared to the apprenticeship of writing and public speaking (with, in Anglo-Saxon countries, an accent on what is called *elocution*), becomes more and more an 'activity of appreciation', 'suitable to cultivate the sentiments and imagination', with the teaching of rhetoric increasingly giving way to a culture of taste and a preparation for reception.[32]

There is a link of mutual dependence between the nature of the texts offered for reading and the form of the reading done of them. The reading of the *lector* assumes a *skholè*, a socially instituted situation of *studious leisure* in which one may 'seriously play' (*spoudaiôs paizein*) and take playful things seriously; and hence the reading is disposed to grant very exactly what playful things demand from the dehistoricized work of university tradition, as well as from the literary work born of the formalist intention.

Pure production produces and presupposes pure reading, and *ready-mades* are just a sort of limit case of all works produced for commentary and by commentary. To the extent that the field gains in autonomy, writers feel themselves increasingly authorized to write works destined to be *decoded*, hence subject to a *repeated reading necessary to explore, without exhausting it, the intrinsic polysemy* of the work. For his part, the 'pure' reader who excludes any reductive reference to the social history of production and producers and any historian's intention to reactivate the polemical and political virtue of the literary work naturally espouses the 'intention' (as Panofsky said) of all works which have no other intention than not to have an intention, except that inscribed in the very form of the work. It follows that the *scholastic view* of which Austin spoke[33] is never so *invisible* as when *scholars* of all countries, shut within the perfect circle unknowingly outlined by their aesthetic theories, plunge (like

Mallarmé's Hérodiade) the pure gaze of a dehistoricizing reading into the mirror of a pure and perfectly dehistoricized work.

Poverty of ahistoricism

It is undoubtedly no accident that the scholastic vision of the world and the set of indisputable (because instituted) premises which it tacitly engages are never as openly betrayed as in the case of philosophy: paradoxically, insertion into a universe placed under the dominion of the *skholè*, of gratuitous study, of finality without purpose, does not necessarily predispose one to objectify all the conditions of possibility of the aesthetic experience, which Kant well characterized as 'the pure exercise of the faculty of feeling' or as a 'disinterested play of the sensibilities'. More precisely, the philosophy of the history of philosophy which professors of philosophy of all theoretical persuasions[34] involve *in practice* in the reading of philosophical texts, and for which Gadamer produces the explicit theory, in no way inclines them to tear themselves away, in their theories of the perception of cultural works (of which theories of reading are a particular case), from the enchanted circle of pure reading of texts purified of any historical attachment.

It would be necessary to bring to light the ensemble of assumptions constitutive of the *philosophical doxa*, a paradoxical reality, rigorously shielded from the most 'radical' challenges posed by the accredited critics of the *doxa*; and in particular all the assumptions involved *in practice* in the 'philosophical' reading of texts that the scholastic tradition designates as 'philosophical', meaning those that call for this reading. In this way one would see that the dehistoricized and dehistoricizing reading by the historian of philosophy tends to bracket out (more or less completely) anything that ties the text to a history and a society and, in particular, to the space of possibles in relation to which philosophical work was originally defined; and also that it ignores the *ensemble* of coexisting systems, which – at least so long as the philosophical field is not yet constituted as such (and undoubtedly even beyond that, as we see clearly, for example, in the case of Heidegger) – cannot all be 'philosophical' in the strict sense the internal definition implies.

We forget that what circulates among philosophers, whether contemporaries or of successive eras, is not only canonic texts, but also titles of books, labels of schools, garbled quotations, and concepts ending in -ism – often entailing polemical denunciations or devastating anathemas (which sometimes function as slogans). There are also the routine wisdoms which are transmitted through courses and textbooks, the invisible and unadmitted props of the 'common sense' of an intellectual generation, and which tend to reduce certain works to a few keywords, a few obligatory quotations. And there is also the immense quantity of information which is linked to belonging to a field and which is immediately invested in exchanges among contemporaries: information on institutions (academies, journals, publishers, etc.) and people, on their physical appearance and their institutional affiliation, on their interrelations, alliances or quarrels, and everything which links them to their times; information on problems and ideas which are current in the ordinary universe, and which are carried by newspapers – has a historian of philosophy, even a Hegelian, ever inspected the philosopher's morning paper? – on the debates and conflicts of the university world which, universalized, are so often at the source of the university vision of the universe.

Reading, and a fortiori the reading of books, and books of philosophy, is but one of the many ways, even for the most bookish of professional readers, to acquire the learning mobilized in writing and reading. And so the greatest part of the immense invisible plinth of great thought, and notably everything taken for granted by contemporaries, risks remaining inaccessible: passing unnoticed, this *doxa* has little chance of being recorded by witnesses' testimony, in chronicles or memoirs – which, whatever their author's actual proneness to amnesia, are always the 'memoirs of an amnesiac', in Satie's phrase. By transporting on to a properly epistemic terrain – if only by the abolition of reference to the realities designated by proper names or by so-called personal allusions – thoughts, judgements and analyses which are partly the product of the universalization of the particular case, ordinary reading transforms into timeless and impersonal answers to timeless and universal problems those position-takings which (on the terrain of politics or morality, but also, even if to a lesser extent, in the order of knowledge or of logic) remain rooted in questions, learning and experiences constituted and acquired according to the mode of doxic knowledge.

The more or less conscious dehistoricization determined by the active or passive ignorance of the historical context is associated with the actualization – always more or less anachronistic – unconsciously performed by any reading, unless a special effort is made, by the sole fact of relating texts to the current space of possibles and to the philosophical problematic inscribed in this space. This 'actualizing' reference is what allows a commentary to be produced, by anachronism, which is both dated and falsely achronic, and which, even when it believes itself faithful to the spirit and letter of thoughts it wants simply to reproduce, actually transforms them, because the space in which it makes them function has been transformed.

It is this common practice of philosophical commentary which is justified and codified by the hermeneutic theory proposed by Gadamer, an application of the Heideggerian philosophy of philosophy to the reading of philosophical texts. According to *Truth and Method*, an adequate comprehension of a philosophical text is an 'application' (one could just as well say an *execution*, as for a musical work or an order), in short, a putting into practice of a programme of action inscribed in the work itself. It is postulated that this programme is endowed with a transhistorical validity and that its implementation is none other than an *actualization*, which, grounded in the essential temporality of the existing, makes it present, historic in the very act of making it acting and efficient. And a radical contrast is made between understanding a philosophical (or legal) text *historically* and understanding something *philosophically* or legally, meaning putting into practice the programme immanent in the text, executing the score and the order which it contains. 'The text that is understood historically is forced to abandon its claim that it is uttering something true. We think we understand when we see the past from a historical standpoint, i.e. place ourselves in the historical situation and seek to reconstruct the historical horizon. In fact, however, we have given up the claim to find, in the past, any truth valid and intelligible for ourselves.'[35] In short, where historical understanding historicizes and relativizes, 'authentic' understanding apprehends a truth torn out of time in and through the detemporalizing act of comprehension.

Effectively it is messages such as philosophical or theological or legal texts, and especially scientific propositions (strangely absent from the 'tradition' as Gadamer defines it), which – even though they are the product of history – 'to speak like Kant, seem to pretend to universal validity', among other reasons because they receive a form of practical eternity from a historical actualization which is continually recommenced. And it is true that the historical apprehension that analyses the conditions of the *emergence* of these normative messages claiming to impose the conditions of their adequate actualization is, in practice, completely different from, if not excluded by, an actualization performed by someone who 'applies' a physical law or who performs a calculation of probabilities – and who could not care less about the historical processes leading to its 'emergence'. But is the same true of a philosophical theory, a juridical law or a theological dogma, and should independence from historical conditions not be, in that case, put to the test, at the risk of identifying truth with *authority* (as the use of the very word 'tradition' suggests)? Must we accept all the political implications of the overthrow of the Kantian hierarchy of the faculties proposed by Gadamer when he suggests 'redefining the hermeneutics of the human sciences in terms of legal or theological hermeneutics'?[36]

It is just such an overthrow that he performs, out of evident concern for conservatism (as much political as intellectual), when, on the basis of a 'rehabilitation of authority and tradition'[37] and a denunciation of the prejudice of refusing prejudice, he means to treat philosophical texts, in the manner of theological or legal texts, as bearers of a 'normative value'. For the philosopher-philologist whom Heidegger put on a pedestal, adequate interpretation is a revelation of truth which consists of saying the truth about a text of truth.

But how is it possible not to see that all the various stakes and interests which may be involved there may mean that the logical rationales which give philosophical or legal or theological constructions the appearance of a universal normativity may only be rationalizations designed to universalize particular interests? How can we not fear that the subjective experience of normativity is only an illusion born of the affinity between habitus and interests (itself grounded in an identity of conditions or, at the very least, a homology of positions) between those who have produced the original message and those who give themselves the mission of 'applying' it? And, at the risk of succumbing to *superstition*, should we not submit and subordinate any application of resources inherited from the past to a historical criticism of their causes and effects, of their conditions of production and conditions of reception?

Double historicization

At the risk of introducing surreptitiously, thanks to the effusion and illusion of immediate understanding, the most obscure layers of beliefs that are always concealed in the cultural arbitrary of a tradition, one must in effect operate a *double historicization*, both of tradition and of the 'application' of tradition. Only the analysis of inherited schemas of thought and of the illusory manifestations they produce can ensure a theoretical mastery (itself a condition of a true practical mastery) of the process of communication. This requires the reconstruction both of the space of possible positions (apprehended through the dispositions associated with a certain position) in relation to which the historical given (text, document, image, etc.) to be interpreted is elaborated, and of the space of possibles in relation to which one interprets it. To ignore this double determination is to be condemned to an anachronistic and ethnocentric 'understanding' which is likely to be fictive and which, in the best of cases, remains unaware of its own principles (the appearance of normative evidence and timeless necessity it procures may be the effect of the homology between the two historical situations, or the result of a labour of unwitting reinterpretation based on the excessive application of the interpreter's categories of thought). This alienated 'understanding', ignorant of its own social conditions of possibility, defines the traditional relationship to tradition, a relationship of immersion and adherence without any distance; the appearance of historical awareness, as a consciousness of the gap between the time of production and the time of 'application', marks the rupture with that 'understanding'. And the traditionalist relationship, which is to the traditional relationship what orthodoxy is to the *doxa*, and of which Heidegger and Gadamer made themselves the theoreticians, aims to mimic this naive relation by a fictive return to the prehistoric experience of tradition.

To understand understanding is to understand why such a tradition associated with a social universe rather distant in time and space – the aesthetic of Kant or, perhaps to a lesser degree, his theory of the 'conflict of faculties' – speaks to us spontaneously in the language of the universal: the 'fusion of horizons' may be purely illusory and rest on nothing but the confusion of horizons which defines anachronism and ethnocentrism, and it remains, in any case, to be explained. The subjective impression of necessity which we experience from a statement which appears to be an answer capable of convincing whomever asks the question at issue must be tested by reconstructing the social genesis of the question, thus its reason for being and its meaning, and the social conditions of its perpetuation as a question, and hence the social genesis of the questioning and the questioner. In short, it is not sufficient to sense transhistoricity in the naiveté of an immediate identification with the text (or the event) – a transhistoricity must be proved. To escape (however slightly) from history, understanding must know itself as historical and give itself the means to understand itself historically; and it must, in the same movement, understand historically the historical situation in which what it labours to understand was formed.

Though one may be convinced that being is history, with no afterlife, and that one must therefore demand of biological history (with the theory of evolution) and sociological history (with the analysis of the collective and individual sociogenesis of forms of thought) the truth of a reason which is historical through and through and yet irreducible to history, it must also be admitted that it is by historicization (and not by the decisive dehistoricization of a sort of theoretical *escapism*) that one may endeavour to extract reason most effectively from historicity. First there is historicization of the known object, of categories of thought and of perception (the 'quattrocento eye', for example) which have been invested in its production, and which differ from those we spontaneously apply to it. Then there is historicization of knowing subjects, of their reading and perception, categories of thought, perception and appreciation, which intervene nowhere more than in the case of the comprehension and (apparently) immediate appreciation which we may (believe we) have, beyond the bounds of historical distance, of a painting by Piero della Francesca or a text by Empedocles or Parmenides, not to mention an African mask.

Unless one is satisfied with the verbal and tautological solutions of the ontology of the *Verstehen* for which Heidegger supplied the model, then it is from the labour of historical science, a collective and cumulative labour, and not from some form of transcendental reflection, that one must expect the solution to the question of the adequate appropriation of products of historical labour – documents, monuments, instruments – which are linked to a greater or lesser extent to determinations of the historical situation. Certain of them, especially instruments of thought (methods, concepts, etc.), orient and organize our present perception of the historical past (thus contributing to the apparent abolition of *distance* with respect to the past).[38] In fact, only a labour of this sort can give us access to an appropriate knowledge of the social conditions of the work's production, offering by the same token the means of explaining it, *giving it reason*, that is, restoring to it its specific rationale and necessity, in short, making its existence felt as necessary (which does not amount, as Gadamer thinks, to resuscitating its historical environment). Only work like this, too, can give us knowledge of, and thereby make us conscious of, the whole collection of assumptions engaged in the way the work is perceived, starting with the principles, intentionally drawn on or not, of hermeneutic technique and the presuppositions concerning the function conferred on 'reading' or on the perception of the work (either as a purely cognitive function of understanding in order to understand or as a purely normative function of the edifying 'application'). It is only at the end of this double test that an accurate understanding may be gained of the lasting *effect* the work exercises, whether it be the 'eternal charm' of Greek art that Marx described (rather casually . . .), or even the *effect of truth*, which may be accompanied or not by a real revelation of truth.

Only social history can effectively supply the means to rediscover the historical truth in the objectivized or incorporeal traces of history which present themselves to awareness in the guise of a universal essence. Reminding ourselves of the historical determinations of reasoning may constitute the principle of a true freedom with respect to these determinations. Free thought must be won by a historical anamnesis capable of revealing everything in thought which is the forgotten product of historical work. Becoming resolutely aware of historical determinations, a true reconquest of the self (which is the exact opposite of the magical flight into 'essential thought') offers a possibility of really controlling these determinations. It is only by mobilizing all the resources of the social sciences that a historicist realization of the transcendental project can be carried to its conclusion. Like souls which, according to the myth of Er, have drunk the waters of Lethe after having chosen their lot of determinations, our thought has forgotten the ontogenesis and the phylogenesis of its own structures; since their roots are to be found in the structures of social fields established by history, they can be restored to our thought by knowledge of history and of the structure of these fields. The effort I have made here to try to advance this knowledge would be justified, to my mind, if I had succeeded in demonstrating (and convincingly) the possibility of a way of thinking about the social conditions of thought which gives thought an opportunity of freedom in relation to those conditions.

2

The Social Genesis of
the Eye

∽

I do not interpret, because I feel at home in the present image.

LUDWIG WITTGENSTEIN

The book by Michael Baxandall, *Painting and Experience in Fifteenth Century Italy*,[1] appeared to me at first as an exemplary realization of what a sociology of artistic perception ought to be, and also as an opportunity to get rid of the traces of intellectualism which might have remained in the exposition I had made some years earlier of the fundamental principles of a science of artistic perception.[2] Describing the comprehension of a work of art as an act of *decoding*, I suggested that the science of the work of art had the goal of reconstructing the artistic *code*, understood as a historically constituted system of classification (or of principles of division)[3] which is crystallized in an ensemble of *words* permitting us to name and perceive differences;[4] that is to say, more precisely, the goal of writing a history of these codes, instruments of perception which vary in time and space, notably as a function of transformations in the material and symbolic instruments of production.[5] I based myself on a systematic analysis of the variations in the preferences of the visitors to European museums according to different social variables (such as level of education, age, place of residence, profession, etc.) in order to demonstrate that the categories of perception (naively held as universal and eternal) applied by art lovers in our societies to a work of art are in fact historical categories, and these need to be reconstructed both in their phylogenesis, by a social history of the invention of the 'pure' artistic disposition and competence, and in their ontogenesis, by a differential analysis of the acquisition of this disposition and this competence. In other words, I reiterated that the disinterested game of sensibility and the pure exercise of the faculty of feeling spoken of by Kant assumed totally particular historical and social conditions of possibility, since aesthetic pleasure – this pure pleasure 'which ought to be able to be felt by any man' – is the privilege of those who have access to the economic and social conditions which allow the 'pure' and 'disinterested' disposition to be durably established.

That being said, even though my intention from the start was to try to make explicit the specific logic of sensory knowledge, analysing it more or less simultaneously with respect to very different empirical objects (such as the Kabyle ritual), I had a great deal of difficulty in breaking with the intellectualist conception which – even in the iconological tradition founded by Panofsky, and especially in the semiological tradition, then at its peak – tended to conceive the perception of the work of art as an act of decoding, or, as one liked to say, a 'reading' (through a typical illusion of the *lector* spontaneously inclined to what Austin called 'the scholastic point of view'). This perspective is the foundation of the 'philologism' which, according to Bakhtin, leads to treating language as a dead letter destined to be *decoded* (and not to be spoken or understood practically); more generally, it is the foundation of the hermeneutism which leads to conceiving any act of comprehension according to the model of *translation* and turns the perception of a cultural work, whatever it may be, into an intellectual act of decoding which presupposes the elucidation and the conscious application of rules of production and interpretation.

Here is, in fact, the paradox of the historical comprehension of a work or a practice of the past – that of Piero della Francesca for example – or of a practice or a work emanating from a foreign tradition – Kabyle ritual: to make up for the absence of the (true) understanding immediately available to an indigenous contemporary, one must perform the task of *reconstructing* the code found invested there; but without meanwhile forgetting that the singularity of the original comprehension is that it in no sense presupposes any such intellectual effort of construction and translation; and that the contemporary native, in contrast to the interpreter, invests in his comprehension practical schemas which never crop up as such in consciousness (in the manner, for example, of grammatical rules). In short, the analyst's theory of the perception of a work of art must involve a theory of the initial perception as a practice, one which has no theory or concept itself and for which he has to find a substitute through the work of trying to construct a framework of interpretation, a model capable of explaining practices and works. This certainly does not mean that he forces himself to *mimic* or reproduce in practice (according to the logic, dear to Michelet and many others, of 'resurrecting the past') the practical experience of comprehension – even if an explicit mastery of the schemas which are in practice involved in the production, and the comprehension, may lead to the possibility of feeling the practical experience of the native contemporary – but *in a somewhat vicarious mode*.

Michael Baxandall's analysis therefore encouraged me to carry to its conclusion – despite all the social obstacles in the path of such a transgression of the social hierarchy of practices and objects – the transfer to the domain of artistic perception of everything which my analyses of the ritual acts of Kabyle peasants or of the evaluative operations of professors and critics had taught me about the specific logic of practical sense, of which aesthetic sense is a particular case. The science of the mode of aesthetic knowledge finds its foundation in a theory of practice *as* practice, meaning as an activity founded on cognitive operations which mobilize a mode of knowing which is not that of theory and concept, without nevertheless being (as those who feel its specificity would often have it) a sort of ineffable participation in a known object.

In the same way that today the most culturally deprived people seem to lean towards a taste described as 'realist' because, unlike lovers of art, they do not possess in a *practical state* the *specific categories* stemming from the autonomization of the field of production (which permit differences in manner and style to be perceived in an immediate manner)[6] and so can apply to works of art only the practical schemas they use in daily existence,[7] so in the same way the contemporaries of Piero della Francesca engaged in their perception of his paintings schemas which stemmed from their daily experience of the sermon, the dance and the market. The immediate comprehension thus offered to them undoubtedly has little in common with that procured for the cultivated amateur of our time by that 'Kantian' eye which was invented in and through the effort of painters to assert their autonomy, notably by asserting their mastery of what they gained as their own in the division of labour of symbolic production – namely manner, form and style.

The Quattrocento eye

The relationship of false familiarity that we entertain with the techniques of expression and the expressive contents of fifteenth-century painting, and in particular with the Christian symbolism whose nominal remoteness masks the deep and real variations with the passing of time, prevents us from perceiving the size of the gap between schemas of perception and appreciation which we now apply to these works and those they objectively demand and which their immediate recipients applied to them.[8] There is no doubt that the comprehension we may have of these works – which are at once too close to disconcert us and to demand a learned decoding, and too far away to offer themselves in an immediate manner to the prereflexive and almost corporeal grasp of the harmonized habitus – may be the source, illusory as it might be, of a very real pleasure. It remains true that only a real labour of historical ethnology may permit us to correct errors of accommodation which are more likely to pass unnoticed here than in the case of the so-called primitive arts – especially African art – where the discordance between the ethnological analysis and the aesthetic discourse cannot escape the attention of even the most hardened aesthetes. In effect there are few cases where scientific construction of the object requires as obviously as here that rare form of intellectual intrepidness which is necessary to break with received ideas and to defy propriety, and to think about works as sacralized as those of Piero della Francesca or Botticelli in their historical truthfulness as paintings for 'shopkeepers' (the nineteenth century, which invented our aesthetic, said out loud what is unthinkable today).

To break with the illusory and partial comprehension that is founded on denial of historicity, the historian must reconstruct the 'moral and spiritual eye' of the Quattrocento mind, meaning in the first place, the social conditions of this *institution* – without which there is no demand, hence no market for painting – called the *interest* in painting and, more precisely, the interest in such and such a genre, manner or subject. 'The pleasure of possession, an active piety, civic consciousness of one or another kind, self-commemoration and perhaps self-advertisement, the rich man's necessary virtue and pleasure of reparation, a taste for pictures: in fact, the client need not analyse his own motives much because he generally worked through institutional forms – the altarpiece, the frescoed family chapel, the Madonna in the bedroom, the cultured wall-furniture in the study – which implicitly rationalized his motives for him, usually in quite flattering ways, and also went far toward briefing the painter on what was needed.'[9]

The brutality, or innocence, with which the requirements of clients (especially their concern to get their money's worth) are asserted in legal contracts constitutes in itself a first important piece of information, both about the attitude of buyers of the fifteenth century with respect to the works and, in contrast, about the 'pure' gaze – purified of any reference to economic value – which today's cultivated spectator, the product of a more autonomous field of production, feels just as bound to bring to bear on 'pure' works of the present as on 'impure' works of the past. As long as the relationship between the patron and the painter can be taken as a simple commercial relationship in which the patron decides what the artist should paint, and over what time period, and with what colours, the properly aesthetic value of the works cannot be really considered as such, meaning independently of their economic value; sometimes still prosaically measured by the painted surface area or the time spent at it, the latter is more and more often determined by the cost of materials utilized and the technical virtuosity of the painter,[10] which is expected to be manifestly evident in the work itself.[11] If, as Baxandall shows, interest in technique continually increases at the expense of attention to materials, it is undoubtedly because gold becomes rare and because the concern of the *nouveaux riches* to distinguish themselves leads to a rejection of the ostentatious display of wealth, in painting as well as in clothing, while the humanist current comes to reinforce Christian asceticism. It is also because, to the extent that the field of artistic production gains autonomy, painters are more and more able to display and attach value to the technique, the manner, the *manifattura*, hence the *form* – in short, everything which (unlike the subject, which is most often imposed) belongs to painters alone.

But an analysis of the 'more or less conscious responses of painters to market conditions', and the advantage they were able to draw in asserting the autonomy of their métier from the growing propensity of their clients to privilege the technical aspect of the work and the visible manifestations of the 'master's touch', refers us back to an analysis of the visual capacities of those clients, and of the situation in which simple lay people could acquire the practical skills which guaranteed them immediate access to pictorial works and allowed them to appreciate the technical virtuosity of their authors.

Reconstructing a 'vision of the world': this project, seemingly routine, reveals itself as perfectly unprecedented, if not impossible, the moment one tries to rely on the old notion of *Weltanschauung*, undoubtedly one of the most overused in scientific tradition. This is first of all because, as Michael Baxandall himself notes, 'a society's visual practices are, in the nature of things, not all or even mostly represented in verbal records';[12] and then because a seemingly mandatory use of such 'testimony of visual activity' as paintings or sketches would merely prejudge the very problem one is asking them to help resolve. In fact, it is on this circular argument that Baxandall the historian relies in postulating that social factors 'lead to the development of distinctive visual skills and habits; and these visual skills and habits become identifiable elements in the painter's style.'[13] The knowledge of dispositions, inseparably cognitive and evaluative, with which he equips himself by drawing on written sources which touch on the uses of arithmetic, on religious practices and representations, or on dance techniques of fifteenth-century Italy, allows him to understand the paintings in their historical logic and, therefore, to treat them as documents of a historical vision of the world, and to find in the visible properties of pictorial representation some indications concerning the schemas of perception and appreciation which painter and spectators engaged in their vision of the world and in their vision of the pictorial representation of the world.

'A moral and spiritual eye' fashioned by 'religion, education, business',[14] the 'Quattrocento eye' is nothing other than the system of schemas of perception and appreciation, of judgement and of pleasure, which were acquired through the practices of daily life (school, church, marketplace) by listening to lectures, speeches or sermons, measuring piles of wheat or lengths of čloth, or by resolving calculations of compound interest or maritime insurance, and which were put to work in ordinary existence and also in the production and perception of works of art. Against the intellectualist error to which an analyst easily falls prey, Baxandall aims to restitute a 'social experience' of the world, understood as practical experience acquired by frequenting a particular social universe, meaning, in the present case, the habitus of a merchant or, as he himself puts it in an intentionally schematic summary of his study, that of a 'church-going businessman, with a taste for dancing'.[15]

These practical schemas, acquired in the practice of commerce and invested in the trade in works of art, are not those logical categories which philosophy loves to lend to a painting. Even in the case of a professional judge of taste, the critic Cristoforo Landino, the terms used to characterize paintings, and which may be understood as the expression of his 'reaction to the paintings, clearly, but also towards the latent sources of his standards',[16] are organized according to a structure, but one which does not have the formal rigour of a properly logical construction: 'Pure, easy, gracious, ornate, varied, prompt, blithe, devout, relief, perspective, colouring and composition, design and foreshortening, imitator of Nature, lover of the difficulties – Landino offers a basic conceptual equipment for addressing Quattrocento pictorial quality. His terms have a structure:

one is opposed to, or is allied with, or is subsumed by, or overlaps another. It would not be difficult to draw a diagram in which these relationships were registered, but the diagram would imply a systematic rigidity which the terms in practice do not and should not have.'[17]

The different dimensions that analysis inevitably isolates for the needs of understanding and explanation are intimately linked inside the *unity of a habitus*, and the religious dispositions of a man who has attended church and heard sermons are completely merged with the mercantile dispositions of a businessman accustomed to the immediate calculation of quantities and prices, as the analysis of the criteria of evaluation of colours shows: 'After gold and silver, ultramarine was the most expensive and difficult colour the painter used. There were cheap and dear grades and there were even cheaper substitutes, generally referred to as German blue. [...] To avoid being let down about blues, clients specified ultramarine; more prudent clients stipulated a particular grade – ultramarine at one or two or four florins an ounce. The painters and their public were alert to all this and the exotic and dangerous character of ultramarine was a means of accent that we, for whom a dark blue is probably no more striking than scarlet or vermilion, are liable to miss. We can follow well enough when it is used simply to pick out the principal figure of Christ or Mary in a biblical scene, but the interesting uses are more subtle than this. In Sassetta's panel of *St Francis Renouncing his Heritage* at the National Gallery, the gown St Francis discards is an ultramarine gown. In Masaccio's expensively pigmented *Crucifixion*, the vital narrative gesture of St John's right arm is an ultramarine gesture.'[18]

The foundation of the charismatic illusion

To love a painting, in the case of the Quattrocento merchant, is to *find a dividend there*, to recover one's outlay, getting something for one's money, in the form of the 'richest' colours, the most obviously costly, and the most clearly exhibited pictorial technique; but it is also – and this might be a definition of the premodern form of aesthetic pleasure – to find there that supplementary satisfaction which consists in finding oneself in it entirely, recognizing oneself, feeling well, feeling at home, finding in the painting one's world and one's relationship with the world. The *well-being* procured by artistic contemplation may result from what the work of art gives an opportunity to achieve, in a form intensified by gratuitousness – acts of successful comprehension which make for happiness, like the experience of an immediate accord with the world, preconscious and prereflexive, like a miraculous encounter between practical sense and objectified meanings. This is to say that the charismatic ideology which describes the love of art in the language of being love-struck is a 'well-founded illusion': it describes very well the relation of mutual solicitation between aesthetic meaning and artistic significations – of which the lexicon of love, if not sex, is an approximate (and doubtless the least inadequate) expression; it passes over in silence the social conditions of the possibility of this experience.

The habitus urges, interrogates, makes the object speak, while for its part, the object seems to incite, call upon, provoke the habitus; of course, as Baxandall remarks, skills, memories or images that manage to blend with the properties directly perceived can only come forth because, for a predisposed habitus, they seem magically evoked by these properties (the magical efficacy which poetry often attributes to itself finds its principle in that sort of almost physical harmony which gives words, and their connotations, the power to call up experiences buried in the folds of the body). In short, if (as aesthetes never stop proclaiming) the artistic experience is a matter of sense and feeling, and not of decoding and reasoning, it is because the dialectic between the constituting act and the constitutive object, mutually soliciting each other, is effected in the essentially obscure relationship between the habitus and the world.

The contract for *The Adoration of the Magi* between Ghirlandaio and the prior of the Hospital of the Innocents in Florence shows that a painting in which economic sense is satisfied is also one which gratifies religious sensibility, by proportioning the economic value of colours to the religious value of their iconographic props, by giving the gold to Christ and to the Virgin and by using ultramarine to *give worth* to a gesture by Saint John. But we know from Jacques Le Goff's research that the calculating mind of the merchant also found something to apply itself to in the properly religious sphere, with the appearance of Purgatory, which introduces accounting into the spiritual order, having coincided with the birth of the bank.[19] One has only to add the moral (and political) satisfactions obtained by the perception of a harmonic and harmonious representation, equilibrated and reassuring, of the visible world, and quite simply, the pleasure of freely exercising a hermeneutic expertise, and one can see that in the case of the Quattrocento man the experience of beauty in what it can have of the miraculous is born of the relation of reciprocal intromission established between the socialized body and a social object which seems made to satisfy all socially instituted senses, sense of sight and sense of touch, but also economic sense and religious sense.

A historical analysis which repudiates the verbal generalities of the analysis of essence in order to immerse itself in the historical particularity of a place and a time represents an obligatory passage – an inevitable moment (against empty theoreticism) and one destined to be surpassed (against blind hyper-empiricism) – for any scientific research into *invariants*. Interpreted in this way, the knowledge of the conditions and historical conditionings of the pleasures of the 'Quattrocento eye' may lead to what undoubtedly constitutes the invariant and transhistorical principle of properly artistic satisfaction, that imaginary achievement of a universally happy encounter between a *historical* habitus and a *historical* world which frequents it, and which it inhabits.

3

A Theory of Reading
in Practice

∼◦∼

Be very careful in this conversation of Jacques and his master
if you don't want to take the true for the false, and the false
for the true. There now! You've been warned and I wash my
hands of the affair.

DENIS DIDEROT

I see only too well in novels that it is me who pays, and gives
force of credence and of 'life' to words, most of which cost
their author *nothing* – (I am speaking of the best novels; 75
per cent of sentences are changeable *ad libitum* as are,
moreover, perceptions in 'life' – *current perceptions*.)

PAUL VALÉRY

'When Miss Emily Grierson died, our whole town went to her
funeral: the men through a sort of respectful affection for a fallen
monument, the women mostly out of curiosity to see the inside of
her house, which no one save an old manservant – a combined
gardener and cook – had seen in at least ten years ...'¹ William
Faulkner's story begins like any story or novel, in conformity with
the rules of the genre. It presents a protagonist, Miss Emily Grierson,
who is discreetly designated as an eminent personage; walk-on parts,
divided by gender and characterized according to stereotype (the
conformity of the men, the curiosity of the women); a narrator who
accepts the customary conventions of the genre and who is discreetly
identified with the group ('*we* found', '*we* said', '*our* town'); and also

a whole set of cues, especially temporal ones ('in at least ten years'), which introduce an air of the unexpected.

To present Emily, a glorious vestige of a vanished past ('fallen monument'), Faulkner piles up details that are apparently innocuous but designed to trigger, like so many springs, the presuppositions of common sense, the very ones that ordinary novelists usually mobilize, almost without realizing it, to produce an effect of the real. He draws, for example, on the idea of nobility – and everything it implies, such as the famous 'noblesse oblige', explicitly invoked in the text – to evoke the image of a venerable and very dignified old lady, the last survivor of a ruined great family and symbol of past traditions, and to arouse all the anticipations that are contained in such a social essence.

The idea of nobility, a favourable prejudice which is socially instituted (and hence endowed with all the force of the social), functions as a principle of the construction of social reality, a principle tacitly accepted as much by the narrator and his characters as by the reader; and it simultaneously functions as a source of anticipations that are ordinarily grounded in facts, since nobility has the status of an essence which precedes and produces existence, opening or excluding by definition a range of possibles. The power of presupposition is so strong, and the hypotheses of the practical induction of the habitus so robust, that they resist what is self-evident: '"I want arsenic." The druggist looked down at her. She looked back at him, erect, her face like a strained flag. "Why, of course," the druggist said. "If that's what you want."' The meaning of the words and actions is predetermined by the social image of the person who produces them and, in the case of a person 'above all suspicion', the very idea of murder is excluded.

The anticipations of common sense are stronger than the evidence of the facts; the official truth ('Like when she bought the rat poison, the arsenic'; 'there was written on the box, under the skull and bones, "For Rats"') is more credible than an ostentatious admission, crazed or cynical ('"I want some poison,' she said to the druggist'). And the same goes for all the suspicious signs the author proffers – the 'smell', Emily's madness in saying that 'her father was not dead', etc. – which are systematically ignored, or repressed, by Emily's fellow citizens as well as by the reader ('We did not say she was crazy then. We believed she had to do that. We remembered all the young men her father had driven away, and we knew that with nothing left, she would have to cling to that which had robbed her, as people will'). And just as it is only after Emily's death, that is to say forty years 'after the event', that the inhabitants of Jefferson discover that Emily has poisoned her lover and kept his body in the house for all those years, so it is only on the last page of the story that readers discover their blunder.

A reflecting story

However, all this would be no more than the well-crafted plot of a realist narrative if it did not appear retrospectively that Faulkner, by a skilful manipulation of chronology, has constructed his tale as a trap enlisting the assumptions of ordinary existence and the conventions of the novelistic genre to encourage an expectation throughout the story of a *plausible meaning* which will find itself brutally belied at the end. Faulkner in effect stages a double abuse of confidence. First there is the deception using Emily when she plays on the more or less imaginary representation of the aristocracy ('*We* had often thought of them as a tableau'), and the consensus on the meaning of the world that arises from the tacit agreement of the habitus, in order to deceive the druggist and all her fellow citizens, especially the men, who are more disposed than the women, with their gossip, to be favourably prejudiced towards the official, public truth. Then there is the author's deception of readers by using everything they tacitly concede in the 'reading contract' to direct their attention towards misleading clues and false trails and to make them overlook the clues, particularly as regards chronology, which he unnoticeably plants in the course of the tale, like an honest author of crime novels, and which only a methodical reading like that of Menakhem Perry[2] can pick up and organize.[3]

In fact, Faulkner covertly breaks this 'reading contract' (if indeed one is justified in speaking of a 'contract' to describe the naive trust that readers place in their reading and the abandoned way they throw themselves into it, along with all their common-sense assumptions). To achieve this breach, he uses procedures which are very similar to those of a detective novel, like the scattering of clues designed to pass unnoticed at first. But far from using these ordinary procedures to allow the reader retrospectively to retrace an apparently extraordinary dénouement back into the logic of the ordinary world, he uses them to encourage the most ordinary expectations all the better to disappoint them and expose them by an ending which is really extraordinary – so unexpected, in any case, that it invites a rereading or, at the very least, a sort of mental recapitulation which obliges the reader to discover, if only in a confused way, the mystification of which he has been the victim, and the accomplice. The reader that 'A rose for Emily' tacitly asks for is really this extra-ordinary reader, the 'arch-reader', as some used to say (without ever questioning the social conditions of possibility of this curious figure), or, better still, the *meta-reader* who will know how to read not only the narrative, quite simply, but the ordinary reading of the narrative, the presuppositions engaged by readers in both their ordinary experience of time and action, and in their experience of reading a 'realist' or mimetic fiction which purports to express the reality of the ordinary world and the ordinary experience of that world.

'A rose for Emily' is a reflexive story, a reflecting story which encloses in its very structure the program (in the computer sense) for a reflection on the novel and on naive reading. In the fashion of an experimental text or device, it calls for repeated reading, but also the divided reading which is needed to combine the impressions of the first naive reading, and the revelations it arouses, with the second reading, the retroactive illumination that the knowledge of the ending (acquired at the end of the first reading) casts on to the text, and especially on to the presuppositions of a naively 'novelistic' reading. Thus, caught in this sort of trap – a veritable provocation to a truly paradoxical *allodoxia* since it results from the natural application of the presuppositions of the *doxa* – the reader is forced to acknowledge openly everything he customarily and unwittingly grants to authors – who are just as unaware of what they are demanding of the reader.

Bringing into play the whole range of presuppositions tacitly engaged in ordinary experience of the world and in ordinary experience of reading, Faulkner brings to the fore a whole set of traits which misdirect the attention of a reader to another meaning, while concealing the true structure, especially in its temporal dimension. By jumbling up the chronological order, he pushes the reader into anticipations which will eventually be deceived. Meanwhile he gives the reader – in a knowingly orchestrated disorder, generally out of phase – temporal markers which might enable the reader to rescue the narrative from pure discontinuity, and so to grasp, through the real order of events, meanings and links of causality and intention which would otherwise only appear retrospectively, based on the final revelation.

To produce this effect, he first plays on the assumptions and procedures of novelistic writing and reading. Like a novelist who pretends to believe what he relates and who asks the reader to read his narrative while feigning to forget that it is a fiction, Faulkner accredits his apparent tale by a constant use of 'we' or of impersonal, unanimous and anonymous expressions like 'the ladies said . . .'; he thus presents himself as a spokesperson for a group whose members grant each other what each of them unknowingly takes for granted, the non-thetic theses which constitute the common vision of the world. Thus, for example, although he duly mentions Emily's bizarre behaviour, he relies on the usual picture of nobility to suggest that it can be imputed not to madness, but to a stance of aristocratic gandeur and pride. By asking the reader to read his narrative according to the accepted convention, as a fictitious true story, Faulkner authorizes and encourages that reader to bring assumptions into the reading that are usually engaged in life and everyday vision, such as the prejudice which means that more credit will be given to the view which is masculine, official and respectful of conventions and proprieties, and less to the view of women, who are sociologically inclined to question official (meaning masculine) certainties, and who will be proved right by the final discovery.[4]

But he also brings to the very writing of the tale his practical mastery of the presuppositions of ordinary writing and reading (such as the fact that one reads a book by going from the front to the back) which are meant to pass unnoticed, as well as his practical knowledge of the gap between the naive reading – submissive, hurried and distracted – which does not bother to reconstruct the overall structure of times and places, and the 'scholastic' reading of the professional reader, which might proceed by doubling back and, by re-establishing the true chronology of events, blow apart the whole construction insidiously suggested to the naive reader. The visible proof of this dual mastery is furnished by all the phrases like 'she looked' and 'her eyes looked' which recall the narrator's point of view and which will restrospectively appear as underlying the ignorance of Emily's fellow citizens as to the truth of the character and her actions. This reflexive writing therefore calls for a reflexive reading which, in contrast to the rereading of a crime mystery whose solution is now known, makes for a discovery not only of a set of misleading clues but of a *self-deception* into which the trusting reader has been led, as well as of the devices and effects, especially those linked to the time structure of the story and its reading, through which the novelist has skilfully awakened the social assumptions underlying the naive experience of the world and time.

Time of reading and reading of time

Looking at this short story alone, it is not certain that one could share Sartre's view of 'Faulkner's temporality' as he described it in a celebrated article.[5] Undoubtedly because his work as a novelist led (or forced) him to pay close attention to the relationship between the time of practice and narrative time, Faulkner adopted the tactic of making a visible break with the traditional conception of the novel and with a naively chronological representation of the experience of time: 'When you read *The Sound and the Fury*,' writes Sartre, 'you are first struck by the oddities of the technique. Why has Faulkner broken up the time of his story and jumbled up the pieces? Why is the first window that opens onto this narrative world the mind of an idiot? The reader is tempted to look for landmarks and to reconstruct the chronology for himself.' But perhaps that is precisely what the author wants to make readers do: take on the effort of identification and reconstruction that is indispensable for 'finding their way' and in doing so discover how much they lose when they find their way too easily, as in novels organized according to current conventions (especially as regards the temporal structure of the narrative), that is, respecting the truth of the ordinary experience of time, and the experience of the ordinary reading of the telling of that experience.

Similar to works of kinetic art which demand the active collaboration of the spectator in order to take on an existence, Faulkner's novels are also veritable machines for exploring time which, far from offering a ready-made theory of temporality which only needs to be made explicit, instead oblige readers to *make* this theory for *themselves*; they make it from material supplied by the narrative about the temporal experience of characters and, more importantly, from reflections on their own temporal experiences as acting agents and as readers, reflections which are aroused by the questioning of their *reading routines*. Indeed, like the experimental interruptions of doxic 'sleep' sometimes induced by ethnomethodologists – when, for example, they suggest to a student whose mother asks him to fetch milk from the kitchen that he respond 'But where's the kitchen?' – Faulkner's narratives denounce the tacit agreements on which common sense is based – for example, the agreement that unites the traditional novelist with his or her reader. They call into question the shared *doxa* which is the basis of doxic experience of the world and of the novelistic representation of that world.

In consciously taking on the task, quite extraordinary in its apparent mundaneness, of *recounting a story*, meaning placing himself in the distanced and neutralized relation to practice and its specific logic that is implied by the social act of narration, Faulkner was led to inscribe into the very structure of his stories a very profound inquiry into the experience we have of temporality, both in our lives and in the narration of our lives or those of other people. This inquiry, and the beginnings of an answer he brings to it through a writer's particular methods, are an invitation to *produce* a theory of temporal experience which is not, strictly speaking, that of Faulkner, nor the one Sartre attributes to Faulkner.

This theory cannot be constructed without repudiating and overcoming the spontaneous philosophy of time shown most typically in the novelistic representation, its biographical variant especially. This spontaneous philosophy of action, and of the narration of action, on which the 'pre-Faulknerian' novelist (and also, often enough, the historian) depends in the writing of a story – and which finds its natural extension in the philosophy of temporal consciousness, Husserl's or Sartre's – prevents access to genuine knowledge of the structure of practice. The production of time that occurs in and through practice has nothing to do with an experience (in the sense of *Erlebnis*) of time, even if it presupposes an experience (in the sense of *Erfahrung*) or, as Searle says,[6] a set of *background assumptions* (Faulkner gives us many examples of these, whether those underlying the hypotheses of Emily's fellow citizens as to the meaning of her relationship with Homer Barron and their prediction of the future of this liaison, or those underlying their unanimous, peremptory judgements: 'So, the next day, we *all* said, "She is going to kill herself", and *we* said that it would be the best thing. When she had first begun to be seen with Homer Barron, *we* had said, "She will marry him." Then *we* said . . .').

Agents temporalize themselves in the very act by which they transcend the immediate present towards the future implicated in the past of which their habitus is the product; they produce time in the practical anticipation of a still-to-come [*à-venir*] which is at the same time the practical actualization of the past. Thus one can reject the metaphysical representation of time as a reality in itself, exterior and anterior to practice, without accepting a philosophy of consciousness which, with Husserl, is associated with the (central) idea of *temporalization*. Temporalization is neither the constitutive activity of a transcendental consciousness torn out of the world, as Husserl would have it, nor even that of a *Dasein* engaged in the world, as with Heidegger, but that of a habitus orchestrated with other habituses (in opposition to Husserl's idea of transcendental intersubjectivity). This practical relation to the world and to time which is common to a set of agents, who bring the same assumptions into the construction of the meaning of the world in which they are immersed, is the basis of the experience of that world as a commonsense world. The habitus, as a practical sense, which is the product of the incorporation of structures of the social world – and, in particular, its immanent tendencies and its temporal rhythms – engenders assumptions and anticipations which, ordinarily being confirmed by the course of events, ground a relation of immediate familiarity or ontological complicity with the familiar world, a complicity totally irreducible to the relation between a subject and an object.

In short, the habitus is the basis of the social structuration of temporal existence, of all the anticipations and the presuppositions through which we practically construct the sense of the world – its signification, but also, inseparably, its orientation towards the still-to-come. This is what Faulkner obliges us to discover by methodically disconcerting the sense of the social game that we apply as much in our experience of the world as in the naive reading of the naive telling of that experience. This sense of the game is also a sense of the history of the game, that is, of the still-to-come which it reads directly into the present state of the game and which it helps to make happen by orienting itself in relation to it, without having to place it explicitly in a conscious project, and hence to constitute it as a contingent *future*.

Illusion and the *Illusio*

To be true consists of giving the complete illusion of truth, following the ordinary logic of facts, and not transcribing them in servile fashion and pell-mell order. I conclude from this that the Realists of talent ought to call themselves illusionists instead [. . .] Each of us simply makes *an illusion of the world*, a poetic, sentimental, joyous, melancholic, dirty, or lugubrious illusion according to our natures. And the writer has no other mission than to reproduce faithfully this illusion, with all the artistic processes which he has learned and has at his command.

GUY DE MAUPASSANT

It has to be acknowledged, therefore, that it is historical analysis which allows us to understand the conditions of the 'understanding', the symbolic appropriation, real or fictive, of a symbolic object which may be accompanied by that particular form of enjoyment which we call aesthetic. But this is not to elevate knowledge of the historical truth to the condition and the measure of aesthetic pleasure (which would amount to condemning those literary or artistic pleasures that, as in the legend of Amphitryon, are the product of a misunderstanding).

The 'impious dismantling of the fiction' – whether it gives itself away as feigned and fictive, as literary fiction does (at least when it achieves an awareness of itself), or whether as Searle observes, it takes seriously what it says and agrees to be accountable for it (and hence, in some cases, agrees to be convinced of an error, as in science fiction) – leads to discovering, along with Mallarmé, that the *foundation of belief* (and of the delectation which, in the case of literary fiction, it procures) resides in the *illusio*, the adherence to the game as a game, the acceptance of the fundamental premise that the game, literary or scientific, is worth being played, being taken seriously. The literary *illusio*, that originating adherence to the literary game which grounds the belief in the *importance* or *interest* of literary fictions, is the precondition – almost always unperceived – of the aesthetic pleasure which is always, in part, the pleasure of playing the game, of participating in the fiction, of being in total accord with the premises of the game. It is also the precondition of the literary *illusion* and of the belief effect (rather than the 'reality effect') which the text can produce.

To understand this belief effect itself, distinguishing it from the one produced by the scientific text, one must observe, following Faulkner's analysis in action, that it rests on the accord between the presuppositions (or, more precisely, the schemas of construction) that the narrator and the reader (or, in the case analysed by Baxandall, the painter and the spectator) engage in the production and reception of the work. Because they are held in common, they serve to construct the world of common sense; the almost universal agreement on these structures, especially spatial and temporal ones, is the foundation of the fundamental *illusio*, the belief in the reality of the world.

Flaubert extends, by making them more profound, both Mallarmé's questioning of the foundations of a belief one could call scholastic (since it is linked to the existence of fields which all presuppose the *skholè*), and Faulkner's questioning of the foundations of a belief in what the text expresses. Flaubert does so in fictions which make use of the belief effect in order to question the foundations of the belief effect. He is not content just to dramatize characters who, like Frédéric or Madame Arnoux, live in a literary way a literary adventure, the myth of a grand impossible passion, and who push the belief in literature, meaning in fiction, into unreality, to the point of really living the most tired, hackneyed tropes of fiction, like the myth of purity in love ('it seems to me you are there when I read passages about love in books'). He links this propensity to take the illusions of art and love seriously and to confront the real only through a literary anticipation (doomed to disillusion) to a sort of pathology of the primordial belief in the reality of social games, to an incapacity to enter into the *illusio* as an illusion of reality collectively shared and approved. Flaubert explicitly connects this irrepressible inclination to escape into fiction – which he shares with Frédéric, and which he actively achieves by writing a work in which he objectivizes it – to a sort of powerlessness to take seriously the most real of society's games, the world of common sense, of the doxic experience of the common world procured by successful socialization, capable of ensuring the incorporation of shared structures, which grounds what Durkheim calls 'logical conformism' and, thereby, the consensus on the world's sense.

In short, in coming back tirelessly, from *Madame Bovary* to *Bouvard and Pécuchet* via *Sentimental Education*, to characters who live life as a novel because they take fiction too seriously, for lack of being able to take the real seriously, and who commit a 'category error' totally similar to that of the realist novelist and his reader, Flaubert reminds us that the propensity to grant the status of reality to fictions (to the point of wanting the reality of existence to conform to fiction, as do Don Quixote, Emma or Frédéric) perhaps finds its foundation in a sort of detachment, an indifference, a passive variant of the stoical ataraxia, which leads to seeing reality as illusion and to perceiving the *illusio* in its truthfulness as a 'well-founded illusion', to take up once more the expression Durkheim uses about religion.

To take the literary illusion seriously is in fact to play one *illusio* off against another: the *illusio* reserved for the *happy few*, the literary *illusio*, the belief of learned people [*clercs*], a privilege of those who live literature and who can, by writing, live life as a literary adventure, is played off against the most common and most universally shared *illusio*, the *illusio* of common sense. Sancho is to Don Quixote what the Thracian servant is to Thales, a permanent reminder of the reality of the world of common sense, of the common world, almost universally shared, unlike special worlds which are microcosms founded, like the universe of literature or of science, on a rupture with common sense and with the doxic adherence to the ordinary world.

But Flaubert achieves this analytic work on the forms of the illusion and the forms of the *illusio*, and on their relations, by means of a properly literary *mode of expression*, thus giving us an opportunity to grasp the difference between literary expression and scientific expression. If he poses the problem of reality's fiction and of reality *as* fiction, it is within a fiction which, undoubtedly more than any other, is able to produce the illusion of reality. This is because, like Faulkner, he mobilizes the most profound structures of the social world, these being at the same time the mental structures which readers engage in their reading and which, as the product of the incorporation of structures of the real world, are granted to this fictional world and are able to ground the most complete belief in the fiction which describes them, just as they ground the belief in the ordinary experience of the world. But these structures are not marked out as such, as in scientific analysis: they inhabit a story, where they are realized and dissimulated at the same time. Literary expression, like scientific expression, relies on conventional codes, socially grounded presuppositions, historically constituted classificatory schemas, such as the opposition between art and money which organizes the whole composition of *Sentimental Education* and the reading of that work. But it delivers these structures and the questions it asks about them, such as those I have just examined, only in concrete stories, singular exemplifications which (to speak like Nelson Goodman) are like samples of the real world. These representative and representational samples, exemplifying very concretely, like swatches of cloth, the reality described, thereby present themselves with all the appearances of the commonsense world, which is also inhabited by structures, but ones dissimulated in the guise of contingent adventures, anecdotal accidents, particular events. This suggestive, allusive, elliptical form is what makes the literary text, like what is real, deliver up its structure, but by veiling it and by snatching it from our gaze. In contrast, science tries to speak of things as they are, without euphemisms, and asks to be taken seriously, even when it analyses the foundations of this quite singular form of the *illusio* which is the scientific *illusio*.

For a Corporatism of the Universal

~∞~

Once the Sophists spoke to a small number of men; today, the periodical press allows them to lead a whole nation astray.

HONORÉ DE BALZAC

Unlike the preceding chapters, this one – intentionally – takes a normative position based on the conviction that it is possible to use a knowledge of the logic of the functioning of the fields of cultural production to draw up a realistic programme for the collective action of intellectuals. Such a programme has a particular urgency in these times of restoration: as a result of a whole set of convergent factors, there is a threat to the most precious collective achievements of intellectuals, starting with the critical dispositions which were simultaneously the product and the guarantee of their autonomy. It is fashionable to proclaim everywhere, amid a great fanfare, the death of intellectuals, that is, the end of one of the last critical countervailing powers capable of opposing the forces of economic and political order. And the prophets of evil are, of course, recruited from among the people who have most to gain from this disappearance: pen-pushers, driven by their 'impatience to see themselves printed, performed, known, vaunted', as Flaubert said, to make every sort of compromise with the powers of the day (journalistic, economic or political), would like to be rid of the people who obstinately defend or incarnate the virtues and values which are endangered, but which are still threatening their nothingness. It is significant that one of the most representative of these 'journalist philosophers', as Wittgenstein called them, expressly attacked Baudelaire, and went on to make a television history of intellectuals in which (like that character of Walter de la Mare's who only saw the lower part of the world – plinths, feet, shoes) he singled out from this immense adventure only the parts he could grasp – cowardice, treachery, baseness, small-mindedness.

Those I am addressing here are not all those who conceive of culture as a patrimony, a dead culture to be made into an obligatory cult of ritual piety, or as an instrument of domination and distinction, cultural bastion and Bastille, to be erected against the Barbarians within and without (who these days often seem to the new defenders of the West to be one and the same), but rather those who conceive of culture as an instrument of freedom presupposing freedom, as a modus operandi *allowing the permanent supersession of the* opus operatum, *of the desolate, cultured 'thing'. These people will grant me, I hope, the right I grant myself here to call for the modern incarnation of the critical power of intellectuals, a 'collective intellectual' who might be capable of making a discourse of freedom heard, a discourse that recognizes no other limit than the constraints and controls which each artist, each writer and each scholar, armed with all the acquisitions of his or her predecessors, enjoin upon themselves and all others.*

Intellectuals are paradoxical beings who cannot be thought of as such as long as they are apprehended through the obligatory alternative between autonomy and commitment, between pure culture and politics. This is because intellectuals are constituted, historically, in and through their overcoming of that opposition: writers, artists and scholars asserted themselves for the first time as intellectuals, at the time of the Dreyfus Affair, when they intervened in political life *as intellectuals*, meaning with a specific authority founded on their belonging to the relatively autonomous world of art, science and literature, and on all the values associated with that autonomy – disinterestedness, expertise, etc.

Intellectuals are two-dimensional figures who do not exist and subsist as such unless (and only unless) they are invested with a specific authority, conferred by the autonomous intellectual world (meaning independent from religious, political or economic power) whose specific laws they respect, and unless (and only unless) they engage this specific authority in political struggles. Far from there existing, as is customarily believed, an antinomy between the search for autonomy (which characterizes the art, science or literature we call 'pure') and the search for political efficacy, it is by increasing their autonomy (and thereby, among other things, their freedom to criticize the prevailing powers) that intellectuals can increase the effectiveness of a political action whose ends and means have their origin in the specific logic of the fields of cultural production.

To be in a position to define what the major directions of a collective action by intellectuals might be it is necessary and sufficient to repudiate the tired alternative between pure art and engaged art which we all have in our minds, and which periodically arises in literary debates. But it is formidably difficult to banish like this the forms of thought we apply to ourselves when we take ourselves as object of thought. This is why, before stating these directions and in order to be able to do so, we must try to make as explicit as possible the unconscious deposited in each intellectual by the very history of which intellectuals are the products. Against the genesis amnesia, which is the basis of all forms of the transcendental illusion, there is no more effective antidote than the reconstruction of the forgotten or repressed history perpetuated in these apparently ahistorical forms of thought structuring our perception of the world and of ourselves.

This is an extraordinarily repetitive history, since its constant change disguises a pendulum swing between two possible attitudes towards politics, either commitment or retreat (at least this was so until this opposition was overcome with Zola and the Dreyfusards). The *'engagement'* of *'philosophes'* which Voltaire in 1765, in the article in the *Philosophical Dictionary* called 'The man of letters', contrasts with the scholastic obscurantism of decadent universities and academies, 'where things are only half said', has a successor in the participation by 'men of letters' in the French Revolution – even though, as Robert Darnton has shown, 'literary bohemia' seized the opportunity of the revolutionary 'disorders' to take revenge on the most consecrated of the followers of the *philosophes*.

In the post-revolutionary period of restoration, 'men of letters', being held responsible not only for the current of revolutionary ideas – through the role of *opinion makers* conferred on them by the proliferation of newspapers in the first phase of the revolution – but also for the excesses of the Terror, are regarded with mistrust and even contempt by the young generation of the 1820s; they are mistrusted most especially by the Romantics who, in the first phase of the movement, challenge and reject the pretension of the *'philosophe'* to intervene in political life and to propose a rational vision of historical evolution. But, once the autonomy of the intellectual field finds itself threatened by the reactionary politics of the Restoration, the romantic poets, led to assert their desire for autonomy in a rehabilitation of feeling and religious sensibility against Reason and the criticism of dogma, hasten to claim, as do Michelet and Saint-Simon, freedom for the writer and the scholar, and to assume in fact the prophetic function which was that of the eighteenth-century philosopher.

But in a new swing of the pendulum, the populist Romanticism which seems to have carried away virtually all the writers in the period before the 1848 revolution does not survive the failure of the movement and the installation of the Second Empire: the collapse of illusions which I will expressly call 'forty-eighter' (to evoke the analogy with the illusions of 1968 whose collapse still haunts our present day) leads to that extraordinary disenchantment, so vigorously evoked by Flaubert in *Sentimental Education*, which provides a favourable terrain for a new assertion of intellectuals' autonomy, this time radically elitist. The defenders of art for art's sake, like

Flaubert and Théophile Gautier, assert the autonomy of the artist by opposing 'social art' and the 'literary bohemia' just as much as they oppose a bourgeois art which is subordinated in matters of art (and also the art of living) to the norms of the bourgeois clientele. They oppose this new-born power which is the cultural industry by refusing the servitude of 'industrial literature' (except as an alimentary substitute for a private income, as with Gautier and Nerval). Not admitting any other judgement than that of their peers, they assert the closing in on itself of the literary field, but also the writer's renunciation of leaving his ivory tower to exercise any form of power whatsoever (thereby making a break with the poet as visionary [*vates*] like Hugo or the prophet-scholar like Michelet).

By an apparent paradox, it is only at the end of the century, at a time when the literary field, the artistic field and the scientific field arrive at autonomy, that the most autonomous agents of these autonomous fields intervene in the political field as intellectuals – and not as cultural producers converted into politicians, like Guizot or Lamartine – that is, with an authority founded on the autonomy of the field and all the values associated with it: ethical purity, specific expertise, etc. In a concrete fashion, intrinsically artistic or scientific autonomy is asserted in political acts like Zola's 'J'accuse' and the petitions designed to support it. These interventions of a new kind tend to maximize the two dimensions constitutive of the identity of the intellectual who is invented through them – 'purity' and 'engagement' – giving birth to a *politics of purity* which is the perfect antithesis of the reason of state. They imply in effect the assertion of the right to transgress the most sacred values of the collectivity – patriotic values, for example, with the support given to Zola's defamatory article against the army, or much later, during the Algerian war, the call for support for the enemy – in the name of values transcending those of citizenship or, if you will, in the name of a particular form of ethical and scientific universalism which can serve as foundation not only for a sort of moral magisterium but also for a collective mobilization to fight to promote these values.

It would suffice to add to this overview of the major stages in the genesis of the figure of the intellectual some indications of the cultural policy of the 1848 Republic or that of the Commune, in order to have an almost complete picture of the possible relations between cultural producers and power such as they might be observed either in the history of a single country, or in the political space of European states today. History carries an important lesson: we are in a game in which all the moves made today, wherever, have already been made – from the rejection of politics and the return to the religious, to the resistance to actions by a political power hostile to intellectual things, via the revolt against the grip of the media, or the disabused abandonment of revolutionary utopias.

But the fact of finding oneself thus at 'end game' does not necessarily lead to disenchantment. It is clear in effect that the intellectual (or, better, the autonomous fields which make the intellectual possible) is not instituted once and for all with Zola, and that the holders of cultural capital may always 'regress', as a result of a disintegration of that unstable combination which defines the intellectual, towards one or another of apparently exclusive positions, either towards the role of 'pure' writer, artist or scholar, or towards the role of political actor, journalist, politician, expert. Moreover, contrary to what the naively Hegelian vision of intellectual history might have us believe, the claim of autonomy which is inscribed in the very existence of the field of cultural production must reckon with obstacles and powers which are ceaselessly renewed, whether we are dealing with external powers such as those of the Church, the state and great economic enterprises, or internal powers, and in particular those which accompany control of the specific instruments of production and distribution (press, publishing, radio, television).

This is one of the reasons – along with the differences in national histories – why the *variations* among countries in the state of relations now and in the past between the intellectual field and political power mask the *constants*, which are nevertheless more substantial and which are the real foundation of the possible unity of intellectuals of all countries. The same *intention of autonomy* can in effect be expressed in opposite position-takings (secular in one case, religious in another) according to the structure and the history of the powers against which it must assert itself. Intellectuals of different countries must be fully conscious of this mechanism if they want to avoid letting themselves be divided by conjunctural and epiphenomenal oppositions which stem from the fact that the same will to emancipation runs up against different obstacles. Here I could take the example of the most visible French philosophers and German philosophers (including Foucault and Habermas) who, since they pit the same concern for autonomy against contrasting historical traditions, seem to oppose each other with apparently inverse relations with truth and with reason. But I could equally well take the example of an issue like public opinion polls, which some in the West take as particularly subtle instruments of domination, whereas to others, in the countries of Eastern Europe, they appear as the conquest of liberty.

In order to understand and master the oppositions which are in danger of dividing them, intellectuals of different European countries can only overcome the oppositions which threaten to divide them if they have a vivid awareness of the structures and the national histories of the powers they must stand up to in order to exist as intellectuals. They must, for example, know how to recognize in the statements of any one of their foreign colleagues (in particular when these statements seem disconcerting or shocking) the effects of historical and geographical distance from the experience of political despotism such as Nazism or Stalinism, or from ambiguous political movements like the student revolts of 1968, or, where internal powers are concerned, the effects of the present and past experience of intellectual worlds which are very unequally subject to open or latent censorship by politics or economics, the university or the academy, and so on.

When we speak as intellectuals, that is, with the ambition to be universal, it is always, at any moment, the historical unconscious inscribed in the experience of a singular intellectual field which speaks through our mouths. I think that we only have a chance of achieving real communication when we objectify and master the various kinds of historical unconscious separating us, meaning the specific histories of intellectual universes which have produced our categories of perception and thought.

I want to come now to an exposition of the particular reasons why it is especially urgent today that intellectuals mobilize and create a veritable *Internationale of intellectuals* committed to defending the autonomy of the universes of cultural production or, to parody a language now out of fashion, *the ownership by cultural producers of their instruments of production and circulation* (and hence of evaluation and consecration). I do not think I am succumbing to an apocalyptic vision of the state of the field of cultural production by saying that this autonomy is very severely threatened or, more precisely, that a threat of a totally new sort today hangs over its functioning; and that artists, writers and scholars are more and more completely excluded from public debate, both because they are less inclined to intervene in it and because the possibility of an effective intervention is less and less frequently offered to them.

The threats to autonomy result from the increasingly greater interpenetration between the world of art and the world of money. I am thinking of new forms of sponsorship, of new alliances being established between certain economic enterprises (often the most modernizing, as in Germany, with Daimler-Benz and the banks) and cultural producers; I am thinking, too, of the more and more frequent recourse of university research to sponsorship, and of the creation of educational institutions directly subordinated to business (as with the Technologiezentren in Germany or the business schools in France). But the grip or empire of the economy over artistic or scientific research is also exercised inside the field itself, through the control of the means of cultural production and distribution, and even of the instances of consecration. Producers attached to the major cultural bureaucracies (newspapers, radio, television) are increasingly forced to accept and adopt norms and constraints linked to the requirements of the market and, especially, to pressure exerted more or less strongly and directly by advertisers; and they tend more or less unconsciously to constitute as a universal measure of intellectual accomplishment those forms of intellectual activity to which they are condemned by their conditions of work (I am thinking, for example, of *fast writing* and *fast reading*, which are often the rule in journalistic production and criticism). One could ask whether the division into two markets characteristic of the fields of cultural production since the middle of the nineteenth century, with on one side the narrow field of producers for producers, and on the other side the field of mass production and 'industrial literature', is not now threatening to disappear, since the logic of commercial production tends more and more to assert itself over avant-garde production (notably, in the case of literature, through the constraints of the book market).

It would be necessary to analyse the new forms of stranglehold and dependence, like the ones introduced by sponsorship, and against which the 'beneficiaries' have not yet developed appropriate systems of defence since they are not fully aware of all their effects; it would also be necessary to analyse the constraints imposed by state sponsorship – even though it seems to escape the direct pressures of the market – whether through the recognition it grants spontaneously to those who recognize it because they need it in order to obtain a form of recognition which they cannot get by their work alone, or whether, more subtly, through the mechanism of commissions and committees – places of negative co-optation which often result in a thorough standardization of the avant-garde, either scientific or artistic.

The exclusion from public debate of artists, writers and scholars is the result of the conjoined impact of several factors: some grow out of the internal evolution of cultural production – like the increasingly narrow specialization which leads researchers to give up the wider ambitions of the intellectual in earlier days – whereas others are the result of the increasingly strong grip of a technocracy which, with the often unconscious complicity of journalists (themselves caught in the game of competition), puts citizens on extended intellectual vacation by favouring 'organized irresponsibility', in the words of Ulrich Beck,

and which finds an immediate ally in a technocracy of communication
– more and more present, via the media, in the universe of cultural
production. One would have to develop, for example, the analysis of
the production and reproduction of technocratic power or, better,
epistemocratic power, in order to understand the almost unconditional delegation, founded on the social authority of educational
institutions, which the great majority of citizens grant, on the most
vital issues, to the 'state nobility' (the best example being the almost
unlimited confidence which those who have been called 'nucleocrats'
enjoy, notably in France).

With less and less to communicate (in fact and by right) the greater
their success, measured by the size of the audience they address, those
who control access to the instruments of communication tend to
spread the emptiness of media droning inside the apparatuses of
communication, and tend increasingly to impose superficial and
artificial problems born of simple competition for the biggest audience on to the political field as well as the fields of cultural
production. The deepest forces of inertia of the social world – not to
mention economic powers which, especially through advertising,
exercise a direct hold on the written and spoken press – can thus
impose a domination all the more invisible in that it is accomplished
only via complex networks of reciprocal dependence, like the *censorship* exercised through the intersection between mutual controls of
competition on the one hand, and the interiorized controls of self-
censorship on the other.

These new masters of thoughtless thought monopolize public
debate to the detriment of professionals of politics (parliamentary
legislators, trade union leaders, etc.); and also to the detriment of
intellectuals, who are subject, even within their own universe, to sorts
of *specific powerplays* such as surveys aiming to produce manipulated
classifications, or the 'top ten' lists which newspapers publish on
anniversary occasions, and so forth, or even publicity campaigns
aiming to discredit productions destined for the narrow (and long-
term) market at the expense of the products of wide circulation and
short cycle which new producers launch on to the market.

It has been shown that the successful political demonstration is the
one which manages to make itself visible in the papers and especially
on television, and hence to impress upon journalists (who may
contribute to its success) the idea that it is successful – with the most
sophisticated forms of demonstration being conceived and produced,
sometimes with the help of communications advisers, with an eye on
the journalists who must take notice of them.[1] In the same way, an
ever larger part of cultural production – when it is not coming from

people who, since they work in the media, are guaranteed the support of the media – is predefined, down to date of appearance, title, format and size, content and style – to catch the attention of journalists who will make it exist by speaking about it.

Commercial literature has not just come into existence recently; nor is it new that the necessities of commerce make themselves felt at the heart of the cultural field. But the grip of the holders of power over the instruments of circulation – and of consecration – has undoubtedly never been as wide and as deep as it is today – and the boundary has never been as blurred between the experimental work and the *bestseller*. This blurring of boundaries to which so-called 'media-oriented' producers are spontaneously inclined (as shown by the fact that the journalistic lists of hits always juxtapose the most autonomous and the most heteronomous producers) constitutes the worst threat to the autonomy of cultural production. The heteronomous producer, whom the Italians magnificently call *tuttologo*, is the Trojan horse by means of which all forms of social stranglehold – that of the market, of fashion, of the state, of politics, of journalism – are imported into the field of cultural production. The basis on which one can condemn these *doxosophes*, as Plato called them, is implicit in the idea that the specific force of the intellectual, even in politics, can rely only on the autonomy conferred by the capacity to respond to the internal requirements of the field. Zhdanovism, which flourishes among mediocre or failed writers and artists, is only one piece of evidence among others that heteronomy arrives in a field through the producers who are the least capable of succeeding according to the norms it imposes.

The anarchic order reigning in an intellectual field which has achieved a high degree of autonomy is always fragile and threatened, to the extent that it constitutes a challenge to the laws of the ordinary economic world, and to the rules of common sense. It is dangerous for it to depend on just the heroism of a few. It is not virtue which can found a free intellectual order; it is a free intellectual order which can found intellectual virtue.

The paradoxical and apparently contradictory nature of the intellectual means that any political action aiming to reinforce the political efficacy of intellectuals' enterprises is fated to give itself an apparently contradictory slogan. On the one hand, the aim is to reinforce autonomy, notably by reinforcing the separation from heteronomous producers and by fighting to guarantee cultural producers the economic and social conditions of autonomy in relation to all forms of power, not excluding those of state bureaucracies (and first of all, in respect to the publication and evaluation of the products of intellectual activity). On the other hand, it must tear cultural producers away from the temptation to remain in their ivory tower, and encourage them to fight, if only to guarantee themselves the power over the instruments of production and consecration and, by involving themselves in their own times, to assert the values associated with their autonomy.

This fight must be *collective* because the effectiveness of the powers which are exercised over them results in large part from the fact that those intellectuals who confront them are dispersed and in competition with each other – and also because efforts at mobilization will always be suspect, and doomed to failure, so long as they can be suspected of being used as part of struggles for leadership by an intellectual or a group of intellectuals. Cultural producers will not find again a place of their own in the social world unless, sacrificing once and for all the myth of the 'organic intellectual' (without falling into the complementary mythology of the mandarin withdrawn from everything), they agree to work collectively for the defence of their own interests. This should lead them to assert themselves as an international power of criticism and watchfulness, or even of proposals, in the face of the technocrats, or – with an ambition both more lofty and more realistic, and hence limited to their own sphere – to get involved in rational action to defend the economic and social conditions of the autonomy of these socially privileged universes in which the material and intellectual instruments of what we call Reason are produced and reproduced. This *Realpolitik of reason* will undoubtedly be suspected of corporatism. But it will be part of its task to prove, by the ends to which it puts the sorely won means of its autonomy, that it is a corporatism of the universal.

Notes

~∞~

Note on the epigraph to the book, 'It is by reading that one becomes readerly': Queneau's play on the proverb includes a pun on the verb *lire*, since *liseron* means 'bindweed'. *Trans.*

Preface

1 D. Sallenave, *Le Don des morts* (Paris: Gallimard, 1991), *passim.*
2 Ibid.
3 Ibid.
4 Ibid.
5 Ibid.
6 H.-G. Gadamer, *L'Art de comprendre, Écrits, II, Herméneutique et Champ de l'expérience humaine* (Paris: Aubier, 1991), p. 17; and also on the irreducibility of historical experience as 'the immersion in a "becoming" excluding knowledge of "what happens"', p. 197.
7 J. W. Goethe, 'Karl Wilhelm Nose', *Naturwiss. Sch.*, IX, p. 195, quoted in E. Cassirer, *Rousseau, Kant, Goethe*, trans. James Guttman, Paul O. Kristeller and John H. Randall (Princeton, N.J.: Princeton University Press, 1947), p. 80.
8 M. Chaillou, *Petit Guide pédestre de la littérature française du XVIIᵉ siècle* (Paris: Hatier, 1990), esp. pp. 9–13.
9 L. Wittgenstein, 'Lecture on ethics', *Philosophical Review* (1965): 3–26. *Trans.*

Prologue Flaubert, Analyst of Flaubert

1 To allow the reader to follow the analysis more easily and to check its

validity against other readings, the appendices to this chapter contain a summary of *Sentimental Education* and some classic interpretations of the novel.

2 For example, it is not without some malign delectation that one learns from Lucien Goldmann that Lukács saw in *Sentimental Education* a psychological (rather than sociological) novel, leaning towards the analysis of the interior life (cf. L. Goldmann, *Introduction to a Sociology of the Novel*, trans. Alan Sheridan (London: Tavistock, 1975), p. 2).

3 The two principal English translations of Gustave Flaubert's novel are *A Sentimental Education: the Story of a Young Man* in Oxford University Press's World's Classics series, trans. Douglas Parmée (Oxford, 1989), and *Sentimental Education* in the Penguin Classic series, trans. Robert Baldick (Harmondsworth, 1964). Henceforward references will be noted as *SE*, O or P, followed by a page number referring respectively to these Oxford or Penguin editions. The quotations here are from *SE*, O, pp. 3–4. *Trans.*

4 This income is for a long while incarnated in his mother, 'who nourishes a high ambition for him' and who never stops recalling him to order and to strategies (matrimonial, in particular) necessary to assure the maintenance of his position.

5 'He protests' when Deslauriers, invoking the example of Rastignac, cynically outlines for him a strategy for assuring him of success: 'Make sure you can get into [Dambreuse's] good books – and his wife's too! Become her lover!' (*SE*, P, p. 29). He manifests towards other students and their common preoccupations a disdain (*SE*, P, p. 33), which, like his indifference to the success of idiots, springs from 'loftier ambitions' (*SE*, P, p. 72). But he evokes with neither revulsion nor bitterness a future as defence attorney or parliamentary orator (*SE*, P, p. 95).

6 *SE*, P, p. 269.

7 *SE*, P, pp. 11, 24, 33, 59, 201.

8 To show to what degree of precision Flaubert pushes the search for a pertinent detail, we need only cite the analysis of the Dambreuse coat of arms offered by Yves Lévy: 'The *senestrochère* (left arm moving on the right side of the shield) is a very rare heraldic charge, which may be considered as the defamed form of *dextrochère* (right arm moving on the left side of the shield). The choice of this charge, its fist closed, and elsewhere the choice of enamels (sable for the field, gold for the arm and silver for the glove) and the ever-so-significant device ('by all accounts') sufficiently indicate the intention of Flaubert to give his character telling armorial signs; it is not the shield of a gentleman, it is the coat of arms of an exploiter.'

9 *SE*, P, pp. 42, 54, 91.

10 *SE*, P, pp. 161, 236, 337, 358.

11 *SE*, P, p. 121.

12 *SE*, P, p. 385.

13 *SE*, P, p. 220.

14 *SE*, P, pp. 65, 96, 142.

15 *SE*, P, p. 261.

16 *SE*, P, p. 29. The eminent position of the Dambreuses may be noticed from the fact that, named very early on (*SE*, P, p. 24), they will not be accessible to Frédéric until relatively late, and thanks to some intercessions. Temporal distance is one of the most insurmountable retranslations of social distance.

17 M. J. Durry, *Flaubert et ses Projets inédits* (Paris: Nizet, 1950), p. 155.

18 *SE*, P, p. 45.

19 'With his passion for pandering to the public, he led able artists astray . . . controlling their destinies by means of his connexions and his magazine. Young painters longed to' see their works in his window . . .' (*SE*, P, p. 50).

20 'A chandelier . . . made this interior look more like a drawing-room than a shop' (*SE*, P, pp. 32–3).

21 *SE*, P, p. 389.

22 *SE*, P, p. 175.

23 *SE*, P, p. 152.

24 *SE*, P, p. 55.

25 Thus, 'more sensible to glory than to money,' Pellerin, whom Arnoux has just cheated over a commission but whom he covered with praise shortly afterwards in *L'Art Industriel*, rushes to the dinner to which he had been invited (*SE*, P, p. 55).

26 'The man's a bore, a philistine, a scoundrel, a ruffian!' says Pellerin (*SE*, P, p. 52). For his part, M. Dambreuse puts Frédéric on his guard against him: 'You don't do business together, I trust?' (*SE*, P, p. 239).

27 *SE*, P, p. 385.

28 'When the liqueurs were served, she [Mme Arnoux] disappeared. The conversation became very free' (*SE*, P, p. 58).

29 *SE*, P, p. 124.

30 *SE*, P, p. 131.

31 The dominant hierarchy, that of money, is never pointed out so well as at Rosanette's: there Oudry has the advantage over Arnoux ('He is rich, the old scoundrel' – *SE*, P, p. 133), Arnoux over Frédéric.

32 On the uses of the notion of *milieu* from Newton, who does not use the word, to Balzac, who introduced it into literature in 1842 in the preface to *La Comédie humaine*, or to Taine, who makes it one of the three explanatory principles of history, passing through the *Encyclopédie* of D'Alembert and Diderot, where it appears with its mechanical meaning, Lamarck, who introduces it to biology, and Auguste Comte, among others, who constitutes it theoretically, one may read the chapter entitled 'Le vivant et son milieu' in the book by Georges Canguilhem, *La Connaissance de la vie* (Paris: Vrin, 1975), pp. 129–54.

33 There are different forms of 'capital' in Bourdieu's work: 'not only "economic capital" in the strict sense (i.e. material wealth in the form of money, stocks and shares, property, etc.), but also "cultural capital" (i.e. knowledge, skills and other cultural acquisitions, as exemplified by educational or technical qualifications), "symbolic capital" (i.e. accumulated prestige or honour), and so on' (John O. Thompson, Introduction to Pierre Bourdieu, *Language and Symbolic Power* (Cambridge: Harvard University Press, 1991), p. 14). *Trans.*

34 The future presents itself in fact as a bundle of unequally probable trajectories situated between an upper limit – for example, for Frédéric, minister and lover of Mme Dambreuse – and a lower limit – for example, for the same Frédéric, clerk to a provincial solicitor, married to Mlle Roque.

35 Flaubert never really succeeds in distinguishing Deslauriers and Hussonnet: at one time associated in the politico-literary enterprise in which they want to interest Frédéric, they are always very close to each other in their attitudes and opinions, even if the former orients his ambitions more to literature and the latter to politics. In the course of a discussion of the reasons for the

failure of the 1848 revolution, Frédéric replies to Deslauriers: 'You were always just tradesmen and shopkeepers, and the best of you were nothing but jumped-up schoolmasters!' (*SE*, O, p. 402). Remember a previous notation: 'Frédéric looked at him; with his shabby frock-coat, his dirty spectacles, and his pale face, the lawyer cut such a poor figure that he could not prevent a contemptuous smile from touching his lips' (*SE*, P, p. 159).

36 *SE*, P, p. 275.

37 *SE*, P, p. 245.

38 G. Flaubert, Letter to Louise Colet, 7 Mar. 1847, in *Correspondance* (Paris: Gallimard, Pléiade Collection, 1973), vol. 1, p. 446. Another comprehensive French edition of the letters is *Correspondance* (Paris: Conard, 1926–33). This particular letter is not included in *The Letters of Gustave Flaubert 1857–1880*, ed. and trans. Francis Steegmuller (2 vols, Cambridge: Harvard University Press, 1982). (Henceforward these three editions will be cited as *Corr.*, P; *Corr.*, C; and *Letters.*)

39 *SE*, P, p. 30.

40 *SE*, P, p. 166.

41 *SE*, P, p. 237.

42 The existence of *structural invariants* such as those which characterize the position of the 'heir', or, more generally, of the adolescent, and which could be the foundation of the relations of identification between reader and character is doubtless one of the fundamentals of the eternal quality which literary tradition lends to certain works or certain characters.

43 Bourdieu's concept of habitus is key to his thought: 'The habitus is a set of *dispositions* which incline agents to act and react in certain ways. The dispositions generate practices, perceptions and attitudes which are "regular" without being consciously co-ordinated or governed by any "rule"' (Thompson, Introduction to Bourdieu, *Language and Symbolic Power*, p. 12). *Trans.*

44 *SE*, P, p. 245.

45 *SE*, P, p. 120.

46 *SE*, P, p. 64.

47 *SE*, P, pp. 69, 92.

48 *SE*, P, p. 159.

49 *SE*, P, p. 117.

50 *SE*, P, p. 245. On the attempt by Sartre to find in the deep structure of Gustave's relation to others, and in particular his father, the root of the proclivity for doubling which would be the foundation of this 'doublet', see J.-P. Sartre, *The Family Idiot: Gustave Flaubert 1821–1857*, trans. Carol Cosman (2 vols, Chicago: University of Chicago Press, 1981–91), vol. 1, pp. 215, 319.

51 Hexis means 'a certain durable organisation of one's body and of its deployment in the world. "Bodily hexis is political mythology realised, *embodied*, turned into a permanent disposition, a durable way of standing, speaking, walking, and thereby of feeling and thinking"' (Thompson, Introduction to Bourdieu, *Language and Symbolic Power*, p. 13). *Trans.*

52 *SE*, P, p. 34.

53 P. Coigny, *L'Éducation sentimentale de Flaubert* (Paris: Larousse, 1975), p. 119.

54 *SE*, O, p. 435.

55 *SE*, P, p. 246.

56 *SE*, P, p. 96.
57 *SE*, P, p. 29.
58 *SE*, P, p. 245 (emphasis added).
59 *SE*, P, p. 245.
60 *SE*, P, p. 245.
61 *SE*, P, p. 88.
62 Thus it is that, for Deslauriers, Mme Arnoux represents a 'society woman': 'the society woman – or what he imagined as such – dazzled the lawyer as the symbol and the epitome of countless pleasures he had never known' (*SE*, P, p. 245).
63 *SE*, P, pp. 158, 216.
64 *SE*, P, p. 312. 'Hussonnet was not at all amusing. Forced to write every day on all sorts of subjects, to read countless newspapers, to listen to a great many arguments, and to produce startling paradoxes, he had ended up by losing all sense of reality, blinding himself with his own damp squibs. The difficulties of what had once been an easy life kept him in a state of perpetual agitation; and his literary impotence, which he refused to acknowledge to himself, made him peevish and sarcastic. Talking about a new ballet called *Ozaï*, he made a violent attack on dancing, and, talking about dancing, on the Opéra; then, talking about the Opéra, on the actors of the Italiens, who had now been replaced by a company of Spanish players, "as if we hadn't had our fill of the Castiles!"' (*SE*, P, p. 212).
65 *SE*, P, p. 343.
66 *SE*, P, p. 359.
67 *SE*, P, p. 416.
68 *SE*, P, pp. 99–100.
69 *SE*, P, pp. 242–3.
70 *SE*, P, p. 100.
71 *SE*, P, p. 55. The first part of the novel is the site of a second coincidence, but one which is resolved happily: Frédéric receives an invitation from the Dambreuses for the very day of Mme Arnoux's party (*SE*, P, p. 88). But the time of incompatibilities has not yet arrived, and Mme Dambreuse will cancel her invitation.
72 *SE*, P, p. 401.
73 *SE*, P, p. 402.
74 *SE*, P, p. 355.
75 *SE*, P, p. 339.
76 *SE*, P, p. 345.
77 *SE*, P, p. 368.
78 *SE*, O, p. 21.
79 *SE*, P, pp. 382–3.
80 *SE*, P, p. 367.
81 *SE*, P, p. 381.
82 It is true that *Sentimental Education* is 'the novel of coincidences in which the characters passively participate, as if they were hallucinating, wide-eyed, before the waltz of their destinies' (J. Bruneau, 'Le rôle du hasard dans *L'Éducation Sentimentale*', *Europe* (Sept.–Nov. 1969): 101–7). But it is a question of necessary coincidences, those occasions when both the necessity inscribed in the 'milieu' and the necessity incorporated in the characters are revealed: 'In this novel where chance seems to reign (meetings, disappearances, occasions which present themselves, occasions

which are missed), there is in fact no place for chance. Henry James, reading this novel as an "epic without air", noted that everything "hangs together", that all the pieces were solidly stitched together' (V. Brombert, 'L'Éducation sentimentale: articulations et polyvalence', in C. Gothot-Mersch (ed.), *La Production du sens chez Flaubert* (Paris: UGE, coll. '10/18', 1975), pp. 55–69).

83 Flaubert notes that there exist profound resemblances between Arnoux and Frédéric (*SE*, O, p. 65). And he gives this character fated to hold double positions some *durable* double dispositions, or split ones: the 'innate combination of sincerity and commercial guile' which, at his apogee, leads him to try to increase his profits 'while preserving artistic appearances' also incites him, when he is weakened by an attack and turns to devotion, to dedicate himself to trade in religious objects, 'to secure both his salvation and a fortune' (*SE*, P, p. 389). (Flaubert leans here, we see, on the homology between the artistic and religious fields.)

84 *SE*, O, p. 213.

85 *SE*, P, p. 182.

86 An example of these fluctuations: 'His return to Paris gave him no pleasure. [. . .] Dining all by himself, Frédéric was overcome by a strange feeling of loneliness; then he thought of Mademoiselle Roque. The idea of marriage no longer struck him as fantastic.' (*SE*, P, p. 254). The day after his triumph at the soirée of the Dambreuses, on the contrary: 'Frédéric's thoughts had never been further removed from marriage. Besides, Mademoiselle Roque struck him as a somewhat ridiculous little thing. What a difference there was between her and a woman like Madame Dambreuse! A very different future awaited him!' (*SE*, P, p. 347). There is a new return to Mlle Roque after his break with Mme Dambreuse (*SE*, P, p. 410).

87 *SE*, P, pp. 360–1.

88 *SE*, O, p. 446.

89 *SE*, P, p. 149.

90 *SE*, P, p. 355.

91 In the contrasting portraits of Rosanette and Mme Arnoux (*SE*, P, pp. 149–50), it is the mother and housewife role of 'Marie' (a first name which, as Thibaudet notes, symbolizes purity) that has the most important place.

92 *SE*, P, p. 356.

93 *SE*, P, p. 254.

94 *SE*, P, p. 409.

95 *SE*, P, p. 361.

96 *SE*, P, p. 369.

97 *SE*, P, p. 186.

98 One finds the same structure in Flaubert's project entitled 'Un ménage moderne': 'That hundred thousand francs around which turn all the vilenesses of the characters, he owed them to the woman, to the first lover, to the husband; the woman extorted them with a "dirty trick" that she committed on the young man infatuated with her; she destined them for her lover; but she gives them to her husband, who is unexpectedly ruined' (Durry, *Flaubert et ses Projets inédits*, p. 102).

99 *SE*, P, p. 185.

100 *SE*, P, p. 194.

101 *SE*, P, p. 402.

102 *SE*, P, p. 409.

103 S. Freud, 'The theme of the three caskets', *Complete Psychoanalytic Works of Sigmund Freud*, ed. James Strachey (London: Hogarth, 1956), vol. 12, pp. 291–302. By means of the three situations of the casket, which belongs successively to Mme Arnoux, to Rosanette and to Mme Dambreuse, its three owners are designated and thus a hierarchy is established among them in the relations of power and money.

104 Thus we understand that he had to be fully reassured of the 'non-negative' character of his 'vocation' as a writer, with the success of *Madame Bovary*, to be in a position to finish *Sentimental Education*.

105 *SE*, P, p. 35.

106 J.-P. Richard, 'La création de la forme chez Flaubert', *Littérature et Sensation* (Paris: Seuil, 1954), p. 12.

107 *SE*, P, p. 22.

108 *SE*, P, p. 212.

109 *SE*, P, p. 320.

110 For example, *SE*, O, p. 202 ('His mortification ... was compounded by rage over his powerlessness'); P, p. 269 ('Frédéric loved her so much that he went out. Soon he was filled with anger against himself, cursing himself for a fool'); and above all, P, pp. 413–14 (the final meeting with Mme Arnoux). More generally, every action appears 'all the more impractical' the stronger the desire, fated, moreover, to exasperation in the imaginary.

111 This is the Oxford version of the famous last line of the novel (p. 464). Penguin renders it: 'That was the happiest time we ever had' (p. 419). *Trans.*

112 *SE*, O, p. 458. *Trans.*

113 G. Flaubert, Letter to Louise Colet, 8 Oct. 1846, in *Letters*, vol. 1, p. 84.

114 G. Flaubert, Letter to his mother, 15 Dec. 1850, in *Letters*, vol. 1, p. 132.

115 'I want to write the moral history of the men of my generation – or, more accurately, the history of their *feelings*. It's a book about love, about passion; but passion such as can exist nowadays – that is to say, inactive' (G. Flaubert, Letter to Mlle Leroyer de Chantepie, 6 Oct. 1864, in *Letters*, vol. 2, p. 78).

116 G. Flaubert, Letter to Louise Colet, 31 Mar. 1853, in *Letters*, vol. 1, pp. 183–4.

117 G. Flaubert, Letter to Louise Colet, 15–16 May 1852, in *Corr.*, P, vol. 2, p. 291, or similarly, 3 May 1853, p. 323.

118 G. Flaubert, *The Temptation of Saint Antony*, trans. Kitty Mrosovsky (Ithaca: Cornell University Press, 1981), pp. 64–5.

119 G. Flaubert, Letter to George Sand, 29 Sept. 1866, in *Letters*, vol. 2, pp. 88–9.

120 These are, to be sure, the 'accepted ideas' that Flaubert vigorously hunted down, in himself and others, as well as the verbal habits which are characteristic of a person; as for example what he called the 'stupid phrases' of Rosanette ('Nothing doing! Go to Jericho! You never can tell', etc.) or the 'ordinary locutions' of Mme Dambreuse ('An innate selfishness revealed itself in her habitual expressions – "What do I care? I'd be a fool if I did. Why should I?"' – *SE*, P, pp. 357, 384).

121 G. Flaubert, *Novembre* (Paris: Charpentier, 1886), p. 329. See also *November*, trans. Frank Jellinek, ed. Francis Steegmuller (New York: Serendipity, 1967).

122 *SE*, P, p. 241.

123 One thinks of the reflection aroused in Frédéric by Martinon's success: 'There is nothing more humiliating than seeing fools succeed where one has failed oneself' (*SE*, P, p. 72). All the ambivalence of the subjective relationship that the intellectual maintains with those who are dominant and their dishonestly acquired powers is encapsulated in the illogicality of this sentence. This avowed contempt for success may be no more than a manner of making a virtue of necessity, and the dream of a lofty viewpoint no more than a form of the illusion of escaping determinations which is itself part of the determinations inscribed in the position of the intellectual.

124 *SE*, P, p. 286 (emphasis added).

125 G. Flaubert, Letter to Louise Colet, 26 Aug. 1849, in *Letters*, vol. 1, pp. 70–1.

126 G. Flaubert, Letter to Louise Colet, 6–7 Aug. 1846, in *Letters*, vol. 1, p. 49.

127 G. Flaubert, Letter to George Sand, 6 Sept. 1871, in *Corr.*, C, vol. 6, p. 276.

128 This strictly internal analysis of the properties of the work will be filled out (in the following chapter) by the findings of the description of the literary field and the position Flaubert occupied in it.

129 Flaubert's *Dictionnaire des idées reçues*, translated by Jacques Barzun as *Dictionary of Accepted Ideas*, with introd. and notes (New York: New Directions, 1968), and also known as *The Dictionary of Platitudes: Being a Compendium of Conversational Clichés, Blind Beliefs, Fashionable Misconceptions and Fixed Ideas*, is often printed at the end of the novel from which it is derived, *Bouvard and Pécuchet* (see also *Bouvard and Pécuchet*, including *Dictionary of Received Ideas*, trans. A. J. Krailsheimer (London: Penguin, 1976)). *Trans.*

130 *SE*, P, p. 295.

131 G. Genette, *Figures* (Paris: Seuil, 1966), pp. 229–30.

132 R. Barthes, *The Pleasure of the Text*, trans. Richard Miller (New York: Hill and Wang, 1975), p. 9.

133 The suspension of disbelief produced by the literary text relies, we shall see, on the agreement between the assumptions it makes and those that we make in ordinary experience of the world.

134 Conferring on *Sentimental Education* the status of 'sociological document', as has been done many times (see for example J. Y. Dangelzer, *La Description du milieu dans le roman français* (Paris, 1939), or B. Slama, 'Une lecture de L'Éducation sentimentale', *Littérature*, no. 2 (1973): 19–38), by sticking to the most exterior indices of the description of 'milieux', means that the specificity of the literary work is lost.

135 Homais is the quack pharmacist and Bournisien the abbot who ignores Emma's entreaty in *Madame Bovary*. *Trans.*

136 *SE*, P, pp. 38ff.

137 *SE*, P, p. 41. In the 1846 map of Paris reproduced here, we have shown with continuous arrows the trajectories of the principal characters and attached their names to their places of residence. The dotted line running from north to south, representing the limit of the zone occupied by the insurgents of 1848, was adapted from C. Simon, *Paris de 1800 à 1900* (3 vols, Paris: Plon and Nourrit, 1900–1).

138 *SE*, P, p. 33.

139 *SE*, P, p. 36.

140 *SE*, P, p. 35.
141 *SE*, P, p. 33.
142 It is doubtless not by chance that one finds in this quartier one of the most flourishing lycées of the era, the Lycée Condorcet, which took in the children of the grande bourgeoisie, destined for the most part, according to a study in 1864, to study law (117 out of 244) or medicine (16), in contrast to the Lycée Charlemagne, more 'democratic', with a higher proportion of students destined for the Grandes Écoles (cf. R. Anderson, 'Secondary education in mid-nineteenth century France: some social aspects', *Past and Present* (1971): 121–46). This financial bourgeoisie, which often combines more substantial titles with nobility (cf. Dambreuse and Frédéric whose eventual pretensions father Roque evokes – *SE*, P, p. 103), is no doubt more given to the accumulation of cultural capital than the old aristocracy.
143 *SE*, P, p. 30.
144 *SE*, P, p. 359.
145 *SE*, P, p. 115.
146 *SE*, P, p. 388.
147 *SE*, P, p. 121.
148 *SE*, P, p. 256.
149 *SE*, P, p. 311.
150 We have situated Deslauriers in the place des Trois-Maries, since we cannot locate the 'rue' des Trois-Maries of which Flaubert speaks.

Part I Three States of the Field

Chapter 1 The Conquest of Autonomy

1 Undoubtedly the hatred of the 'bourgeois' and 'philistines' had become a literary commonplace with the Romantics who, whether writers, artists or musicians, never stopped proclaiming their distaste for high society and the art it commissioned and consumed (cf. the journal *Romantisme*, nos. 17–18 (1977)), but one cannot help noticing that during the Second Empire indignation and revolt take on an unprecedented violence, which has to be put in relation to the triumphs of the bourgeoisie and the extraordinary development of the artistic and literary bohemia.
2 L. Bergeron, *Les Capitalistes en France (1780–1914)* (Paris: Gallimard, coll. 'Archives', 1978), p. 77.
3 Ibid., p. 195.
4 Quoted by A. Cassagne, *La Théorie de l'art pour l'art en France chez les derniers romantiques et les premiers réalistes* (Paris, 1906; Geneva: Slatkine Reprints, 1979), p. 342.
5 In a note found among the papers of the imperial family 'on the subject of encouragements to offer people of letters', Sainte-Beuve writes: 'Literature in France is also a democracy, or at least it has become one. The vast majority of people of letters are hard workers, labourers in a manner of speaking, living from their pens. We are not referring here to lettered men who belong to the University, or to those who belong to the Académie, but to the very great majority of writers comprising what we call the literary press' (Sainte-Beuve, *Premiers Lundis* (Paris: Calmann-Lévy, 1886–91),

vol. 3, pp. 59ff.; see also *Nouveaux Lundis* (Paris: Calmann-Lévy, 1867–79), vol. 9, pp. 101ff., where Sainte-Beuve speaks of the 'literary worker'; in English *Sainte-Beuve: Selected Essays*, trans. and ed. Francis Steegmuller and Norbert Guterman (New York: Doubleday, 1963)).

6 The Parnassians were opposed to Romanticism, especially its didacticism. An outgrowth of art for art's sake, this poetic movement stressed form, and its major figures were Théophile Gautier, Théodore de Banville, Charles Leconte de Lisle, and José María de Heredia. *Trans.*

7 J. Richardson, *Princess Mathilde* (London: Weidenfeld and Nicolson, 1969), and also F. Strowski, *Tableau de la littérature française au XIXe siècle* (Paris: Paul Delaplane, 1912).

8 Cassagne, *La Théorie de l'art pour l'art*, p. 115.

9 Ibid.

10 On this point, see especially L. O'Boile, 'The problem of excess of educated men in Western Europe, 1800–1850', *Journal of Modern History* 42, no. 4 (1970), pp. 471–95, and 'The democratic Left in Germany, 1848', *Journal of Modern History* 32, no. 1 (1961): 374–83.

11 A. Prost, *Histoire de l'enseignement en France 1800–1967* (Paris: A. Colin, 1968).

12 Letter from Jules Buisson to Eugène Crépet, quoted in C. Pichois and J. Ziegler, *Baudelaire* (Paris: Julliard, 1987), p. 41.

13 This homology of position undoubtedly contributes to explaining the propensity of the modern artist to identify his social destiny with that of the prostitute, 'a free worker' in the market of sexual exchanges.

14 Here one sees an example of the simplification committed by those who think of the transformations of modern societies as linear and unidimensional processes, such as Norbert Elias's 'process of civilization': they reduce to a unilateral process the complex evolutions that, when dealing with modes of domination, are always ambiguous, doubled-faced, with the regression of a recourse to physical violence being, for example, compensated by a progression in symbolic violence and in all other gentler forms of control.

15 H. de Balzac, *Traité de la vie élégante* (Paris: Delmas, 1952), p. 16.

16 C. Baudelaire, 'Pierre Dupont', in *Baudelaire as a Literary Critic*, selected essays trans. Lois B. Hyslop and Francis E. Hyslop Jr (University Park: Pennsylvania State University Press, 1964), p. 52.

17 *Corr.*, C, vol. 6, p. 161.

18 G. Flaubert, Letter to George Sand, 29 Apr. 1871, in *The George Sand–Gustave Flaubert Letters*, trans. A. L. McKenzie (Chicago: Academy, 1979), p. 200.

19 E. Bazire, *Manet* (Paris, 1884), pp. 44–5, quoted in *Manet, 1832–1883*, catalogue of the 1983 exhibition (New York: Museum of Metropolitan Art/Abrams, 1983), p. 226.

20 G. Flaubert, Preface to *Les Dernières Chansons* by L. Bouilhet, 20 June 1870, cited in *Corr.*, C, vol. 6, p. 477.

21 G. Flaubert, Letter to Louise Colet, 22 Sept. 1853, in *Selected Letters of Gustave Flaubert*, ed. Francis Steegmuller (New York, Farrar, Straus and Cudeby, 1953), p. 164.

22 Cassagne, *La Théorie de l'art pour l'art*, pp. 212–13.

23 E. Casamaraschi, *Réalisme et Impressionnisme dans l'oeuvre des frères Goncourt* (Pisa: Libreria Goliardica; Paris: Nizet, n.d.), p. 96.

24 G. Flaubert, 26 Jan. 1862, in *Corr.*, P, vol. 3, p. 203.

25 G. Flaubert, Letter to J. Sandeau, 26 Jan. 1862, in *Corr.*, P, vol. 3, p. 202.

26 C. Baudelaire, Letter to G. Flaubert, 31 Jan. 1862, quoted in C. Pichois and J. Ziegler, *Baudelaire*, trans. Graham Robb (London: Hamish Hamilton, 1989), p. 185.

27 On the candidature to the Académie, as on everything concerning the Baudelairean enterprise, in particular his relations with editors, see Pichois and Ziegler, *Baudelaire*, and also H. J. Martin and R. Chartier (eds), *Histoire de l'édition française* (4 vols, Paris: Promodis, 1984), and on Flaubert, R. Descharmes, 'Flaubert et ses éditeurs, Michel Lévy et Georges Charpentier', *Revue d'histoire littéraire de la France* (1911): 364–93 and 627–63.

28 Baudelaire, *Baudelaire as a Literary Critic*, p. 142; see also, on Gautier, ibid., p. 340.

29 C. Baudelaire, *Oeuvres Complètes* (Paris: Gallimard, coll. 'Pléiade', 1976), vol. 2, pp. 231–4.

30 Baudelaire, *Baudelaire as a Literary Critic*, p. 65.

31 C. Baudelaire, Letter to Mme Aupick, 4 Dec. 1847, in *Selected Letters of Charles Baudelaire: the Conquest of Solitude*, trans. Rosemary Lloyd (Chicago: University of Chicago Press, 1986), p. 30.

32 Baudelaire, *Baudelaire as a Literary Critic*, p. 143; see also, with respect to Gautier, ibid., p. 341.

33 Ibid., p. 356.

34 C. Baudelaire, *Charles Baudelaire: a Self Portrait*, ed. L. B. Hyslop and F. E. Hyslop Jr (New York and London: Oxford University Press, 1957), p. 101.

35 Baudelaire, *Baudelaire as a Literary Critic*, p. 70.

36 It has to be said that Flaubert had many disputes with Lévy, while he maintained friendly relations with Charpentier whose publishing house is one of the gathering places of the literary and artistic avant-garde (see E. Bergerat, *Souvenirs d'un enfant de Paris* (Paris: Charpentier, 1911–13), vol. 2, p. 323).

37 G. Flaubert, Letter to Ernest Feydeau, mid-Nov. 1872, in *Corr.*, C, vol. 6, p. 448.

38 G. Vapereau, *Dictionnaire universel des contemporains* (Paris: Hachette, 1865), article on 'E. About', and L. Badesco, *La Génération poétique de 1860* (Paris: Nizet, 1971), pp. 290–3.

39 F. Strowski, *Tableau de la littérature française au XIXᵉ siècle*, pp. 337–41.

40 Cassagne, *La Théorie de l'art pour l'art*, pp. 115–18.

41 Baudelaire, *Baudelaire as a Literary Critic*, p. 66.

42 Pierre Dupont was, after Béranger, the most celebrated songwriter of the mid-century. A romantic poet in his youth, laureate of the Académie in 1842, he proves himself a 'village poet' in 1845, notably with his song *Les Boeufs*, which became widely known. He recites his poems in the literary cafés frequented by bohemia and, entering into the working-class movement, writes revolutionary songs on the eve of 1848, becoming the bard of the new republic. He is arrested and condemned after the coup d'état. His work is published in 1851, under the title *Chants et Chansons*, with a preface by Baudelaire. Gustave Mathieu, friend and imitator of Dupont, born in Nevers and member of the Berrichon group which gathered around George Sand, enjoys a great literary reputation after 1848, notably on

account of his political poems that, like those of Dupont, were sung by Darcier in the cabarets of the Left Bank (see E. Bouvier, *La Bataille réaliste 1844–1857* (Paris: Fortemoing, 1913)).

43 The 'worker-poets' flourished in the years before 1848. Charles Poncy, a mason from Toulon, publishes poems in *L'Illustration* which are very successful, triggering the appearance of a whole series of socialist chants which are often only pale or clumsy imitations of Hugo, Barbier and Ponsard.

44 Pichois and Ziegler, *Baudelaire* (Paris), p. 219.

45 P. Martino, *Le Roman réaliste sous le second Empire* (Paris: Hachette, 1913), p. 9.

46 Bouvier, *La Bataille réaliste 1844–1857*.

47 G. Flaubert, *Madame Bovary* (Paris: Conard, 1921), pp. 577, 581, 629, 630.

48 C. Pichois, *Baudelaire: Études et témoignages* (Neuchâtel: La Baconnière, 1976), p. 137.

49 B. Russell, 'The superior virtue of the oppressed', *The Nation*, 26 June 1937, and Champfleury, *Sensations de Josquin*, p. 215, quoted in R. Cherniss, 'The Antinaturalists', in G. Boas (ed.), *Courbet and the Naturalistic Movement* (New York: Russell and Russell, 1967), p. 97.

50 C. Baudelaire, *The Poems of Baudelaire*, trans. Roy Campbell (New York: Pantheon, 1952).

51 We have seen, in a letter of 31 January 1862, replying to Flaubert's expression of astonishment at his candidature to the Académie, that Baudelaire manifests consciousness of a solidarity.

52 G. Flaubert, Letter to Edma Roger des Genettes, 30 Oct. 1856, quoted by Francis Steegmuller in *Flaubert and Madame Bovary: a Double Portrait* (New York, Farrar, Straus, 1950), pp. 376–7.

53 G. Flaubert, Letter to E. de Goncourt, 1 May 1879, in *Corr.*, C, vol. 8, p. 263.

54 G. Flaubert, Letter to Renan, 13 Dec. 1876, in *Corr.*, C, vol. 7, p. 368.

55 G. Flaubert, Letter to George Sand, May 1867, in *Letters*, vol. 1, p. 105.

56 G. Flaubert, Letter to Ernest Feydeau, 17 Aug. 1861, in *Corr.*, P, vol. 3, p. 170.

57 T. Gautier, *Histoire du romantisme*, quoted in P. Lidsky, *Les Écrivains contre la Commune* (Paris: Maspero, 1970), p. 20.

58 Cassagne, *La Théorie de l'art pour l'art*, pp. 154–5.

59 G. Flaubert, Letter to George Sand, 19 Sept. 1868, in *Selected Letters*, p. 215.

60 G. Flaubert, Letter to Mme Roger des Genettes, Summer 1864, in *Letters*, vol. 2, p. 76.

61 C. Baudelaire, Letter to Barbey, 9 July 1860, quoted in Pichois, *Baudelaire: Études et témoignages*, p. 177.

62 G. Flaubert, Letter to George Sand, 12 Dec. 1872, in *The George Sand–Gustave Flaubert Letters*, p. 281.

63 G. Flaubert, Letter to Count René de Maricourt, 4 Jan. 1867, in *Corr.*, C, vol. 5, p. 264. The ambivalent relationship they maintain with the bourgeois public and with writers who agree to serve it may no doubt explain in part why, with the exception of Bouilhet and Théodore de Banville, the proponents of art for art's sake experience resounding failures in the theatre, as did Flaubert and the Goncourts, and also why, like Gautier and Baudelaire, they kept boxfuls of librettos and scenarios.

64 M. Du Camp, *Théophile Gautier* (Paris: Hachette, 1895), p. 120, quoted by M. C. Schapira, 'L'Aventure espagnole de Théophile Gautier', in R. Bellet (ed.), *L'Aventure dans la littérature populaire au XIX siècle* (Lyons: PUL, 1985), pp. 21–42 (on the relations between Gautier and Girardin, see esp. pp. 22–5).

65 G. Flaubert, Letter to Louis Bouilhet, 30 Sept. 1855, in *Corr.*, P, vol. 2, p. 598. This letter is a chance to verify once more the importance of Flaubert's social capital: Mme Stroehlin, a close .friend of his mother's and her neighbour in Rouen, was 'well in favour with the imperial authorities'. Bouilhet, in contrast to Flaubert, seems to have been totally devoid of social capital and, as is often the case, of the dispositions that allow its acquisition (as Flaubert reproached him on many occasions).

66 G. Flaubert, Letter to Ernest Feydeau, 15 May 1859, in *Letters*, vol. 2, p. 17.

67 Just by the effect of thematic grouping, the very fine study by Albert Cassagne gives an overwhelming proof of this – one may consult, for example, their various judgements on universal suffrage or on popular education: see *La Théorie de l'art pour l'art*, pp. 195–8.

68 Thus the Goncourts, who evoke at length the contradictions of the modern artist (E. and J. de Goncourt, *Charles Demailly* (Paris: Fasquelle, 1913), pp. 164–71), represent bohemia as a sort of literary proletariat who, 'condemned to misery by the decline of literary salaries', offer the 'small journal' a sort of revolutionary army, 'naked, malnourished, without shoes', ready to go to war against the 'aristocracy of letters' (ibid., pp. 24–5).

69 G. Flaubert, Letter to Ernest Chevalier, 23 July 1839, in *Corr.*, C, vol. 1, p. 54; see also a letter to Gourgaud-Dugazon, 22 Jan. 1842, ibid., p. 93.

70 A.-C. Flaubert, Letter to Gustave Flaubert, 29 Aug. 1840, in *Corr.*, P, vol. 1, p. 68. And an example of the anti-Prudhommean pleasantries offered by the very young Gustave: 'I am going to reply to your letter and, as certain waggish writers say, put my hand to my pen to write to you' (G. Flaubert, Letter to Ernest Chevalier, 28 Sep. 1834, in *Corr.*, P, vol. 1, p. 15; see also ibid., pp. 18 and 27).

71 In fact, it appears that Flaubert was rather a good student (without being as 'brilliant' as Bouilhet). And he might have been especially marked by the very bitter experience of his years at a boarding school (boarder from 1832 to 1838, then a day student, he quits the Collège in 1839 after leading a revolt): 'When I was twelve, they put me in a college: there I saw the world in a microcosm, its vices in miniature, the seeds of its ridicule, its petty passions, small cliques, little cruelties; I saw there the triumph of force, mysterious emblem of the power of God' (G. Flaubert, *Oeuvres de jeunesse*, vol. 2, p. 270, quoted by J. Bruneau, *Les Débuts littéraires de Gustave Flaubert 1831–1845* (Paris: A. Colin, 1962), p. 221). 'I was at college from the age of ten and there contracted at an early age a profound aversion to men. This society of children is as cruel for the victims as that other small society, that of men. The same crowd justice, same tyranny of prejudices and force, same egotism' (G. Flaubert, 'Memories of a madman', in *Oeuvres de jeunesse*, vol. 1, p. 490, quoted by Bruneau, *Les Débuts littéraires*, p. 221).

72 In contrast to Flaubert, Baudelaire – whose father, a cultivated civil servant (he practised painting) and descended from a family of magistrates, died

when he was a child, and whose father-in-law, General Aupick, pursued a brilliant career – had a very conflictual relationship with his family; by opposing his literary ambitions and forcing a judicial career on him, they imprint on his whole life the stigmata of the excluded. As C. Pichois and J. Ziegler have remarked, for him prodigality is a method of rejecting the family who had rejected him, by refusing to honour the limits it had imposed on his spending. This rupture with his family (suffered and yet willed), and especially the break with his mother, is without doubt at the root of a tragic relationship with the social world, that of the excluded person forced to exclude, in and through a permanent rupture, that which excludes him.

73 G. Flaubert, Letter to George Sand, 2 Feb. 1869, in *The George Sand–Gustave Flaubert Letters*, pp. 121–2.

74 Letter from Paul Alexis to Flaubert, quoted in A. Albalat, *G. Flaubert et ses Amis* (Paris: Plon, 1927), pp. 240–3. The outline titled 'Le hibou philosophe, notes pour la composition et la rédaction d'un journal' gives an idea of what Baudelaire's response would have been in 1851. Clearer in his rejections than his approbations, he expresses his horror of commercial literature (G. Planche, J. Janin, A. Dumas, E. Sue, P. Féval – 'Conseils aux jeunes littérateurs', in C. Baudelaire, *Oeuvres complètes* (Paris: Gallimard, 1976), vol. 2, pp. 50–2; the article 'Les Drames et les romans honnêtes' adds to this list Ponsard, Augier and the neoclassicals), his esteem for the literature of realist manners (Ourliac), his respect for legitimate writers (Gautier, Sainte-Beuve), but at that time he shows himself still hostile to art for art's sake, no doubt under the influence of the pre-1848 bohemia (ibid., vol. 2, pp. 38–43). The short text titled 'De quelques préjugés contemporains', however, written at the same time, marks his break with the ideals of 1848 and romantic idealism (Hugo, Lamennais) (ibid., vol. 2, p. 54). In 1855, he affirms his break with realism in a text titled 'Puisque réalisme il y a' (ibid., vol. 2, pp. 57–9).

75 'When the novel of manners is not leavened by an author's high natural taste, it very much risks being flat and even [. . .] completely useless. If Balzac made of this routine genre an admirable thing, always curious and often sublime, it is because he threw his whole being into it' (ibid., vol. 2, p. 121). In short, Baudelaire holds that 'this bastard genre whose domain is truly limitless' (ibid., vol. 2, p. 119) should be saved by the application of some special talent, such as the 'art of saying things well'.

76 Martino, *Le Roman réaliste sous le second Empire*, p. 98. In a savage critique of a speech by Musset at the Académie, Flaubert criticizes the hierarchy of genres – and Musset's docility with respect to it (cf. G. Flaubert, Letter to Louise Colet, 30 May 1852, in *Letters*, vol. 1, pp. 159–60).

77 G. Planche, *Portraits littéraires*, vol. 2, p. 420, quoted by J. Bruneau, *Les Débuts littéraires de Gustave Flaubert*, p. 111.

78 Bruneau, *Les Débuts littéraires*, pp. 72ff.

79 G. Flaubert, Letter to Louise Colet, 20 June 1853, in *Corr.*, P, vol. 2, p. 358.

80 Quoted by Bouvier, *La Bataille réaliste 1844–1857*, p. 329.

81 It can be shown, by analysing the choice between different 'grandes écoles', that the opposition between art and money, between culture and the economy, is one of the most fundamental schemas of perception and

appreciation of the matrix of preferences that is the habitus (cf. P. Bourdieu, *La Noblesse d'État: Grandes écoles et esprit de corps* (Paris: Minuit, 1989), pp. 225ff.; in English as *The State Nobility: Grandes Écoles and Esprit de Corps* (Cambridge: Polity, 1995)).

82 E. Zola, *Oeuvres complètes* (Paris: Bernouard, 1927–39), vol. 41, p. 153.

83 Ibid., p. 157.

84 W. Asholt, 'La question de *L'Argent*: Quelques remarques à propos du premier texte littéraire de Vallès', *Revue d'Études Vallésiennes*, no. 1 (1984): 5–15.

85 G. Flaubert, Letter to Edma Roger des Genettes, 30 Oct. 1856, quoted by Steegmuller, *Flaubert and Madame Bovary*, pp. 376–7.

86 G. Michaut, *Pages de critique et d'histoire littéraire*, 1910, p. 117, quoted by Martino, *Le Roman réaliste sous le second Empire*, pp. 156–7.

87 E. Duranty, *Le Réalisme*, no. 5 (15 Mar. 1857), p. 79, quoted by R. Descharmes and R. Dumesnil, *Autour de Flaubert* (Paris: Mercure de France, 1912).

88 G. Flaubert, Letter to Louise Colet, 20 Sept. 1851, in *Letters*, vol. 1, p. 145.

89 G. Flaubert, Letter to Louise Colet, 13 Sept. 1852, in *Corr.*, P, vol. 2, p. 156.

90 G. Flaubert, Letter to Ernest Feydeau, end Nov./beginning Dec. 1857, in *Corr.*, P, vol. 2, p. 782.

91 G. Flaubert, Letters to Louis Bouilhet, 2 and 10 Aug. 1854, in *Corr.*, P, vol. 2, pp. 563–4.

92 Quoted by Albalat, *Gustave Flaubert et ses Amis*, p. 68.

93 To take but one example, Eugène Scribe, who enjoyed enormous success on the Boulevard from the beginning of the 1830s until the Second Empire, presents, in *Bertrand et Raton*, produced in 1833, and in *La Camaraderie*, produced in 1837, situations (for example, the debates and rivalries at the core of a political and literary circle in the latter) and observations (the disenchanted speeches of the Comte de Rantzau about revolutions in the former) in which one may recognize in crude form certain Flaubertian themes (cf. B. Froger and S. Hans, 'La Comédie-Française au XIXe siècle: un répertoire littéraire et politique', *Revue d'Histoire du Théâtre* 36, no. 3 (1984): 260–75).

94 É. Zola, *Les Romanciers naturalistes* (Paris: Fasquelle, 1923), pp. 184–96.

95 'He thought himself endowed with a gift for broad comedy and he boasted he could make the belts around the paunches of the gawkers shake with laughter at the goings-on at the Pont-Neuf. His masterpiece was for him the lurid slapstick routine dubbed "the creditor's step" that he had taught Gautier and that they danced together at Neuilly with the contortions of twirling dervishes. "This is theatre," he would cry, collapsing in a sweat on the divan, "and the real stuff!"' (Bergerat, *Souvenirs d'un enfant de Paris*, p. 132).

96 G. Flaubert, Letter to Louise Colet, 12 Sept. 1853, in *Corr.*, P, vol. 2, p. 429. This theme returns in an almost obsessional fashion during the whole period of the composition of *Madame Bovary*.

97 G. Flaubert, Letter to Count René de Maricourt, Aug.–Sept. 1865, in *Corr.*, C, vol. 5, p. 179.

98 Thus, in the *Revue des Deux Mondes* of June 1874, Duvergier de Hauranne denounces Manet and his fellows as a political *danger*: 'Here we touch on what one could call the democracy of art. This democracy protests

bourgeois platitudes and the corrupt fantasies of bourgeois luxury; but most of the time it only knows how to imitate these platitudes, and it is often as unwholesome as the art it wants to reform. The claim is to idealize triviality by the excess of that very triviality and to escape banality by the very affectation of commonness' (quoted by J. Lethève, *Impressionnistes et Symbolistes devant la presse* (Paris: A. Colin, 1959), pp. 73–4).

99 G. Flaubert, Letter to Louise Colet, 27 Mar. 1853, *Selected Letters*, p. 148.

100 Quoted in B. Weinberg, *French Realism: the Critical Reaction 1830–1870* (New York and London: Oxford University Press, 1937), p. 165. An analysis of the arguments, minutely inventoried by the author, employed by adversaries and defenders of realism shows that discussion and disagreement are only possible because the adversaries tacitly agree on a cluster of common presuppositions, such as the opposition between the real and the poetic, the copy, imitation or reproduction and style, the search for elegance, choices, etc.

101 The industrial novels that today are called best-sellers seem to obey (though the hypothesis would have to be verified) a logic which is the strict inverse of the Flaubertian intention: they paint the extraordinary (in its most ordinary definition) mediocrely, evoke unusual situations and characters, but according to the logic of common sense and in the most ordinary language, designed to give them a familiar aspect.

102 A. Claveau, *Courrier franco-italien*, 7 May 1857, quoted in Flaubert, *Corr.*, P, vol. 2, p. 1372.

103 Albalat, *Gustave Flaubert et ses Amis*, p. 43.

104 C. Baudelaire, 'Madame Bovary' in *Charles Baudelaire as a Literary Critic*, p. 143. *Trans.*

105 Badesco, *La Génération poétique de 1860*, p. 204, n. 74.,

106 Albalat, *Gustave Flaubert et ses Amis*; Badesco, *La Génération poétique de 1860*. It is clear that history takes a place, and an important one, in the literary field: its efforts to become more 'veracious', more 'impartial', as they said in those days, did not preclude the will to also become more 'literary'. Critical judgements on different historians – Thiers, Mignet or Michelet – always take their style into account, and Michelet is congratulated for being 'a magician of style'.

107 In an article analysing in detail the controversy between the author of *Salammbô* and the archaeologist Froehner, and in particular everything revealed by Flaubert's response about the question of the status of literature with respect to science, Joseph Jurt shows that Flaubert seeks in science a stylistic ideal (precision) and a cognitive model (the ideal of impartiality) (J. Jurt, 'Le statut de la littérature face à la science', in *Écrire en France au XIXe siècle* (Montreal: Longueuil, 1989), pp. 175–92).

108 G. Flaubert, Letter to Louise Colet, 7 Oct. 1853, in *Corr.*, P, vol. 2, p. 450.

109 Bruneau, *Les Débuts littéraires de Gustave Flaubert*, pp. 112ff.

110 P. G. Castex (Flaubert, *L'Éducation sentimentale* (Paris: CDU, 1962)) compares the attitude of Rastignac in the Père-Lachaise cemetery (the famous challenge to the capital by the petit-bourgeois provincial on the rise: 'To us two now!') with the conduct of Frédéric who, in the same circumstances, limits himself to 'admiring the countryside while they made speeches', grows bored and who, in contrast to Rastignac's going to dine

with Mme de Nuncingen when the ceremony was over, omits seizing the chance represented for him by Mme Dambreuse.

111 G. Flaubert, Letter to Caroline Flaubert, 14 Oct. 1869, in *Corr.*, C, vol. 6, p. 82.

112 'This is exactly how we were in our youth; all men of our generation could find themselves in it' (G. Flaubert, Letter to Mlle Leroyer de Chantepie, 13 Dec. 1866, in *Corr.*, C, vol. 5, p. 256.

113 A close friend of Flaubert's (they travel together to the Orient in the course of which they seal a relationship that Maxime cultivates with care and Flaubert ignores), Maxime Du Camp becomes for him, little by little, a sort of ethical and aesthetic foil (he breaks off with him in 1852). In a sense, he is the exact antithesis of Flaubert: the one who, instead of making the field, is made by the forces of the field, who, while proving profoundly conservative in his own universe, always presents himself (and thinks of himself) as of the avant-garde in the political domain. Hence, governed by ambition, he thinks of nothing but social art and useful poetry; he celebrates steam and the locomotive, becomes director of a review and runs around the salons to 'promote himself'.

114 G. Flaubert, Letter to George Sand, Dec. 1875, in *The George Sand–Gustave Flaubert Letters*, p. 349.

115 Albert Thibaudet had already spotted the 'tendency to symmetries and to antitheses' that he called the 'binocular vision' of Flaubert: 'His manner of feeling and thinking consists of grasping, as if joined into a pair, contraries, extremes of the same genre, and of composing from these two extremes of a given genre, from these two flat images, an image in three-dimensional relief' (A. Thibaudet, *Gustave Flaubert*, p. 89, quoted in L. Cellier, 'L'Éducation sentimentale', *Archives des Lettres Modernes* 3, no. 56 (1964): 2–20). And Léon Cellier adds to the series of pairs I had found in my analysis of *Sentimental Education* the one formed by Sénécal and Deslauriers. He observes that Sénécal is to Deslauriers what Deslauriers is to Frédéric: Deslauriers protects Sénécal, harbours him, as Frédéric had protected him; Sénécal separates from him, comes back to him, uses him (reproducing the attitude which had been Frédéric's towards him); they both place themselves at the service of the dictatorship, one as prefect, the other as police agent.

116 This refusal to participate, to belong or be classified is constantly expressed, notably when Louise Colet tries to dragoon Flaubert into the creation of a review: 'But as to actually participating in anything at all in this world, no! no! a thousand times no! I no more want to be associated with a review, or to be a member of a society, a club, or an academy, than to be a city councillor or an officer in the national guard' (G. Flaubert, Letter to Louise Colet, 31 Mar. 1853, in *Letters*, vol. 1, p. 184; or again, to Louise Colet, 3 May 1853, in *Corr.*, P, vol. 2, p. 323).

117 Martino, *Le Roman réaliste sous le second Empire*, p. 25.

118 G. Flaubert, Letter to Louise Colet, 25 June 1853, in *Corr.*, P, vol. 2, p. 362; or again: 'The Ganges is not more poetic than the Bièvre, but the Bièvre is not more so than the Ganges. Let's be careful not to fall back, as in the era of classical tragedy, into the aristocracy of subjects and the preciosity of words. It will be found that coarse expressions have a fine effect on style, as formerly it was embellished for you with choice terms.

Rhetoric is *back again*, but it is still rhetoric' (G. Flaubert, Letter to J. K. Huysmans, Feb.–Mar. 1879, in *Corr.*, C, vol. 8, p. 225).

119 This is what was not understood by the realists Flaubert fights against, and since them, by all commentators who, as we see today with regard to official art, hold that an aesthetic revolution is necessarily associated, in its causes and effects, with a political revolution (in the ordinary sense of the term); they can thus fight over whether those who accomplish an aesthetic revolution inseparable from a political revolution which is specific (meaning that it is accomplished *inside* the field), such as the Impressionist revolution against the Académie and the Salon, are more or less progressive or conservative politically than those whose power they overthrow – with the use of a vocabulary of political origin, like the notion of the avant-garde, greatly contributing to this confusion. The solution to this false problem can no longer depend, then, only on the political dispositions of historians who are in a position to oppose each other only because they have in common an ignorance of the autonomy of the field and the specificity of the fights taking place there.

120 Letter to Louise Colet, 16 Jan. 1852, in *Letters*, vol. 1, p. 154.

121 Baudelaire, *Charles Baudelaire as a Literary Critic*, p. 162.

122 Ibid.

123 Ibid., pp. 167–8.

124 Quoted in B. Weinberg, *French Realism: the Critical Reaction*, p. 162.

125 Badesco, *La Génération poétique de 1860*, pp. 304–6.

126 G. Merlet, *Revue Européenne*, 15 June 1860, quoted by Weinberg, *French Realism: the Critical Reaction*, p. 133.

127 G. Flaubert, Letter to George Sand, 23–4 Jan. 1867, in *The George Sand–Gustave Flaubert Letters*, p. 51.

128 G. Flaubert, Letter to Ernest Feydeau, first fortnight of Oct. 1859, in *Selected Letters of Gustave Flaubert*, p. 202. Monet will evoke, in almost the same terms, this absolute detachment of the artist's eye: 'One day, finding myself at the bedside of a dead person who had been and was still dear to me, I surprised myself with eyes fixed on the tragic brow, in the act of mechanically searching for the sequence, the appropriation of shades of colour which death had put on that immobile face. Tones of blue, yellow, grey, what else? This is the state I had reached . . .' (G. Clemenceau, *Claude Monet, Les Nymphéas*, 1928, pp. 19–20, quoted by L. Venturi, *De Manet à Lautrec* (Paris: A. Michel, 1953), p. 77).

129 G. Flaubert, Letter to Louise Colet, 22 Apr. 1853, in *Corr.*, P, vol. 2, p. 313.

130 G. Flaubert, Letter to Louise Colet, 11 May 1853, in *Corr.*, P, vol. 2, p. 330.

131 G. Flaubert, Letter to George Sand, 4 Dec. 1872, in *The George Sand–Gustave Flaubert Letters*, p. 278.

132 Flaubert, who always refused to marry, takes the marriage of his close friends, Alfred Le Poitevin, Ernest Chevalier, as a submission to conformity, which arouses in him reprobation and sometimes sarcasm. Starting a family is engaging in a 'grocer's' existence (cf. M. Nadeau, *Gustave Flaubert écrivain* (Paris: Les Lettres Nouvelles/Maurice Nadeau, 1980), pp. 75–6).

133 G. Flaubert, Letter to George Sand, 28 Oct. 1872, in *The George Sand–Gustave Flaubert Letters*, p. 267.

134 Weinberg, *French Realism: the Critical Reaction*, p. 172 and also p. 164.
135 G. Flaubert, Letter to Huysmans, Feb.–Mar. 1879, in *Corr.*, C, vol. 8, p. 224.
136 Descharmes and Dumesnil, *Autour de Flaubert*, p. 48. The same analysis of the failure of the *Education* is found in his correspondence: 'Aesthetically speaking, *the falseness of perspective is lacking*. By devising the plan well, the plan disappears. Every work of art has to have a point, a summit, *form a pyramid*, or else the light should focus at one point. Nothing like that in life. But Art is not Nature!' (G. Flaubert, Letter to Mme Roger des Genettes, in *Corr.*, C, vol. 8, p. 309).

Chapter 2 The Emergence of a Dualist Structure

1 Cf. A. Viala, *Naissance de l'écrivain* (Paris: Minuit, 1984). One must be careful of reading clues of a sort of absolute beginning into the first signs of the institutionalization of the personage of the writer, such as the appearance of specific apparatuses of consecration. In effect, for a long time this process remains ambiguous, even contradictory, to the extent that artists must pay with a statutory dependence on the state for the recognition and official status that it accords them. And it is only at the end of the nineteenth century that the system of characteristics constitutive of an autonomous field is found assembled together (without ever excluding completely the possibility of regressions to heteronomy, such as the one starting today, thanks to a return to new forms of patronage, public or private, and because of the encroachment of journalism).
2 If, Courbet apart, painters have rarely invoked populist justifications, it is perhaps because they are not confronted by the problem of mass diffusion, since their products are unique and of a relatively high unit price, and since the only success they can know is worldly success, close in its social effects to success in the theatre.
3 On the prestige of science around 1880, see D. Mornet, *Histoire de la littérature* (Paris: Larousse, 1927), pp. 11–14.
4 Notably with writers linked to the Théâtre de l'Oeuvre such as Félix Fénéon, Louis Malaquin, Camille Mauclair, Henri de Régnier or Saint-Pol-Roux.
5 Cf. C. Charle, *La Crise littéraire à l'époque du naturalisme* (Paris: PENS, 1979), pp. 27–54.
6 Cf. R. Ponton, 'Naissance du roman psychologique: Capital culturel, capital social et stratégie littéraire à la fin du XIXe siècle', *Actes de la Recherche en Sciences Sociales*, no. 4 (July 1975): 66–81.
7 From 1876 to 1880, Zola defended a naturalist theatre under his byline as theatre critic (cf. É. Zola, *Le Naturalisme au théâtre*, in *Oeuvres complètes* (Paris: Bernouard, 1927–39), vol. 30; *Nos auteurs dramatiques*, in ibid., vol. 33).
8 J.-J. Roubine, *Théâtre et Mise en scène, 1880–1980* (Paris: PUF, 1980).
9 Cf. R. Ponton, *Le Champ littéraire en France de 1865 à 1905*, EHESS thesis, Paris, 1977, and J. Jurt, 'Synchronie littéraire et rapport de forces: Le champ poétique des années 80', *Oeuvres et Critiques* 12, no. 2 (1987): 19–33.
10 J. Huret, *Enquête sur l'évolution littéraire* (Paris: Charpentier, 1891); re-

edited with notes and preface by Daniel Grojnowski (Vanves: Thot, 1982), p. 158.

11 Florian-Parmentier, *La Littérature et l'Époque: Histoire de la littérature française de 1885 à nos jours* (Paris: Eugène Figuière, 1914), pp. 292–3.

12 Ibid.

13 Typical of the new regime established in the literary field, the survey of sixty-four writers (published in *L'Écho de Paris* between 3 March and 5 July 1891) spells out the new philosophy of history, that of perpetual outmoding, in the three questions posed: '1. Is naturalism sick? Is it dead? 2. Can it be saved? 3. By what will it be replaced?'

14 Notably Florian-Parmentier, *La Littérature et l'Époque*; J. Muller and G. Picard, *Les Tendances présentes de la littérature française* (1913); G. Le Carbonel and C. Vellay, *La littérature contemporaine* (Paris: Mercure de France, 1905).

15 Cf. R. Wohl, *The Generation of 1914* (Cambridge: Harvard University Press, 1979). The prototypical expression of this theory of generations, which has become one of the 'methods' admitted into literature (with the study of 'literary generations') and into politics (the 'political generations'), is the book by François Mentré, *Les Générations sociales* (Paris, 1920), that constructs the notion of 'social generation' as the 'spiritual unity' constituted around a 'collective stage'.

16 J. Huret, *Enquête sur l'évolution littéraire*, p. 160.

17 Cf. C. Charle, 'Champ littéraire et champ du pouvoir: Les écrivains et l'affaire Dreyfus', *Annales ESC*, no. 2 (Mar.–Apr. 1977): 240–64.

18 On the elaboration of the notion of 'reason of state' as a specific rationale, irreducible either to 'ethical reason' or to 'theological reason', see E. Thuau, *Raison d'État et Pensée politique à l'époque de Richelieu*, thesis, University of Paris, 1966.

19 We note in passing the complete irreality of the great tendential laws such as the one which maintains that intellectuals lose political power as they gain in autonomy: in fact, as we see, it is the very form of power that changes to the point that it does not make sense to compare the critical and negative power of a Zola or a Sartre with the dependent power of a Corneille or a Racine.

20 On the specific logic of the political field, see P. Bourdieu, 'La représentation politique: Éléments pour une théorie du champ politique', *Actes de la Recherche en Sciences Sociales*, nos 36–7 (1981): 3–24.

21 C. Baudelaire, quoted by A. Cassagne, *La Théorie de l'art pour l'art en France chez les derniers romantiques et les premiers réalistes* (Paris, 1906; Geneva: Slatkine Reprints, 1979), p. 81.

22 C. M. Leconte de Lisle, Letter to Louis Ménard, 7 Sept. 1849, quoted by P. Lidsky, *Les Écrivains contre la Commune* (Paris: Maspero, 1970).

23 Cf. É. Zola, *Mes Haines* (Paris: Fasquelle, 1923), pp. 322 and 330. And also, about Courbet and Proudhon: 'A canvas, for him, is a subject: what does it matter if it is painted in red or in green! [. . .] He comments, he makes the painting mean something; but not a word about the form.' Or again: 'My art, on the contrary, is a negation of society, an affirmation of the individual, outside all rules and all social necessities' (ibid., pp. 35–6, 39).

24 Here I rely on the research that I undertook regarding the *symbolic revolution* achieved by Manet; the first results (on the Académie and the academic eye) were presented in P. Bourdieu, 'L'Institutionnalisation de

l'anomie', *Les Cahiers du Musée National d'Art Moderne*, nos 19–20 (1987): 6–19. I wanted here to propose a *simplified schema* of the exchanges between painters and writers, which it is up to the reader to enrich and qualify.

25 C. Baudelaire, *Oeuvres complètes* (Paris: Gallimard, 1976), vol. 2, p. 312.

26 J. C. Sloane, *French Painting between the Past and the Present: Artists, Critics and Traditions, from 1848 to 1870* (Princeton: Princeton University Press, 1951), p. 77.

27 Zola, *Mes Haines*, p. 34.

28 C. Pissarro, *Lettre à son fils Lucien* (Paris: Albin Michel, 1950), p. 44.

29 D. Gamboni, *La Plume et le Pinceau* (Paris: Minuit, 1989).

30 A. Gide, *Les Faux-Monnayeurs* (Paris: Gallimard, coll. 'Folio', 1978), p. 30.

31 Analyses of essence and formal definitions can only in effect dissimulate the fact that the affirmation of the specificity of the 'literary' or the 'pictorial' and of its irreducibility to any other form of expression is inseparable from the affirmation of the autonomy of the field of production that it both presupposes and reinforces. Thus it is that, as we shall see, the analysis of the pure aesthetic disposition which is elicited by the most advanced forms of art is inseparable from the analysis of the process of autonomization of the field of production.

32 Zola, *Mes Haines*, pp. 68 and 81. The logic of the transfer to literature of categories invented with respect to painting can be clearly seen in the principle that he enunciates regarding Hugo and that undoubtedly defines the *modern* aesthetic, as radical subjectivism, against the absolutism of the academic aesthetic: 'There should be no literary dogma; each work is independent and demands to be judged on its own' (ibid., p. 98). Artistic activity is not governed by pre-existing rules and cannot be measured by any transcendent criterion. It produces its own rules and itself supplies the measure of its appreciation.

Chapter 3 The Market for Symbolic Goods

1 Even though the data on which they rely are dated – they were collected in 1976 – the analyses offered here remain fully valid for the present period (this is conveyed by indicating every now and again some current equivalents for defunct agents or institutions, or by presenting some indices of the changes undergone by those which have persisted). The changes occurring in the domain of the theatre, as in the world of galleries or publishing, do not seem to have had a profound effect on the structure revealed by empirical analyses undertaken in an earlier state of these universes. (In order to disentangle the constants and to grasp similarities, I have ignored or relegated to the background the *specific characteristics* of different fields, literary and artistic especially, in favour – in this *exploratory* work – of elucidating the principles of division which the different fields have in common and which shape both the functioning of the different fields of cultural production and the perception we have of them.)

2 The quotation marks will henceforth denote that we are speaking of the 'economy' in the restricted sense of economism.

3 The very unequal lengths of the duration of the production cycle make the

comparison of the annual reports of different publishing houses virtually meaningless: the idea of the actual situation of the enterprise given by the annual report becomes more and more inadequate the further away one goes from businesses with a rapid turnover, that is, with the growth of the share of long-cycle products. In effect, taking as an example the evaluation of stocks, one could take account of the *manufacturing cost*, the (uncertain) *sales price*, or the *price of the paper*. Each mode of evaluation may or may not be appropriate depending on whether you are looking at 'commercial' firms whose stock reverts very rapidly to the state of printed paper or at firms for whom it constitutes a capital that tends to increase steadily in value.

4 Pierre Bourdieu himself was with Éditions de Minuit before moving to Le Seuil. *Trans.*

5 At Laffont (and also at other publishers less completely subordinated to market logic, such as Albin Michel), translations of foreign books seem to obey a logic which is more properly literary.

6 The time that has elapsed since the date of the study allows us to see that Éditions de Minuit, attaining the status of consecrated institution (with, especially, Nobel Prizes for Samuel Beckett and Claude Simon), can try to accumulate for a while (according to a logic observed in the case of the Denise René gallery) both the prestige of avant-gardist asceticism and the profits of commercial success; a good example of this double game strategy is the novel by Jean Rouaud, crowned with the Goncourt Prize (cf. B. Simonot, 'Prix Goncourt: une liberté surveillée', *Liber, Revue Européenne des Livres*, no. 8 (Dec. 1991), p. 21).

7 The same logic makes the publisher/talent-spotter (of whom Maurice Nadeau is undoubtedly one of the most typical examples) always liable to see his 'discoveries' tempted away by better-placed or more consecrated publishers who offer their name, notoriety and influence on prize-giving juries, as well as greater publicity and higher royalties.

8 If one concentrates on some key points along a continuum (there are evidently intermediary positions between Durand-Ruel and Denise René), one observes that, in contrast to the Sonnabend gallery, which assembles young painters (the oldest is fifty) but ones who are already relatively recognized, and to the Durand-Ruel gallery, which has almost no painters who are not either dead or famous, the Denise René gallery occupies (in 1976) that particular point in the time–space of the artistic field where the profits of the avant-garde and of the consecrated – usually mutually exclusive – manage *for a while* to combine forces. It puts together a set of painters who are already highly consecrated (abstractionists) and an avant-garde group, or a group just behind the avant-garde (kinetic art), as if it had succeeded in escaping for a while the dialectic of distinction that carries schools into the past (in 1990 the Éditions de Minuit occupies a similar position in the publishing field).

9 It is well known that the head of one of the largest French publishing firms almost never reads any of the manuscripts he publishes and that his working day is taken up with purely managerial tasks (meetings of the production committee, meetings with lawyers, with executives of subsidiaries, etc.).

10 Robert Laffont acknowledges this dependence when he explains the declining ratio of translations to original books by citing, in addition to the rise

in the advances for translation rights, 'the determining influence of the media, particularly radio and television, in the promotion of a book'. 'The author's personality and eloquence are a weighty factor in these media's choice and hence in access to the public. In this respect, foreign authors, with the exception of certain celebrated figures, are naturally at a disadvantage' (*Vient de paraître*, information bulletin of Robert Laffont Publications, no. 167, Jan. 1977).

11 This is particularly clear with respect to the theatre, where the market for classics ('classical matinées' at the Comédie-Française) obeys very special laws by virtue of its dependence on the education system.

12 R. Kanters, in *L'Express*, 15–21 Jan. 1973.

13 P. Marcabru, in *France-Soir*, 12 Jan. 1973.

14 For an analysis of the temporal structure of gift exchanges, see P. Bourdieu, *Le Sens pratique* (Paris: Minuit, 1980), pp. 178–83; in English as *The Logic of Practice*, trans. Richard Nice (Stanford: Stanford University Press, 1980).

15 On trade within Indo-European societies as a 'nameless skill', unnameable, see É. Benveniste, *Le Vocabulaire des institutions européennes* (Paris: Minuit, 1969), pp. 139ff.; on the pre-capitalist economy as a denied 'economy', see P. Bourdieu, *Algérie 60* (Paris: Minuit, 1977), pp. 19–43.

16 B. Demory, 'Le livre à l'âge de l'industrie', *L'Expansion*, Oct. 1970, p. 110.

17 This is to bear in mind that there might be an arbitrariness in characterizing a gallery by the paintings it acquires – which may lead to conflating the painters that it has 'made' and that it 'holds' with those of whom it possesses only some works without having a monopoly on them. The ratio of these two categories of painters varies, moreover, according to the gallery, and would undoubtedly permit us to distinguish, separate from any judgement of value, between 'sales galleries' and movement galleries.

18 It goes without saying that, as has been shown elsewhere, the 'choice' between the risky investments required by the economy of denegation and the sure investments in worldly careers (for example, the choice between artist and art teacher of drawing, or between writer and writer-professor) is not independent of social origin and its influence on a readiness or otherwise to take risks according to the securities it guarantees.

19 Cf. *Peintres figuratifs contemporains* (Paris: Galerie Drouant, last quarter, 1967).

20 None of the writers associated with the Nouveau Roman has received the Prix Goncourt or the Prix de l'Académie, and, until the Nobel Prize was won by Claude Simon, they were only distinguished by the most 'intellectual' of these instances of consecration, the Prix Fénéon and, especially, the Prix Médicis (cf. J. Ricardou, *Le Nouveau Roman* (Paris: Seuil, 1973), pp. 31–3).

21 R. Laffont, *Éditeur* (Paris: Laffont, 1974), p. 302.

22 Fewer than 5 per cent of 'intellectuals with intellectual success' are also found among the authors of bestsellers (and they are all highly consecrated authors, such as Sartre, Simone de Beauvoir, etc.).

23 These are the Grandes Écoles, training grounds for various French elites, and the subject of Bourdieu's study *The State Nobility: Grandes Écoles and Esprit de Corps* (Cambridge: Polity, 1995). *Trans.*

24 Denise René, Presentation of the *Catalogue du premier salon international*

des galeries pilotes (Lausanne: Musée cantonal des Beaux-Arts, 1963), p. 150 (emphasis added).

25 To eliminate a number of discussions on a number of 'concepts' current in art, literature and even philosophy, it is enough to perceive that it is usually a question of *classificatory notions*, sometimes retranslated into words that seem more neutral and objective ('objectal literature' being used, for example, instead of 'Nouveau Roman', itself used for the 'set of novelists published by Éditions de Minuit'), which serve the primary function of identifying groups united in *practical* terms, such as painters assembled in a notable exhibition or a consecrated gallery, or writers published by the same publisher, or else of activating simple and loose characterizations (of the type 'Denise René means abstract geometric art', 'Alexandre Iolas means Max Ernst', or 'Arman is trashcans' and 'Christo is wrapping').

26 As an avant-garde painter says in response to a questionnaire on photography, tastes may be 'dated' with reference to what the taste of the avant-garde was at different periods: 'Photography is old-fashioned. – Why? – Because it is no longer in fashion; because it is linked to the conceptual framework of two or three years ago [. . .]. – Who would say the following: when I look at a painting, I am not interested in what it represents? – These days, the kind of people who have little knowledge about art. It is typical of someone who has no idea about art to say that. *Twenty years ago*, I'm not even sure that twenty years ago, abstract painters would have said that. It is very much the guy who doesn't know and who says: me, I am not an old fart, what matters is whether it looks pretty.'

27 Interview reprinted in *VH 101*, no. 3 (Autumn 1970): 55–61.

28 This is why it would be naive to think that the relation between proximity in time and inaccessibility of works disappears in the case where the logic of distinction induces a return (at the second degree) to an older mode of expression (as today with 'neo-Dadism', the 'new realism', or 'hyperrealism').

29 To stay within the limits of available information (furnished by the very fine study by Pierre Guetta, *Le Théâtre et son Public*, 2 vols, mimeo, Ministry of Cultural Affairs, Paris, 1966), we have cited only theatres considered in that study. Of 43 Parisian theatres surveyed in 1975 in the specialized papers (subsidized theatres excluded), 29 (or two-thirds) offer plays clearly belonging to boulevard theatre; 8 present classical or neutral (in the sense of 'unmarked') works; and 6, all located on the Left Bank, present plays that could be considered as belonging to the intellectual theatre. (Some of the theatres have disappeared since the period of the study, but others have arrived to occupy the equivalent positions in the space.)

30 Here, as throughout the text, 'bourgeois' is shorthand for 'occupants of dominant positions in the field of power' when it is employed as a noun or, when it is an adjective, as 'structurally linked to these positions'. In the same way, 'intellectual' signifies 'dominated positions in the field of power'.

31 Even though it adopted its 'modern' form in the last quarter of the nineteenth century with the appearance of a theatre of 'research', the structure observed in the space of theatre is not of recent origin. When Françoise Dorin, in the 1973 *Le Tournant*, one of the big boulevard hits, places an avant-garde author in the most typical vaudeville situations, she is only rediscovering (the same causes producing the same effects) the

strategies employed back in 1836 by Scribe, in *La Camaraderie*, against Delacroix, Hugo and Berlioz: then, to reassure the high-minded public in the face of the audacities and extravagances of the Romantics, he denounced the character Oscar Rigaut, famous for his mournful poetry, as a *bon vivant*, meaning a man like any other and in no position to attack the bourgeois as 'grocers' (cf. M. Descotes, *Le Public de théâtre et son Histoire* (Paris: PUF, 1964), p. 298). These attacks would not be as frequent as they are in the plays themselves (one thinks, for example, of the parody of the Nouveau Roman in *Haute-fidélité* by Michel Perri, 1963), and even more so among the critics, if they were not guaranteed to attract the complicity of the 'bourgeois' audience which feels itself defied or condemned by the 'intellectual theatre'.

32 A. de Baecque, 'Faillite du théâtre', *L'Expansion*, Dec. 1968.

33 The logic of the functioning of fields of production of cultural goods as fields of struggle favouring strategies of distinction means that the products of their functioning, whether creations of fashion or works of art, are predisposed to act differentially, as instruments of distinction.

34 J.-J. Gautier, *Théâtre d'aujourd'hui* (Paris: Julliard, 1972), pp. 25–6.

35 J.-J. Gautier, *Le Figaro*, 11 Dec. 1963.

36 The same position in a homologous structure engenders the same strategies: A. Drouant, the art dealer, denounces the 'leftist hacks, the pseudo-geniuses in whom false originality takes the place of talent' (Galerie Drouant, *Catalogue 1967*, p. 10).

37 L. Dandrel, *Le Monde*, 13 Jan. 1973. The 'Restoration' atmosphere conferring a certain lustre on (politically) conservative positions favours the return in force of regressive position-takings in the fields of cultural production – with, for example, the return to the 'story' in the domain of the novel or in a recent survey in *Le Figaro* which abandons the defensive strategies it was condemned to in earlier days and readily proposes a list of 'over-rated writers', which includes most of the cultural heroes of the avant-garde: Duras, Beauvoir, Simon, Bataille, etc. (cf. *Le Figaro*, 16 Mar. 1992).

38 'We are dealing with a sort of talent denigrated by the new cinema, which on this point imitates the new literature, a hostility easy to understand. When an art presupposes a determined talent, impostors feign to despise it, finding it too arduous; the mediocre ones choose the most accessible paths' (L. Chauvet, *Le Figaro*, 5 Dec. 1969).

39 'A film is not worthy of the new cinema if the term protest does not figure in the list of its themes. But when it is there, it doesn't mean a thing' (L. Chauvet, *Le Figaro*, 4 Dec. 1969).

40 'Would he not be pleased to pile up the crudest erotico-masochistic provocations heralded by the most emphatic lyrico-metaphysical professions of faith, and to see the Parisian pseudo-intelligentsia swoon before these sordid banalities?' (C.B., *Le Figaro*, 20–1 Dec. 1969).

41 'You are not informed just like that, these are things that you feel ... I didn't know exactly what I was doing. There are people putting stuff out but I didn't know it [...]. Information, you sort of feel it, you want to say things and you fall into it ... It's full of little what-nots, it is feelings and not messages' (avant-garde painter).

42 J.-J. Gautier, *Théâtre d'aujourd'hui*, p. 26. Publishers are also extremely conscious that the success of a book depends on who publishes it: they know how to recognize what is 'for them' and what is not, and they observe

that a book 'which was for them' (for example Gallimard) has done badly with another publisher (for example Laffont). The adjustment between the author and publisher, and then between the book and the public, is thus the result of a series of choices in which the brand image of the publisher always intervenes. It is as a function of this image that authors choose the publisher, who chooses them as a function of the idea that he himself has of his publishing house, and the image of the publisher also figures in the minds of readers when they choose an author, which undoubtedly helps to explain the failure of 'displaced' books. It is this mechanism which makes a publisher justly say: 'Each publisher is the best in its own category.'

43 The numerous works in which corporate owners, bankers, high-ranking civil servants or politicians expound their amateurish philosophy are just so many homages made to culture and to cultural production. Of one hundred people named in *Who's Who* who have produced literary works, more than a third are non-professionals (industrialists, 14 per cent, senior civil servants, 11 per cent, doctors, 7 per cent, etc.), and the share of part-time producers is still larger in the domain of political writings (45 per cent) and general writing (48 per cent).

44 It is not by chance that the role of symbolic security incumbent on the art dealer is particularly visible in the domain of painting, where the 'economic' investment of the buyer (the collector) is incomparably more substantial than in the area of literature or even theatre. Raymonde Moulin observes that 'the contract signed with an important gallery has a commercial value' and that the dealer is, in the eyes of amateurs, the 'guarantor of the quality of the works' (R. Moulin, *Le Marché de la peinture en France* (Paris: Minuit, 1967), p. 329).

45 According to the same logic, philosophical 'questioning' of philosophy will be accepted, even celebrated, by those same philosophers who would regard any sociological objectification of the philosophical institution as intolerable.

Part II Foundations of a Science of Works of Art

Chapter 1 Questions of Method

Epigraph: 'Research is the art of taking the next step.' *Trans.*

1 P. Bourdieu, 'Le couturier et sa griffe: contribution à une théorie de la magie', *Actes de la Recherche en Sciences Sociales*, no. 1 (1975): 7–36.

2 E. Auerbach, *Mimesis: the Representation of Reality in Western Literature*, trans. from German by Willard R. Trask (Princeton: Princeton University Press, 1953), p. 547.

3 Cf. E. Panofsky, *Architecture gothique et Pensée scolastique*, preceded by *L'Abbé Suger de Saint-Denis*, trans. and afterword by P. Bourdieu (Paris: Minuit, 1970), pp. 133–67. The Panofsky texts are separate in English: *Gothic Architecture and Scholasticism* (New York: Meridian, 1957) and *Abbot Suger on the Abbey Church of St. Denis and its Art Treasures*, ed., trans. and annotated by E. Panofsky, 2nd edn (Princeton: Princeton University Press, 1979).

4 It can be seen here that I was unequivocally opposed to the 'structuralist'

philosophy of the agent and of action. Those who would doubt this may refer to an article of mine which still seems to me today to be a rather accurate objectification of the state of the field of philosophy and the social sciences as it was in the 1960s. This article, by the very fact that it was written *in those same years* (cf. P. Bourdieu and J.-C. Passeron, 'Sociology and philosophy in France since 1945: death and resurrection of a philosophy without subject', *Social Research*, no. 34 (1967): 162–212), testifies to a freedom in relation to the constraints of the field which is not acknowledged in me, in their sociologism, by those who (at the price of many misinterpretations, some truncated or faked quotations and an amalgamation appropriate to the dirtiest tricks of political polemics) can speak of 'the thought of '68'.

5 It is clear that (at least when it is applied to contemporaries, that is to say, to competitors) the search for sources, which is never the best hermeneutic strategy in any case, is inspired not so much by a concern to understand the meaning of a contribution as to reduce it or destroy its originality (in the sense of information theory), while enabling the 'discoverer' of unknown sources to distinguish himself in a cunning way from the naive folk who, through lack of culture or blindness, allow themselves to be taken in by the illusion of the never-before-seen. The ruses of polemic reasoning are innumerable, and someone who (like so many other 'genealogists') would never have paid the least attention to the notion of habitus or to the uses made of it by Husserl, if I had not used it, rushes to exhume the Husserlian usages in order to reproach me, as if in passing, for having betrayed the magisterial thought – in which the same person wants nevertheless to discover a destructive anticipation.

6 This would be sufficient to distinguish the notion as it is employed here from soft and vague usages ('field of writing', 'theoretical field', etc.) which make it a noble surrogate for notions just as banal as those of 'domain' or 'order'.

7 Cf. J. Proust, *Questions de forme, logique et proposition analytique de Kant à Carnap* (Paris: Fayard, 1986).

8 E. Cassirer, *Substance et Fonction* (Paris: Minuit, 1977). One could equally well invoke Bachelard (especially *Le Rationalisme appliqué* (Paris: PUF, 1949), pp. 132–3, and *La Philosophie du non* (Paris: PUF, 1940), pp. 133–4), which proposes a 'structural' epistemology (G. Canguilhem, *Études d'histoire et de philosophie des sciences* (Paris: Vrin, 1968), p. 202), insisting notably on the formal, operational and structural character of modern mathematics. I have tried to separate out, in an article written during the peak of structuralism, the conditions for applying to the social sciences the relational mode of thought which has established itself in the natural sciences (cf. P. Bourdieu, 'Structuralism and theory of sociological knowledge', *Social Research* 25, no. 4 (1968): 681–706).

9 On the link between the Russian Formalists and Cassirer, one should consult P. Steiner, *Russian Formalism: a Metapoetics* (Ithaca: Cornell University Press, 1984), pp. 101–4.

10 P. Bourdieu, 'Champ intellectuel et projet créateur', *Les Temps Modernes*, no. 246 (1966): 865–906, translated as 'Intellectual field and creative project', *Social Science Information* 8, no. 2 (April 1969): 89–119.

11 Cf. P. Bourdieu, 'Une interprétation de la sociologie religieuse de Max Weber', *Archives Européennes de Sociologie* 12, no. 1 (1971): 3–21, see

'Legitimation and structural interests in Weber's sociology of religion', trans. C. Turner, in *Max Weber: Rationality and Modernity*, ed. S. Whimster and S. Lash (London: Allen and Unwin, 1981), pp. 119–316.

12 I have tried to separate out the general properties of fields – by taking the different analyses performed to a higher level of formalization – in the courses I gave at the Collège de France from 1983 to 1986 and which will be the subject of a later publication.

13 Thus, when it comes to analysing the social usages of language, it is the rupture with the abstract notion of 'situation' – itself introducing a rupture with the Saussurean or Chomskian model – which obliged me to think of the relations of linguistic exchange as so many markets defined in each case by the structure of the relations between the linguistic or cultural capitals of interlocutors and the groups to which they belonged.

14 I have tried to make a first step in this direction with the analysis of the market for the private home (cf. P. Bourdieu et al., 'L'économie de la maison', *Actes de la Recherche en Sciences Sociales*, nos 81–2 (1990): 2–96).

15 Here I could take the example of the study of the academic field, where the absolute necessity of situating this field within the field of power required a recourse to crude and obviously inadequate indicators; or the study of the episcopacy, where the structuring relation of bishops to theologians (and, more generally, to clerics) could not be grasped except in a very rough and qualitative manner; or the study, this one paradigmatic, of the field of institutions of higher education, where the concern to apprehend the field as a whole – as against the minutiae, both irreproachable and theoretically and empirically absurd, presented in monographs devoted to a single institution – leads to immense difficulties, sometimes practically insurmountable.

16 Those whom I might have thus injured ought to have read what I wrote at the end of *Distinction* regarding the perverse pleasures of 'lucid vision' (cf. P. Bourdieu, *Distinction: a Social Critique of the Judgement of Taste*, trans. Richard Nice (Cambridge: Harvard University Press, 1984), pp. 485–6.

17 I had given a first provisional presentation of the methodological principles of research on literary, artistic and philosophical fields which grew out of a seminar held at the École Normale Supérieure between the 1960s and the 1980s, in three complementary articles: 'Champ intellectuel et projet créateur', *Les Temps Modernes*, no. 246 (1966): 865–906; 'Champ du pouvoir, champ intellectuel et habitus de classe', *Scolies*, no. 1 (1971): 7–26; and 'Le marché des biens symboliques', *Année Sociologique*, no. 22 (1971): 49–126. I owe it to the eventual users of these labours to say that the first of these texts (translated in *Knowledge and Control: New Directions for the Sociology of Education*, ed. Michael F. Young (London: Collier and Macmillan, 1971), pp. 161–88) seems to me essential and yet outmoded. It advances central propositions concerning the genesis and structure of the field, and certain of the most recent developments of my work, since it prefigures everything about the pairs of oppositions functioning as matrices of common places and of topics. However, it contains two errors which the second article tries to correct: it tends to reduce the objective relations between positions to interactions between agents, and it omits to situate the field of cultural production within the field of power, so it lets slip the real principle of certain of its properties. As for the third

(translated as 'The market for symbolic goods', in *The Field of Cultural Production* (Cambridge: Polity Press; New York: Columbia University Press, both 1993)), it sets out, sometimes in a rather abrupt form, the principles which served as the basis for the work presented here and for a whole body of research conducted by others.

18 I will take up later the analysis of the belief, inherent in the scholarly point of view, which is accorded to cultural works and which is itself at the basis of the completely singular belief in the very content of these works, 'that voluntary and provisional suspension of disbelief that constitutes poetic faith', according to Coleridge, and which leads to the acceptance of the most extra-ordinary experiences (cf. Coleridge, *Biographia Literaria*, no. 2, p. 6, quoted by M. H. Abrams, *Doing Things with Texts: Essays in Criticism and Critical Theory* (New York and London: W. W. Norton, 1989), p. 108).

19 Cf. D. Gamboni, 'Méprises et mépris: éléments pour une étude de l'iconoclasme contemporain', *Actes de la Recherche en Sciences Sociales*, no. 49 (1983): 2–28.

20 R. Wellek and A. Warren, *Theory of Literature*, 2nd edn (New York: Harcourt, Brace, 1956), p. 75.

21 In ordinary language, a life is inseparably the set of events of an individual existence conceived as a story [*histoire*] and the telling of that story; it describes life as a path, a career, with its crossroads and dead-ends, or as a progress, a path that is made and that has to be made, a course, an accumulation, a voyage, a route, a linear and unidirectional displacement composed of a beginning ('a start in life'), several stages and then an end, in the double meaning of term and of goal ('he will make his way' signifies: he will succeed in life) – an end to the story.

22 An example encountered recently of this philosophy of biography: 'I attempt [. . .] to present his life (part of it, at first) as an *intelligible whole*, something capable of being seen as *a unity*, as *the development of just such a Daimon* as Goethe describes in a favourite poem of Wittgenstein's . . .' (B. McGuiness, *Wittgenstein: a Life*, vol. 1: *Young Ludwig, 1889–1921* (Berkeley: University of California Press, 1988), p. xi (emphasis added)).

23 J.-P. Sartre, 'La conscience de classe chez Flaubert', *Les Temps Modernes*, no. 240 (1966): 1921 (emphasis added).

24 Ibid., p. 1935.

25 Ibid., pp. 1945–50.

26 J.-P. Sartre, *Being and Nothingness: an Essay on Phenomenology*, trans. Hazel E. Barnes (New York: Philosophical Library, 1957), pp. 557–75, and esp. p. 562.

27 Cf. C. Becker, 'L'offensive naturaliste', in C. Duchet (ed.), *Histoire littéraire de la France*, vol. 5: *1848–1917* (Paris: Éditions Sociales, 1977), p. 252.

28 Undoubtedly, we needed to read with more care the small, youthful work where Sartre proposes a reinterpretation, or rather a radicalization, of the Cartesian theory of freedom: what is involved is neither more nor less than restoring to Man the radical freedom of creating eternal truths and values which Descartes had granted to God (J.-P. Sartre, *Descartes* (Geneva: Traits; Paris: Trois Collines, 1946), pp. 9–52).

29 An appendix (p. 209) contains an analysis of the position and the trajectory of Jean-Paul Sartre and furnishes the elements for understanding why and in what way he found himself predisposed to give an exemplary expression

to the defence of the myth of the uncreated creator (which has received so many other formulations throughout the history of philosophy).

30 An appendix to chapter 2 below (p. 278) contains an analysis of the ethical and political dispositions of the two major categories of conservative discourse in relation to the positions and the trajectories of those who produce them.

31 To pursue this method to its end, with its presumption of the existence of an intelligible relation between position-takings and positions in the field, it would be necessary to gather the sociological information necessary to understand how, in a determined state of a determined field, different analysts are distributed among different approaches, and why, among the different possible methods, they appropriate one rather than another. One might find some elements for creating such a relation in the analysis I offered of the debate between Roland Barthes and Raymond Picard (cf. P. Bourdieu, *Homo Academicus*, trans. Peter Collier (Cambridge: Polity; Stanford: Stanford University Press, 1988), and especially the postscript to the second French edition (Paris: Minuit, 1992)).

32 A defence of the New Criticism against the critiques that have been levelled at it (notably its esoteric aestheticism, its aristocratism, its ignorance of history, its scientific pretensions) may be found in R. Wellek, 'The new criticism: pro and contra', *Critical Inquiry* 4, no. 4 (1978): 611–24. One should also read the desperate and competent speech for the defence that the old theoretician of literature makes to those who, according to him, point to the 'end of art' and the 'death of literature' or of 'culture' – in random order, Marxists, semiologists (Roland Barthes saying that 'literature is constitutively reactionary'. . .), deconstructionists, etc., etc. (cf. R. Wellek, 'The attack on literature', *American Scholar* 42, no. 1 (1972–3): 27–42). There he gives a fair idea of the 'great fear' which the verbal terrorism ('language is fascist', etc.) of the *conservative revolutions* of the 1970s succeeded in arousing in the protected and privileged universe of the *American Scholar*, provoking, as a counterattack, the efforts at the *restoration* of culture (with Allan Bloom especially) to which we are subject today.

33 J. C. Ransom, *The World's Body* (New York and London: Scribner's, 1938).

34 P. Szondi, *Introduction à l'herméneutique littéraire* (Paris: Le Cerf, 1989); see in English, P. Szondi, *On Textual Understanding and Other Essays*, trans. Harvey Mendelsohn (Minneapolis: University of Minnesota Press, 1986).

35 P.-M. de Biasi, foreword to G. Flaubert, *Carnets de travail*, critical and genetic edition by P.-M. de Biasi (Paris: Balland, 1988), p. 7.

36 R. Debray-Genette, *Flaubert à l'oeuvre* (Paris: Flammarion, 1980).

37 P.-M. de Biasi, 'La critique génétique', in *Introduction aux méthodes critiques pour l'analyse littéraire* (Paris: Bordas, 1990), pp. 5–40; R. Debray-Genette, 'Esquisse de méthode', in *Essais de critique génétique* (Paris: Flammarion, 1979), pp. 23–67; C. Duchet, 'La différence génétique dans l'édition du texte flaubertien', in *Gustave Flaubert*, vol. 2 (Paris, 1986), pp. 193–206; T. Williams, *Flaubert, L'Éducation sentimentale, Les Scénarios* (Paris: José Corti, 1992); and especially the two collections, L. Hay (ed.), *Essais de critique génétique* (Paris, Flammarion, 1979), and A. Grésillon (ed.), *De la genèse du texte littéraire* (Tusson: Du Lérot, 1988).

38 P.-M. de Biasi, in Flaubert, *Carnets de travail*, pp. 83–4.

39 M. Foucault, 'Réponse au cercle d'épistémologie', *Cahiers pour l'analyse*, no. 9 (1968), pp. 9–40 (citations from pp. 40, 29, 37).

40 Only historical observation can determine in each case if there exists a privileged orientation of the transfers between fields and why; but everything permits us to suppose that it is neither a matter of relations of pure historical conditioning such as those which Burckhardt endeavoured to sketch in the *Reflections on History* (London: George Allen and Unwin, 1943) (with Islam an example of a culture conditioned by a religion, and Athens, the French Revolution, etc., as examples of the State conditioned by the culture, etc.), nor a matter of relations of pure logical determination. In every case, logical reasons and social causes are mixed together to make up that complex of necessities of different orders that is the basis of symbolic exchanges between different fields.

41 On the rampant Hegelianism in art history, see E. H. Gombrich, *In Search of Cultural History* (Oxford: Clarendon Press, 1969) and also, on the opposition to be overcome between Hegelianism and positivism, 'From the revival of letters to the reform of the arts', in *The Heritage of Apelles: Studies in the Art of the Renaissance, III* (Oxford: Phaidon Press, 1976), pp. 93–110.

42 *Kunstwollen*, that 'artistic will' belonging to the ensemble of works of a people and an epoch, and transcendent, as Panofsky shows, in relation to the individual will of a historically definable subject, was never very far, even in Alois Riegl, from that sort of autonomous force that a mystical history of art described (cf. E. Panofsky, 'The concept of *Kunstwollen*', in *Perspective as Symbolic Form*, trans. Christopher S. Wood (New York: Zone, 1991), and P. Bourdieu, 'Postface', in Panofsky, *Architecture gothique et Pensée scolastique*). In reality, it is always just the addition, performed by the retrospective gaze of the scholar, of innumerable *Künstler-Wollen* (or, if you want to be Nietzschean, *Künstler-Wille*) expressing the interests and the dispositions of individual artists.

43 It can be seen how interesting it is from this perspective to have studies of figures who have participated in a more or less 'creative' manner in several fields (such as Galileo, for example, studied from this very point of view by Panofsky), and have produced, according to the typically Leibnizian method of possible worlds, several realizations of the same habitus (just as, in the order of consumption, the different arts give rise to objectively systematic expressions, as 'counterparts' in Lewis's sense, of the same taste).

44 Cf. in particular C. J. Tynianov and R. Jakobson, 'The problem of literary and linguistic studies', in *The Theory of Literature: Texts of the Russian Formalists*, presented and trans. by T. Todorov (Paris: Seuil, 1965), pp. 138–9; F. V. Erlich, *Russian Formalism* (The Hague: Mouton, 1965); Steiner, *Russian Formalism*; F. W. Galan, *Historic Structures: the Prague School Project, 1928–1946* (Austin: University of Texas Press, 1984); P. Steiner (ed.), *The Prague School: Selected Writings, 1929–1946* (Austin: University of Texas Press, 1982); and finally I. Even-Zohar, 'Polysystem theory', *Poetics Today* 1, nos. 1–2 (1979): 287–310.

45 Cf. Steiner, *Russian Formalism*, esp. pp. 108–10, and also F. Jameson, who shows that 'Tynianov retains Saussure's basic model of change, in which the essential mechanisms at work are the ultimate abstractions of Identity and Difference' (F. Jameson, *The Prison-House of Language: a Critical Account of Structuralism and Russian Formalism* (Princeton: Princeton University Press, 1982), p. 96).

46 J. Tynianov, quoted by Steiner, *Russian Formalism*, p. 107.
47 On the ambiguity of the notion of *ustanovka*, see Steiner, ibid., esp. p. 124.
48 M. Faure, 'L'Époque 1900 et la résurgence du mythe de Cythère', *Le Mouvement Social*, no. 109 (1979): 15–34, at 25.
49 R. Ponton, *Le Champ littéraire en France de 1865 à 1905*, EHESS thesis, Paris, 1977, pp. 223–8.
50 P. Bayle, entry on 'Catius', in *Dictionnaire historique et critique*, 3rd edn (Rotterdam, 1720), p. 821, a, b, quoted by R. Koselleck, *Le Règne de la critique* (Paris: Minuit, 1979), p. 92.
51 Cf. H. S. Becker, 'Art as collective action', *American Sociological Review* 39, no. 6 (1974): 767–76; 'Art worlds and social types', *American Behavioral Scientist* 19, no. 6 (1976): 703–19.
52 I take up here once more the themes, and sometimes the terms, of an article written several years ago (cf. P. Bourdieu, 'Sartre', *London Review of Books* 2, no. 22 (20 Nov.–2 Dec. 1980): 11–12) without including all the textual references I allude to, referring the reader to the book by Anna Boschetti, *Sartre et 'Les Temps Modernes'* (Paris: Minuit, 1985), which sharpens and deepens through a systematic study of the field and the work the analysis I had only sketched.
53 This propensity to merge in the same logical class the 'bourgeois' and the 'people' is a constant of the vision of the social world of writers and artists, and more generally of intellectuals. One observes it especially in Flaubert.
54 A more complete understanding of the 'Sartre effect' would require an analysis of the social conditions of the appearance of the social demand for a prophecy for intellectuals: conjunctural conditions, such as the experiences of rupture, tragedy and anguish associated with the collective and individual crises produced by the war (the Occupation, the Resistance and the Liberation); structural conditions, such as the existence of an autonomous intellectual field endowed with its own institutions of reproduction (the École Normale Supérieure) and legitimation (journals, circles, publishers, academies, etc.), and hence able to sustain the independent existence of an 'aristocracy of intelligence' which was separated from power, if not against all powers, and able to impose and sanction a particular definition of intellectual accomplishment.

Chapter 2 The Author's Point of View

1 This chapter, which aims to draw out of the historical analyses of the literary field presented above some propositions which are valid for the whole set of fields of cultural production, tends to leave aside the specific logic of each of the specialized fields (religious, political, juridical, philosophical, scientific) that I have analysed elsewhere and which will be the subject of a forthcoming book.
2 Similarly, 'he' should be taken to refer to female agents as well, and vice versa. *Trans.*
3 The notion of field of power has been introduced (cf. P. Bourdieu, 'Champ de pouvoir, champ intellectuel et habitus de classe', *Scolies*, no. 1 (1971): 7–26) in order to account for the *effects* which may be observed at the very heart of the literary or artistic field and which are exercised, with different strengths, on the ensemble of writers or artists. The content of the notion

has been made gradually more precise, notably thanks to the research carried out on the Grandes Écoles and on the set of dominant positions to which they lead (cf. P. Bourdieu, *Noblesse d'État* (Paris: Minuit, 1989), pp. 375–6; in English as *The State Nobility* (Cambridge: Polity, 1995)).

4 Cf. M. Weber, *Ancient Judaism*, trans. Hans Gerth and Don Martindale (Glencoe: Free Press, 1952), pp. 278ff.

5 The status of 'social art', in this respect, is completely ambiguous: even if it refers artistic or literary production to external functions (for which the proponents of 'art for art's sake' do not fail to reproach it), it shares with 'art for art's sake' a radical challenge to worldly success and that 'bourgeois art' which recognizes it while looking down on the values of 'disinterestedness'.

6 It can be understood how by this logic, at least in certain sectors of the field of painting at certain times, the absence of any training and any scholarly consecration may appear as a form of glory.

7 P. Casanova, *Liber*, no. 9 (Mar. 1992): 15.

8 The form taken by the dependence of fields of cultural production with respect to economic and political powers undoubtedly very much depends on the real distance between the universes (which may be measured by objective indices such as the frequency of inter- and especially intragenerational movements from one to another, or by the social distance between the two populations, from the viewpoint of social origins, places of education and training, matrimonial and other alliances, etc.), and also on the distance between mutual representations (which may vary from the anti-intellectualism of Anglo-Saxon countries to the intellectual pretensions, equally threatening, of the French bourgeoisie).

9 As we see, autonomy does not come down to the independence tolerated by those in power: a high degree of freedom may be left to the world of art without being automatically marked by assertions of autonomy (one thinks for example of English painters of the nineteenth century, of whom one could say that the reason they did not precipitate the same ruptures as French painters of the time was because, unlike the latter, they were not subject to the tyrannical constraints of an all-powerful academy); conversely, a high degree of constraint and control – through strict censorship, for example – does not necessarily lead to the disappearance of any assertion of autonomy so long as the collective capital of specific traditions, original institutions (clubs, journals, etc.) and their own models is sufficiently great.

10 On this question which has been often studied, see H. Rosenberg, *Bureaucracy and Aristocracy: the Prussian Experience 1660–1815* (Cambridge: Harvard University Press, 1958), esp. p. 24; J. R. Gillis, *The Prussian Bureaucracy in Crisis, 1840–1860: Origins of an Administrative Ethos* (Stanford: Stanford University Press, 1971); and especially R. Berdahl, *The Politics of the Prussian Nobility: the Development of a Conservative Ideology 1770–1848* (Princeton: Princeton University Press, 1989).

11 Cf. P. Bourdieu and L. Boltanski, 'La production de l'idéologie dominante', *Actes de la Recherche en Sciences Sociales*, nos. 2–3 (1975): 4–31.

12 See the Appendix, p. 278.

13 The same goes, of course, for studies trying to establish the '*best of*' lists of writers or artists when they predetermine the classification by determining the population worthy of participating in its establishment (cf. P. Bourdieu,

Homo Academicus, trans. P. Collier (Cambridge: Polity; Stanford: Stanford University Press, 1988), appendix 3, 'The hit parade of French intellectuals, or who will be the judge of the legitimacy of judges?').

14 F. Haskell, *Rediscoveries in Art: Some Aspects of Taste, Fashion and Collection in England and France* (Ithaca, NY: Cornell University Press, 1976).

15 There is an example of such an analysis, for the American philosophical pantheon, in the study by B. Kuklick, 'Seven thinkers and how they grew: Descartes, Spinoza, Leibniz; Locke, Berkeley, Hume; Kant', in R. Rorty, J. B. Schneewind and Q. Skinner (eds), *Philosophy in History: Essays on the Historiography of Philosophy* (Cambridge: Cambridge University Press, 1984), pp. 125–39.

16 Thus little more than a third of the writers in the sample studied by Rémy Ponton had had higher education, whether successfully completed or not (cf. R. Ponton, *Le Champ littéraire en France de 1865 à 1905*, EHESS thesis, Paris, 1977, p. 43). For a comparison in this respect between the literary field and other fields, see C. Charle, 'Situation du champ littéraire', *Littérature*, no. 44 (1981): 8–20.

17 Cf. S. Miceli, 'Division de travail entres les sexes et division du travail de domination: une étude clinique des Anatoliens au Brésil', *Actes de la Recherche en Sciences Sociales*, nos 5–6 (1975): 162–82.

18 V. Pareto, *Manual of Political Economy*, trans. Ann S. Schwier (New York: A. M. Kelley, 1971).

19 It is only exceptionally, especially in moments of crisis, that certain agents may develop a conscious and explicit representation of the game as a game, one which destroys the investment in the game, the *illusio*, by making it appear what it always objectively is (to an observer foreign to the game, indifferent to it) – that is, a historical fiction or, in Durkheim's terms, a 'well-founded illusion'.

20 In order to explain the explosion in the prices of paintings since the end of the nineteenth century, Robert Hughes invokes (besides the purely economic factors such as the much greater liquidity of fortunes) a numerical growth in all professions engaged in the artistic field, and the associated differentiation in the operations which aim to constitute a work of art as a sacred treasure (cf. R. Hughes, 'On art and money', *New York Review of Books* 21, no. 19 (6 Dec. 1984): 20–7).

21 We shall see that the constitution of the aesthetic gaze as the 'pure' gaze, capable of considering the work in itself and for itself, meaning as 'finality without end', is linked to the establishment of the work of art as object of contemplation, with the creation of private and then public art galleries and museums and with the parallel development of a body of professionals responsible for conserving the work of art, materially and symbolically; and it is also linked to the progressive invention of the 'artist' and of the representation of artistic production as 'creation' purified of all determination and all social function.

22 There is nothing to be gained by replacing the notion of literary field with that of 'institution': besides the fact that it risks suggesting, by its Durkheimian connotations, a consensual image of a very conflictual universe, this notion causes one of the most significant properties of the literary field to disappear – its *weak degree of institutionalization*. This is seen, among other indices, in the total absence of arbitrage and legal or institutional

guarantee in conflicts of priority or authority and, more generally, in the struggles for the defence or conquest of dominant positions. Thus, in the conflicts between Breton and Tzara, the former, during the 'Congress for the determination of directives and the defence of the modern spirit' which he organized, has no other recourse than to anticipate the intervention of the police in case of disruption, and during the final assault on Tzara on the occasion of the soirée at the Coeur à Barbe, he resorts to insults and blows (he breaks the arm of Pierre de Massot with a blow of his cane), while Tzara appeals to the police (cf. J.-P. Bertrand, J. Dubois and P. Durand, 'Approche institutionnelle du premier surréalisme, 1919–1924', *Pratiques*, no. 38 (1983): 27–53).

23 Cf. especially R. Darnton, 'Policing writers in Paris circa 1750', *Representations*, no. 5 (1984): 1–32.

24 As we have seen, that sociology which links the characteristics of works directly to the social origins of authors (cf. for example R. Escarpit, *Sociologie de la littérature* (Paris: PUF, 1958)) or to groups to whom they were addressed, either real (patrons) or supposed (cf. for example F. Antal, *Florentine Painting and its Social Background* (Cambridge: Harvard University Press, 1986), or L. Goldmann, *Le Dieu caché* (Paris: Gallimard, 1956)), conceive of the relationship between the social world and cultural works in terms of the logic of *reflection*, and ignore the *refraction* exercised by the field of cultural production.

25 While an event such as the Black Death of the summer of 1348 determines the general direction of a global change in the themes of painting (the image of Christ, relations among figures, exaltation of the Church, etc.), this direction is reinterpreted and translated as a function of specific traditions, associated with local particularities of the field in the course of being established, as is shown by the fact that they appear in different forms in Florence and Sienna (cf. M. Meiss, *Painting in Florence and Sienna after the Black Death* (Princeton: Princeton University Press, 1951)).

26 Cf. D. Lewis, 'Counterpart theory and quantified modal logic', *Journal of Philosophy*, no. 5 (1968): 114–15, and J. C. Pariente, 'Le nom propre et la prédication dans les langues naturelles', *Langages*, no. 66 (1982): 37–65.

27 This holds true for all fields of cultural production, and in particular the scientific field, where the confrontation of 'programmes of scientific research', as Lakatos says, exercises a powerful structuring effect on scientific representations and practices.

28 The example of the 'Incohérents' perfectly illustrates this mechanism: they invented loads of things which conceptual painters reinvented after them, but, not being taken seriously, they could not take themselves seriously and so, by the same token, their inventions passed unnoticed, including in their own eyes. Cf. D. Grojnowski, 'Une avant-garde sans avancée: les "Arts incohérents", 1882–1889', *Actes de la Recherche en Sciences Sociales*, no. 40 (1981): 73–86.

29 To 'feel' what is represented by these historical inventions which have now become familiar – for example, the 'salon des refusés', the 'vernissage', the 'pétition' and so on – one must think of them by analogy with a phenomenon like the introduction of the word *jogging* and the corresponding practice, which means that a figure in brightly coloured shorts, T-shirt and cap who runs on sidewalks, through passers-by (and who, ten years

earlier, would have been regarded as eccentric, if not crazy) now passes almost *unnoticed*.

30 In using the term *framing* to make myself understood, I risk evoking in the reader's mind Goffman's notion of *frame*, an ahistoric concept I wish to dissociate myself from: where Goffman sees fundamental structuring alternatives, we should instead see historical structures stemming from a social world which is situated and timebound.

31 It is on this basis of common premises that the *reading contract* is established between the sender and receiver. In denouncing this contract, those responsible for the great cultural revolutions undermine ordinary readers in their *mental integrity*, in the vital principles of their vision of the natural and social world.

32 This is what one of the Symbolist poets questioned by Huret spells out: 'In every case, I consider the worst Symbolist poet as far superior to any of the writers under the naturalist regimen' (J. Huret, *Enquête sur l'évolution littéraire* (Paris: Charpentier, 1891), re-edited with notes and preface by Daniel Grojnowski (Vanves: Thot, 1982), p. 329). And another, Moréas: 'A poem by Ronsard or Hugo is pure art; a novel, whether by Stendhal or Balzac, is qualified art. I like our psychologists [authors like Anatole France, Paul Bourget or Maurice Barrès who belong to the current called 'psychological novel'] very much, but they must stay in their place, that is, beneath the poets' (ibid., p. 92). Another example, less glaring, but nearer to the experience which really guides choices: 'At fifteen, nature tells a young man if he is a poet or if he must be content simply with prose . . .' (J. Huret, ibid., p. 299, emphasis added). We see the significance, for someone who has strongly internalized these hierarchies, of the passage from poetry to the novel. (The division into separate castes by absolute boundaries oblivious to real continuities and overlappings has the same results everywhere – for example, in the relations between disciplines, philosophy and the social sciences, pure sciences and applied sciences, and so on – including *certitudo sui* and a refusal to lower oneself, automatic promotion or devaluation, and so forth.)

33 A. Cassagne, *La Théorie de l'art pour l'art en France chez les derniers romantiques et les premiers réalistes* (Paris, 1906; Geneva: Slatkine Reprints, 1979), pp. 75ff. It would be worth reproducing entire pages where A. Cassagne evokes the juvenile enthusiasms of Maxime Du Camp and Renan, Flaubert and Baudelaire or Fromentin.

34 E. and J. de Goncourt, *Manette Salomon* (Paris: UGE, coll. '10/18', 1979), p. 32.

35 It is necessary to recall here the whole analysis (cf. part I, chapter 2) of the logic according to which artistic movements temporalize themselves, and which furnishes the *model of change* as observed in other fields.

36 Cf. Bertrand, Dubois and Durand, 'Approche institutionnelle du premier surréalisme, 1919–1924'.

37 Cf. J. Cohen, *Structure du langage poétique* (Paris: Flammarion, 1966). One notes in passing that the logic described here dooms all those false analyses of essence which try to extract transhistoric definitions of genres whose nominal constancy disguises the fact that they continually construct themselves by a rupture with their own definition in a previous state.

38 'My thinking, despite the ever greater sales of the novel, is that the novel is a worn-out and hackneyed genre which has said everything it had to say, a

genre in which I have done everything to kill the novelistic, to turn it into a sort of auto-biography of people who do not have a story' (E. de Goncourt, in Huret, *Enquête sur l'évolution littéraire*, p. 155).

39 This passage from the preface to *Chérie* reminds us that the rejection of the novelistic is inseparable from an effort to ennoble the genre, which can be understood with reference to the position of the novel and novelists in the field (and notably in relation to poetry), and to the link between this inferior genre and a doubly inferior public (at least in the minds of writers), since it is 'feminine' and 'popular' and/or 'provincial'. Obviously, we cannot see this as a simple effect of the concern for ennoblement, since that may lead novelists in a completely different direction – with Bourget and the psychological novel for example, that is, towards ennobling evocations, thanks above all to an effort of composition (cf. P. Bourget, 'Note sur le roman français en 1921', in *Nouvelles Pages de critique et de doctrine*, vol. 1 (Paris: Plon, 1922), pp. 126ff.), whether of locations, milieux or characters, or to an evocation of sentiments which are socially noble.

40 When the history and the theory of literature become part of literary production to such an extent, it is understandable why exchanges of roles are so frequent: between critics and writers, between theoreticians (or historians) of literature and littérateurs (and, at least in France, between film-makers and film critics).

41 Cf. R. Lourau, 'Le manifeste Dada du 22 mars 1918: essai d'analyse institutionnelle', *Le Siècle Éclaté* 1 (1974): 9–30. Another more common effect of this closing in upon itself is the sort of collective narcissism affecting intellectual groups, from Saint-Germain-des-Prés to Greenwich Village (and often described in the numerous books in which they dramatize their own existence), inclining them to turn a complacent gaze on themselves, with even an appearance of self-critical lucidity which is one of the major obstacles to scientific objectification.

42 R. Leibowitz, *Schoenberg et son École* (Paris: J.-B. Janin, 1947), p. 78.

43 Ibid., pp. 87–8.

44 R. Daval and G.-T. Guilbaud, *Le Raisonnement mathématique* (Paris: PUF, 1945), p. 18.

45 The same is true of Brisset, the 'naive' philosopher, whom his discoverers André Breton and Marcel Duchamp tried in vain to provide with a biography: 'His whole life is unknown to us, except for the date of one lecture (1891 in Angers), another at a scholarly society (3 June 1906) and seven other key points: seven books signed by a certain Jean-Pierre Brisset. No descendants or known heirs, despite active research undertaken by the Surrealists (Marcel Duchamp especially); uncertain birth and death dates; no trace of him among publishers ...' (jacket notes for *La Grammaire logique*, followed by *La Science de Dieu* (Paris: Tchou, 1970)).

46 On the frequently cruel treatment that patented artists and writers inflicted on le Douanier Rousseau, one may consult R. Shattuck, *The Banquet Years: the Origins of the Avant-Garde in France, 1885 to World War I*, rev. edn (New York: Vintage, 1968), pp. 45–112, and especially the pages devoted to 'Rousseau's banquet' (pp. 66–71) where we see the painter-object, turned into a toy of mystification, giving in to the game with whole-hearted submission (going as far as to withstand for a while drops of hot wax falling from one of the lanterns placed above him); but without

according the mockery and farces of his 'friends' an adherence quite as 'naive' as they might have thought, as some observations by Fernande Olivier bear witness: 'So his face turned purple the minute he was *thwarted or bothered. He generally acquiesced to everything people told him, but one had the feeling that he held back and did not dare say what he thought'* (p. 61). For other accounts of the banquet, see J. Siegel, *Bohemian Paris, Culture, Politics and Boundaries of Bourgeois Life 1830–1930* (New York: Viking Penguin, 1986), p. 354.

47 Submission to the most academic norms and conventions is a constant in works – published or not, public or private (I am thinking of love letters) – of members of the working class. Thus, even though from the end of the nineteenth century on the break with the mass public has been almost total – it is one of the sectors where many publications are paid for by the author – poetry today still incarnates the idea which the least cultivated of consumers have of literature (no doubt under the influence of primary school, which tends to identify literary initiation with learning poetry). As can be verified by an analysis of a writer's Who's Who (*L'Annuaire national des lettres*, for example), the members of the working class and the petit-bourgeoisie who embark on writing have (almost without exception) too high an idea of literature to write 'realist' novels; and, in fact, their production consists essentially of poetry – very conventional in form – and secondarily of historical studies.

48 On all these points, see D. Vallier, *Tout l'Oeuvre peint du Douanier Rousseau* (Paris: Flammarion, 1970).

49 One recognizes here all the traits of the 'popular aesthetic' expressed in photography (cf. P. Bourdieu, *Photography: a Middle-Brow Art*, trans. Shaun Whiteside (Cambridge: Polity; Stanford: Stanford University Press, 1990)).

50 A. Rimbaud, *Complete Works*, trans. Paul Schmidt (New York: Harper and Row, 1967), p. 204.

51 The canonization of outsider art found its limit in the fact that, in contrast to naive art, its producers could not be constituted as artists.

52 Vallier, *Tout l'Oeuvre peint du Douanier Rousseau*, p. 5.

53 Cf. M. Thevoz, *L'Art brut* (Paris: Skira, 1980); R. Cardinal, *Outsider Art* (New York: Praeger, 1972).

54 W. S. Rubin, *Art Dada et surréaliste*, French translation by R. Revault d'Allones (Paris: Seghers, n.d.), p. 22.

55 The increasingly marked historicization of aesthetic judgement has been observed (cf. R. Klein, *La Forme et l'Intelligible* (Paris: Gallimard,1970), pp. 378–9, and 408–9), but without relating it to the logic of the functioning of a field which has achieved a high degree of autonomy and to its specific historicity.

56 Cf. C. Charle, *La Crise littéraire à l'époque du naturalisme* (Paris: PENS, 1979), pp. 181–2.

57 Cf. E. B. Henning, 'Patronage and style in the arts: a suggestion concerning their relations', *Journal of Aesthetics and Art Criticism* 18, no. 4, pp. 464–71.

58 It goes without saying that I do not constitute as a transhistorical essence (as do so many authors who put Proust, Marinetti, Joyce, Tzara, Woolf, Breton and Beckett into the same net) a notion which, like that of the avant-garde, is *essentially relational* (in the same way as conservatism and

progressivism are), and is definable only at the level of a field at a determined moment. That said, the dream of reconciling political vanguard-ism and avant-gardism in matters of art and the art of living in a sort of summation of all revolutions – social, sexual, artistic – is undoubtedly a constant of literary and artistic avant-gardes. But this ever-recurring utopia, which undoubtedly had its Golden Age before the First World War, keeps running up against evidence of the practical difficulty of overcoming, other than in the ostentatious impostures of. *radical chic*, the structural gap (despite the homology) between 'advanced' positions in the political field and those in the artistic field and, by the same token, the discrepancy, even the contradiction, between aesthetic refinement and political progressivism (cf. for example the history of the New York avant-garde sketched in relation to *Partisan Review* in the book by James Burkhart Gilbert, *Writers and Partisans: a History of Literary Radicalism in America* (New York: John Wiley, 1968), or the ferocious description of radical chic in the book by Tom Wolfe, *Radical Chic and Mau-Mauing the Flak-Catchers* (New York: Farrar, Straus and Giroux, 1970)).

59 Among the factors determining the transformation of demand, one must also take into account the global rise in the level of education (or the increase in the time spent in school) which acts independently of the preceding factors, and notably through the intermediary of the effect of statutory assignment: the bearer of a certain diploma owes it to himself – 'noblesse oblige' – to carry out practices inscribed in the social definition (the status) assigned him by this title.

60 A. Anglès, *André Gide et le Premier Groupe de la 'Nouvelle Revue française': la formation d'un groupe et les années d'apprentissage, 1890–1910* (Paris: Gallimard, 1978), p. 18 (emphasis added).

61 F. Bourdon, *La Haute Parfumerie française,* mimeo, Paris, 1970, p. 95.

62 Although it has to be admitted that the slow process which made possible the *emergence* of different fields of cultural production and the full social recognition of corresponding social figures (the painter, the writer, the scholar, etc.) reached its culmination only at the end of the nineteenth century, there is no doubt that one could push back its first manifestations as far as one likes, even to the moment when cultural producers first appeared, fighting (almost by definition) to have their independence and particular dignity be acknowledged. Among the innumerable studies which add to the description and analysis of this slow movement of autonomiza-tion, in relation to the aristocracy and the Church especially, a special place must be reserved for the articles collected in the *Storia dell'arte italiana* (Turin: Einaudi, 1979), and a very fine book by Francis Haskell, *Patrons and Painters: a Study in the Relation Between Italian Art and Society in the Age of the Baroque* (London: Chatto and Windus, 1963). Without explicitly taking on such a project, Francis Haskell describes in the most rigorous manner the progressive construction of an artistic field obeying its own norms, and the appearance of a socially distinct category of pro-fessional artists, who are less and less inclined to recognize any rules other than those of the specific tradition they have received from their prede-cessors, and more and more capable of freeing their production from all external servitude, whether to the moral censorships and the aesthetic programmes of a church concerned with proselytism or to the academic controls and commands of political powers – and who are especially

concerned to assert and to gain acceptance for special criteria of evaluation for their products.

63 Ponton, *Le Champ littéraire*, pp. 69–70.

64 An example of this can be found in the case of Anatole France who acquired social capital and a familiarity with the world of letters from the position of his father, a Parisian secondhand bookseller, and this compensated for his weak economic and cultural capital.

65 Ponton, *Le Champ littéraire*, p. 57, and J. Cladel, *La Vie de Léon Cladel*, followed by *Léon Cladel en Belgique*, ed. E. Picard (Paris: Lemerre, 1905).

66 P. Vernois, 'La fin de la pastorale', in C. Duchet (ed.), *Histoire littéraire de la France*, vol. 5: *1848–1917* (Paris: Éditions Sociales, 1977), p. 272.

67 L. Cladel, quoted by Vernois, ibid.

68 L. Cladel, quoted by Ponton, *Le Champ littéraire*, p. 98. To measure how much the regionalist novel, paradigmatic expression of one form of populist intention, owes to the fact that it is the product of a negative vocation, linked to relegation or disillusionment, it would be necessary to compare those who ended up with the populist novel after this kind of trajectory with those who are exceptions, like Eugène Le Roy, a minor Périgord official coming to Paris, author of *Moulin du Frau* (1895), *Jacquou le croquant* (1899), etc., and especially with Émile Guillaumin, a tenant farmer from the Bourbon region, author of *La Vie d'un simple* (1804).

69 M. Schapiro, 'Courbet et l'imagerie populaire', in *Style, Artiste et Société* (Paris: Gallimard, 1982), p. 293 (emphasis added).

70 Ibid., p. 299. 'Just think,' wrote Champfleury to his mother in 1850, 'that with a natural wit which could have made me a humorous vaudeville writer, I aimed at something higher' (quoted by P. Martino, *Le Roman réaliste sous le second Empire* (Paris: Hachette, 1913), p. 129). We know that after a forced detour Champfleury ends up writing comedy in the style of Paul de Kock (see, for example, *Les Enfants du professeur Turck ou Le secret de M. Ladureau*).

71 Cf. Schapiro, 'Courbet et l'imagerie populaire', pp. 315ff. Hussonnet in *Sentimental Education* follows a very similar path.

72 Among the determinants of dispositions one must take into account, besides family position which is defined synchronically and diachronically (a propensity), is the position (older, younger) within the family itself as a field.

73 Realism defines itself fundamentally, with Courbet, by the desire to depict 'the vulgar and the modern'. Champfleury claims for the artist the right to represent the contemporary world with truthfulness (cf. Martino, *Le Roman réaliste*, pp. 72–8).

74 B. Dort, in Duchet (ed.), *Histoire littéraire de la France*, p. 617.

75 Ibid., p. 621. We see how these qualifications attributed to Lugné-Poe's activity characterize the relatively 'invariant' tendencies of a privileged habitus.

76 Cassagne, *La Théorie de l'art pour l'art*, pp. 103–34.

77 The solidarities which form within artistic groups between the most endowed and the most deprived are one of the means which permit certain poor artists to survive despite the absence of resources offered by the market.

78 See, among other case studies, M. Rogers, 'The Batignolles group: creators of Impressionism', *Autonomous Groups* 14, nos 3–4 (1959), reprinted in M. C. Albrecht, J. H. Barnett and M. Griff (eds), *The Sociology of Art and Literature* (New York: Praeger, 1970), pp. 194–220.

79 'The Decadents did not want to make a *tabula rasa* of the past. They advocated indispensable reforms, carried out with *method* and *prudence*. The Symbolists, on the contrary, wanted to *keep none* of our old customs and strove for the creation of a totally new mode of expression' (E. Reynaud, *La Mêlée symboliste I* (Paris: La Renaissance du Livre, 1918), p. 118, quoted by J. Jurt, *Symbolistes et Décadents, deux groupes littéraires parallèles*, mimeo, 1982, p. 12, emphasis added). We know the affinity which linked the representatives of the young poetry, the Décadents more than the Symbolists, to the anarchists, from whom they drew encouragement in their struggle against rules and masters, against the market and commercial literature. Verlaine published in *Le Décadent* a 'Ballade en l'honneur de Louise Michel' and Laurent Tailhade devoted a study to her under the title 'La grande sœur des pauvres' (cf. J. Jurt, 'Décadence et poésie: à propos d'un poème de Laurent Tailhade', *Französisch Heute*, no. 4 (1984): 371–82).

80 Cf. Ponton, *Le Champ littéraire*, pp. 248–9. The evolution of the Surrealist group towards a greater social homogeneity (by the elimination or estrangement of extremes) obeys the same logic (cf. Bertrand, Dubois and Durand, 'Approche institutionnelle du premier surréalisme, 1919–1924'). Another observation: a more elevated social recruitment occurs when the group achieves consecration.

81 E. and J. Goncourt, *Journal*, quoted by Cassagne, *La Théorie de l'art pour l'art*, p. 308.

82 Cf. P. Lidsky, *Les Écrivains contre la Commune* (Paris: Maspero, 1970), pp. 26–7.

83 Cf. A. M. Thiesse, 'Les infortunes littéraires: carrières des romanciers populaires à la Belle Époque', *Actes de la Recherche en Sciences Sociales*, no. 60 (1985): 31–46.

84 Cf. Ponton, *Le Champ littéraire*, pp. 80–2.

85 See among others, K. Popper, *Objective Knowledge: an Evolutionary Approach* (Oxford: Oxford University Press, 1972), esp. ch. 3.

86 Cf. Anglès, *André Gide et le Premier Groupe de la 'Nouvelle Revue française'*, pp. 163–5.

87 Cf. ibid., pp. 334–9.

88 S. Mallarmé, 'La musique et les lettres', in *Oeuvres complètes*, ed. H. Mondor and G. Jean-Aubry (Paris: Gallimard, coll. 'Pléiade', 1970), p. 647.

89 '[I am] . . . reminded of certain orchestral phrasings in which we hear, first, a withdrawal to the shades, swirls and uneasy hesitation, and then suddenly the bursting, leaping, multiple ecstasy of Brilliance, like the approaching radiance of a sunrise . . .' (Mallarmé, 'Music and letters', in *Mallarmé: Selected Prose Poems, Essays and Letters*, trans. Bradford Cook (Baltimore: Johns Hopkins University Press, 1956), p. 49; 'Grands faits divers', in *Oeuvres complètes*, p. 402).

90 Mallarmé, *Oeuvres complètes*, p. 400.

91 Ibid., p. 645.

92 Mallarmé, 'Music and Letters', p. 46.

93 Mallarmé, *Oeuvres complètes*, p. 405.

94 Ibid., pp. 573–4.

95 Ibid., p. 647.

96 Ibid., p. 655.

97 Such as 'the most inane sunset' (ibid., p. 574).
98 By an abstraction or, better, an extraction of their essence – cf. 'Le Ten O'Clock de M. Whistler' (ibid., pp. 574–5).
99 Mallarmé, *Mallarmé: Selected Prose Poems*, p. 133.
100 Mallarmé, *Oeuvres complètes*, p. 646.
101 'In truth, what is Literature but this mental chase, undertaken, as a discourse, in order to define or to find, with respect to oneself, proof that the spectacle responds to an imaginative comprehension, it is true, in the hope of gazing at one's reflection there' (ibid., p. 648).
102 It is not an exaggeration to say that he was not heard, since he more than anyone has been pressed into the service of the exaltation of 'creation', of the 'creator' and the Heideggerian mystique of poetry as 'revelation'.
103 The same effects of a double bind position may be observed, as we have seen (cf. part I, chapter 3), among the theatre critics of 'bourgeois' newspapers.
104 As a typical example of this constant, the bourgeois theatre designated itself towards the middle of the nineteenth century as the school 'of common sense' (cf. Cassagne, *La Théorie de l'art pour l'art*, pp. 33–4).
105 Even if it permits the mimicry of 'axiological neutrality' and objectivity, the aptitude to adopt all perspectives for the practical purposes of polemics has nothing in common with the knowledge of perspectives as such, which implies the capacity to grasp each of them (and most especially one's own) at its source, namely its necessity.
106 A typical example of this attitude can be seen in Hubert Bourgin: H. Bourgin, *De Jaurès à Léon Blum, l'École Normale et la politique*, presented by Daniel Lindenberg (Paris, London and New York: Gordon and Breach, 1970).
107 Cf. M. Godman, *Literary Dissent in Communist China* (Cambridge: Harvard University Press, 1967).
108 Here is it necessary to mention actual specific coups d'état, that is, efforts to impose principles of external hierarchization by using political power (state intervention, including by commissions and administrative bodies, in the internal affairs of fields of cultural production), economic power (all forms of sponsorship), the power of the press (for example, the 'prize-winners lists', especially those based on 'opinion polls' which are – unconsciously – manipulated), etc.

Part III To Understand Understanding

Chapter 1 The Historical Genesis of the Pure Aesthetic

1 See P. F. Strawson, 'Aesthetic appraisal and works of art', in *Freedom and Resentment* (London: Methuen, 1974), pp. 178–88, and T. E. Hulme, *Speculations* (London: Routledge and Kegan Paul, 1960), p. 136.
2 See H. Osborne, *The Art of Appreciation* (London: Oxford University Press, 1970). The interest of this definition lies in the fact that it collects a whole ensemble of characteristic traits offered by other definitions: thus, for example, Hulme observes that the object of aesthetic contemplation is 'framed apart by itself' (Hulme, *Speculations*).

3 R. Jakobson, *Questions de poétique* (Paris: Seuil, 1973); and 'Closing statement: linguistics and poetics', in T. A. Sebeok (ed.), *Style in Language* (Cambridge: MIT Press, 1960). In a more recent variant we have the alternative of the text as a pretext (for subjective projections) or as an all-powerful constraint, with the former branch corresponding more to the vision of the *auctor*, and the latter to a vision of the *lector*, more scientistic.

4 R. Wellek and A. Warren, *Theory of Literature* (Harmondsworth: Penguin, 1949).

5 E. Panofsky, *Meaning in the Visual Arts* (New York: Doubleday/Anchor, 1955), p. 13.

6 There is an exposé of the Wittgensteinian critique of essentialism, and of the critique of this critique, in M. H. Abrams, *Doing Things with Texts* (New York and London: W. W. Norton, 1989), pp. 31–72.

7 A. Danto, 'The artworld', *Journal of Philosophy* 61 (1964): 571–84.

8 On the confusion besetting the most culturally deprived museum visitors for lack of a minimal mastery of the instruments of perception and appreciation, and in particular of reference points such as names of genres, schools, epochs, artists, etc., see P. Bourdieu and A. Darbel, with D. Schnapper, *Love of Art: European Art Museums and Their Public*, trans. Caroline Beattie and Nick Merriman (Stanford: Stanford University Press, 1990), and P. Bourdieu, 'Outline of a sociological theory of art perception', in *The Field of Cultural Production*, ed. Randal Johnson (Cambridge: Polity; Stanford: Stanford University Press, 1992).

9 And if one wants to exhaust the analysis of the social conditions of the possibility of this extra-ordinary experience, one must add in further the prophetic intervention of that artist (in these circumstances, Marcel Duchamp) who was the first to expose the effect of the aesthetic institution of the museum and the artist, in his case by exhibiting a urinal or a bottle rack.

10 This rapid and at best schematic sketch of what might make up a social history of the aesthetic disposition with respect to painting relies in part on the observations of M. H. Abrams, *Doing Things with Texts*, esp. pp. 135–58, and also on those of W. E. Houghton Jr, 'The English *virtuoso* in the seventeenth century', *Journal of the History of Ideas*, no. 3 (1942): 51–73 and 190–219.

11 A deeper view of this history of aesthetic theory is to be found in M. H. Abrams, *Doing Things with Texts*, especially in the chapter entitled 'From Addison to Kant: modern aesthetics and the exemplary art', pp. 159–87.

12 See R. Shusterman, 'Wittgenstein and critical reasoning', *Philosophy and Phenomenological Research*, no. 47 (1986): 91–110.

13 Cf. P. Bourdieu, *Distinction: a Social Critique of the Judgement of Taste*, trans. Richard Nice (Cambridge: Harvard University Press, 1984), p. 194.

14 This means that when the philosopher offers a definition of the essence of the judgement of taste or when he concedes the universality it claims to a definition, such as Kant's, that matches his own dispositions, he is less removed than he imagines from the ordinary mode of thinking and from a propensity to make an absolute out of the relative.

15 E. Delacroix, *Oeuvres littéraires* (Paris: Grès, 1923), vol. 1, p. 76.

16 The fact that around the 1880s music becomes the art of reference, at least for the defenders of pure art, has to be related to the progress towards

aesthetic *formalism* which, at least in poetry, accompanies the autonomization of the field stemming from the logic of specific revolutions.

17 M. Riffaterre, *Essais de stylistique structurale* (Paris: Flammarion, 1971).

18 S. Fish, 'Literature in the reader', *New Literary History*, no. 2 (1970): 123ff.

19 W. Iser, *The Act of Reading: a Theory of Aesthetic Response* (Baltimore: Johns Hopkins University Press, 1978).

20 Any cultural good – literary text, pictorial or musical work – is the object of apprehendings which vary with the dispositions and cultural expertise of receivers, that is, today, according to educational background and the time since it was acquired (cf. Bourdieu and Darbel, with Schnapper, *The Love of Art*, in which a model of the variations in the reception of pictorial works is offered, one which is valid for the whole set of cultural works).

21 H.-G. Gadamer, *Wahrheit und Methode*, 2nd edn (Tübingen: Mohr, 1965), p. 246; in English as *Truth and Method*, 2nd rev. edn, trans. Joel Weinsheimer and Donald Marshall (New York: Crossroads, 1989).

22 I recall here an interview when I tried to point out the difference between the logic of denunciation and the logic of comprehension by saying, against all the prosecutors and public accusers who have stood up to condemn Heidegger, that 'I would be his best lawyer' (cf. P. Bourdieu, 'Ich glaube ich wäre sein bester Verteidiger', *Das Argument*, no. 171 (Oct. 1988): 723–6).

23 Among all those who have tried to ground creative reading in theory, one can cite, for literature, Gérard Genette (G. Genette, 'Raisons de la critique pure', in *Figures*, vol. 2 (Paris: Seuil, 1969), pp. 6–22), and for philosophy, H.-G. Gadamer (H.-G. Gadamer, *Truth and Method*, and *Philosophical Hermeneutics*, trans. David E. Linge (Los Angeles: University of California Press, 1976)), someone who, against historicist reduction, refuses to see in the author's intentions the ultimate measure of interpretation and who considers that 'understanding is an enterprise which is not only reproductive, but productive.' But it is in the writings of Heidegger on poetry (especially his essays 'On the nature of language' and 'Origins of the work of art') that this theory of reading as a mystical offering has found its full expression: to abandon oneself to words is to grasp the revelation of the being which is carried out in the poem and continues to be carried out there; 'to let words be' in the manner of the poet, whose call to being is a gift and a giving, is to reproduce the creating act which gives being, by giving speech to being.

24 G. Bachelard, *L'Eau et les Rêves* (Paris: J. Corti, 1942), p. 37.

25 This is just as true for the interpretation of the text of an interview with a simple layperson as for the understanding of the work of a celebrated author (which does not mean that the latter does not pose particular problems, notably the belonging of its author to a field).

26 Very close to what was, in other times, the historical critique of sacred texts (here again, one must mention Spinoza), the analysis of the social uses of cultural goods does not have as its purpose – or even, it seems to me, have as its effect, as defenders of the established cultural order feign to believe – a destruction of culture through relativization; it encompasses a critique of the cultural *superstition* and *fetishism* which turn works from instruments of production, hence of invention and possible freedom, into a heritage, routinized and reified.

27 Cf. R. Chartier (ed.), *Pratiques de la lecture* (Marseilles: Rivages, 1985), esp. 'Du livre au lire', pp. 61–82.

28 Durkheim shows, for example, that the humanist tradition reduced the Graeco-Roman world to an 'unreal and idealised environment peopled by personalities who had undoubtedly existed historically and who were presented in such a way that they had, so to speak, nothing historical about them', and he imputes this dehistoricization to the need to somehow neutralize pagan literature in order to be able to make it the basis of a pedagogic enterprise aiming to inculcate a Christian habitus (E. Durkheim, *The Evolution of Educational Thought: Lectures on the Formation and Development of Secondary Education in France*, trans. Peter Collins (London and Boston: Routledge and Kegan Paul, 1977), p. 507).

29 We know that in France until the revolution, classical languages and literature formed the basis of teaching, with modern subjects like physics only appearing in the final year of secondary school (cf. F. de Dainville, 'L'enseignement scientifique dans les collèges de jésuites', in René Taton (ed.), *Enseignement et Diffusion des sciences en France au XVIIIe siècle* (Paris: Hermann, 1964), pp. 27–65; P. Costabel, 'L'oratoire de France et ses collèges', in ibid., pp. 67–100). On the United States and England, see L. Gossman, 'Literature and education', *New Literary History* (University of Virginia), no. 13 (1982): 364–5, n. 8.

30 E. Durkheim, *L'Évolution pédagogique en France* (Paris: PUF, 1938), vol. 2, p. 128.

31 Cf. M. Arnold, *A French Eton, or Middle Class Education and the State* (London and Cambridge, 1864) (an account of a study of a lycée in Toulouse in 1859), and A. Vuillemain, 'Rapport au roi sur l'instruction secondaire', *Le Moniteur Universel*, 8 Mar. 1843, pp. 385–91, quoted by Gossman, 'Literature and education', p. 365. See also A. Prost, *L'Enseignement en France, 1800–1867* (Paris: A. Colin, 1968), pp. 52–68.

32 Gossman, 'Literature and education', pp. 341–71, esp. p. 355.

33 I have shown elsewhere that the propensity to extend almost limitlessly the posture of *lector*, which has characterized certain forms of ethnological and semiological structuralism, and to deliver up to 'reading' 'things' which were not made (solely) to be read (roughly speaking, rites and strategies of kinship, works of art or even certain forms of discourse) is the basis of systematic errors. The paradigm of these errors is what Bakhtin calls philologism, the lettered relation to the dead letter which leads to constituting language as a code allowing the decoding of a message implicitly considered as deprived of any other function than the one it holds for the expert – to be deciphered. One cannot avoid *épistémocentrisme* except at the cost of a reflection which is epistemological to the highest degree since it takes as object the epistemic posture itself, the theoretical point of view, and everything which separates it from the practical point of view.

34 The best demonstration of the universality of this professional disposition is undoubtedly the absence (also grounded in the fear of erring by sliding into 'historicism') of any effort on the part of those who lay claim to Marxism to 'historicize' 'Marxist' concepts, even those most visibly linked to historical conjunctures.

35 H.-G. Gadamer, *Truth and Method*, p. 270.

36 Ibid., p.277.

37 For example: 'Everyone knows that curious impotence of our judgment

where the distance in time has not given us sure criteria. Thus the judgment of contemporary works of art is desperately uncertain for the scientific consciousness. Obviously we cannot approach such creations with prejudices that we are not in control of, presuppositions that have too great an influence over us for us to know about them; these can give to contemporary creations an extra resonance [*eine Uberresonanz*] that does not correspond to their true content and their true significance' (ibid., p. 265).

38 A symbolic revolution (the one effected by Manet, for example) may be incomprehensible as such to us because the categories of perception which it produced and imposed have become natural to us and because those it overthrew have become strange to us.

Chapter 2 The Social Genesis of the Eye

1 M. Baxandall, *Painting and Experience in Fifteenth Century Italy: a Primer in the Social History of Pictorial Style* (Oxford: Oxford University Press, 1972); French edition, *L'Oeil du quattrocento: l'usage de la peinture dans l'Italie de la Renaissance*, trans. Y. Delsaut (Paris: Gallimard, 1985).

2 P. Bourdieu, 'Éléments d'une théorie sociologique de la perception artistique', *Revue Internationale des Sciences Sociales* 20, no. 4 (1968): 640–64; the English translation 'Outline of a sociological theory of art perception' first appeared in *International Social Science Journal* 20 (Winter 1968): 589–612, and was reprinted in P. Bourdieu, *The Field of Cultural Production* (Cambridge: Polity, 1993), pp. 215–37.

3 Bourdieu, 'Éléments d'une théorie sociologique de la perception artistique', p. 648.

4 Ibid., p. 656.

5 Ibid., p. 649.

6 Ibid., p. 646.

7 Ibid., p. 642.

8 The pages which follow are a modified version of an article written in collaboration with Yvette Delsaut (cf. P. Bourdieu and Y. Delsaut, 'Pour une sociologie de la perception', *Actes de la Recherche en Sciences Sociales*, no. 40 (1981): 3–9).

9 M. Baxandall, *Painting and Experience in Fifteenth Century Italy*, p. 3.

10 Ibid., p. 16.

11 Ibid., p. 23.

12 Ibid., p. 109.

13 Ibid., Preface.

14 Ibid., p. 109.

15 Ibid.

16 Ibid., p. 110.

17 Ibid., p. 150. This concern to avoid giving things logic for logic's sake is well seen in the prudence with which Baxandall greets any search for the historical sources, especially philosophical ones, of the words in which painters or their friends expressed their 'ideas' on painting and on art. (Cf. M. Baxandall, 'On Michelangelo's mind', *New York Review of Books* 27, no. 15 (8 Oct. 1981): 42–3.)

18 Baxandall, *Painting and Experience in Fifteenth Century Italy*, p. 11.

19 J. Le Goff, 'The usurer and purgatory', in *The Dawn of Modern Banking*

(Los Angeles: Yale University Press, 1979), pp. 25–52, and *The Birth of Purgatory*, trans. Arthur Goldhammer (Chicago: University of Chicago Press, 1984).

Chapter 3 A Theory of Reading in Practice

1 W. Faulkner, 'A rose for Emily', in *Thirteen Stories* (New York: Random House, 1950).
2 M. Perry, *Literary Dynamics, How the Order of a Text Creates Its Meanings (Poetics and Comparative Literature)* (Tel-Aviv: Tel-Aviv University, 1976).
3 So, in the first three pages of the story: 'Dating from that day in 1894 when Colonel Sartoris . . .', 'dating from the death of her father', 'the next generation', 'On the first of the year' – but with no indication of which year – 'eight or ten years earlier', 'Colonel Sartoris had been dead almost ten years', 'thirty years before', 'That was two years after her father's death and a short time after her sweetheart had abandoned her.'
4 It goes without saying that we do not need to lend the author an explicit consciousness of the mechanisms he puts to work, and of which he has, like any social agent, a practical mastery. Thus it is probable that he does not pose the question of the gender of the *postulated reader*. And why should he, since in all probability the apparatus would work equally well if the reader were a woman?
5 J.-P. Sartre, 'On *The Sound and the Fury*: time in the work of Faulkner', in *Literary and Philosophical Essays*, trans. Annette Michelson (New York: Criterion, 1955), pp. 79–87.
6 Cf. J. R. Searle, *Intentionality: an Essay in the Philosophy of Mind* (Cambridge: Cambridge University Press, 1983).

Postscript For a Corporatism of the Universal

1 P. Champagne, *Faire l'opinion: le nouveau jeu politique* (Paris: Minuit, 1990).

Index of Names

Subject Index